GUERRILLA
MARKETING

Other books by Jay Conrad Levinson

The Most Important $1.00 Book Ever Written

Secrets of Successful Free-Lancing

San Francisco: An Unusual Guide to Unusual Shopping
(with Pat Levinson and John Bear)

Earning Money Without a Job

555 Ways to Earn Extra Money

150 Secrets of Successful Weight Loss
(with Michael Lavin and Michael Rokeach)

Quit Your Job!

An Earthling's Guide to Satellite TV

Guerrilla Marketing

Guerrilla Marketing Attack

The Investor's Guide to the Photovoltaic Industry

Guerrilla Marketing Weapons

The 90-Minute Hour

Guerrilla Financing
(with Bruce Jan Blechman)

Guerrilla Selling
(with Bill Gallagher and Orvel Ray Wilson)

Guerrilla Marketing Excellence

Guerrilla Advertising

Guerrilla Marketing Handbook
(with Seth Godin)

Guerrilla Marketing Online
(with Charles Rubin)

Guerrilla Marketing for the Home-Based Business
(with Seth Godin)

Guerrilla Marketing Online Weapons
(with Charles Rubin)

The Way of the Guerrilla

Guerrilla Trade-Show Selling
(with Mark S. A. Smith and Orvel Ray Wilson)

Get What You Deserve: How to Guerrilla-Market Yourself
(with Seth Godin)

Guerrilla Marketing with Technology

GUERRILLA MARKETING

THIRD EDITION

Secrets for Making Big Profits from Your Small Business

Jay Conrad Levinson

Houghton Mifflin Company
Boston   New York.

For information about permission to reproduce
selections from this book, write to Permissions,
Houghton Mifflin Company, 215 Park Avenue South,
New York, New York 10003.

Library of Congress Cataloging-in-Publication Data

Levinson, Jay Conrad.
    Guerrilla marketing : secrets for making big profits from your small
business / Jay Conrad Levinson. — 3rd ed.
        p. cm.
    Includes bibliographical references and index.
    ISBN 0-395-90625-3
    1. Marketing.   2. Small business — Management.   3. Advertising.
I. Title.
HF5415.L477 1998
658.8 — dc21   98-24984   CIP

Printed in the United States of America

QUM 20 19 18 17 16 15 14 13

I dedicate this book to:

Mike Lavin

Thane Croston

Alexis Makar

Lynn Peterson

Wally Bregman

Bill Shear

Michael Larsen

Elizabeth Pomada

Marnie Patterson Cochran

Leo Burnett

Steve Savage

Sidney Mobell

Norm Goldring

Elaine Petrocelli

Bill Gallagher, Jr.

Bill Gallagher, Sr.

Chet Holmes

Charles Kessler

Allan Caplan

Charles Rubin

Robert Pope

Jeff McNeal

Liz Hymans

Jay Abraham

Al Ries

Mark Drevno

Dottie Ioakimedes

Terri Lonier

Seth Godin

Howard Gossage

Orvel Ray Wilson

Peter Schofield

Debra Kahn Schofield

Jack J. Freeman

guerrillas each and every one

Contents

I
The Guerrilla Approach to Marketing — Updated

Although marketing concepts continue to change so fast that there are daily publications devoted solely to chronicling the advances, the soul of guerrilla marketing remains unchanged. It is updated and amplified, to be sure, but its principles stand up. In our ever-evolving world of marketing, in real space and cyber-space, the guerrilla thrives by adapting to the myriad changes.

Guerrillas know that changes are usually in their favor because they *respond* to them rather than resisting them.

The marketing industry is evolving dramatically as computer technology asserts itself, as communication by satellites enables guerrilla marketers to advertise on television in prime time, as the Internet becomes as familiar to consumers as the supermarket, as an inflationary economy strengthens the bond between people and their money, and as social causes such as domestic violence, our rain forests, protecting children, and finding a cure for AIDS influence the marketing scene.

Although you'll learn about the most important changes, I hope your enlightenment is enhanced by the security of knowing that this updated guerrilla approach to marketing *works* and is *proven* in action. Fifteen years of success for tens of thousands of guerrilla businesses throughout the world underscore this truth. Successful guerrillas want to know how to use the latest changes to their advantage, and this edition explains it all.

If your business is exceptionally well funded and you have stockpiles of money allocated to marketing your products, you might take the standard approach and handle the marketing function with big bucks and textbook tactics. But if you can allocate only a modest amount of money to marketing, I advise you to take a radically different approach and handle the marketing function with big ideas and guerrilla tactics.

Who this book is for

Goals and shortcuts

You'll best understand the guerrilla approach to marketing if you read a standard marketing textbook. There you'll learn how to establish marketing goals and how to reach those goals. In this book, you'll learn of similar marketing goals and shortcuts to attaining them. Guerrilla tactics do not put textbook tactics to shame. But they do provide you with an alternative to standard expensive marketing so that you can increase your sales with a minimum of expense and a maximum of smarts. You'll learn how to do what the big spenders do without having to spend big. Since very little comes to us for nothing, you'll have to do some extra work. And instead of relying on money power, you can rely on brainpower.

Big imaginations instead of big budgets

It's a Herculean feat to keep abreast of the daily changes that occur in marketing. I write a guerrilla marketing newsletter and several monthly guerrilla marketing columns to accomplish all that Hercules would. The bare-bones essence of marketing has changed only in that we've become more enlightened by it. The weapons of marketing have undergone a revolution. This updated edition of *Guerrilla Marketing* is to keep you abreast of the current state of its art and its science. Although the true nature of guerrilla marketing remains the same, the breadth and technology of marketing have changed dramatically.

The mandatory weapon

Technology now gives small-business owners a blatantly unfair advantage. It allows them to produce first-rate marketing materials that used to require big budgets but now require only a big imagination. Technology has changed the playing field, leveling it more than some people like. Everybody can be a desktop publisher. And don't make the mistake of thinking that technology is for young people. Americans in their 40s are considered to be the most technologically adept people in the nation.

Another major change for the good is the use of environmental issues in marketing. If you tell prospects about your environmentally sound manufacturing practices, you give them an additional reason to buy from you.

Cable and satellite television, the Internet, fax machines, and delightful software for the small-business owner give guerrillas a crucial advantage. Guerrillas know that the computer is a mandatory weapon in today's world. If you are technophobic, make an immediate appointment with your technoshrink, because technophobia is fatal today!

In the late 1970s, 75 percent of marketing budgets went into advertising. During the late 1990s, 50 percent goes into trade promotions, 25 percent into consumer promotions, and a bit less than 25 percent into advertising. Many of these expenditures are being shifted to marketing on-line, and more will shift with each tick of the clock.

Do guerrillas welcome change? They thrive on it—because they know that their competitors have a tough time keeping up. This edition informs you about the marketing changes that will give you a leg up on your competition so that you will prosper.

Here are some important facts that guerrillas should keep in mind as we begin the twenty-first century:

Important facts
for guerrillas

- Millions of baby boomers will enter middle age.
- The 18- to 34-year-old market will lose more than $100 billion worth of spending power.
- Dual-income households and aging Americans will put a premium on time-saving products and services.
- Discretionary income will increase because of the trend toward smaller families and the fact that fewer households are being formed.
- The shrinking middle class will force retailers to aim more for the top and bottom. Some guerrilla companies will successfully manage to do both.
- Health care for those older than eighty-five will expand, opening up new opportunities to serve people.
- Home remodeling will enjoy boom times because of the high cost of housing. Fitness products will be nearly as commonplace as furniture.
- Cosmetics and skin-care products will help oldsters look like youngsters. Middle-aged models will become commonplace.
- Persons aged seventy-five or older will move to Florida, Nevada, Alaska, and Arizona. This age group will become a lucrative market.
- Satellite and cable TV will grow rapidly, as will the galaxy of choices available, enabling guerrillas to aim directly at their market, geographically and demographically.
- VCRs will become so widespread that video brochures will be recognized as high-powered weapons, proving their effectiveness to all types of businesses. In 1998, nearly 90 percent of Americans own VCRs.

Warmth in a cold world

- Tomorrow's marketplace will be populated by customers who are more demanding, less forgiving, and who appreciate warmth and attention to detail.
- America will learn to purchase products and services on the Internet. The Internet's speed and convenience will turn it into a forum in which most commerce is conducted—a universe unto itself.
- The American mindset will move toward voluntary and involuntary simplicity, which is characterized by thrift and anti-materialism along with a plantation economy that has the nation's wealth, albeit, the world's wealth, concentrated in the hands of a few.
- New industries will develop, such as full-spectrum fitness, which include holistic fitness for the mind, spirit, and body. Integrative medicine, which combines Eastern and Western medicine, will come to the fore.
- Clean-food diets will feature food free of artificial preservatives, coloring, irradiation, synthetic pesticides, drug residues, and growth hormones.
- The new counterculture will emerge, a generation that holds the antiestablishment sentiment of the '60s and that appreciates the luxuries afforded by the technology of the '90s.

The ultimate winners

- The ultimate winners in the future will be companies that are totally accessible to buyers at the time the buyers want to buy. Not easy, but possible. Your product or service will often be considered exactly the same as that of your competitors. This is because an enormous influx of marketing will create mass confusion and the perception that all offerings are created equal.
- Supermarkets will sell shelf space to companies just for the privilege of being displayed. Those same supermarkets scan your purchases and then produce a profile on your purchasing habits. Therefore, if you buy a box of Cheerios, you may then be sent a coupon for Wheaties.
- Ads will invite consumers to phone in or send for a free sample, enabling guerrillas to compile a list of consumers who have expressed interest in their product.
- New ways to influence consumer purchases, ranging from in-store TV to high-tech coupon machines and on-line couponing, will be developed for use at the point-of-sale. That point will often be smack dab in front of a computer monitor.

- There will be a growth spurt in frequent-buyer clubs, modeled after frequent-flier programs. There will also be a noticeable increase in the numbers of businesses forming strategic alliances.
- People are more mobile than ever, and mobile to different parts of the country. The ten fastest-growing cities in the United States in 1996 were Henderson, Nevada; Chandler, Arizona; Pembroke Pines, Florida; Palmdale, California; Plano, Texas; Las Vegas, Nevada; Scottsdale, Arizona; Laredo, Texas; Coral Springs, Florida; and Corona, California. Notice the switch to warmer and sunnier climate? Notice a movement westward and southward? Is there information here that you can use to enhance your marketing strategy?

  Warm and sunny
- People are leaving big cities in the Northeast and Midwest and moving west—with the sun. The cities experiencing the most shrinkage in 1996 were St. Louis, Norfolk, Washington, D.C., Baltimore, Philadelphia, Milwaukee, Kansas City, Buffalo, Pittsburgh, and Providence. The populations in these bigger cities are declining, while the growing cities are primarily suburbs of other big cities.
- The shopping mall concept will be expanded to include more products and more services, including recreation and fitness clubs, theaters and nightclubs, and nutritious fast-food restaurants.
- The millennium generation (people born from 1979 to 1987, blessed with an evolved social conscience) will appear less radical than the flower children of the '60s but will affect equally rich changes in our culture.
- Businesses that offer culturally oriented activities such as travel to historic places and museums will boom, for a maturing society will seek this kind of entertainment. More consumers will demand premium products such as coffees, breads, microbrewed beers, and a wide variety of foods and snacks.
- We will learn of an impending energy revolution that is based on fossil fuels. Advancements in cold fusion, photovoltaics, and zero-point energy will allow scientists to extract energy from apparent vacuums.
- Marketing will reflect the new reality that is causing people to look beyond their own lives and businesses and realize they are part of a whole.

The burgeoning markets

Guerrilla Marketing will open your mind to the burgeoning markets in the United States: suburbanites, working women, the elderly, gays and lesbians, and ethnic groups (especially Hispanics and Asians). The new marketing weapons discussed are Web sites, E-mail, video brochures, newsletters, toll-free numbers, cellphones, infomercials, and postcard decks. And the classic marketing weapons—direct mail, telemarketing, free publicity, trade shows, and catalogs—are evolving, too.

Because advances in the marketing industry are inevitable, it will always be necessary to update the methods and tactics of guerrilla marketing while maintaining its essence. In 1993, *Guerrilla Marketing* called to your attention the *three* most important marketing secrets. This updated edition gives you even more of a head start by imparting the *thirteen* most important marketing secrets.

Three is now thirteen

Stop for a moment and ask yourself if you're marketing properly right now. You can be pretty certain that the answer is a resounding "No!" if any of these seven danger signals are present:

1. My sales are driven mostly by price.
2. Customers cannot distinguish my products or services from those of my competitors.
3. I use disconnected sales gimmicks.
4. I do not have a unified plan for imparting my message to my customers and to the trade.
5. Most sales leads come from my sales staff.
6. Longtime customers say, "I didn't know you offered that."
7. I do not have a customer or prospect database.

This book is reaching you just in time if these symptoms are yours. And remember, you can't be too rich, too thin, have too much computer-processing power, or know too much about marketing.

One of the seven habits practiced by effective people is called "sharpening the saw"—improving the things that you do best. This edition continues to sharpen the saw of guerrilla marketing. In doing so, it provides the guerrilla with a keener edge than ever. With more than 2 million new businesses launched in America each year, the guerrilla needs all the ammunition available to achieve victory. This edition was written to restock your guerrilla arsenal with ammunition. But don't listen for the sound of triggers being pulled as much as the sound of mouses being clicked.

A keener edge than ever

Even with the changes in marketing, markets, and the media, the guerrilla approach remains the sensible one for all marketers. For entrepreneurs, for small businesspeople, and for all businesspeople, the guerrilla approach is crucial. Ask the successful small-business owners who have prospered in the face of a limited budget and a torrent of competitors and they'll tell you it *is* crucial that you make the attitude and smarts of the guerrilla part of your permanent mindset.

If I ran a small or even a gigantic business, I'd take comfort in knowing that my marketing techniques were effective and successful and had been proven on the front lines. I'd feel confident knowing that my marketing mindset was state-of-the-moment. I'm delighted to share the insights that make guerrilla marketing so effective. I'm even more gratified to understand the high level of success you will attain when you act upon what you learn. From one guerrilla to another, I wish you fame and fortune—especially fortune!

1

What Is Guerrilla Marketing?

Marketing is everything you do to promote your business, from the moment you conceive of it to the point at which customers buy your product or service and begin to patronize your business on a regular basis. The key words to remember are *everything* and *regular basis.*

What marketing includes The meaning is clear: marketing includes the name of your business, the determination of whether you will be selling a product or service, the method of manufacture or servicing, the colors, size, and shape of your product, the packaging, the location of your business, the advertising, the public relations, the sales training, the sales presentation, the telephone inquiries, the problem solving, the growth plan, the referral plan, and the follow-up. If you gather from this that marketing is a complex process, you're right.

You should look at marketing as a circle that begins with your idea for generating revenue and is complete when you have the blessed patronage of repeat and referral business. If your marketing doesn't come full circle, then it's a line that may lead you to the bankruptcy courts.

Marketing as a circle

Guerrilla marketing tactics differ from traditional marketing tactics in twelve important ways. I used to compare guerrilla marketing with textbook marketing, but today, because *Guerrilla Marketing* is often used as a textbook, I compare it to traditional marketing.

Guerrilla marketing versus traditional marketing

1. Traditional marketing practice requires that you invest money in the marketing process. The theory of guerrilla marketing is that your primary investments should be *time, energy,* and *imagination.*
2. Traditional marketing practice is geared to big business, recommending tactics associated with huge corporations and their traditionally large budgets. Guerrilla marketing is geared to *small business.* Every word of every sentence on every page

of every guerrilla marketing book is directed at the small-business owner with a big dream but not a big bankroll.

3. Traditional marketing practice measures how well it's doing by sales. Guerrilla marketing is based on the reality that anybody can find a way to drum up high sales. But high sales, fast turnover, strong response rates, and heavy store traffic are meaningless if you aren't generating consistent profits. The primary measuring stick to guerrillas is *profits*.

4. Traditional marketing practice is based on experience and then judgment, which involves guesswork. Wrong guesses are too expensive for guerrillas, so guerrilla marketing is based on the *science of psychology*—laws of human behavior. There are certainties we can assume regarding purchase patterns, and guerrillas focus on these certainties.

5. Traditional marketing practice suggests that you increase your business's production rates and then diversify by offering allied products and services. Guerrilla marketing suggests that you veer away from diversification and look at your *focus*. Your job is to create a standard of excellence with an acute *focus*, and excellence falls by the wayside when diversification occludes it.

6. Traditional marketing practice encourages you to grow your business linearly by adding new customers. Guerrilla marketing never scoffs at new customers and makes a concerted effort to add them continually, but encourages you to *grow your business geometrically*. Guerrilla marketers must aim for more transactions with existing customers, larger transactions, and referral transactions by using the immense power of customer follow-up and outrageously good service.

Growing geometrically

7. Traditional marketing practice asks that you look around for opportunities to obliterate the competition. Guerrilla marketing asks you to forget competition temporarily and to scout opportunities to *cooperate* with other businesses and support one another in a mutual quest for profits.

8. Traditional marketing practice would have you believe that advertising works *or* that direct mail works *or* that a Web site works. The guerrilla marketing theory proves that that is nonsense. The days of single weapon marketing are behind us. Marketing *combinations* are what work. If you combine advertising with direct mail and a Web site, each one will help each other to work better.

9. Traditional marketing practice urges you to count your re-

ceipts at the end of the month to see how many sales you've made. Guerrilla marketing suggests that you concentrate on how many *relationships* you've made each month. Each relationship can lead to a plethora of receipts and sales.

10. Traditional marketing practice doesn't encourage the use of technology because the technology of yesterday was too complicated, too expensive, and too limited. Guerrilla marketing urges you to *embrace* the technology of today because it is simple to use, inexpensive to purchase, and limitless in its ability to empower your business on the marketing front.

11. Traditional marketing practice identifies a handful of weapons that promote your business, all of which are relatively costly. Guerrilla marketing identifies at least *100 weapons you can use to boost your profits*, and half of them are free.

12. Traditional marketing practice intimidates many small-business owners because it is enshrouded by mystique and complexity. Guerrilla marketing *removes the mystique* and exposes marketing for exactly what it is, putting *you* in control.

No more mystique and complexity

Every type of entrepreneurial enterprise must have a marketing plan—it's not possible to succeed without one. There are no exceptions.

Assume that you have a fine business background and are well versed in the fundamentals of marketing as practiced by the giant corporations. Admirable. Now forget as much as you can. Your marketing agenda as an entrepreneur is vastly different than that of an esteemed member of the *Fortune* 500. Some of the principles may be the same, but the *details* are different. A good analogy is that of Adam and Eve. In principle, they were very much the same, but they varied in crucial ways—and thank heaven for that.

You're about to become a master of guerrilla marketing, the type of all-out marketing necessary for entrepreneurial success. Guerrilla marketing is virtually unknown to the large corporations, though some of them are catching on. Be grateful that guerrilla marketing tactics are rarely practiced by the titans . . . for the large corporations have the benefit of big bucks, and you don't.

Your size is an ally

You must rely on something just as effective but less costly. I'm happy to report that your size is an ally when it comes to marketing. If you're a small company, a new venture, or a single individual, you can use the tactics of guerrilla marketing to their fullest. You have the ability to be fast on your feet, to employ a vast array of marketing tools, to gain access to the biggest marketing brains and get them at bargain-basement prices. You may not need to use every weapon in your potential marketing arsenal, but you will need some of them. Therefore, you should know how to use them all.

Your business may not need to advertise. But it will need a marketing plan. Word of mouth may be so favorable and spread so rapidly that your venture can reap a fortune simply from it. If this is the case, the word of mouth was most likely motivated by an effective marketing strategy. In fact, a strong word-of-mouth campaign is part of marketing. And so are business cards, stationery, hours of operation, and the clothes you wear. Location is also important in marketing.

Marketing is the painfully slow process by which you move people from their place in the sun to their place on your customer list, gently taking a grasp of the inside of their minds and never letting go. Each component that helps you sell your product or service is part of the marketing process. No detail is too insignificant. In fact, the smaller the detail, the more important it is to a customer. The more you realize that, the better your marketing will be. And the better your marketing is, the more money you will make. I'm not talking about sales; I'm talking about profits—the bottom line.

The painfully slow process

That's the good news. The bad news is that one day you'll no longer be an entrepreneur. If you successfully put the principles of guerrilla marketing into practice, you'll become rich and famous and will no longer have the lean, hungry mentality of the entrepreneur.

The good news and the bad news

Once you've reached that stage, you may resort to the textbook forms of marketing, for you may feel too encumbered with employees, traditions, paperwork, management levels, and bureaucracy to be flexible enough for guerrilla marketing. However, you probably won't mind that state of affairs too much. After all, Coca-Cola, Standard Oil, Procter & Gamble, and General Motors were all started by entrepreneurs. You can be certain that they practiced guerrilla marketing techniques as much as possible in their day. And you can also be sure that they do their marketing by the numbers these days. And I doubt if they complain about it.

In time, large companies may be surpassed in size by companies that are today being founded and nurtured by entrepreneurs such as you. This will happen due to the result of a combination of factors. Marketing genius will be one of them. Count on it.

I am assuming you understand that you must offer a quality product or service to be successful. Even the best marketing in the world won't motivate a customer to purchase a poor product or service more than once. In fact, guerrilla marketing can speed the demise of an inferior offering because people will learn of the shoddiness that much sooner. Do everything in your power to ensure the quality of your product or service. If you're selling quality, you are ready to practice guerrilla marketing.

It is also mandatory that you have adequate capitalization — that is, money. Note that I didn't say that you need a lot of money. Sufficient capitalization to engage in guerrilla marketing will be enough. This means you'll need enough cash or cash reserves to promote your business aggressively for at least three months and ideally for a full year. It might take $300; it might take $30,000. It depends on your goals.

There are thousands of small businesses in the United States. Many of them offer superb products and highly desirable services. But fewer than one-tenth of 1 percent of those businesses will make it to the point of phenomenal financial success. The elusive variable that makes the difference between merely being listed in the Yellow Pages and being listed on the New York Stock Exchange is the *marketing* of the product or service.

You now hold in your hand the key to becoming part of that tiny percentage of entrepreneurs who go all the way. By realizing that many facets of your business can fall into the category of marketing, you have a head start on competitors who don't see the difference between *advertising* and *marketing*.

The more aware of marketing you are, the more attention you will pay to it. And the increased attention will result in better marketing of your offerings. I'd venture a bold guess that fewer than 10 percent of the new- and small-business owners in America have explored as many as a dozen of the marketing tools available to them. These methods include a Web site, canvassing, personal letters, telephone marketing, circulars and brochures, signs on bulletin boards, classified ads, outdoor signs, direct mail, samples, seminars, demonstrations, sponsoring of events, exhibitions at trade shows, T-shirt ads, public relations, using searchlights, advertising specialties such as imprinted ballpoint pens, and advertising in the Yellow Pages, newspapers, and magazines, and on radio, television, and billboards. Guerrilla marketing *demands* that you scrutinize *each* of these marketing methods, and then use the combination that is best suited to your business.

Once you've launched your guerrilla marketing plan, keep track of which weapons are hitting your target and which are missing. Merely knowing can *double* the effectiveness of your marketing budget.

How to double your effectiveness

There are absolutely no advertising agencies that specialize in guerrilla marketing. When I worked as a senior executive at some of the world's largest (and smallest) advertising agencies, I found that the agencies didn't have a clue as to what advertising or marketing tactics make an entrepreneur successful. They could help the big guys, but they were helpless without the brute force of big bucks. So where can you turn to for help? The first place is *Guerrilla Marketing*. Next, take advantage of your own ingenuity and energy. And finally, you will probably have to seek the advice of a marketing or advertising professional in the areas where guerrilla marketing overlaps standard marketing. But don't expect the pros to be as tough in the trenches as you are. Most likely, they operate best from high in a posh skyscraper.

Where to get help

The guerrilla marketing approach requires you to comprehend every facet of marketing, experiment with many of them, winnow out the losers, double up on the winners, and then employ the marketing tactics that prove themselves to you in the battleground of real life.

To understand the nature of this idea, it's useful to examine the reason why Japan knocked the United States off its perch as world leader in the TV, stereo, automobile, and electronics industries.

Industry in the United States has been able to turn out excellent products with a low percentage of rejects—5 percent. That means that of 1 million manufactured items, only 50,000 were rejects. Industry leaders recognized that the cost to lower that number would be greater than the profit industry would realize by achieving perfection. So it became an economic truism that you could run a successful manufacturing operation if you limited your rejects to 50,000 per million units. And the public became used to the concept—it complained about lemons but wasn't all that surprised at them.

After World War II, Japan suffered from an identity of poor quality. For years the phrase "Made in Japan" was enough to elicit

Solving an identity crisis

a frown from a sophisticated purchaser. How did the Japanese overcome this problem? Japan decided to fly in the face of the economic truism that allowed for a 5 percent reject rate. Japan figured that if the public accepts products even though 50,000 per million are inferior, it might happily embrace products of which fewer than 50,000 were unacceptable. But according to the economists, this would cost a ton of money.

The Japanese, having nowhere to go but up, figured it was worth it. They improved the quality of what they made to the point that right now, they have only 200 rejects per million units. Two hundred rejects versus our 50,000 rejects! And Japan is still working on methods for lowering this figure.

How did Japan become the leader in the TV, stereo, automobile, and electronics industries? By reducing mistakes. Every error that could possibly be construed as a mistake was noticed by people actually hired by industry to count mistakes. In the category of mistakes were included shoddy workmanship, tardiness, breaks that lasted too long, minor flaws in detail work, low morale, and anything at all that impeded production. Weekly, departments within Japanese industrial firms would meet with their hired mistake counters. They were told the number of mistakes made that week, and they worked to reduce that number. By working at it assiduously, they dramatically cut the number of mistakes.

Counting mistakes

By eliminating most mistakes, Japan took over leadership. And as the number of mistakes went down, productivity went up. In all businesses, there are numerous opportunities and numerous problems. The Japanese exploited their opportunities and solved their problems. This is what guerrilla marketing is all about.

Exploiting every opportunity

Guerrilla marketing involves recognizing the myriad opportunities out there and *exploiting every one of them*. In the marketing of any product, problems are certain to arise. Solve these problems and continue to look for new problems to solve—problems of prospects and customers. Businesses that solve problems have a greater chance of success than those that don't. Today and in the twenty-first century, businesses that save time for people will flourish. Why? Lack of time is a problem, and growing numbers of people in industrialized societies see it as such. The time-saving industry will become an important one in our society.

You must seize the important opportunities, yet you cannot neglect the smaller opportunities or overlook the minor problems.

You've got to go all out. This is one of the foundations of successful guerrilla marketing. By going all out, the Japanese reversed the consumer's reaction to "Made in Japan." The phrase now means excellent craftsmanship and attention to detail.

Energy alone is not enough, however. Energy must be directed by intelligence. Intelligent marketing is marketing that is first and foremost focused on a core idea. All your marketing must be an extension of this idea: the advertising, the stationery, the direct mailings, the telephone marketing, the Yellow Pages advertising, the package, the Internet presence, the whole thing. It isn't enough to have a better idea; you need to have a focused strategy. Today many large and supposedly sophisticated companies go to one expert for a trademark, another expert for an advertising program, yet another expert for direct-mail planning, and possibly one more professional for location selection. This is nonsense. Nine times out of ten, each of these experts will pull the company in a different direction.

Energy alone is not enough

What must be done is to have all the marketing pros pull in a common direction—a preagreed, long-term, carefully selected direction. When this is done, a synergistic effect is automatically created and five types of marketing tactics do the work of ten. The preagreed direction will always be clear if you encapsulate your thoughts in a core concept that can be expressed in a *maximum* of first, seven sentences, then seven words. That's right, a *maximum* of seven. Think it can't be done? Try it for your own business.

Pulling in the same direction

Here's an example. An entrepreneur wanted to offer courses in computer education, but knew that most people suffer from "technophobia"—fear of things technical. His advertisements for proposed courses in word processing, accounting by computer, and the electronic spreadsheet produced little response, so he decided to restate the basic premise of his offering. At first, he stated it thus: "I wish to alleviate the fears that people have regarding computers so that they will recognize the enormous value and competitive advantages of working with computers." He then reduced this thought to a seven-word core concept: "I will teach people to operate computers." This brief statement clarified his task—clarified it for himself, his sales staff, and his prospective students.

Later he developed a name for his company, one that reduced his core concept to three words: Computers for Beginners. This bypassed the problem of technophobia, stated his premise, and attracted hordes of beginners. Originally his concept was six pages long. By condensing his ideas, he was finally able to achieve the succinctness necessary to assure clarity. And clarity led to success. It usually does.

Focusing on a core idea

The concept of focusing your marketing on a core idea is a simple one. When you begin to market your offering this way, you are a member of an enlightened minority and you're well on your way to marketing success—a prerequisite for financial success.

Guerrilla Marketing simplifies the complexities, eliminates the mystique, and explains how entrepreneurs can use marketing to generate maximum profits from minimum investments.

Put another way, this book can help make a small business big. It can aid an individual entrepreneur in making a lot of money as painlessly as possible. Often, the only factor that determines success or failure is the way in which a product or service is marketed. The information in these pages will arm you for success and alert you to the shortcomings that lead to failure.

What guerrilla marketing is not

Here is what guerrilla marketing is not: expensive, easy, common, wasteful, taught in marketing classes, found in marketing textbooks, practiced by advertising agencies, or known to your competitors. Be grateful that it is not these things. If it were, all business owners would be guerrillas, and your path to success would be a paved one rather than a secret route to the end of a rainbow with a bigger pot of gold than you ever imagined.

2

Entrepreneurial Marketing:
The Guerrilla Difference

In an article in the *Harvard Business Review*, John A. Welsh and Jerry F. White remind us that "a small business is not a little big business." An entrepreneur is not a multinational conglomerate but a profit-seeking individual. To survive, he must have a different outlook and must apply different principles to his endeavors than does the president of a large or even medium-size corporation.

Not only does the scale of small and big businesses differ, but small businesses also suffer from what the *Harvard Business Review* article calls "resource poverty." This is an opportunity that requires an entirely different approach to marketing. Where large ad budgets are not necessary or feasible, where expensive ad production squanders limited capital, where every marketing dollar must do the work of two dollars, if not five dollars or even ten, where a person's company, capital, and material well-being are all on the line—that is where guerrilla marketing can save the day and secure the bottom line.

A large company can invest in a full-scale advertising campaign run by an ad agency, and that company has the resources to switch to a different campaign if the first is not successful. And if the company ad manager is smart, he or she will hire a different agency the second time around. This luxury is not available to entrepreneurs, who must get it right the first time. Entrepreneurs who are guerrillas get it right because they know the secrets—and so will you.

Get it right the first time

This is not to say that I hold the techniques employed by the big corporations in contempt; quite the contrary. While creating advertising for companies such as Alberto-Culver, Quaker Oats, United Airlines, Citicorp, Visa, Sears, and Pillsbury, I frequently employed big-company marketing techniques. I was acting properly. But to suggest that the individual entrepreneurs I advise employ the same techniques would be irresponsible, not to mention financially wasteful. Instead, I resort to the techniques of guerrilla marketing, techniques that might get me laughed out of a Procter & Gamble or IBM conference room.

Many of the approaches and some of the techniques overlap. Entrepreneurs need to govern tactical operations by marketing strategy and to weigh their marketing efforts against that strategy. They also need to examine all of the marketing avenues available to them. The critical difference is the bottom line — entrepreneurs must keep a far keener eye on the bottom line than do the giant firms.

The critical difference

Entrepreneurs have to spend far less money testing their marketing tactics; their marketing must produce results at a fraction of the price paid by the biggies. The entrepreneur's use of marketing will be more personalized and realistic.

Large companies think nothing of producing five television commercials for testing purposes only. Small companies wouldn't dare do this. Large companies employ many levels of management to analyze the effectiveness of their advertising. Small companies entrust the judging to one individual. Large companies look first to television — the most far-reaching of all the advertising media. Small companies usually look first to small newspaper ads in local papers. Big companies hire expensive consultants to maximize their presence on the Internet. Small companies do this themselves. Both are interested in sales that generate profits, but each will achieve its goals in a dramatically different way.

Large companies often aim to lead an industry or to dominate a market or large market segment, and they use marketing ploys designed to attain those lofty ambitions. However, small companies or individual entrepreneurs can flourish merely by gaining a tiny slice of an industry, a fraction of a market. Different wars require different tactics.

Flourishing with a tiny slice

Large companies must advertise from the outset and continue to advertise with virtually no interruption, but smaller enterprises may advertise only during the start-up phase and then rely solely on guerrilla weapons and word-of-mouth advertising. Can you imagine what would happen if Budweiser depended on word-of-mouth advertising? Miller would sell many more six-packs.

An individual entrepreneur may be able to get enough business just by dealing with one gigantic company. An acquaintance of mine was able to survive financially (and in gracious style, I might add) merely by conducting small seminars for one large banking firm. No large company could exist off the income he was generating, but my friend was able to target that one firm until he was given his first assignment. Then there were others, and still others. This year, he is conducting his seminars for a large chemical company. Working with companies of that size, he needs very few customers. Needless to say, his marketing was tailored to this reality.

A descriptive brochure sent to a single large corporation may result in enough business to keep an energetic telephone marketing trainer in the chips for a long time. Try to find a New York Stock Exchange–listed company that could do the same. Impossible!

Very few customers may be enough

Many entrepreneurs get all the business they need by posting signs on bulletin boards. A large company would never consider such a possibility. If it did, it would be known as Shrinking, Inc., in short order. The point is obvious: sauce for the small goose is not necessarily sauce for the large goose. And vice-versa.

For example, an executive at a large company may carry business cards that are plain and straightforward. The executive's name, company name, address, and phone number are suitable. Perhaps a title is necessary. For a smart practitioner of an individual enterprise, however, the business card should contain more information. For example, a typist I know has a business card with the above information along with the message "Legal, theses, statistical, manuscript, resume, and business typing." Her card does double duty, and it needs to. That is what guerrilla marketing is all about.

The guerrilla business card

A business card can double as a brochure, a circular, a wallet-size advertisement, and a listing of your services or products. It can open up to become a mini-brochure. Customers appreciate such mini-brochures: their time and space are at a premium, and your card saves them time while taking up little space. The cost to produce such a card is not much more than that for a standard card. A business card can be more than a mere listing of one's name, address, and phone number; it can be a marketing weapon. To see how valuable a weapon it can be for you, call InfoCard at 512-327-3385.

A huge corporation can run radio or television commercials and tell the audience, at the end of each message, to get the address of the nearest dealer by consulting the Yellow Pages. But the individual entrepreneur dare not direct listeners or viewers to the Yellow Pages. That would only alert his prospective customers to the competition or to the dominance of certain competitors. Instead, the astute entrepreneur directs his prospects to the white pages, where there will be no competitive ads, where his organization's small size will not appear as a detriment, and where recognizable promotion themes and symbols will not woo a customer away.

You have more flexibility

Perhaps the biggest difference between an individual businessperson and a large corporation is in the degree of flexibility each possesses. Here the balance tips in favor of the small business. Because the small business hasn't indoctrinated numerous levels of management and a gigantic sales organization in the tactics and strategies of its marketing plan, it can make changes on the spot. It can be fast on its feet and can react to market changes, competitive ploys, undeveloped service niches, economic realities, new media, newsworthy events, and last-minute offers.

I recall how a major advertiser once was offered an unbelievably good media buy for a fraction of its normal price. Because the offer did not fit into the company's engraved-in-bronze plan, and because the person to whom the offer was made had to check with so many bosses, the company turned down the offer. A tiny business then accepted it: a thirty-second commercial just before the Super Bowl, for the incredible price of $500. The cost of this commercial slot (in the San Francisco Bay area) normally sold for ten times that amount. Due to a lack of flexibility, the giant corporation was unable to take advantage of the bargain. Speed and flexibility are the essence of guerrilla marketing.

A single burning concept

Business in each decade is fueled by a single burning concept. In the '80s, that concept was quality. Quality was so important that it became the ticket to admission to doing business in the '90s. The concept of the '90s became flexibility. The more you can offer, the better service you can provide and the more customers you can satisfy. Word-of-mouth marketing will flourish from the spring of flexibility. During the first decade of the twenty-first century, the key concept will be innovation. However, guerrilla marketers should first develop a reputation for flexibility and live up to their praises consistently. Then they can focus on innovation.

A success-bound entrepreneur must learn to think about marketing and advertising on a different wavelength than does a corporate advertising executive. While you must think about the primary marketing tools much as the executive does, you must also develop a sixth sense for the other opportunities available to entrepreneurs. It may be that a personal letter or visit is in order. A corporate manager might never consider such mundane tactics. Perhaps a telephone marketing campaign is in order. Can you picture Coca-Cola getting involved in telephone marketing to customers? Can you imagine Chevron going one-on-one with their prospects?

The one-on-one capabilities of the small business represent an extraordinary opportunity to the business owner who recognizes a good thing when it stares him in the face. Small businesses can win and keep business; they build and grow the business by focusing on seemingly tiny details. The small business can get up close and *personal* with its customers.

Up close and personal

There's a certain warmth associated with being a mom and pop business. And even though you may run yours with the acumen of the multinational conglomerates, most of which are not run with much acumen or they'd focus more acutely on their prime talents, you can benefit from the close personal connection associated with small business simply by injecting an extra dollop of warmth into your modus operandi.

You have the flexibility, the speed, and the disregard of image that enable you to use radio commercials and to hire high school students to distribute printed circulars on street corners. You don't have a body of rules to follow, a committee to answer to, a set structure to follow. You're a guerrilla. You *are* the organization. You answer to yourself. You make the rules and you break the rules. That means you get to be amazing, outrageous, surprising, unpredictable, brilliant, and quick.

You also may be able to enjoy the rare luxury of relying upon consistent word-of-mouth advertising. If you're really good at your work and know how to generate word-of-mouth marketing and referral business, it might be enough to keep your coffers brimming. I know of no *Fortune* 500 companies that can enjoy that amenity.

Incidentally, please understand that what appears to be word-of-mouth advertising is often a combination of newspaper, magazine, radio, direct-mail, and word-of-mouth advertising. It's the mouth that gets the credit, not the media. Don't delude yourself: you cannot succeed without media advertising. Succeeding with

It's not really word of mouth

this strategy would be like winning the lottery with your first ticket. It can happen, but don't bet your boots or your business.

Still, it is possible to generate word-of-mouth advertising. There are several ways to accomplish this. The first is to be so good at what you do and to offer products that are so obviously wonderful that your customers will spread the good word about you. Another way to get the ball rolling is to give *brochures* to your new customers. This reminds them why they patronized you in the first place and spurs word-of-mouth endorsements. A third way to obtain positive recommendations is literally *to ask for them*. Nobody is better equipped to talk up your company than you—or perhaps your best customer. Tell all your customers: "If you're really satisfied with my service or products, I'd sure appreciate it if you'd tell your friends." Finally, you can *bribe* your customers. Tell them, "If I get any customers who mention your name, I'll send you a free gift (or give you a 10 percent discount) next time you're in."

The magic question

Another glorious way of obtaining enthusiastic word-of-mouth marketing is by asking yourself the magic question: What other businesses in the area do my customers patronize? I know a restaurateur who asked this question just after opening the business. The answer the owner came up with: hairstyling salons. So the owner gave a free dinner-for-two coupon to all the salon owners within a two-mile radius of his eatery. It wasn't a "Buy one, get one free" or "Eat for free between 5:15 P.M. and 5:23 P.M. on a Wednesday" kind of deal. The restaurateur was offering *two free* dinners. The salon owners checked out the restaurant, enjoyed their meals, and talked it up in the styling salon. The result was an influx of customers, all of whom heard about it while having their hair styled. The cost of all this business? Not a whole lot. I promise.

Which of these methods should you employ to generate your own word of mouth? As a guerrilla, you should use all of them. Testing will tell.

What you can do that big companies can't

The point to remember is that no large corporation can succeed by means of word-of-mouth advertising alone, and some entrepreneurs can. Do yourself a favor and don't leave everything up to the recommendations of your happy customers. They probably have more important things to talk about. Even for a guerrilla, consistent marketing is crucial to success.

An overall marketing plan for a person engaged in individual enterprise might consist of a listing in the Yellow Pages, a Web site, a mailing of circulars and business cards, a posting of signs, and a follow-up telephoning to prospects to whom the promotional material was sent. That five-pronged effort (Yellow Pages, Web site, mailing, sign-posting, and telephoning) might be all it takes to get a business off and running. You can be certain that no big company has a marketing plan so short, simple, and inexpensive.

Imagine that a staple gun and a handful of circulars were the only marketing tools necessary to conduct a business. IBM would boot me out of its corporate offices for suggesting such a thing. However, many a successful typing service uses only these devices. I know a word processor who started out by typing her circulars, thereby lending credibility to her typing ability. She posted them with her staple gun on bulletin boards on local college campuses. Today she no longer posts circulars, and her staple gun gathers dust. Word of mouth has taken over, and she gets all the business she needs through referrals.

Armed with a staple gun

Entrepreneurs can enjoy month after month of profitable business merely by advertising in the classified pages and in the many classified sections now on-line. I'm sure you've seen rafts of ads by independent contractors while perusing the classified ads. You do look through them, don't you? The classified ads are recommended reading for entrepreneurs. They give you ideas. They alert you to the competition. They clue you in as to current prices. You'll read more about them in Chapter 13. The point I'm making here is that classified ads are an important tool for independent businesspeople. They are not a tool for large companies. I doubt if the most professional advertising agencies in the world are well versed in proper use of the classified pages, but the classifieds may be invaluable to freelance earners.

An important tool for independent businesses

The author Peggy Glenn, who lives and writes of the guerrilla life, lists an eleven-point advertising program for a freelance word processor:

1. Hang fliers on campuses and near student gathering places.
2. Ask each school department to allow you to post your fliers.
3. Post a flier in the faculty lounge.
4. Post your flier at placement offices and counseling centers.
5. Leave fliers at the graduate study office.
6. Advertise in the campus newspaper.
7. Post a small sign on the community library bulletin board.
8. Post fliers for special groups such as engineers.
9. Visit a few college departments to see if they need your help.

10. Visit the principals of schools in your community with fliers.
11. Visit private and special schools in your area, leaving fliers.

She admits that this is a lot of marketing. It is to a word-processing freelancer, but not to a large company. This illustrates clearly that marketing works differently for entrepreneurs—it can be inexpensive yet comprehensive.

Inexpensive yet comprehensive

There are thirteen highly significant marketing secrets that must be known by all advertisers, large and small. Even the tiniest of entrepreneurs must be aware of them. Your awareness will begin the moment you begin reading the next chapter.

3

The Thirteen Most Important Marketing Secrets

It floors me that these secrets are secrets at all. Instead, they ought to be truisms, engraved on brass plaques in the offices of all who market or plan marketing. Yet these proven gems of marketing wisdom have somehow escaped the ken of large and small marketers alike. I sincerely believe that it is next to impossible to market a product or service successfully unless these secrets are known and put into practice. I also believe that merely by learning these secrets, then living by them, you're 80 percent of the way toward success with your marketing.

If you have a small business and want it to become a large business, forget it—until you put these secrets into practice. If you allow these concepts to become part of your mental marketing framework, you've got a giant head start on those who do not.

So as not to keep you in suspense any longer, I'll reveal the secrets right here and now. They can be summarized in thirteen words, each ending in the letters "ent": commitment, investment, consistent, confident, patient, assortment, subsequent, convenient, amazement, measurement, involvement, dependent, and armament.

The big thirteen

1. You must have *commitment* to your marketing program.
2. Think of that program as an *investment*.
3. See to it that your program is *consistent*.
4. Make your prospects *confident* in your firm.
5. You must be *patient* in order to keep a commitment.
6. You must see that marketing is an *assortment* of weapons.
7. You must know that profits come *subsequent* to the sale.
8. You must aim to run your firm in a way that makes it *convenient* for your customers.
9. Put an element of *amazement* in your marketing.

10. Use *measurement* to judge the effectiveness of your weapons.
11. Establish a situation of *involvement* between you and your customers.
12. Learn to become *dependent* upon other businesses and they upon you.
13. You must be skilled with the *armament* of guerrillas, which means technology.

If you're not committed, it probably won't work

Let's start with the first rule. If you're not committed to a marketing or advertising program, it's probably not going to work for you. I tell my clients that the single most important word for them to remember during the time they are engaged in marketing is *commitment*. It means that they are taking the marketing job seriously. They're not playing around, not expecting miracles. They have scant funds to test their marketing—they must act. Without commitment, marketing becomes practically impotent.

You evolve a marketing plan, revise and rerevise it until it is *a powerful plan for your purposes*. You put it to work and you stay with it, no matter what (in most cases). You watch it slowly take effect, rise and falter, take a bit more effect, slide back a bit, start taking hold even more, stumble, then finally grab on and soar, taking you with it. Your plan is working; your cash register is ringing; your bank balance is swelling. And this is because you were *committed to your marketing program*.

What happens if you're not patient enough?

Let's examine that last paragraph. What if you weren't patient enough during the time your plan "slowly" took effect? You might have changed the plan. Many entrepreneurs do. What if you dropped the plan the moment it faltered? You would have lost out. Many marketers do. What if you lost your cool when your sales slid backward? You might have scrubbed the plan. Suppose you dropped it when it stumbled, as virtually all marketing plans do, at least temporarily. Disaster would have ensued. However, because you stayed with the plan, because you were committed to it, it took

Understanding the meaning of commitment

hold. Your success was very much due to your understanding of the concept of commitment. If you hadn't been in touch with the essence of the concept, you probably would have killed the plan— and killed your chances along with it. If you understand the meaning of *commitment*, it will pay off for you.

A new sleep shop was opening in Boulder, Colorado. The owner of the business had heard about me, so he flew out to northern California to talk. We hit it off. We discussed the idea of commitment to a marketing program. He admitted that he knew zilch about marketing and turned the whole thing over to me. I developed a marketing plan, secured his approval, then reiterated the importance of his commitment to the program. Mind you, I'm talking about a guy with one small store.

The marketing strategy was implemented. Six weeks later, my new client called me to tell me he was still committed to the program, but that he hadn't seen much proof of it working for him. He said that he was completely relaxed about the whole thing because he felt he understood about commitment. After twelve weeks, he called to tell me he was beginning to see hints that the program was taking effect. After six months, he opened his second store. After nine months, he opened his third, and at the end of the year, he had five stores. He remained committed to the marketing program, and within six years had forty-two stores in Colorado, Iowa, Kansas, Wyoming, and Missouri.

I doubt my client would have progressed to the point where he could have justified a second store if he hadn't stayed with the plan. He could have wavered and veered from the plan. But it was a well-conceived plan, a plan that was tailored to his needs. At the outset, you won't have any way of knowing if your plan is good or bad, except for low-cost testing, your own intuition, and the counsel of others in whom you believe. But once you believe in your plan, you've got to back your belief with *patience*. Patience is commitment.

Backing your belief with patience

My client's plan called for weekly newspaper advertising, daily radio advertising, strong in-store signs, weekly sales training, consistent customer follow-up, and free gifts for customers during promotions. That was in the '70s. In the '80s, it was augmented by daily TV advertising three weeks out of every four. And for the '90s, though the business was sold for an obscene sum, it might be supported even more by a video brochure and certainly a Web site connected to other local and global businesses. But the framework would remain the same—because the mindset of the owner would remain that of a guerrilla.

Create a sensible plan, then stick with it until it proves itself to you. How long might that take? Three months, if you're lucky. Probably six months. Possibly as long as a year. But you will never, ever know whether the plan is working within the first sixty days. Commitment is directly related to time. The longer you live by a plan, the deeper your sense of commitment. If your boat sinks in

How long does it take to work?

Swimming to a distant beach

the ocean and you start swimming to shore, you shouldn't give up if you don't hit the beach within one hour—or even five hours. To survive, you've got to be *committed* to swimming to that beach. Think of this when you consider altering your marketing plans after a short time. Lest you misunderstand, think about the following list each time you run an ad and get a response that doesn't meet your expectations:

1. The first time a man looks at an ad, he doesn't see it.
2. The second time, he doesn't notice it.
3. The third time, he is conscious of its existence.
4. The fourth time, he faintly remembers having seen it.
5. The fifth time, he reads the ad.
6. The sixth time, he turns up his nose at it.
7. The seventh time, he reads it through and says, "Oh brother!"
8. The eighth time, he says, "Here's that confounded thing again!"
9. The ninth time, he wonders if it amounts to anything.
10. The tenth time, he will ask his neighbor if he has tried it.
11. The eleventh time, he wonders how the advertiser makes it pay.
12. The twelfth time, he thinks it must be a good thing.
13. The thirteenth time, he thinks it might be worth something.
14. The fourteenth time, he remembers that he wanted such a thing for a long time.
15. The fifteenth time, he is tantalized because he cannot afford to buy it.
16. The sixteenth time, he thinks he will buy it someday.
17. The seventeenth time, he makes a memorandum of it.
18. The eighteenth time, he swears at his poverty.
19. The nineteenth time, he counts his money carefully.
20. The twentieth time he sees the ad, he buys the article or instructs his wife to do so.

The guerrilla from 1885

The above was written by one Thomas Smith in London back in 1885. So much for commitment. Now let's talk about another "ent" word, the second of the thirteen most important secrets of all—*investment.*

Marketing and advertising should be considered *conservative investments.* They are not miracle workers. They are not magic formulas. They are not instant gratifiers. If you don't recognize that marketing is a conservative investment, you'll have difficulty committing yourself to a marketing program.

The nature of a conservative investment

Suppose you buy a blue-chip stock. If it drops after a few weeks, you don't sell it. You hold on to it in hopes that its value will increase. And in all likelihood, it will. Such is the nature of a conservative investment. Look at marketing in the same way. If it doesn't produce instant results, it's because most marketing doesn't. If it does produce instant results, excellent—but don't expect this to happen every time.

Marketing will contribute to slow but steady increases for you. At the end of a year, you'll be able to say that you've invested X dollars in marketing and received X plus Y in sales. Don't expect marketing to suddenly double your sales. Although that has happened, it is unusual. Recognizing this, you'll feel good about making a conservative investment in marketing the next year, and the year after that. If you expect more from marketing, chances are you'll be disappointed. If you expect only that, chances are you'll be gratified. And successful.

Here is an example of a nearsighted business decision: I worked with a client who had never engaged in newspaper advertising. We developed a marketing plan for his four eyeglass stores, a creative strategy, and a media plan. We discussed commitment. Then we ran the ads. After four weeks, my client called to tell me he was dropping the entire advertising program. When I asked why, he told me he had expected his sales to at least double by this time. He admitted that I had explained that advertising does not work this way. But he said that he'd decided he didn't want to spend money that didn't produce instant sales.

A sad example

I wish I had informed him early on that his advertising expenditure was a conservative investment. Perhaps he would have better understood its powers. But instead he dropped the plan and he lost his money. He didn't understand the investment concept. He was expecting miracles, instant results, dramatic changes. Marketing does not work that way. Don't expect it to. Don't lose money because of it. Whenever you spend one dime for any type of marketing, use the term *investing* to describe your expenditure. By *investing* your money in marketing, you'll earn more money than by *spending* your money in marketing. See the difference?

Expecting miracles that never happen

The third major marketing secret is to make your marketing *consistent*. Don't change media. Don't change messages. Don't vary your graphic format. Change your offers and headlines if you wish, even your prices, but do not change your identity. Don't drop out of the public eye for long periods. When you are ready to market your product or service, be prepared to put the word out consistently. Consistently means regularly—and for a goodly period of time. It means that instead of running a couple of large newspaper ads once every few months, you'll run smaller newspaper ads, and run them frequently. Instead of airing fifty-five radio commercials in one week every few months, run twelve radio commercials per week every week. You can even drop out of sight one week out of four. As long as you are a consistent marketer, you can pull out of the media for brief periods.

Familiarity breeds confidence

Consistency breeds familiarity, familiarity breeds confidence, and confidence breeds sales. If your products or services are of sufficient quality, your confidence and your offering will attract buyers more than any other attribute.

Therefore, the fourth secret is to make prospects *confident* in your offering. Confidence is extremely important to you—more important than quality, than selection, than price, than service. Confidence will be your ally. And commitment, as proven by consistent marketing, will breed confidence.

I have a retail furniture client who has been with me for close to thirty years. When she first began to market her product, she spent a fortune advertising on television. Could she afford it? Of course not. But she believed that television was her key to success. But with the number of dollars she had to invest, television was doom because she could afford to run only two commercials per week, even though they were on the highest-rated show at the time. Ratings are virtually meaningless with only two spots a week. It doesn't take a guerrilla to know that one can't expect TV to produce profits with so few commercials. Today my client runs lots of commercials on TV, investing only a tiny portion of her marketing budget and enjoying exceptionally gratifying profits as a result. We'll discuss TV in greater detail later, but for now, suffice it to say that unless you can use a medium *effectively*, you shouldn't use it at all.

Using a medium effectively or not at all

My client was able to salvage her business from her disastrous TV experience. When she met with me, we talked about commitment, investment, and consistency. We talked about the other guerrilla secrets as well. Since that day she has run a tiny ad in the newspaper every Sunday, and her sales have continued to rise. She dramatically increased her sales without increasing her marketing expenses as a percentage of her gross revenue. It happened over a period of several years. Her store has quadrupled in size, and her profits have followed suit. As I mentioned, she's also back on television—running ten commercials per day, two weeks out of every four. The key to her glittering success was consistent advertising. She calls her Sunday newspaper ad, now not so tiny, her "meal ticket." And she's right. She tells me that almost everyone who comes into her store says they've seen the original ad. You'd find that hard to believe if you saw the size of the original ad, but you'd find it easy to believe if you knew that she's been running that and similar ads in the same newspaper on the same day for years. People are *familiar* with her operation. They're *confident* in her offerings. And they buy from her.

Guerrillas have meal tickets

She is committed, she sees her marketing as an investment, she is consistent and patient, and she has since added a multitude of weapons to her marketing arsenal. This *assortment* of weapons generates many new, higher-than-projected profits for her. The wider the assortment of weapons in your marketing arsenal, the wider the grin on your face when you review your financial statements.

Does my client send follow-up mailings to all of her customers? Of course she does. She has learned that marketing doesn't end with the sale. It's the marketing done *subsequent* to the sale that leads to the juicy profits. It costs six times more to sell a product or service to a new customer than it does to an existing customer. My client always mails to existing customers, and she benefits from the repeat sales, which are the inevitable payoff.

The inevitable payoff

Her store is known as a very *convenient* place to buy. It's open seven days a week. Hours are extended for the convenience of her customers—not for her own convenience. She accepts every credit card under the sun. She takes checks, arranges partial payment plans, delivers, installs, is accessible twenty-four hours a day via voice-mail, E-mail, and fax. And parking is convenient.

Although she takes much of her business for granted, she knows that her marketing must *amaze* people. So her marketing mentions that her custom-designed furniture is available at factory-direct prices because she has her own factory. The prices are amazing and so is the homemade touch. It enables her to custom-design furniture and offer it at an off-the-floor price. This element of *amazement* attracts attention to her ads.

Most amazing of all, she has doubled the effectiveness of all her marketing! How did she do such a wondrous thing? The answer is *measurement*, as if you didn't know. She measured the effectiveness of all her marketing, asking people where they first heard of her. In this way she was able to eliminate the weapons and newspapers that weren't pulling their weight, and she doubled those that gave her the biggest bang for her bucks. The result: a doubling of her profits. The reason: measurement (also called "sourcing" by those in the know).

Doubling your marketing effectiveness

One of the most delightful daily aspects of her showroom is the return of satisfied customers. They are always treated warmly and helpfully. There is a powerful feeling of *involvement*, the eleventh secret, between these people and the business. The business proves that it's involved with customers by means of its constant follow-up, by sending mailers, inviting customers to private sales, offering a selection tailored to their needs, providing a helpful Web site for them, and being especially nice to them, almost always remembering their names. The customers prove that they're involved by coming back several times during the year to see what's available for their homes and usually finding something to buy. They prove it by referring the store to their friends and frequently bring friends in tow when they're making a shopping foray. They show their involvement by providing testimonials and by completing questionnaires.

The dependent guerrilla

My client does not see herself as a freestanding, self-contained, independent business owner. She instead views herself as quite *dependent* on her manufacturing business, on her suppliers, on nearby furniture showrooms carrying noncompeting lines, on the media that alert her to special opportunities and open their minds to bartering time and space for a comfy sofa or two, and on competitors from distant places, with whom she trades war stories during trade shows. These people are, in turn, dependent on her for information, business, and referrals. Everybody is learning that the more dependent they are, the higher their profits will be. Dependency is another guerrilla secret. Many small-business owners view themselves as independent souls, but guerrillas know that power comes from teamwork more than from rugged individualism.

When the first edition of this book was published, my client knew as much about computers as I know about what you ate for dinner last night. But today, her computer is an integral part of her business, enabling her to boost her profits while cutting down on her marketing expenses. Dictionaries describe the equipment necessary to wage and win battles as *armament*. Armament of the guerrilla is technology. Armament is your computer, your on-line presence, your electronic connections within your business and within the entire world, voice-mail, fax machines, and wireless connections to delivery vans. It also means equipment within your factory that allows you to produce more and better for less and with fewer. All of these marketing weapons you can now create with an inexpensive desktop publishing system. The list is long and imaginative, lethal to those who deign to compete, regardless of their size and bankroll.

What you need to wage and win battles

These thirteen secrets—as embodied by thirteen words—are the most valuable secrets you'll learn in this book. They are also extremely difficult rules to follow.

Valuable rules but difficult to follow

Your friends, employees, co-workers, partners, family, and suppliers may advise you to change your marketing plan when they don't see instant results. These same well-meaning people will question a marketing program that does not produce a dramatic increase in sales over a short period of time. And they'll be the first to tire of your marketing, to become bored with your ads or commercials. But your customers won't feel this way. They'll go through the process of developing confidence in your offering, and you should do everything in your power not to undermine that process.

The moral: when you do develop your marketing plan, don't give it your stamp of approval until you are ready to commit yourself to it. Don't approve it until you are ready to invest in it with a realistic expectation of return. And don't implement it until you are prepared to stick with it consistently. This isn't to say that you can't make changes. Of course you can. But make changes while remaining consistent.

Your mission is clear

In review:

- Your task: make prospects *confident* in you.
- Your secret weapon: *commitment* to your plan.
- Your personality: *patience* describes it.
- Your marketing: an *assortment* of at least twenty weapons.
- Your format: the spirit of *consistency*.
- Your finances: some wisely *invested* in marketing.
- Your energy: apparent *prior to* and *subsequent to* the sale.

- Your operation: the essence of *convenience*.
- Your creative message: it always *amazes* readers.
- Your unglamorous but extremely profitable chore: *measurement* of who your customers are and where the heck they heard of you.
- Your relationship with customers: *involvement* is the only word for it.
- Your relationship with other businesses: you're *dependent* on each other for mutual profitability.
- Your arsenal for marketing: brimming with the *armament* of guerrillas — easy-to-use technology.

There. Now you can never say you weren't made fully aware of the thirteen most important marketing secrets. By knowing them, by making them a cornerstone of your business, you have a head start on your competition. Now let's increase that head start. Let's examine what it takes to develop a successful plan in the first place.

4

The Blueprint: Developing a Guerrilla Marketing Plan

In order to engage in successful marketing, you absolutely must start out with a marketing plan. But how do you develop one? You engage in research, attend to all details, and give the matter quite a bit of deep thought. Rest assured, the difference between many a success and failure is market planning and nothing else. Whether you're a one-person band or you work from a home office, you must operate according to a strategy, just like the big corporations.

A word that you should now start to use and understand is *positioning*. To position is to determine the specific niche that your offering is intended to fill. What will you stand for in the minds of your prospects and customers? I once read of an airline that commenced operations during a time when most airline business was drastically down. By establishing a solid marketing plan, the new airline took off with astounding speed. It positioned itself as a high-frequency, no-frills airline that specialized in flights of less than two hours and in connecting passengers with long-distance routes of other airlines. It was a unique position, because there wasn't another airline in the region that offered such benefits. Success came rather easily.

Positioning

To attract further attention, the airline held seat-clearance sales, offered free fifths of Chivas Regal scotch and Jack Daniel's bourbon, and introduced other innovations into a rather staid industry. *Each* of these marketing ideas was a result of intelligent market planning and brilliant positioning.

One of the best-known names in American advertising circles is David Ogilvy. After spending several billion dollars on advertising, Mr. O. listed thirty-two things his advertising agency had learned. Of the thirty-two, he said that the single most important decision involved *positioning the product*. He claimed that marketing results depended less on how advertising was written than on how the product or service was positioned.

The guerrilla marketing plan or strategy should serve as the springboard for marketing that sells. When doing your own market planning, review your offering with regard to your objectives, the strengths and weaknesses of your offering, your perceived competition, your target market, the needs of that market, and the trends apparent in the economy. This should be instrumental in your establishing a proper position. Ask yourself these basic questions: What business am I in? What is my goal? What benefits do I offer? What competitive advantages? What do I fear?

The springboard for marketing that sells

When you fully understand the true nature of your business, your goal, your strengths and weaknesses, your competitors' strengths and weaknesses, and the needs of your target market, your positioning will be that much easier to determine and your strategy that much easier to plan.

Small businesses have an advantage over large businesses in that they can occupy smaller niches and prosper by dominating them. A small business's specialty might be palm trees rather than a full-scale plant and tree nursery. Not a huge niche, but perfect for the small company that operates such a firm very successfully in my neck of the galaxy.

A question to ask and answer

Ask yourself, Who is my target market? The answers you had when you started in business may be different today and in the twenty-first century. Many enormous new markets are being identified in the United States, and many guerrilla marketers are enjoying record-breaking profits by aiming at these markets. Guerrilla fact: the more markets you target, the more profits you receive.

Be careful that you don't limit your marketing to only one target market. Recently the largest copying company in the San Francisco Bay Area, marketing to business in general, allocated a portion of its marketing funds to target the legal industry, because that's where the most copies are generated. This effort led to a 31 percent increase in profits in one year without spending an extra cent in marketing costs. You must identify *all* of your target markets. Then take careful aim at each.

Four relatively new markets emerged as viable target audiences in the '90s. They are now bombarded with marketing—an effort that is certain to continue throughout much of the twenty-first century. The markets are older people; women; ethnic groups, especially Asian-Americans and Hispanics; and small businesses, especially home-based businesses.

The University of Michigan informs us that older people rely on mass-media marketing even more than on friends and family when it comes to consumer information. Surveys from several sources show that older folks rank health first, financial security second, a closer relationship with God third, and a closer relationship with family fourth. In the past, when people got old, they died. Today, they control the pursestrings of a $1.5 trillion pocketbook.

Marketing to older people

When communicating with older people, guerrillas use the term "older" rather than "elderly" or "senior citizen." And instead of saying "55 and older," say "55 and better." No games, please! When using graphics, show older people as *actively old* and living life to its fullest. Avoid anything trendy. Older people respond well to products and services that appeal to their autonomy and independence. Their eyesight is faltering, so use large type in your printed material. Do you know which magazine has the largest circulation in the United States? It used to be *Reader's Digest*; then it was *TV Guide*; now it's *Modern Maturity*.

Today, more than half of the new businesses in the United States are started by women, and these businesses have higher success rates than those started by men. The kinder, gentler, entrepreneurial woman of the 1990s is very different from the woman of the 1950s. Today, one in six businesses in this country is owned by a woman. Research shows that 57 percent of women have nurtured the dream of running their own firm, with 48 percent saying that being their own boss is the reason why. We're learning more and more about this market:

The woman of today

- 61 percent of women think that kids are the best part of life.
- 8 percent of women eat three regular meals a day with no snacks.
- 16 percent of women think society could thrive without marriage.
- White women outnumber white men by 2.2 percent.
- Black women outnumber black men by 5.2 percent.
- 22 percent of computer scientists are women, up from 14 percent in 1970, but 99 percent of assistants are women, the same percentage as in 1970.
- Women spend three and one-third hours per weekday watch-

Feminine statistics

ing television. Women are less likely than men to change channels during commercials but are more likely to mute the sound.

- 41 percent of the network audience for baseball are women over the age of 18. For NBA basketball, the percentage is 37 percent; for NFL football, it's 36 percent. All of these percentages are rising.

The woman of today has more interests and can be reached through more marketing vehicles than ever before. Women have power. Examples: although 79 percent of bed purchase decisions are made by women, a man pays for the bed 77 percent of the time. Similar percentages can be found regarding other expensive items, including houses and cars, which are typically the most expensive purchases people will make in their lifetime.

Guerrillas not only include women as a target audience in their general marketing, they also direct much of their marketing directly to women and only to women. Women's purchasing power is on the incline, as is their stature in business. It's important to know the powers and the myths about women.

The powers and myths about women

Let's talk about the powers of women. They control more than 60 percent of all wealth and influence in the United States. The U.S. Bureau of Labor Statistics reports that 25 percent of working wives are paid more than their husbands. This is up 17 percent from ten years ago.

Women control or influence 80 percent of all new vehicle purchases; 46 percent of all menswear purchases; 66 percent of home computer buys; 82 percent of supermarket purchases; 53 percent of investment decisions; and 70 percent of home appliance choices.

They also handle 75 percent of family finances. The majority of single adults in the United States are women. Where 1 percent of business travelers were women in 1970, 40 percent of them were women in 1997. The Internet supersource Jupiter predicts that women will account for 50 percent of Internet use within two years.

Seven myths about women come to us courtesy of futurist Faith Popcorn:

- *Myth 1: You can market to women on product differentiation alone.* This isn't true because women want a relationship.

They'd rather buy dishwashing liquid from a company that sponsors after-school programs. Relationship innovation is more important to them than product innovation.

- *Myth 2: Products are finite and self-contained.* Another myth. Marketers need to create a dialog. Each communication needs to become two-way.
- *Myth 3: Women like to shop.* A recent report by the *Wall Street Journal* reveals that 60 percent of women feel that shopping is a negative experience.
- *Myth 4: Single exposure advertising research is a useful guide to women's' preferences.* Ms. Popcorn says that it isn't possible to gauge an ad's ability to build a long-term relationship with just one isolated viewing.
- *Myth 5: Corporation policies are unimportant.* A company's values are inseparable from their marketing activities.
- *Myth 6: Service is the preserve of the service department.* Service is the ultimate marketing function. It is everybody's preserve—or else.
- *Myth 7: Women aren't entrepreneurial.* Women start companies at twice the rate of men and employ more people than the *Fortune* 500 combined.

Unfortunately, work brings stress. *Working Woman* magazine asked its readers to name the best cures for stress. The response indicated that more money would do the trick in 61 percent of the cases and more time in 56 percent. Might you be able to offer something to alleviate this stress? If so, 82 percent might want it because they feel work has become more stressful during the past two years and 92 percent rated their stress level at three or higher on a scale of one to five. But this market is not going to diminish, because 67 percent of the readers say they are happier than their mothers were.

Ethnic groups are a potential lode of purchasing power. Asian-Americans today number 10 million, many of whom are affluent, educated, and, happily for the guerrilla, have no brand loyalties—yet.

Don't overlook ethnic groups

The Hispanic and Asian markets have a combined purchasing power of $216 billion, and they don't assimilate as they used to. They know they don't have to if they don't want to. Changes in communication technology allow new arrivals to retain their cultural and linguistic identities and allow guerrillas to target these markets with extreme accuracy. A few other facts to ponder:

Ethnic insights

- Members of the nation's population born in foreign countries accounted for 9.7 percent in 1997, a total of 25.8 million people. This is a larger segment than at any time in the past five decades.
- Half of foreign-born residents were from Central America, South America, or the Caribbean. One in four was born in Asia and one in five was born in Europe. More than 7 million residents, a full 27 percent of the foreign-born population, were from Mexico.
- The second highest number came from the Philippines, followed by China and Hong Kong.
- One-third of foreign-born residents had become U.S. citizens as of March 1997.
- California has the most foreign-born residents, 24.9 percent of its population. Next comes New York at 19.6 percent, Florida at 16.4 percent, New Jersey at 15.4 percent, and Texas, 11.3 percent.

Although the Asian market segment is the smallest of the major ethnic groups, it is growing rapidly, and statistics prove that this segment's median household income is above average in the United States.

Emphasizing the proper values

Guerrillas emphasize the values deemed traditionally important to Asians: *independence, leisure, and family unity as a means to achieve financial success and social status.* Guerrillas emphasize their product's or business's *stability.* Asian-Americans are attracted to businesses that have credibility and experience. The Asian-American market segments include the Chinese, Koreans, Japanese, Vietnamese, and the Laotians.

How to reach ethnic markets

To reach ethnic communities, consider placing ads in their newspapers, running spots on their cable TV channels, interacting with their on-line forums, becoming a presence in their on-line chat groups and conferences, experimenting with direct mail, sponsoring events aligned with the groups that are your target audiences, and linking to their Web sites if you can add value to them. Many ethnic groups rely on native language media for their consumer information.

Some marketing honchos are terrified of ethnic markets, foreign cultures, and unfamiliar languages. Guerrillas accept that challenge, working with ethnic ad agencies. Specialized advertising agencies can help you gain access to and communicate with virtually any ethnic market. More firms with this type of specialization are springing up. There are now several advertising agencies that specialize in serving the huge African-American market. You can find more information about them in publications such as *Adweek*.

Today, small business represents over 90 percent of all business in America, and 24 percent of Americans consider themselves to be telecommuters. More than 40 million Americans work from home, according to IDC/Link, a marketing research firm. And the number of home-based businesses is growing by about 20 percent each year. In 1993, there were 12.4 million home-based companies. In 1997, that number exceeded 17 million.

The average worker from home is 40.2 years old, has a household income of $59,200, is white collar, and lives in or around a major metro area. An impressive 48 percent of home workers are college graduates, and 65 percent are married. What kind of work do they do at home? The most common careers of home workers are management consultant, financial adviser, technology consultant, graphic artist, sales rep, writer, wholesaler or retailer, marketing consultant, and Internet counselor.

Workers from home

Sound like a reasonable target market to you? It should, because technology is making it easier to succeed as a small business, to work at home, and to prosper as never before.

When you have clearly focused on your market or markets, you can clarify your market position. Then you should measure the position against four criteria: (1) Does it offer a benefit that my target audience really wants? (2) Is it an honest-to-goodness benefit? (3) Does it truly separate me from my competition? (4) Is it unique and/or difficult to copy?

Four criteria to meet

Unless you are completely satisfied with your answers, continue searching for a proper position. When you've answered the questions to your own satisfaction, you'll have a sensible position—and that should lead you to your goal. An accurate market position requires clear, constructive goals and effort. Positioning is the key to marketing. No guerrilla would think of doing a speck of marketing without a proper marketing plan that includes a positioning statement.

The guerrilla marketing plan

Before writing your marketing plan, practice thinking big. At this time your imagination is not a limiting factor, so open your mind to all the possibilities for your venture.

You may write your finished plan in ten pages. At first, though, try to state it in one paragraph.

Guerrillas create strategies with seven sentences:

1. Sentence one explains the purpose of the strategy.
2. Sentence two explains how you'll achieve this purpose. It describes your competitive advantage and benefits.
3. Sentence three describes your target market—or markets.
4. Sentence four, the longest, outlines the marketing weapons you'll employ.
5. Sentence five describes your niche.
6. Sentence six reveals the identity of your business.
7. Sentence seven states your budget, which should be expressed as a percentage of your projected gross revenues.

An example of a marketing plan

Suppose you call your business Prosperity House and you intend to sell books about freelancing. Let your strategy start with the words:

"The purpose of Prosperity House marketing is to sell the maximum number of books at the lowest possible selling cost per book. This will be accomplished by positioning the books as being so valuable to freelancers that they are guaranteed to be worth more to the reader than their selling price. The target market will be people who are or plan to be engaged in freelance earning activities."

Next, the paragraph might say, "The marketing tools we plan to use include classified advertising in magazines, newspapers, and on-line, direct mail, sales at seminars, publicity in newspapers and on radio and television, direct sales calls to bookstores, mail-order display ads in magazines, weekly postings on on-line bulletin boards oriented to freelancers, E-mailings to known freelancers, and a Web site linked to many others that serve freelancers. The niche that Prosperity House occupies is a business that provides valuable information for freelancers. Our identity will be one of expertise, readability, and quick response to customer requests. Thirty percent of sales will be allocated to marketing."

That's a long paragraph. And it's a simplistic paragraph. But it does the job. It's for a product rather than a service, for an earning venture that entails hardly any contact with the public. This mail-order venture requires very little in the way of marketing, considering all the options. It works beautifully in real life; it has worked since 1974.

The plan starts with the purpose of the marketing—that is, it starts with the bottom line. Then it connects with the benefits that will beautify that bottom line and with those who will contribute to that line—the target audience. The marketing tools are then listed. Next comes the positioning statement, which explains what the product stands for—why the offering has value and why it should be purchased. The identity (not the image, which is phony compared with the honesty of an identity) comes next. And the cost of the marketing wraps it up.

Dissecting the plan

Take a moment to understand clearly the crucial difference between an *image* and an *identity*. *Image* implies something artificial, something that is not genuine. *Identity* defines what your business is really about.

The difference between an image and an identity

A business owner gets together with his staff and they develop an image, which is defined by many dictionaries as "a façade." Their marketing plan reflects the image they choose. However, if customers find that the business isn't exactly what they expected, they will feel distrustful of the company.

Another business owner gets together with his staff and they identify their identity—they base it on truth. Their marketing reflects this identity. People come in and see that the business is exactly what they expected. They feel relaxed. They know they can trust this company.

Which of these two business owners is the guerrilla? What's better for your company, a phony image or an honest identity? We both know the right answers. This is the marketing strategy of the company Computer Ace: the goal of Computer Ace marketing is to fill 100 percent of the company's available time for computer education at the lowest possible cost per hour. This will be done by establishing the credentials of the educators, the location of the operation, and the equipment. The target market will be local businesspeople who can benefit from learning how to operate a small computer. The marketing tools that will be used include a combination of personal letters, circulars, brochures, signs on off-line and on-line bulletin boards, classified ads in local newspapers, Yellow Page advertising, direct mail, advertising specialties,

Choosing between phoniness and honesty

free seminars, sampling, and publicity in local newspapers, on radio, and on television. The company will be positioned as the prime source of one-on-one, guaranteed instruction in the operation of small computers; positioning will be intensified by an on-line presence in the local community, office decor, employee attire, telephone manners, and location selection. Our company's identity will be a blend of professionalism, personal attention, and warm human regard for our students. Ten percent of sales will be allocated to marketing.

**Deceptively
simple**

Most marketing plans, especially if they are reduced to one paragraph, seem deceptively simple. A complete marketing plan, which can run as short as three paragraphs—the marketing plan, the creative plan, and the media plan—or as long as 10 or even 110 pages (not recommended), should serve as a *guide*. It need not spell out all the details.

The chairman and chief executive officer of the Coca-Cola Company recognized this need for simplicity when he said, "If I had to state our business plan in one sentence, it would be this: 'We are going to build on our marketing strength in order to achieve profitable growth in the decade ahead.'"

**The framework
for creating the
advertising**

Naturally, the marketing plan identifies the market. It provides the framework for creating the advertising—as will be seen in the next chapter. It specifies the media to be utilized, along with costs, as will be seen in Chapter 6. And that's all it really has to do.

A business plan

A business plan may require support documents such as results of research, the overall competitive situation, financial projections, and other details. However, you shouldn't include these details in the marketing plan itself. Guerrilla marketing plans are brief. A good road map lists the name or number of the highway wherever appropriate, not wherever possible.

**The briefer
the better**

The marketing plan should be the essence of simplicity. The briefer your plan, the easier it will be to follow. Bolster it with as many support documents as you wish. But don't include support information in the plan itself. Leave the details for other documents.

When your employees read the plan, they should understand your goals immediately, because your strategy is clear and direct.

Once you've given your plan the proper focus, you can expand it in those areas pertinent to your business. As you do so, remember that your main purpose is to obtain maximum profits. Profits are very different from sales. Anyone can achieve sales but it takes a guerrilla to consistently turn honest profits. You'll turn profits if you clearly list all your goals—including timing, budgets for *all* business-related plans, and projections. Without projections, you won't have a measuring stick. Your expanded plan should first address your long-term vision, then your vision for the near future.

Your main purpose

Consider the market share you are targeting, what key personnel may be necessary to command that share, which inside services you'll need, and which outside services you can use to negate the need for inside services. Whether or not you list the potential pitfalls, think about how you'll deal with them. If you're prepared for obstacles, you'll be better able to surmount them as they surface. And surface they will.

Many expanded marketing plans include a situational analysis. This includes information about your key customers, your expected competition, and the possibilities, probabilities, and reality of the marketplace at the moment. As you analyze your situation, always keep your eye on your bottom line. Don't let business get in the way of the *purpose* of business. The means should not interfere with the end.

Computers now enable us to project results based upon hypothetical instances. An expanded marketing plan or business plan may examine these "what-if" situations. It should have the framework for incorporating alternative courses of action based on contingencies. An expanded marketing plan can embrace lists of objectives, priorities, monitoring methods, problems, opportunities, and responsibilities. However, it is more of a luxury than a necessity. Many entrepreneurs get bogged down and datalogged with details to the point that the flame of their initial thrust grows dim. Huge corporations also get carried away with technology, and then they are distracted from their original dreams.

Expanded marketing plans

You should reexamine your marketing plan yearly, whether it is brief or expanded. Your goal should be to maintain it. The conservative philosophy should apply: if it is not necessary to change, it is necessary not to change.

The conservative philosophy

But whatever bells and whistles you have attached to your basic plan, whatever MBA documentation you have affixed to it, you must still know who you are, where you are going, and how you will get there. You must start with a bare-bones marketing plan, short and simple. And you should not confuse a marketing plan with a business plan. A longer plan can go into details of growth, exact expenditures, and management details. But the plans I include in this chapter will enable you to start and succeed. The first example is for a real company; the second is for a fictional company. These plans can be implemented by entrepreneurs who have a bent toward mail-order book marketing (you can write or buy the books) or computer education (you can do or delegate the teaching). Both follow a simple formula that can serve as the basis for virtually any venture. Best of all, both plans can be easily adapted to fit your business.

Such plans allow for some flexibility, but not a great deal. For example, Computer Ace may run one magazine ad only once in one regional edition and run radio commercials every day of the year. The marketing plan would still be fulfilled.

A good marketing plan should not allow for too much flexibility. After all, the plan is created to be followed. If you want changes, make them *before* you write the plan. And you must *commit* yourself to the plan.

When to make changes

When you've positioned your business with a marketing plan, what do you do next? You develop a creative plan that explains what your advertising will say—what the message is. Finally, you should create a media plan that provides exact media details: costs, names of newspapers or radio stations, dates and sizes of ads, frequency of advertising, advertising specialties to be employed, tracks for obtaining free publicity, on-line marketing strategy, and the identity of your business.

So, you've established a marketing plan that describes how you'll promote your earning endeavor. You have a creative plan that dictates your message and your identity. You have a media plan that explains exactly where you'll spend your money. Now, if you put the rest of your earning act in order—the financial side, management, legal issues, accounting, the ability to offer a lot of quality in either your products or your services, the appropriate technology, and the right mental attitude—you can start earning money.

Guerrillas begin at this point, but they sometimes get cold feet when they see the early results and then halt the marketing plan so they can think things over. This is not a good idea. If after starting a business and launching a marketing program—this entails investing serious cash in promoting the business (serious being between $100 per month and $1,000,000 per month)—you decide to halt your marketing plan, immediately read the following list of reasons why you *should* continue to market:

Why you should continue to market

1. *The market is constantly changing.* New families, new prospects, and new lifestyles change the marketplace. Nearly 21 percent of the people in America changed residences in 1996. Nearly 6 million Americans get married each year. If you stop advertising, you miss evolving opportunities and you are no longer part of the process—you aren't in the game.
2. *People forget fast.* Each and every day, Americans are bombarded with approximately 2,700 advertisements and marketing messages. In one study, a specific advertisement was shown on TV once a week for thirteen weeks. After the thirteen weeks, 63 percent of the people surveyed remembered the ad. One month later, 32 percent recalled it. Two weeks after that, 21 percent remembered it. This means that 79 percent forgot the ad after six weeks.
3. *Your competition won't quit.* People spend money to make purchases, and if you don't make them aware that you are selling something, they'll spend their money elsewhere.
4. *Marketing strengthens your identity.* If you halt your marketing program, you shortchange your reputation and reliability, and your customers will lose confidence in you. When economic conditions turn sour, smart companies continue to advertise. The bond of communication is too precious to break capriciously.

Most people don't know you exist

5. *Marketing is essential to survival and growth.* With very few exceptions, people won't know that your business exists unless you get the word out. And when you cease marketing, you're on the path to nonexistence. Just as you can't start a business without marketing, you can't maintain one without it.
6. *Marketing enables you to keep your customers.* Many enterprises survive on repeat and referral business. Loyal customers are the key to both. When your customers cease to hear from you or about you, they tend to forget you.
7. *Marketing maintains morale.* Your morale improves when you see your marketing at work, and your employees' morale is similarly uplifted. Also, some customers who actively follow your advertising may see your lack of marketing as a signal of failure.

8. *Your marketing program gives you an advantage over competitors who have ceased to market.* A troubled economy can offer a superb advantage to a marketing-minded entrepreneur. If your competitors stop marketing, you can pull ahead of them and attract some of their customers. In ugly economic situations, there are always winners and losers.

9. *Marketing allows your business to continue operating.* You still have some overhead: telephone bills, Yellow Page ads, rent and/or equipment cost, and possibly a payroll. Marketing creates the air that overhead breathes.

The air your overhead breathes

10. *You stand to lose out on the money, time, and effort you've invested.* If you halt your marketing plan, you lose all the money you spent for ads, commercials, and advertising time and space. Also, you lose consumer awareness. Sure, you can buy it again, but you'll have to start from scratch. Unless you're planning to go out of business, it is rarely a good idea to cease marketing completely.

Consider this: if you put an end to your marketing program, will you save money? You will in the way that stopping your wristwatch saves time. In other words, don't kid yourself.

I hope I've persuaded you to keep your commitment to your marketing program. Consider your marketing investment mandatory. A marketing plan is necessary—in fact, crucial—for a company or an entrepreneur. However, the plan is like a fancy, comfortable, powerful, great-looking car without gas. The fuel that powers your vehicle is the marketing itself: what it says and how it looks. The creative process comes into play in marketing, and it must be used with style and power. There are ways to make the creative juices flow. I'll let you in on the secrets in the following pages.

The fuel that powers your business

5

Secrets of Developing a Creative Marketing Program

The most enjoyable aspect of the marketing process is usually the creativity that's involved. If you want to make your small business big, you should realize that creativity applies to every aspect of the process. We'll begin by explaining how you can make your advertising itself creative. Then we'll explore how you can be creative in media selection, marketing planning, and public relations.

Almost any marketing person worth his or her salt will tell you that *marketing is not creative unless it sells.* You can be fairly certain that you will have creative marketing if you first devise a *creative strategy.* Such a strategy is similar to a marketing plan but is limited to marketing materials only—and directed solely at their content.

The creative strategy

If you think there's a simple formula for establishing such a strategy, you're absolutely right. Here, in the simplest terms possible, is a typical three-sentence creative strategy:

> The purpose of Mother Nature breakfast cereal advertising will be to convince our target audience, mothers of children twelve years of age and younger, that Mother Nature breakfast cereal is the most nutritious and healthful boxed cereal on the market. [This is the purpose of the creative message.] This will be accomplished by listing the vitamins and minerals in each serving of the cereal. [This explains how the purpose will be achieved.] The mood and tone of the advertising will be upbeat, natural, honest, and warm. [This tells the mood and tone—the personality—of the product.]

In this paragraph we listed the purpose of the advertising, the method by which the purpose can be achieved, and the personality of the ads/commercials.

You've undoubtedly seen Energizer's ad campaign with the pink bunny that "keeps on going," even into "commercials" for

The Energizer Bunny

fictitious products. The creative strategy for this marketing campaign may have read:

> The purpose of Energizer battery advertising will be to convince our target audience, primarily males eighteen to fifty-four, that Energizer batteries last an inordinately long time. This will be accomplished by creating an Energizer bunny that marches on and on through the years, powered by an Energizer battery. The mood and tone of the advertising will be humorous and single-minded, to embed the idea of Energizer's durability, while making the TV commercials fun to watch.

When you create your marketing program, your first step is to write a simple creative strategy. Practice first by writing creative strategies for current advertisers. Pick a newspaper advertiser, a television advertiser, a Web site, and a direct-mail advertiser; then compose three-sentence creative strategies that apply to each of them. Do the same for your competitors. This will guide you in establishing your own positioning and prevent you from imitating other marketing campaigns.

After you've devised your strategy—one to which you've devoted much time and thought—you can embark on a seven-step program to assure yourself of successful marketing. Let's check all seven steps.

Seven steps to creative marketing

1. *Find the inherent drama within your offering.* After all, you plan to make money by selling a product or a service or both. The reasons people will want to buy from you should give you a clue as to the inherent drama in your product or service. Something about your offering must be inherently interesting; otherwise you won't sell it. In Mother Nature breakfast cereal, it's the high concentration of vitamins and minerals.

2. *Translate that inherent drama into a meaningful benefit.* Always remember that people buy benefits, not features. People do not buy shampoo; people buy great-looking or clean or manageable hair. People do not buy cars; people buy speed, status, style, economy, performance, and power. Mothers of young kids do not buy cereal; they buy nutrition, though many will buy anything that they can get their kids to *eat*. Find the major benefit of your offering and write it down. It should come directly from the inherently dramatic feature. And even though you have four or five benefits, stick with one or two—three at most.

People do not buy shampoo

3. *State your benefits in as believable a way as possible.* There

is a world of difference between honesty and believability. You can be 100 percent honest (as you should be) and people still might not believe you. You must break the barrier that advertising has erected by its tendency toward exaggeration and state your benefit in such a way that it will be accepted beyond doubt. The company producing Mother Nature breakfast cereal might say, "A bowl of Mother Nature breakfast cereal provides your child with almost as many vitamins as a multivitamin pill." This statement begins with the inherent drama and turns it into a benefit. The word *almost* lends believability.

4. *Get people's attention.* People do not pay attention to advertising; they pay attention only to things that interest them. Sometimes they find those things in advertising. Therefore, you must grab the attention of potential customers and spark their interest. And be sure you interest them in your product or service, not just your advertising. I'm sure you're familiar with advertising that you remember for a product you do not remember. Many advertisers are guilty of creating advertising that's more interesting than whatever it is they are advertising. You can prevent yourself from falling into that trap by memorizing this: *Forget the ad. Is the product or service interesting?* The Mother Nature company might create an interesting image by showing a picture of two hands breaking open a multivitamin capsule from which pour flakes that fall into an appetizing-looking bowl of cereal.

What people pay attention to

5. *Motivate your audience to get involved.* Tell your audience to visit the store. Tell them to make a phone call, fill in a coupon, write for more information, ask for your product by name, take a test drive, or come in for a free demonstration. Don't stop short. To make guerrilla marketing work, you must tell people exactly what you want them to do.

Tell them what you want them to do

6. *Be sure you are communicating clearly.* You may know what you're talking about, but do your readers or listeners? Recognize that people aren't thinking about your business and that they'll only give about half their attention to your ad—even when they are paying attention. Knock yourself out when putting your message across. The Mother Nature company might show its ad to ten people and ask them what the main point is. If one person misunderstands, that means 10 percent of the audience will misunderstand. And if the ad goes out to 500,000 people, 50,000 will miss the main point. That's unacceptable. You want 100 percent of the audience to understand the main point. The company might ac-

complish this by stating in a headline or subhead, "Giving your kids Mother Nature breakfast cereal is like giving your kids vitamins—only tastier." Zero ambiguity is your goal.

It's lousy even if you love it

7. *Measure your finished advertisement, commercial, letter, or brochure against your creative strategy.* The strategy is your blueprint. If your ad fails to fulfill the strategy, it's a lousy ad, no matter how much you love it. Scrap it and start again. Always use your creative strategy to guide you, to give you hints as to the content of your ad. If your ad is in line with your strategy, you may then judge its other elements.

The test of creative advertising

The key to creative advertising is a smart creative strategy. The test of creative advertising is sales and profits. If what you want to sell doesn't generate profits for your business, you are not truly being creative.

How guerrillas use marketing weapons

Creativity doesn't end with the creation of your advertising. Once you've established your marketing weapons—in the form of ads, commercials, signs, circulars, and/or store decor—you must be creative in the way you use them. I know of a deodorant company that introduced its product via TV advertising during the winter. Why advertise in the winter, when people aren't buying as much deodorant? Because this company lacked the funds to go head-to-head with the big guys. So instead of vying for public attention during the summer, when its competition would be fierce, the company advertised its product and attracted attention during the winter, when it had the stage to itself.

Other ways to be creative

There are other ways to be creative. Have your personal letters hand-delivered or send them via Express Mail, Federal Express, or via an out-of-the-ordinary delivery service. Canvass creatively by wearing a unique outfit and handing a small gift to each prospect. Put your signs in unusual places, such as in the hands of paid picketers (this is a unique advertising vehicle). In the Yellow Pages, you can be creative with the size of your ad, its message, color, and its graphic treatment. Be creative in the use of newspaper advertising by running six small ads in one issue rather than one large one. Be creative in your E-mail and on your Web site. If your advertisements generate profits for your company, you're succeeding at being creative. If not, you've got more work to do.

As you can see, there are limitless ways to exercise creativity in all facets of marketing. In one of my earlier books, *Earning Money Without a Job*, I wrote about a couple who got married in their boutique after they informed the local newspapers and TV station about the wedding. Naturally, they received a lot of free coverage.

A former boss of mine, the late Leo Burnett, used to remind his staff that a person can be creative by coming downstairs with his or her socks in their mouth—but what's the point? There must be a reason for your creativity, and your creativity should never detract from your message. The Budweiser Clydesdales ad campaign is both creative and directed squarely at the target audience. Such well-directed creativity is difficult to find, to develop, and to compete against. That's why guerrillas place great emphasis on *creativity* with a *point to it*. **Your socks in your mouth**

When practicing guerrilla marketing, you must be more creative than your competition in every aspect of marketing. Be sure that you create your marketing plan properly, intelligently, clearly, creatively, and consistently. Then you can assure yourself that you are successfully marketing your product or service. You don't have to know how to write or draw to be creative. All you have to do is supply the creative idea. You can always hire someone to write or draw for you—but it's not easy to hire someone to be creative about your business for you. That task should fall to you. And you should revel in it. Let's look at a few examples of creativity in action: **Who will be creative for you**

- A CPA wanted to create more business, so he wrote a tax newsletter and sent it every three months, free of charge, to a long list of prospects. By doing so he established himself as an authority and dramatically improved his business. This isn't an earthshaking act of creativity, but it was an extremely successful plan.
- A waterbed retail store wanted to cast off its counterculture identity, so it relocated to an elegant shopping center, required its staff to dress impeccably, and hired a man with a strong, intelligent voice to serve as the announcer on its radio commercials. The results were excellent.
- A jeweler wanted to attract attention to his business during the holiday season, so he invented outlandishly expensive gift ideas, such as a Frisbee with a diamond in the center. Price: $5,000. One was a miniature hourglass that used real diamonds instead of sand. Price: $10,000. Another was a jewel-encrusted backgammon set with a price tag of $50,000. The

jeweler rarely sold such items, but he attracted national publicity, and his holiday sales soared.

Notice that in none of these examples did I talk about the creativity one usually associates with ads themselves. That's the obvious place to be creative. But these examples describe how to be creative in your prospecting, store decor, employee attire, methods of gaining free publicity. Train yourself to think that the opposite of creativity is mediocrity, and you'll force yourself to use marketing tools in the most creative manner possible.

How creativity flourishes
How does creativity flourish? With *knowledge.* You must have knowledge of your own product or service, knowledge of your competition, knowledge of your target audience, knowledge of your marketing area, knowledge of the economy, knowledge of current events, and knowledge of the trends of the time. With this knowledge you'll develop a creative marketing program *and* you'll produce creative marketing materials.

I gain knowledge by keeping abreast of world events in the usual manner. I read one weekly newsmagazine and ten monthly special-interest magazines. I often watch the late TV news. And I read one daily newspaper. I also surf the Net for about an hour a month. This isn't enough for an aggressive business owner. Guerrillas should be attuned to world happenings, to the world situation, the local situation, and up-to-the-minute trends. It's important to take a look at competitors' marketing campaigns. If you're

Keeping up or falling behind
not keeping up, you're falling behind. And guerrillas can't afford to fall behind.

Armed with this knowledge, you can do what many people define as the essence of creativity: you can combine two or more elements that haven't ever been combined. For instance, when 7UP wanted to boost its sales up there with Coca Cola and Pepsi-Cola, it referred to itself as "The Uncola." This put it in the category of the colas, yet proudly proclaimed that it was different. By combining the prefix un, which means "not," with the word *cola*, 7UP exercised great creativity. The advertising person who dreamed up the concept used his knowledge of popular art and chose psychedelic art for print and television advertisements. By using their knowledge of their product, competition, target audience, and the trends of the day, 7UP produced an exceptionally creative advertising campaign. The proof of that creativity was in the increased sales enjoyed by 7UP. And the seed was basic knowledge.

The Marlboro cigarette company exercised creativity when it combined the ideas of a cowboy and a cigarette. The AT&T telephone company used creativity when it combined the ideas of an emotionally charged situation and a telephone ("Reach out and touch someone"). Avis Rent-a-Car showed creativity when it capitalized on being the second largest, rather than the largest, car rental company, and flatly stated, "We try harder." Microsoft showed creativity in TV commercials that demonstrated many of the business and personal capabilities of owning a computer, then asked, "Where do you want to go today?" Nike, in aiming to be a global leader, established its name not with words but with a simple line it calls a "swoosh," creatively crossing all language barriers. In all of these cases, creativity started with plain and simple knowledge.

Swooshing across language barriers

It's not just in mass media marketing that you can exert creativity. When customers of Crystal Fresh Bottled Water request to have the water delivered, they receive a thank-you note signed by Jeanettte, Lee, Joyce, Diane, Jered, Nancy, Chet, Tim, Walt, Raye, Shelly, and Dan. Customers probably mention this to several of their friends and neighbors. Guerrilla marketing takes time, energy, and imagination. But you can see that it doesn't have to take much money.

As a guerrilla, you are obligated to become knowledgeable about a broad range of topics. Guerrillas are generalists, not specialists. Guerrillas know that to remove the mystique from the creative process, they must think backward. They must start by picturing the mind of their customer at the moment that customer makes a decision to purchase. What led to that decision? What were the thought processes? What made them take place? What were the customer's buttons and what did you do to push them? Thinking backward takes you to the needs and desires that are crucial to motivation.

Thinking backward

Let's take a moment to examine marketing in the light of psychology. "Skinnerian marketing" would dictate that the customer modifies his or her behavior—this kind of marketing says, shows, or does something that causes a customer to change his or her behavior (so as to act in the way you want that customer to act). You gently nudge the customer to buy, to call, to visit, to compare, to clip a coupon, to follow your command.

"Freudian marketing" is addressed to the subconscious—the most powerful part of a person's mind. "Skinnerian marketing" is addressed to the conscious—less powerful, but more easily activated. Guerrilla marketing is addressed to the conscious *and* the subconscious. It changes attitudes while modifying behavior. It comes at the customer from all directions. It persuades, coerces, tempts, compels, romances, and orders the customer to do your bidding. It leaves little to chance. It is the essence of precise planning.

What guerrilla marketing does

As technology evens the playing fields in all the marketing arenas, guerrilla marketers understand their role in the community. I quote from a very successful ice cream company's brochure: "At Ben and Jerry's, we're as concerned about our responsibility to the community, both local and global, as we are about making great ice cream." Then they prove their devotion to humanity by sponsoring altruistic causes such as the Children's Defense Fund, voter registration, peace on earth, saving rain forests, less military spending, and more recycling. Ben and Jerry sponsor concerts to spread the word—not about their ice cream as much as about their desire to save the planet. Ben and Jerry say, "Business has the responsibility to give back to the community." This is their creative platform. It sells sanity. It sells honesty. It sells nobility. It sells ice cream.

From crazy to brilliant

In the 1950s, this creative platform would have been considered crazy. In the '90s, it's considered brilliant marketing as well as humanitarian. Ben and Jerry's is famous for its good deeds. But what about Sears? Sears is pushing for recycling these days. And so are Safeway, Bank of America, Coca-Cola, American Airlines, 3M, Anheuser-Busch, DuPont, UPS, and guerrilla marketers across the nation whose businesses are not yet famous. A creative strategy in the '90s is to back a noble cause.

Cause-related marketing

Apparel-maker Liz Claiborne buys ads aimed at helping victims of domestic violence. Patagonia, the outdoor clothing company, promotes environmental awareness. Esprit, the clothing maker, urges people to vote. In 1996, more than $500 million was spent on "cause-related marketing." This includes causes such as AIDS, breast cancer, multiple sclerosis, domestic violence, healthy eating, and helping the homeless. Corporate philanthropy dawned years ago—in the mid '80s, American Express promoted restoration of the Statue of Liberty.

Are creative strategies based on noble causes successful? In one survey, 83 percent of shoppers said they had changed brands based solely on environmental concerns, and 80 percent of shoppers said a company's environmental reputation is important.

Consumers even said they'd spend a 5.5 percent premium for "green" products.

Along with this new public and corporate conscientiousness, we see a strong move toward products stamped "Made in the USA," primarily among women and older consumers on the East Coast and in the Midwest. Consumers aged eighteen to thirty-five are not as influenced by it, having grown up with foreign-made products in their homes.

Retailers report that "Made in America" promotions of apparel made domestically increase sales from 25 to 50 percent. These are numbers to be taken seriously. And so should cause-related marketing.

Made in the USA

A word of caution: be wary about basing your creative strategy on rapid societal changes that are more anecdotal than factual. The guerrilla is alert but knows the difference between a real change and a media-perceived change.

Guerrillas adapt their marketing, their creative message, and their entire philosophy to the realities of the times. Instead of fighting change, they adapt to it. And their profitability attests to the wisdom of this attitude.

Adapting to reality

6

Secrets of Selecting Marketing Methods

If you are conscientious, you can create a brilliant creative strategy and promote a noble cause. However, there are many ways you can go wrong, and one is to run the right advertising in the wrong media. How do you tell the right from the wrong? Every method of marketing has its own particular strength. Radio is the most *intimate* of the media, allowing you to spend chunks of time in one-on-one situations with your audience. Sometimes the listeners will be in crowded restaurants. But other times they'll be in their cars or in their homes—alone.

The strengths of the media

The newspaper is a prime medium for disseminating the *news*. And that strength can become your strength. Advertising in the newspaper, other than in the classified section, should be newsy, interruptive, and to the point.

Magazines are a medium with which readers become *involved*, the one that bestows upon you the greatest credibility. Whether readers buy individual newsstand copies or subscribe, they take a good, long time to read them. In your magazine ad you can attempt to capture the editorial "mood" of the magazine. You can put forth more information because readers will be willing to take more time reading a magazine ad than a newspaper ad. The credibility of the magazine becomes partly linked to you.

TV lets you demonstrate

Television is the most comprehensive medium: it enables you to convince your prospects by means of actual *demonstrations*. Demonstrations—powerful selling devices—are not possible by any other means except seminars, fairs, and live contact with audiences. Television allows you to combine words with pictures and music, to get into the minds of your potential customers. It is a *visual* medium. In fact, because so many viewers mute the commercials with their remote controls, advertisers *must* tell the story visually; otherwise, they're not telling their story at all and therefore not selling their products. Television advertising can also be very costly, so it must be done properly. This is not a medium with which to dabble.

Cable and satellite TV have put the medium within the reach of *all* advertisers. To a guerrilla, this is glorious news. A prime-time TV spot for under $20? It wasn't possible in the '70s and '80s. Today it is. And many a small business is becoming a big business as a result. Think of advertising on cable and satellite TV as an invitation to give serious consideration to what some describe as "the undisputed heavyweight champion of marketing."

Prime time for guerrillas

Direct mail allows you to take *the most careful aim* at your target audience. Created skillfully, direct-mail advertising enables you to go through the entire selling process—from securing your prospects' attention to actually obtaining sales by means of coupons the prospects can complete and toll-free phone numbers they can call. Like TV, direct mail can be very costly when misused, especially as postage rates continue to rise and the number of mailed pieces increases. To a guerrilla, postage rates aren't as important as response rates. If it costs twice as much postage to get three times the response, only a nitwit would save on postage rates. Also, guerrillas know that they should follow their direct-mail campaign with follow-up mailings, ultra-selective targeting, telemarketing, and unique mailing packages.

Outdoor signs and billboards are superb at *reminding* people of your existence and your reason for being. They aren't successful as a sole means of marketing except in rare instances. However, they work well in combination with other marketing methods. Indoor signs are a different matter altogether because they generate impulse reactions exactly where they ought to—at the place of purchase, where about 76 percent of purchase decisions are made, according to a 1996 study. Worded and designed successfully, indoor signs *capitalize on the momentum generated by your other means of marketing*. Leo Burnett, founder of one of the three best ad agencies in the world, always reminded us to "plan the sale when you plan the ad." He loved the immense power of indoor signs. They should be designed to pick up where your other ads leave off. An indoor sign might be a video message, a hologram, or a moving sign. Don't limit your advertising areas to your own inside premises—the inside of many other premises will work very well. If your prospects are there, you should try to be there. Consider airports, hotel lobbies, club bulletin boards, and stores

The power of indoor signs

owned by people with whom you've established tie-in arrangements.

The marketing medium of your dreams

On-line marketing presents guerrillas with the marketing medium of their dreams—a blend of action, connectivity, targetability, community, and economy—if they go about things in the proper manner. Guerrilla marketing on-line encompasses E-mail, postings on bulletin boards of special interest groups, chat rooms, and the World Wide Web. The great strengths of the on-line medium are interactivity, involvement, and the ability to provide as many details as your prospect wants. Do not think of your site as a thing, as you'd think of a TV spot, but instead as a *session*, because people visit you and stay as long as they wish. And then they leave. Will they ever return? That depends on the nature of your content and how quickly you reciprocate. To market on-line success-

Equally emphasizing eight elements

fully, you must equally emphasize eight elements: planning, content, design, involvement, production, follow-up, promotion, and maintenance. Regardless of the techno bells and whistles that Silicon Valley dreams up, the keys to success on-line are the content of your site, the speed of your response, the change of your data, and the personalization of your message. And as soon as you go on-line, promote your site off-line. In cyberspace, people come to you, and then you have their names. Guerrillas use those names!

Although canvassing takes more time than any other marketing method, it is highly effective. There are few limitations and it provides *personal contact*. It will often be difficult to manage canvassing on your own, so you may want to delegate the job to a professional salesperson or a college or high school student, depending on the complexity of your sales presentation.

The hottest of prospects

Canvassing should be backed by mass-marketing methods. Yellow Pages marketing and classified advertisements hit the *very hottest* of prospects. People who use these sources are searching for the kind of information you're offering, so you don't have to expend much energy to get their attention or to sell the general benefits of your product or service. This advertising also places you in direct confrontation with your competition, which should inspire you to be more precise with your message.

Going into detail

Brochures offer the greatest opportunity to go into *detail* about your product or service. People expect a lot of information from a brochure, and you should feel encouraged to provide it— you can be very informative. With today's computer software, it's easier and less expensive to design and produce a compelling brochure. And if you have a brochure, you should have a Web site on which to provide and display your brochure.

Telephone marketing provides opportunities to be more intimate than you can be in radio advertising and also offers you *great flexibility*. Your telephone marketing campaign can be supplemented by direct mail or any other marketing method, or it can stand alone. A telephone campaign can change a person who is apathetic about your product or service into someone who is prepared to purchase. And you can take orders if your prospects have credit cards. As a guerrilla, take credit cards—all of them. If folks have reached their limit on Visa and MasterCard, take American Express, Discover, Carte Blanche, Diners Club, and even Shell Oil and Macy's, if possible. This may seem mercenary, but you are offering *convenience* to your prospects, and they will appreciate the fact that you make it easy for them to buy from you.

Which credit cards guerrillas accept

Tiny signs on bulletin boards serve to make you part of *the community*, and they heighten people's confidence in you. They are also extremely inexpensive, and if your product or service meets unfulfilled needs, these signs often prove to be the most fruitful of marketing methods. As do Yellow Page and classified ads, signs on bulletin boards tend to attract serious browsers. This is not the case with, for example, television advertising.

Becoming part of the community

Advertising specialties such as T-shirts, calendars, mousepads, and baseball caps work like billboards and signs to *remind* people of your existence. They won't perform the entire selling job, but they can pave the way to acceptance of your offering when used in conjunction with other marketing vehicles. The same goes for the sponsorship of teams and events.

Many businesses get a terrific shot in the sales curve by marketing at trade shows and exhibits. They find the opportunity there to *make contacts with purchase-minded people* who are thinking about the primary topic of the show or exhibit. It is highly advantageous to reach people who have this mindset. There are fewer barriers preventing completed sales. Some companies and entrepreneurs get all the business they need by this one method of marketing. If you fall into this category, your life will be simpler.

A shot in the sales curve

Public relations, which encompasses community relations, publicity, and memberships in clubs and organizations, is a marketing method that should be seriously considered. Public relations works well with virtually all other methods, and it is often the

key to success. By becoming involved in community relations—
service to your community—you make powerful contacts, especially if you work your tail off for the community (and not merely
to serve your business needs). You can better prove your conscientiousness with your *deeds* than you can with your words. When
potential customers learn that you're working for the community
on an unpaid basis, they'll assume you work twice as hard for your
business. This, naturally, attracts them to you.

*Proving your
conscientiousness*

Publicity adds a great deal to your *credibility* and, at worst,
puts your name in the public eye. Guerrillas, however, do not buy
into the saying, "Even bad publicity is good publicity as long as
they spell your name right." Bad publicity is harmful to your
company and your goals. Avoid it at all costs.

If you join clubs and organizations, you'll be in contact with
people who can help you. It seems somewhat self-serving to join
with this purpose in mind, but many do. And it serves their purposes well. A subtle point: *guerrillas are aggressive in their marketing, but they are never crass.*

*People who
can help you*

With all of these marketing methods available, and all are
examined in this book with chapters devoted to them, which do
you, as a guerrilla, choose? *Choose as many as you can do well. The
process of guerrilla marketing begins by being aware of all the
marketing weapons available, then launching many of them, keeping careful track of which are failing and which are working wonders, then eliminating those that miss the target and doubling those
that hit the bull's-eye.*

*How the
guerrilla
marketing
process
begins*

Once you've selected the marketing vehicles that can propel
you to your goal, be sure you use them in an orderly, logical
manner. This can best be accomplished by using a *marketing
calendar.* A marketing calendar will help make all the elements in
your program mesh. It enables you to plan your budget and helps
you avoid unforeseen expenditures. It prevents you from engaging
in hit-or-miss marketing, protects you from marketing lapses, pre-
cludes surprises, and aids enormously in planning, buying, and
staffing. Clients who operate from one report that their marketing
calendar is their most precious business asset. They tell me it's
akin to getting into heaven without the inconvenience of dying.

Most marketing calendars address themselves to the weeks of
the year, to the marketing vehicles that will be employed during
those weeks, to the specific promotions or events in which you will
be engaged, to the length of each promotion, and, when applicable, to whether co-op funds from manufacturers will be available

*The guerrilla
marketing
calendar*

to help pay the tab. In addition, some calendars include the cost of the marketing for each promotion.

Armed with a marketing calendar, as all guerrillas should be, you can see far into the future. The marketing process will come into clearer focus for you. And you will find it considerably simpler to be committed to your marketing program, to see it as the investment it is, and to recognize its consistency.

A moment ago I stated that a guerrilla makes use of as many marketing vehicles as he or she can implement effectively. A marketing calendar indicates whether or not you can use these methods properly because it forces you to come to terms with the costs and realities of the media you select.

Let's examine the marketing calendar on page 64. Note that the calendar runs fifty-two weeks. The owner of this small retail store can infer, by looking at the calendar, which ads are best to run, which products should be in inventory, what costs to project, and what sales to plan. **Examining the calendar**

The calendar projects the use of the *Chronicle* every single week but staggers the monthly use of the *Sun*, the *News*, the *Independent-Journal*, and the *Gazette*. It also allows for a testing of the *Times* and the *Reporter*. This seems like a lot of newspapers, but it is clear that the *Chronicle* will be the marketing flagship.

The lengths of the marketing activities vary from one to five weeks, with a healthy balance of long, short, and medium-length events; this prevents the marketing from being too predictable. Radio is used, but not every week. With such a calendar, Electronic Galaxy is following a well-conceived plan. Promotions and sales are balanced.

Do not employ a marketing vehicle unless you are going to use it like a pro. You must put time, energy, money, and talent into it. This means that you should select marketing tools that are compatible with your business. All of the compatible marketing methods that you can possibly employ with skill, and on a regular basis, should be put to work for you. In Chapter 4, we saw that the entrepreneur named Computer Ace committed to using fourteen methods of marketing—and that didn't include decor, attire, and location. Computer Ace has the option of being a single individual or a multi-employee company, yet its marketing plan calls for the use of personal letters, circulars, brochures (we'll explain the difference in Chapter 12), signs on bulletin boards, classified ads in local newspapers, display ads in local newspapers, magazine advertising, radio advertising, direct-mail advertising, advertising **The compatibility factor** specialties, free seminars, sampling, on-line classified ads, and publicity in newspapers, on radio, and on television. Sounds like this is going to cost Computer Ace a huge sum of money. It won't. You don't have to spend a double bundle to market like a guerrilla—in fact, you may be doing it wrong if you do spend too much money. Mind you, you won't get all that marketing for free. You'll have to invest. However, it's possible to engage in a large number of marketing methods and save money with each.

Begin the process of selecting marketing methods by identifying your target audience. The better you understand your prospects, the easier it will be to attain accuracy with your marketing

ELECTRONIC GALAXY MARKETING CALENDAR

Weeks of	Marketing Thrust	Length	Co-opable	Radio	Newspapers	Cost Per Promotion
9/13	Giant Screen TV	1 wk	Yes	Yes	Chron/Sun	$615
9/20–10/4	New TV Set	3 wks	Yes	Yes-2	Chron/News	$1750
10/11–10/18	Video Experience	2 wks	No	No	Chron/IJ	$984
10/25–11/15	Names to Drop	4 wks	Yes	Yes-2	Chron/Gaz	$2044
11/22	Thanksgiving Sale	1 wk	Yes	Yes	Chron/Sun	$615
11/29	VCR Promotion	1 wk	Yes	No	Chron/News	$450
12/6–12/20	Xmas Promotion	3 wks	Yes	Yes	Chron/IJ	$2076
12/27	Last Week to Save	1 wk	Yes	Yes	Chron/Gaz	$611
1/3–1/17	TV Rut	3 wks	No	No	Chron/Sun	$1245
1/24–2/7	Trade-in Time	2 wks	No	No	Chron/News	$900
2/14–2/21	Clearance Sale	2 wks	Yes	Yes	Chron/IJ	$1384
2/28–3/28	Solve TV Problems	5 wks	No	Yes-2	Chron/Gaz	$2455
4/4–4/18	Giant Screen TV	3 wks	Yes	Yes-2	Chron/Times	$2044
4/25–5/2	People Who Love TV	2 wks	No	No	Chron/News	$900
5/9–5/16	Component TV	2 wks	Yes	No	Chron/IJ	$984
5/23	Memorial Day Sale	1 wk	Yes	Yes	Chron/Gaz	$611
5/30–6/13	Credit Is Easy	3 wks	No	Yes-1	Chron/Sun	$1445
6/20–6/27	VCR Promotion	2 wks	Yes	No	Chron/Rep	$976
7/4–7/11	Video Experience	2 wks	No	No	Chron/IJ	$984
7/18–7/25	Videotape Rentals	2 wks	No	Yes	Chron/Gaz	$1222
8/1–8/8	Free Home Demo	2 wks	No	No	Chron/Sun	$830
8/15–8/29	Giant Screen TV	3 wks	Yes	Yes-2	Chron/News	$1750
9/5	Satellite TV	1 wk	No	No	Chron/IJ	$492
9/12	Video Experience	1 wk	No	No	Chron/Gaz	$411

plans. Kids don't read newspapers. Teen-age girls rarely read business magazines, but they do listen to certain radio stations. Adult males rarely subscribe to *True Romance.* Those are the realities of the marketplace, and you have to tailor your selection of marketing methods to them.

Teenage girls and business magazines

Select as many methods as you can, but select only the ones that will be read, seen, or heard by your target audience.

Although marketing budgets are as unique as snowflakes, you might get a better bead on your target if you study the budgets of three fictitious companies. One is a small contracting company, Super Handyman, a year old, located in a town of 40,000 but within a marketing area of 150,000. The second is a two-person computer education organization, Computer Ace, three years old, outside a city of 500,000, in a market area of 600,000 people. The third is a retail stereo store, Cheerful Earful, five years in business, smack-dab in a city of 1 million people.

Suppose that Super Handyman grosses $4,000 monthly in sales. The owner is willing to spend 7.5 percent of his sales dollars for marketing—a total of $300 per month, or $3,600 per year. Computer Ace takes in $20,000 in monthly sales and invests 10 percent of that in marketing: $2,000 monthly, or $24,000 per year. Cheerful Earful grosses an average of $54,000 in monthly sales. An aggressive 12.5 percent is put back into marketing, permitting $6,750 for marketing each month, or $81,000 per year.

Let's play make-believe

Because these companies are not brand-new, they needn't invest heavily in advertising to get public attention. They already have a logotype; they have business cards, stationery, and invoice forms. They even invested from $500 (Super Handyman) to $5,000 (Cheerful Earful) for professional marketing consultation before they got started in marketing. So they each have a marketing plan, a creative strategy, and a media strategy. Their investment with the consultants has also netted them advertising themes, clear identities, and a visual format. Super Handyman obtained such a large amount of consultation for such a low price by building a sun deck for the marketing consultant in a barter arrangement. Computer Ace and Cheerful Earful worked a similar agreement, if I know my guerrillas. Look at the tables on pages 66 and 67 to see how these guerrillas would apportion their funds.

Super Handyman has selected many marketing methods. His primary marketing medium is newspapers, yet he finds quite a bit of business through his signs posted on bulletin boards and his free seminars. His on-line classified ads are beginning to net new business for him as more people discover the ease and convenience of selecting service providers on-line. His signs, seminars, and on-line postings didn't cost him any extra money, and all three are successful, according to Super Handyman, because of his newspaper advertising. Super Handyman installed a skylight for a graphic artist, who in return gave him nearly $1,000 in artwork: layouts, illustrations, type, and a finished mechanical—all ready for the printer. Super Handyman set up his trade-show booth at the Home Improvement Show, where he distributed his circulars freely and established a mailing list. Super Handyman's $300 monthly investment in marketing runs 7.5 percent of his sales this year. He projects that $300 will represent only 5 percent of his

SUPER HANDYMAN ($300 MONTHLY)

Marketing Method	Monthly Cost	Comments
Canvassing	$0	Main investment is time
Personal Letters	$0	Main investment is time
Circulars	$20	Cost of $240 yearly, amortized
Brochures	$50	Cost of $600 yearly, amortized
Signs on Bulletin Boards	$0	Posts his own circulars
Classified Ads	$40	Runs ads in two newspapers, once weekly
Yellow Pages	$20	Small listing, one directory
Newspaper Display Ads	$100	Runs ads in one newspaper, once weekly
Direct Mail	$10	Postage only, since he mails his circulars
Free Seminars	$0	Distributes his brochures at seminars
Trade-Show Booth	$10	Built booth himself, one-time cost amortized
Public Relations	$20	Cost of materials only, handles his own publicity
Production	$30	Amortized over one year, traded for a painting
On-line Classified Ad	$0	Listed in four separate areas

sales next year, indicating that he expects his sales to increase as a result of his consistent marketing program. (The prices quoted here were from 1984; they are remarkably similar fifteen years later. I guess competition from the on-line world keeps them down. It's tough to compete against free classified ads.)

This is Computer Ace's marketing budget:

COMPUTER ACE ($2,000 MONTHLY)

Marketing Method	Monthly Cost	Comments
Personal Letters	$0	Uses these to gain corporate jobs
Circulars	$30	Cost of $360 yearly, amortized
Brochures	$80	Cost of $960 yearly, amortized
Signs on Bulletin Boards	$30	Monthly fee to have company's flier posted
Classified Ads	$40	Uses one newspaper twice a week
Yellow Pages	$30	Medium listing, one directory
Newspaper Display Ads	$940	One ad weekly, two newspapers
Magazine Ad (One Time)	$100	One full-page ad in *Time*, amortized over one year
Radio Spots	$400	Spends $100 weekly; on one FM station
Direct Mail	$100	Postage only, since company mails circulars
Advertising Specialties	$30	Cost of computer-oriented calendars
Free Seminars	$0	Distributes brochures at these
Sampling	$0	Offered to corporations
Public Relations	$20	Amortized for one publicity push yearly
Production	$200	Amortized over one year—all production of circulars, brochures, ads, commercials
On-line Classified Ads	$0	Placed in four different categories

Computer Ace receives a lot of referral business. The brochures spur word-of-mouth recommendations, and the newspaper ads sell prospective customers completely, inspiring them to phone Computer Ace, where they receive a sales pitch and are encouraged to send for a free brochure. The radio spots direct people to make a phone call. Although Computer Ace spends little for telephone marketing, it engages in a good deal of it as a result of responses to the newspaper and radio advertising.

Computer Ace would love to demonstrate its proficiency on TV but simply cannot afford it. Each year, a publicity stunt such as free computer lessons for city-hall employees results in free TV coverage. The figure of 10 percent of sales invested in marketing will drop to 7.5 percent next year because of an increase in sales. Actual marketing outlays will remain the same.

An ambitious guerrilla   The marketing expenditures for Cheerful Earful are even more ambitious:

CHEERFUL EARFUL ($6,750 MONTHLY)

Marketing Method	Monthly Cost	Comments
Brochures	$200	General brochures with no prices
Point-of-Purchase Signs	$205	One-time cost, amortized over one year
Yellow Pages	$200	One large listing in two directories
Newspaper Display Ads	$2800	Two large ads weekly, two newspapers
Radio Spots	$1400	Consistently run on three FM stations
Television Spots	$500	Two one-week TV splashes, amortized
Direct Mail	$300	Three yearly mailings, amortized
Free Seminars	$0	Held at store, sales made afterward
Searchlight	$20	For one yearly promotion, amortized
Production	$625	Amortized over one year
Web Site	$500	For design, promotion, and maintenance

It's interesting to note that Cheerful Earful, which has the largest of the three budgets examined here, employs the fewest marketing methods. However, it uses two methods seriously: radio and newspaper advertising. The radio rates are very low, since spots are purchased through the company's internal ad agency (more about that in Chapter 7) at a very favorable one-year contractual rate. The newspaper ads are also available at one-year contract rates, at a substantial discount. Television advertising is used with force two times a year: the cost is $3,000 for each week. The Web site costs pay for an attractive and comprehensive multipage site; it is updated weekly and provides price lists for many categories of products, not to mention color photos.

Like other guerrillas, Cheerful Earful is presently spending a large amount—12.5 percent—on marketing. This tactic has eliminated several competitors who spent less boldly (although they enjoyed higher annual sales than Cheerful Earful, their marketing did not reflect this). Cheerful Earful, like all smart guerrilla marketers, plans to spend the same amount on marketing next year, but expects that it will represent only 10 percent of sales. The following year, that amount should represent 7.5 percent of sales. The plan is to spend no less than 7.5 percent on marketing, because the stereo business is highly competitive.

Desktop publishing

Desktop publishing can cut some of the costs, especially if the costs include newsletters and a lot of direct mail. In the past I've alerted small-business owners to the fact that marketing is not a do-it-yourself process (see Chapter 27), and desktop publishing is best left to experts who are savvy. Listen to the music: existing computer software makes desktop publishing so incredibly easy (read *The Desktop Publisher's Idea Book* by Chuck Green or *Web Design and Desktop Publishing for Dummies* by Roger Parker) that I consider desktop publishing to be the guerrilla's secret weapon. It's simple to use, and it creates materials that earn so much credibility that I sincerely believe it gives small-business owners an unfair, yet welcome, advantage. The price of first-rate credibility has dropped considerably since guerrilla marketing was invented and codified. So run—don't walk—to new computer software if you want to save big money on the production and design of newsletters, fliers, brochures, circulars, signs, direct mail, Web sites, and more.

Reach and frequency

When advertisers discuss media, they talk of *reach* and *frequency*. Reach refers to the number of people who will be exposed to the message; frequency refers to the number of times each person will be exposed. Although you'll strive for reach in certain endeavors, frequency is best. Remember, familiarity breeds confidence, and confidence serves as the springboard to sales.

Before you select a marketing method, remember these ideas: it is not necessary to say everything to everybody, nor is it possible. If you try to say everything to everybody, you'll end up saying everything to nobody or nothing to everybody. Instead, you should strive to say something to somebody. Your marketing message is the "something." Your target audience is the "somebody." Just as you take care in selecting what you will say, you should take equal care in selecting to whom it will be said. It is not acceptable to say the right thing to the wrong people. Although TV advertising does wonders for the ego, if your prospective customers don't watch much television, it is folly.

Say something to somebody

I suggest that you embrace the idea that you'll employ absolutely every marketing method listed in this chapter. Then cut the list on the basis of who your audience is, whether you can use the method properly, and whether you can afford the method. With the methods that are left on your list, go for glory. Maximize your utilization and mastery of each. When you combine two surefire marketing methods with two other surefire marketing methods, the total is greater than four—a synergistic effect is created whereby two plus two equals five and six and seven. And when you combine five marketing methods with five others, your possibilities for success increase manyfold.

The more methods of marketing you employ, and the greater your skill at employing and selecting them, the greater your bank balance. The idea is to combine the right marketing message with the right marketing media. That's the guerrilla truth.

7

Secrets of Saving Marketing Money

Saving money is important to everyone—to consumers, to large companies, and to entrepreneurs—*especially* to entrepreneurs. Entrepreneurs are, for the most part, suffering from resource poverty, and not a penny can be wasted. And all money should pull more than its own weight. But is this possible? Bright entrepreneurs make it possible. This chapter suggests several ways to stretch your marketing dollars without decreasing their effectiveness one iota.

Dollar stretching

First of all, *don't feel that you must constantly change your marketing campaigns*. This requires you to spend more production money and it dilutes the overall effect of your marketing. Stick with one campaign until it loses its pulling power. This is difficult to do. In the beginning, most people will like your ad. Then you'll become bored with it. Next, your friends and family will get tired of it. Soon your fellow workers and associates will be bored, and you'll want to change the ad. Don't do it! Let your accountant tell you when to change ads. That's right, your accountant—the person who takes long looks at your profit picture. You can be sure your accountant won't get tired of an ad that continues to pull in business over the long term. The public's reaction to your ad is most important, and it takes a long, long time for the public to get tired of an advertising campaign. If you always keep this in mind, you'll stretch your media money and save production dollars. I'll be telling you several ways to save money in this chapter, but all of them pale in comparison with the way I've just mentioned. The best way to save money marketing is to stick with your marketing program. Abandoning your program too soon is the best way to waste money. Can I say it more clearly?

Who should tell you when to change your ads

Another way to save impressive sums is to make use of the concept of *barter*. Your local radio station or newspaper may not

Bartering

want what you are selling, but they do want *something*. In all likelihood, you can trade with someone who has what they want. If so, you'll get your media ads for a fraction of their usual cost, since you'll be paying with your own services or goods at their *full retail price*. Guerrillas learn of the exciting world of barter by calling 714-831-0607 and closely examining *Barter News*.

Here's an example of bartering: a stereo dealer wanted to advertise on radio but he couldn't afford the cost. He offered to trade recording equipment, but the station wasn't interested. The station was interested, however, in constructing a new lobby. The stereo dealer found a contractor who wanted new stereo equipment. Result: the contractor received $5,000 worth of stereo and television equipment; the radio station got its new lobby; the stereo dealer received $5,000 worth of radio time. Yet the dealer's cost was only $2,500 in equipment. In fact, his cost was less than that because he traded discontinued merchandise that he otherwise would have discounted.

There are many barter houses in the United States that specialize in such trades, sometimes between as many as ten companies. Look in the Yellow Pages for barter houses in large metropolitan areas, listed under "Barter Services" and "Media-Buying Services." At least 500 magazines will trade ad space for whatever it is they need. Policies vary at publications, however, and trades must be individually negotiated. Remember that everyone needs something. By learning what your selected media need, you may be able to set up a money-saving trade.

When I discovered the world of barter, it was much like the first time I went scuba diving. An entire world existed within my own world and I wasn't aware of it. To give you an inkling of the magnitude of barter in today's economy, consider that in 1996 more than 55 percent of media was not purchased but obtained by barter.

Gaining access to co-op funds　　You can also save money by gaining access to *cooperative advertising funds*. Many large advertisers pay cash fees to small advertisers who mention their name or show their logo in their ads. I know a woman who owns a small furniture store. When she mentions the name of a large mattress company in her ads, she receives a small sum of money from that company. Naturally, most of her ads mention the name of a large manufacturer that offers co-op ad funds. Look into co-op advertising—it not only helps save money for entrepreneurs, but also lends credibility to their offerings by mentioning the name of a nationally known company. Some companies that offer co-op funds insist that they be the only company mentioned. Others don't care, just as long as you spell their name correctly. Still others demand that you include their theme line or logo in your ad. A smart entrepreneur, interested in saving marketing money, will include the names of several co-op-oriented companies, thereby saving a large percentage of the ad cost—frequently more than 50 percent. This requires research and organization, but if you're interested in saving money, it's worth it.

Spell their name correctly

Talk to your suppliers and simply ask them about their co-op program. If they don't have one, ask them to start one. One of my clients consistently has more than half of his marketing costs covered by co-op funds. His business is video rentals; the co-op funds come from movie studios. Very few advertising agencies will help you obtain co-op funds, so it's your job. Because it significantly reduces your investment in marketing, it's worth every minute you or your designated guerrilla devote to it. Who says you can't get something for nothing?

Ask and you might get

I also suggest that you set up a *P.I. or P.O. arrangement with an advertising medium.* This is a fairly common method that entrepreneurs use to save and make money. P.I. means "per inquiry" and P.O. means "per order."

P.I. and P.O.

Here's an example of how it works. You contact a television station to ask if it's interested in establishing a P.I. or P.O. arrangement with you (the station gives you television time, and in return, you give a prearranged sum of money per inquiry or per order). Suppose you want to sell books for $10 by mail. You strike up a deal with a TV station whereby the station gives you commercial time and you give the station, say, $3 per order. At this point, no money has changed hands. Now, the TV station provides you with the equipment to produce a commercial heralding your book. Normally, it might charge $100 to run a one-minute commercial, but it gives you the time for free. Then the commercial runs and fifty people order the book. That means the TV station receives $150 (at $3 per order), which is a good deal for the station. You also do well because you receive fifty orders ($500) and risk no marketing costs. Now, if you can make that same arrangement with one hundred other TV stations, you can clearly make very substantial profits without risking marketing outlay.

P.I. and P.O. arrangements are possible to establish with many magazines, radio stations, and television stations. I've never heard of such arrangements to be possible with newspapers, but I imagine that some farsighted publishers would welcome the idea. All it takes is a letter to the medium of your choice, outlining the arrangement you're proposing. If the medium feels it can make money on your offer, you're in business. In this way, you can engage in high-level marketing with virtually no up-front costs other than minimal production costs. The TV station might unfortunately put your commercial in a time slot after midnight—or a time slot that couldn't be sold to another advertiser—but you can bet that the TV station wants to make money on the arrangement. Therefore, it will go all out. And if it makes money, you make money.

If it makes money, you make money

Many an entrepreneur has made many a dollar with this little-known method of saving marketing dollars. A client of mine sold $3,000 worth of his newsletters through a P.I. arrangement with a magazine publisher. The publisher gave free ad space (a full-page ad typically would cost $900) in return for a $50 cut of a $100 subscription price. Thirty subscribers signed up. Result: $1,500 for the publisher and $1,500 for my client—the first year. Renewals will increase his profits.

The magazine wanted to repeat the ad—on the same P.O. basis. Naturally, my client nixed the offer and paid the magazine full price for the full-page ad.

People enjoy being asked about themselves; they enjoy talking about themselves. Take advantage of this human characteristic by *asking questions of your customers*. You'll get expensive research data for free. Prepare a survey that asks your customers all sorts of questions. Some will toss your questionnaire in the wastebasket. Others will answer it thoroughly and provide you with a wealth of information. If you were to get this research through standard research-company channels, it would cost you a fortune. But when obtained the way I've just described, this same information costs very little. More about this in the next chapter.

Free research

If you are a patient sort, you can save money, lots of it, by taking advantage of "gang runs." Some printing companies often run huge amounts of full-color printing on large presses all at once, and occasionally they can run a bit more printing than is scheduled. If you need to have something printed and wish to save money, let a large printer know that you're interested in being included in a gang run and are patient enough to wait until they have one. Furnish the printer with the press-ready materials and the paper: eventually, the printer will have that gang run and you'll be the happy recipient of a mass of full-color brochures, obtained at a fraction of the normal price. To take advantage of this money-saving opportunity, all you have to do is be patient. I've seen clients too impatient to wait for gang runs. They paid five times the price they would have if only they hadn't been in a hurry. And, unfortunately, their rush was often unnecessary.

Impatience is a deterrent to good marketing and to inexpensive marketing as well. If you wish to gain the maximum effect from your marketing and to save money at the same time, avoid rushes like the plague. If you have a solid marketing calendar, a program that is planned ahead for a year, it will be quite easy to avoid them. **Slow down**

In order to save money in marketing, you must be aware of three variables—quality, economy, and speed. Select *any two* of them. Guerrillas opt for the first two. Their penchant for planning means they are rarely in a rush, and they focus on quality and economy. **The three variables**

You can also save considerable sums of money if you realize that the cost of radio and TV time is nothing if not negotiable. Of course, prime time or drive time is difficult to buy and difficult to negotiate. However, if radio or TV time is not sold, it is wasted forever. Therefore, stations will usually accept prices far below their normal rate-card prices. Deals abound.

To entice new advertisers—that is, entrepreneurs—TV stations will ordinarily offer attractive prices. Large advertisers know that rate cards are works of fiction, but small advertisers often believe what they read on rate cards. Don't you believe it. Remember that you can save media money by *making an offer you can afford.* You'll be surprised at how many radio and TV stations will accept your offer. **An offer you can afford**

While we're on the subject of radio and television, let me emphasize that a vast amount of research has proven that you can accomplish almost as much with a thirty-second commercial as you can with a sixty-second commercial. So save money by cutting the verbiage and saying your message in half a minute. If your message is concise and specific, it can be shorter than thirty seconds. In 1996, more than 80 percent of national TV commercials were less than thirty seconds long. The briefest messages are termed "electronic billboards" rather than TV commercials. **Ad size**

You'll save money by applying this truism to your print efforts. Unless you feel it is absolutely necessary to run large, expensive newspaper or magazine ads, you can attract business just as successfully by running small, inexpensive, but routine newspaper or magazine ads. You may not look as important as the purchasers of full-page ads, but you'll end up making more money. Don't forget: consistency is one of the most important factors in marketing. You can achieve that consistency with small ads as well as large ones. The size of your ad does not produce the consumer confidence that consistency does—this truth will save you impressive sums.

It is axiomatic that shoddy production gives you a shoddy image. Therefore, when running print ads, especially newspaper **A silly savings** ads, it is usually silly to save money on production by having the newspaper or other medium design your ads. Instead, hire a professional do this.

There are basically two types of professionals: high-cost and low-cost. To save the most money and achieve the greatest exposure, hire a high-cost designer to lay out your first ad and create a visual format for you. Then hire a low-cost to create all of your follow-up materials, telling him or her to follow the format used in the original ad. This will not infuriate the inexpensive designer, who will probably be thrilled with the business, and it won't anger the expensive designer, who received a fair sum for the talent expended. You will always have sharp-looking ads, even though you paid through the nose only once. You have the best of two worlds: a classy look and format throughout the life of your marketing campaign and a low price for the production of all the ads except the first. You shouldn't have to spend high production fees more than one time, and believe me, it's well worth it. Ask any entrepreneur who has employed this tactic.

Tapping the It's a good idea to tap the power of a pro for your magazine or
power of newspaper ad, your Web site or TV spot. But you can save an
pros ... extraordinary amount of money and reap generous profits if you create marketing materials with your own computer. Open your
... or doing it mind to posting fliers, offering brochures, providing catalogs, de-
yourself signing point-of-purchase and trade show materials, making multimedia presentations, marketing with newsletters, and marketing aggressively on the Web. *You can create these guerrilla marketing weapons right at your desk.*

Half an hour. That's all it takes today to design a newsletter that would do any small-business owner proud. With easy-as-pie software, it's not a matter of creating new designs—you can choose from a generous selection of past designs. Select page designs, artwork, formats, mastheads, and typefaces by pointing and clicking. You'll be absolutely amazed at how creative you can be, at how much money you can earn by creating a broad array of weapons, and at how much money you can save by doing it on your own. Your kid can probably do it for you. In the year 1996, for the first time there were more computer-literate first-graders than computer-literate first-grade teachers.

Save bundles by finding multiple uses for your marketing materials. That photo you used for your ad in the trade magazine? Use it in your brochure, at trade shows, in your catalog, in a PR story, on your Web site, on a calendar you distribute. The cost of the photo, which you may have thought to be high at first, becomes astonishingly low when amortized over time and multiple materials. **Finding multiple uses**

Save even more by writing timeless marketing materials. In your brochure, don't say your business is five years old, because then you'll have to update the information next year. Instead, say your business was founded in 1993—this will always be true. And don't show pictures of your employees, because one of them might be a competitor next year. Timelessness is the name of the economy game.

Another name is *experimentation*. Before you commit yourself to a campaign, experiment and test. Test your idea in a mailing, in a chat room, a Web-site survey, an inexpensive newspaper. Run the same ad in five local papers to see which paper evokes the greatest response, then run five different ads in that paper to see which is most successful. Pray you don't get a five-way tie! Mail the same letter to five different lists and see which is most receptive to your offer. Then mail five different kinds of letters to your winning list to learn which one generates the greatest response for you. You must be willing to fail during the testing. Your goal during this phase is *solid information* rather than high profits. When you've got the right data, the bank deposits will follow.

Have you ever heard of remnant space? Probably not, unless you're in the marketing business. Many national magazines publish regional editions. When doing so, they sell advertising space to regional advertisers. Because of the way magazines are printed, publishers think in terms of four-page units, because it takes one **Remnant space** large piece of paper folded in half to make four pages that fit comfortably into a magazine format. Often a magazine will have sold only three of its four pages as publication date draws near. What does the publisher do with that extra page—that remnant space? Sells it at an astounding discount to a local advertiser. If you wish to be that local advertiser, contact the publication well in advance of the date you wish your ad to appear, or get in touch with Media Networks, Inc., a company devoted to selling remnant space to local advertisers. The company is national, and its toll-free number, from which you should request a free rate book, is 1-800-225-3457. Media Networks can put your ad in most national magazines, in the regional issues, at a far lower cost than you may think.

For example, a full-page, black and white ad in *Time* magazine costs approximately $85,000. Media Networks, Inc., can sell you a full-page black and white ad in *Time* magazine in Tucson, El Paso, Wilmington, Savannah, or many other cities for under $3,000—an $82,000 savings. Some difference!

An efficient money-saving strategy

While we're on the subject of advertising space, we should look at one of the most efficient money-saving strategies in all of marketing—a house advertising agency. Advertising agencies earn their money by receiving a 15 percent discount from publications and broadcast stations where they place advertising. If an ad or commercial costs an advertiser $1,000, that same ad space or commercial time costs an advertising agency only $850. This is known as an agency discount, and advertising agencies are entitled to every cent of it. The advertiser would have to spend $1,000 anyhow. By using an ad agency, the advertiser receives professional help at no extra cost, since the advertisement will cost $1,000 with or without an agency. And the ad agency picks up $150 for its efforts.

You are the advertising agency

What do you do if your business is too small to require the service of an advertising agency? And what if you don't *want* to use an advertising agency? Establish your own in-house ad agency. To create an ad, you usually need only to tell the advertising medium that you are an in-house or internal agency for your business. In some cases, the medium may require that you have a checking account in your agency's name (ten dollars in an account will do nicely). And you may need agency stationery. Again, this is no problem. If your business is called Atlantic Manufacturing, just call your agency Atlantic Advertising and print the name on inexpensive stationery that you order in the minimum amount.

With a checking account and stationery, you are ready to

establish your own in-house advertising agency. And you can save 15 percent on almost all the advertising you place for yourself. You can save on virtually everything but newspaper advertising, for which you pay only the retail rate, which is low to begin with. It's so easy to set up an internal agency that I'm surprised more entrepreneurs don't do so. You can save a considerable sum of money—your $3,000 *Time* regional ad will cost you only $2,500.

If you ever use local television, start out with tight, well-written scripts. Plan a rehearsal session or two prior to the shooting date, then try to shoot three or four commercials in one session. Although the average thirty-second TV commercial costs around $200,000 to produce (thanks to the soft drinks, beers, fast-food chains, and celebrity endorsements), you can reduce the cost to less than $1,000 if you shoot several spots at once, work with thought-out scripts, and avoid paying high talent fees to actors and actresses. Again, some difference! There are several reasons for the difference: full-scale TV productions usually involve large crews for lighting, props, makeup, hairstyling, and transportation of cameras, and this ordinarily involves union and inflated costs. Guerrillas work with skeleton crews and do not work with unions unless absolutely necessary. They're not anti-union; they're pro-efficiency.

TV production on a shoestring

The editing process is one of the most expensive aspects of TV production, especially if videotape is used. With well-planned scripts, your ad will require little editing.

Some advertisers feel that they must hire a celebrity to sell their wares. This adds from $5,000 to $500,000 to the tab. Two Michaels command even more: Jackson and Jordan. It's true that Nike committed X millions of dollars to Tiger Woods for his endorsement and may end up earning 10X in profits as a result. But guerrillas rely on the power of an idea and save the cash.

Production devices such as complex scenery, special effects, and ornate sets make commercials extremely expensive. Because many people are involved in the actual shooting, each scene may be shot four or five different ways to stroke four or five different egos. Guerrillas shoot each scene one way and get their ego kicks through sizable bank deposits.

In addition, TV professionals tend to shoot commercials to suit their own tastes and needs. They can spot flaws that most viewers would never see. So they reshoot and reshoot and reshoot. Guerrillas accept minor flaws and get on with the commercial.

All of these strategies add up to a whale of a difference in money—but not in quality. I have a reel of commercials, each costing under $500. TV pros who have seen them have estimated that the cost of each spot was $10,000 or more. In my opinion, unnecessary TV production costs are murdering many large-company production budgets. Amazingly, they are easy to avoid. So avoid them.

Vampire marketing

Guerrillas are always very careful to avoid vampire marketing, which sucks attention away from their primary message. Viewers remember the special effects but they don't remember the advertiser. It's the funny joke that people recall as they forget who paid to tell it. It's the clever presentation that bleeds dry the motivating offer by directing focus to itself and not the benefit to the prospect.

I've told you that the best way to save money is to commit to a marketing program and give it time to sprout wings and fly. Now I'll tell you the second best way to save your valuable cash: market primarily to *customers* and not to prospects. It costs one-sixth as much to sell something to a customer than to sell it to a prospect. Direct your marketing funds toward follow-up, toward surpassing customer expectations, toward gaining repeat business, toward earning referral business, toward enlarging the size of your transactions. Your growth will pay off in profits even more impressive than the money you'll save by the inward, rather than outward, thrust in your marketing.

Two kinds of advertising

In the final analysis, there are two kinds of advertising: expensive and inexpensive. Expensive advertising doesn't work. Inexpensive advertising is the kind that works—regardless of cost. You'll save the most if you always make sure to run inexpensive advertising—the kind that gives you the results you want. It has more to do with *results* than cost.

8

Secrets of Obtaining Free Research

Marketing pros will tell you that the three most important things you need to do to market anything successfully are to test, test, and test. That is good advice. And the big secret is that you need not shell out any money to learn about your market. If you know what to look for and where to find it, you can obtain crucial information for nary a cent. Let's examine some of the things you might want to find out:

Twenty crucial questions

1. What should you market—your goods, your services, or both?
2. Should your marketing feature some sort of price advantage?
3. Should you emphasize yourself, your quality offerings, your selection, your service, or only the existence of your business?
4. Should you take on your competition or ignore all competitors?
5. Exactly who are your competitors?
6. Who are your best prospects?
7. What income groups do they represent?
8. What motivates them to buy?
9. Where do they live?
10. What do they read, watch, and listen to in the way of media?
11. Do they have fax machines?
12. Are they on-line?
13. Do they have children? If so, what are their ages?
14. What are their favorite sports teams?
15. What are their hobbies?
16. What does their spouse do for a living?
17. What activities most interest their kids at school?
18. Where did they attend high school and college?
19. What are their purchase plans for the coming year?
20. What do they most like about your company?

Complete answers to these questions can prove invaluable to a marketing effort. A lack of answers can prove disastrous. Do what you must to get the answers.

In most cases, great advertising is preceded by great research. There are four inexpensive research methods that will provide you with the information that can make the difference between success and failure.

Enlist your library as an ally

The first is to go to your local library. The reference librarian, one of America's greatest untapped resources, can steer you to just the books and other publications that contain a raft of money-making information for you. Also, many reference librarians know the Internet intimately. Some of the sources to which you'll be directed have market studies of your area, conducted by companies that paid impressive sums for the data. Others contain studies of products or services such as yours and indicate the level of their acceptance by the public. Still others include census reports, research reports, and industry studies. Whenever I wrote a book, I found myself in libraries ferreting out information. And I am always dazzled by the expertise of the reference librarians who not only know where to find information but also seem to delight in the searching. And all the information to which they lead you is free for the asking.

The more customer information you have, the better equipped you'll be to serve those customers. This is where inquisitiveness pays off big. When I write a book these days, I get my information from the Internet. I lean heavily on search engines, which are becoming easier to use and better at their job on a regular basis. Who is a true expert on those search engines? You've got it—your reference librarian.

Your customers have the answers

A second, and commonly overlooked, way to get information is to ask your own customers. If you have a new business, I strongly suggest that you prepare a lengthy questionnaire for them. On it, ask them everything under the sun.

Large corporations that enclose brief questionnaires with their manufactured items such as TV sets, electric razors, or blow dryers report that fewer than half the questionnaires are returned. These questionnaires often consist of only five or six questions. On the other hand, I had a client who gave each of his customers a fifteen-question survey. Seventy-eight percent of the forms distributed were completed and returned. It seems that many people enjoy providing personal information, just as long as they can remain anonymous.

Suppose you want to establish a company that provides auto mechanical services at people's homes rather than in a garage. You might prepare and distribute a survey that asks the following questions of your prospects—namely, motorists:

We are establishing an automotive service that makes "house calls." To help us serve you most effectively, please provide the following information:

What type of car do you drive?_____

What year is it?_____What model?_____

How long have you owned it?_____

Who usually performs mechanical services for your car?_____

Would you want these services to be performed where you live?____

List the three main reasons you would want "house calls" made to service your car:_____

_____

Would you pay more to have "house calls" for your car?_____

What is your sex?_____ Your age?_____

Your household income?_____

What newspapers do you read?_____

What radio stations do you listen to?_____

What TV shows do you watch?_____

Which magazines do you read?_____

What type of work do you do?_____

Do you have a fax machine?_____ What is your fax number?

_____

Are you on-line?_____ What is your E-mail address?

_____

Do you have a Web site? _____ What is your Web address?

_____

Would you purchase products as well as service from a traveling automotive service?_____

Who do you consider to be our competition?_____

Where would you expect us to advertise?_____

Do you have any other comments?_____

_____

In this game of twenty questions, you always emerge the winner. By studying the *questions only,* you can easily see how much you'll learn. Think of how informed you'd be by studying the answers! This kind of questionnaire should be distributed for a number of months, and the answers should be studied each month so that trends can be spotted after the business is established. Note that the questionnaire doesn't ask the name or address of the customer. Anonymity is preserved, enabling you to ask many personal questions. Some questionnaires do ask for names and addresses, sacrificing the promise of anonymity in the quest for more detailed personal information. Guerrillas employ both, knowing that the more personal data they have, the better they can target their marketing.

What you'll learn

When you analyze the completed questionnaires, you'll learn specifics about your prospects, how best to reach them through the media, how to appeal to them, and what kinds of cars they drive. You can analyze the questionnaires by grouping the responses to each question. Perhaps you'll learn that the majority of people interested in patronizing your business drive foreign cars. This alerts you to the possibility of sending a mailing to foreign-car owners. Their names are available from mailing-list brokers. It might be that your customers are owners of older cars. Again, you can reach these people with a targeted mailing. The questionnaire will help you focus your advertising to the right people.

From the questionnaire, you can learn who your competition is by learning who usually performs mechanical services for your prospects. You can determine what it is you offer that is most enticing to your customers—again helping you choose the proper emphasis for your advertising. You'll discover the sex and age of your customers, and you'll learn exactly how and where to communicate with them once you ascertain the newspapers, radio stations, TV shows, and magazines that interest them. If your customers are primarily white-collar workers, the questionnaire will inform you of that fact, and you can tailor your media selection to that reality. You can learn which marketing vehicles will work most effectively for you and you can get a report on your own service.

Customers change

This analysis greatly helps you in determining your marketing thrust, and yet it's extremely inexpensive. Use the information to update or revise your marketing plan. And just think, your only expense was for the duplication of the questionnaire—well under $100. This is free research at its best, and, frankly, you're nuts if you don't take advantage of it. Repeat it every few years to keep abreast of your market. Things change lightning fast, including details about your customers.

The third way to take advantage of inexpensive research is to prepare a questionnaire similar to the preceding one and give it to people using the kinds of services you provide. By doing so you research serious, rather than potential, prospects. You'll receive fewer returns than the 78 percent my client enjoyed, but you'll learn something—which is much more valuable than knowing nothing. Naturally, you won't hand your questionnaire to motorists if you're selling computer education. If that's your business, you'll want your questionnaires in the hands of people entering or departing computer stores. If you are a traveling hairstylist who makes house calls, hand your questionnaires to people leaving beauty salons or barbershops. Whatever your business, you can find prospective customers somewhere: with their kids at the playground; at the beach; in the park; downtown; at the hardware store; at the ballpark. Chances are, you've already got a line on where they are. All you have to do is go there and distribute your long list of questions.

How to get answers to your questions

How do you ensure that the prospective customers will return your questionnaires? You can furnish them with stamped envelopes. You can tempt them with offers of free (but inexpensive) gifts. You can offer them discounts if they complete and return your questionnaire. And you can use pure honesty by explaining, at the beginning of the questionnaire, exactly why you are asking so many questions. Just be sure to include your address so that the questionnaires will be mailed (or brought) to the right place.

You should have an introductory paragraph atop your questionnaire, which could read, "We're trying to learn as much as possible from motorists in the community so that we can offer them the best possible service. We apologize for asking you so many questions in this questionnaire, but we're doing it so that you can benefit in the long run. We promise that your answers will remain anonymous (note that we are not asking for your name). And we also promise that we'll use the information to help you enjoy better automotive service." An honest introduction such as this serves to disarm people who resent being asked so many questions, and it explains *exactly* why you are distributing the survey.

Once again, you end up with valuable information. And again, it costs you hardly a cent. A true guerrilla will use *all three methods* to get free research. Then he or she will put the information to work to create a first-rate marketing plan, using reliable data that can aid in the selection of marketing methods, the evaluation of the competition, and the framing of the creative message.

The fourth method of research is to tap the greatest informa-

The greatest source of information in history

tion source ever developed: the Internet. It truly is, as Bill Gates said, the information superlibrary. And it is more conveniently located than your local library. If you can't find what you're looking for on the Internet, you're probably not looking in the right places. (However, I want to remind you that the *most crucial* information is not and probably never will be on the Internet—that is personal information about your customers. As much as I laud the Net, as much as I implore you to engage in a weekly surf to learn the intricacies and secrets of the Net, I realize that it can't tell me Thing One about my customers. Only my questionnaire can accomplish that.)

There are insights about Internet research known to all cyberguerrillas. These are the most important insights:

- If you're using the Internet to locate information about anything related to an industry, first locate the Web sites of businesses involved in that industry. You'll find them to be a treasury of information. When I wrote a chapter about computer networking for a recent book, I found more substantial and easy-to-understand information on the 3Com Web site than I did in technical journals. 3Com manufactures computer networking hardware, so it was in their best interest to present information clearly. Same for Cisco Systems.

Search engines

- Use *several* search engines. Search engines undergo constant improvement and vie with each other to be easiest to use and most comprehensive. No one search engine is best for all purposes—each seems to have its own areas of specialization. Check a few if you want to get the most valuable and most recent information.
- Look beyond the Web when you're searching for information on-line. There are millions of documents and files available via Gopher, WAIS (Wide Area Information Servers), and FTP, and you can use search utilities like TurboGopher, WinGopher, Archie, Anarchie, and Veronica to find them. Gopher servers store university or government documents such as trade statistics or opinion-poll results. WAIS store the full text of articles, reports, and speeches by famous people, among other facts. FTP servers store files containing lengthy reports, graphics, charts, demo programs, and video clips. Much of this data may never be available on the Web. Use these searching methods to avoid missing important information.

- Never overlook the importance of chat rooms for quick responses to ideas, products, and marketing thoughts. Bright people are on-line chatting, and they are quick to render opinions. You can learn significant information by simply asking in a chat setting. Look for chat rooms where your questions might be appropriate and then ask away.   **Chat rooms**
- Use E-mail for customer surveys. It is so simple to respond to them that response rates for on-line surveys are appreciably higher than for mailed surveys. Don't worry about asking too many questions, but don't overdo a good thing. Offer to send responders the results of your survey, for they are probably inquisitive people if they're willing to answer your questions.

These are not the only methods of conducting inexpensive research; they are simply the most common and effective. You can also get information from your local chamber of commerce, your state chamber of commerce, any industry organizations to which you belong, and any industry publications of which you are aware. Make a field trip or two to poke around and talk to people in your business who are not in your geographic area. Guerrillas abet their primary research with these additional sources of knowledge. Knowledge is the currency of the twenty-first century.   **More sources of inexpensive insight**

When questioning your target audience, it might help to list some of the basic needs people have. Ask them to make check marks by those that pushed their particular buttons. Most people will react to one or more of the following basic needs (known as "appeals" in advertising lingo):   **The basic needs**

Achievement	Style
Pride of ownership	Social approval (status)
Convenience	Health and well-being
Comfort	Profit
Love	Savings or economy
Friendship	Conformity (peer pressure)
Security	Ambition
Self-improvement	Power
Saving time	Independence

If you believe that people patronize you because you offer convenience and economy, you may be surprised to learn, via your questionnaires, that they actually give you their business because your work adds to their sense of security.

Talking with your competitors

You can engage in more free research by conscientiously studying the other advertising that is going on in your community—not only that of your competitors but that of *everyone*. Engage in frank conversations with your customers. Talk with your competitors. If they're from a noncompeting area, tell them about a marketing tactic that worked for you, then ask about any that worked for them. Most likely, they'll talk their heads off because you're obviously a person who understands the business. Guerrillas call this "sharing." The way it works is, the more you give the more you get.

Talk with other businesspeople in your community. You'll find that they'll provide you with useful information and won't charge you for it. Research will help you save money and earn money, and free research will help you save and earn even more.

II
Mini-Media Marketing

Guerrillas shine in mini-media marketing. Standard marketers rarely, if ever, resort to such marketing methods as canvassing, writing personal letters, marketing by telephone, distributing circulars, posting signs on bulletin boards, running classified ads, using signs other than billboards, and putting the Yellow Pages to work. Fortunately, because the titans don't practice mini-media marketing, you'll come across very little competition in these arenas—except from fellow guerrillas. And be warned, there are more guerrillas *daily*, and your close attention to the media will alert you to their presence—as well as educate you by their examples. Be prepared to respond—giant companies aren't as quick on their feet as you. You can respond faster.

More guerrillas every day

Your mini-media marketing must adhere to your marketing plan. It must be accomplished with talent and style. It must still follow many of the fundamentals. But it can break the rules, too. For instance, you can make letters highly personalized. You can post unique signs. You can take advantage of the smallness of your business when making telephone calls. Make them personal, friendly, informal, yet professional.

I urge you to use as many media as you can use correctly, and I urge you to use the mini-media to the max. Mini-media will rarely put a strain on your budget, as production costs are low. You'll have an opportunity to star in the mini-media more than in the maxi-media, where you may be outspent even if you're not outthought. In the mini-media, your size is an advantage, not a disadvantage.

I hope you'll put all of these marketing methods to work while you're still small. If you do, you'll know which to use as your business grows.

The advantages of being small

Your small size enables you to offer advantages in the area of customer service. Your geographic proximity—including the fact that you're a true-blue local—if your market is your own locality, is a big weapon, possessed by few of the behemoths. You know folks on a first-name basis. You see them regularly. You can provide extremely individualized service, tailored to the realities of your customers' budgets. Few big companies can match you. By necessity, they're forced to run customer service by company policy, and that deprives them of flexibility.

As a guerrilla, you're reeking with flexibility—and it can be translated into service that customers crave. A score for your team! The mini-media includes maxi-service. Used properly, they can make you a juggernaut. The '90s have brought a multitude of changes in the mini-media, all of which work to the advantage of the entrepreneur.

No "spamming" please

- E-mail facilitates the fastest of all communication and interactivity. Steer clear of "spamming" (junk E-mail), but don't worry about E-mailing your customers and prospects who say they want info from you.
- Faxes allow you to render speedier service than snail mail (but don't use faxes for marketing; people resent "junk faxes").
- Computer bulletin boards enable you to zero in on specific target audiences and communicate by posting notices or E-mailing members of the audience.
- You can run free classified ads on-line through a wide variety of venues and on-line services.
- Toll-free numbers (800, 888, 876, and 866) are less expensive than ever, so you can increase your response rates anywhere from 30 to 700 percent.
- Catalogs, newsletters, and brochures are simpler than ever to produce, thanks to desktop publishing.
- Desktop publishing is simpler, more inexpensive, and more attractive than ever for small businesses, which use computers to create expensive-looking marketing materials without incurring the expense. The creative genius lurking within you can stop lurking and start working!
- A 900 number can be used both as a marketing weapon and as a new profit center.
- More magazines today offer inexpensive regional editions, offering you first-rate credibility at cut-rate prices. They also offer classified sections.
- More newspapers today offer low-cost zone editions that reach prospects in targeted neighborhoods.

- Computer technology allows entrepreneurs to tap into computer networks, communicate with many people at once, and keep accurate databases.
- TV time, due to the growth of cable companies, has dropped in price to a point that almost any small business can (and should) consider it.
- Satellite TV transmission allows advertisers to home in on extremely specialized markets.
- Home shopping networks encourage viewers to buy instantly, providing advertisers with instant gratification.
- Car phones, cellphones, pagers, and airphones offer more sophisticated communication options, saving time and opening the door to more personalized service.
- VCR penetration is nearing 90 percent, adding to the attractiveness of a video brochure.
- New breakthroughs in psychology are giving us a clearer view of human behavior, so that we can create more effective marketing.
- New media are springing up all over the place: on airport luggage carousels, on airplane movie screens, at grocery checkout counters, in postcard decks, integrated in major movies and TV shows, throughout cyberspace, on blimps in the sky, and even on rockets in space.
- People are being marketed to while on telephone hold, and some appreciate the data while they wait.
- Special-effects technology in television allows small advertisers to get a big-advertiser look without spending big bucks.

Instant gratification for all

I'm just scratching the surface regarding the advances in mini-media that have taken place since the original edition of this book. The maxi-media, once the domain of the big spenders, are now your domain, too. As a guerrilla, your eyes must be open to the marketing options of the twenty-first century. These lovely marketing weapons, which are arriving in the marketing arena on a daily basis, are byproducts of the age of the entrepreneur. Each represents an opportunity for you.

Their domain is now your domain

Whether or not you capitalize on the opportunity is up to you; whether or not you learn of the opportunities is up to me. And learn you will—as soon as you turn the page.

9

Canvassing: Marketing on an Eye-to-Eye Basis

Canvassing can be the most inexpensive marketing method of all. In fact, it can be free, except for the time you devote to it. And if you're just starting out, time is something you have a great deal of in your inventory. After all, canvassing is merely asking prospective customers for business. If ever there was an interactive medium, canvassing is it. There's little question that it was the first of all interactive media, if not the first of all media. During a canvass, which the dictionary defines as "a soliciting of sales," you should engage in three steps.

First impressions count

The first step, called the *contact*, is when you first meet your prospect. That first impression counts like crazy. So make your contact friendly, upbeat, customer-oriented, honest, and warm. *Try to establish a relationship.* Smile, look directly into the person's eye, and if at all possible, *use the person's name.* You need not talk about business if you don't want to. And you really shouldn't. Some *Fortune* 500 companies require that their salespeople ask at least three nonbusiness questions before actually getting down to business. You can talk about personal matters, about the weather, about a current event, about sports, or—hopefully, about your prospective customer. That's probably his or her favorite subject. It's best to avoid politics and religion, but everything else is fair game.

The second step of a canvass is called the presentation. It usually takes longer than the other steps, yet it need take no longer than one minute. During the presentation, you outline the features of your offering and the benefits to be gained from buying from you. Some pro canvassers say, "The more you tell, the more you sell." I'm not sure about that; it depends on what you're selling. If you're selling a home security system, your presentation might take fifteen minutes. If it's an offer to wash your prospect's car, the presentation might take a minute or less. Presentations to sell personal computers may take a few hours; presentations to sell home satellite systems take a day and a half; presentations to sell million-dollar computer switchers take up to a year and a half. The price of your product or service will dictate the time you should spend presenting it.

The third step of a canvass—the close—is the most important; it's the magical moment when you complete the sale. It's when your prospect says "yes" or signs on the dotted line or reaches for his or her wallet or merely nods affirmatively. If you are a poor closer, it doesn't really matter how good you are at the contact and the presentation. You've got to be a good closer to make canvassing work.

The most important step

The canvass existed before any other marketing methods. In fact, the very first sale in history probably occurred when one caveman asked another, "Want to trade me an animal skin for this fruit I picked?" Advertising wasn't necessary. Nor was a marketing plan. Life has become more complicated.

There are different ways to canvass. You can go from door to door. You can canvass in residential neighborhoods, in commercial neighborhoods, and at trade shows. Or you can presell your canvass by first calling or writing the people you intend to canvass. You have a choice of telling them you'll come by at some point, or you can actually set up an appointment. The latter is more like a sales presentation. Most guerrillas canvass with little or no advance warning to the customer. Sure, it helps if you advertise so that the prospective customers have heard of you when you come calling, but you don't have to advertise. If you make a good contact, a crisp presentation, and a dynamite close, and if you are offering a good value, canvassing may be the only marketing tool you ever need.

Canvassing with intelligence

I mentioned that canvassing can be free, and I wasn't kidding. But it will help if you do invest a bit of money in it. For one thing, you want to look good so as to inspire confidence. That means you should look the part. If you are canvassing store owners with the idea of getting them to sign up for your window-washing business, you need not wear a coat and tie. But it helps if you're wearing spotless work clothes, and even if you have a clean rag dangling from your rear pocket.

Dress as your prospects dress

The investment increases a bit more if you offer a business card to the person you are canvassing. The card establishes that you are for real and enables a person to give you business later, if not now. It also helps your referral business — if you do a good job. Your investment will be even greater if you decide to canvass using a brochure or circular. If you do produce such materials, use them as sales aids while you are making your presentation or give them away after you have closed the sale. Don't expect a person to read your literature and listen to your sales talk at the same time. Generally I frown on presenting a circular during this contact

If they don't buy now they won't buy later

because it gives your prospect an opportunity to avoid buying by telling you he or she will "study" your circular and get back to you. If they don't buy now, figure that they won't buy later. Usually they won't. Another way to look at it is that someone *will* buy. Some entrepreneurs give free demonstrations or samples while they canvass. Although this adds to your investment, it is often a smart addition. Some companies say that it's akin to purchasing a customer.

Once you learn the best way to accomplish your canvassing, you'll be confronted with several choices. First, will you want to continue using this method of marketing? Second, are you doing it as well as it can be done? Third, should you be delegating the canvassing job to someone else or to several other people? To an organization of sales reps (called distributors)? The advantages of canvassing are readily apparent. It doesn't cost much, if anything. It's a great way to get a brand-new business going. It strengthens

A canvassing campaign

your contacts, because looking a person directly in the eye is more personal by a long shot than writing a letter, making a phone call, or attracting attention with an ad. Canvassing is also a good way to learn the objections, if any, to your offering. It provides instant results and guarantees that your message is being heard. Like television advertising, it enables you to demonstrate. Like radio advertising, it enables you to be intimate. Like newspaper advertising, it allows you to be newsy. Like magazine advertising, it allows you to involve your prospect. And like direct-response marketing, it is geared to get you a direct response of the positive kind.

The success of canvassing depends upon you and you alone. You can't blame the media if you mess up. And if you succeed, you deserve all of the credit. Furthermore, canvassing is very accountable, meaning that you know darned well whether it's working or not. Results aren't as accountable when you use the more sophisticated media.

Let's say you have a brand-spanking-new home security company. You sell and install burglar and smoke alarms. You've named your company Always Alert, and you've printed up business cards, but nothing else. Your marketing plan calls for you to spend the first two months canvassing for business. The first month, you'll canvass commercial establishments. The second month, you'll canvass homes. Then you'll decide whether to concentrate on businesses or homes and whether to continue canvassing for new business. Let's assume you're so short of cash that you cannot afford to run even one ad. I hope that is never the case, but, for now, let's stack the deck against you.

You're ready to make your detailed canvassing plans. What to wear? As a general rule, dress exactly as your prospects dress, whether it be Levi's or a three-piece suit. If you're calling on businesses, I suggest you wear a dark business suit, whether you are male or female. The dark colors—navy blue, black, deep gray, or charcoal—lend authority to what you say. The suit itself implies professionalism. Stay away from any accessories that detract from the professional look you wish to convey. Be sure your hair is neat and your hands are clean, and that you have a handsome case to carry either samples or sales literature provided by the manufac-turer. I'd feel so good that a smile would come easily. You can pick up a lot of details about presenting yourself in *Get What You Deserve: How to Guerrilla Market Yourself* by Seth Godin and me.

Once you're properly attired, you'll need to decide what to say during the contact, that first precious moment. It's usually best to make a comment first about the store you're visiting: "I like your window display. It seems just right for this location. My name is Tim Winston. My company is Always Alert. We offer security systems to businesses such as yours. What type of security system do you have now?"

During this contact, you complimented the prospect on his or her window display, thereby indicating that you *noticed* it in the first place. I hope you were smiling and making eye contact as you announced your name and the name of your company. Fi-nally, you qualified your prospect with one single question. By "qualified," I mean you determined your prospect's need for your product. If the prospect has a security system and tells you that it consists of both a burglar alarm and a smoke alarm, you can save time by making no presentation whatsoever and leaving after first thanking the person for the information imparted. You might in-quire if the person is happy with the current security system, and be sure to leave your card behind just in case he or she wishes to make a change later. You are best off keeping the time spent with

Qualifying your prospect

nonprospects to a minimum. Once your prospect indicates that he or she already has what you're selling, don't waste your time or theirs.

At the next store, following a similar contact, the prospect may

Features and benefits

tell you that they have no security system. That's your cue to make your presentation. While giving it, remember that whenever you mention a feature, *follow* it with a *benefit*. Hardly anyone buys features, but most of us buy benefits to ourselves. For instance, you could say, "Always Alert features security systems that run on solar power. They never need batteries. They use no expensive electrical power, and they are maintenance free." The feature is the solar power. The benefits are freedom from purchasing batteries, from spending money for electrical power, and from maintaining the devices.

Continue your presentation, making it as long as it must be yet as short as it can be. After all, both you and your prospect have other things to do. While presenting, always be on the lookout for closing signs. It may be that you've made the sale and that the prospect wants to buy. But if you don't look for signs that you've said enough, you could lose the sale. As the most successful sales-

Ask and ye shall close

people say, ABC—always be *closing*.

When you've finished your presentation, try to close with a question that requires more than a yes or no answer. Such a question might be, "Well, that about does it. Will it be better for me to install your alarm system Wednesday or Thursday?" Another could be, "Do you intend to pay for your alarm system at the time of installation, or should I bill you?"

Many excellent books on salesmanship carefully dissect the sale, examining the contact, the presentation, and the close. For reasons of enlarging your bank account rather than catering to my ego, I recommend that you read *Guerrilla Selling* by Bill Gallagher, Orvel Ray Wilson, and myself. If you're going to be a guerrilla, go all out; don't merely play at part of it.

Canvassing requires salesmanship. It requires a contact, a presentation, and a close. Furthermore, it requires *quality* in that salesmanship. And it requires far greater salesmanship in terms of quantity. A great car salesman may make ten contacts, presentations, and closes in one good day. You may make ten in one good hour. To succeed at canvassing, you must have an enthusiasm about your product, an honest enjoyment of people, and a load of determination.

If you're to succeed as an entrepreneur, however, if you're to build your small business into a large one, you must move beyond canvassing, even though it may remain as part of your marketing mix. The disadvantages of canvassing are that it takes much of your time, that you can't reach enough prospects even in one high-energy day, and that it is limited in scope geographically. These disadvantages disappear when you delegate the canvassing to others. And if you succeed at canvassing, you'll soon become itchy to reach more people.

The disadvantages of canvassing

I want to make you the best canvasser possible; so let's examine the contact, the presentation, and the close in more detail.

First, realize that *somebody* is going to close a sale with your customer. It might be a competitor of yours. It might be a friend of the customer. But it will be somebody. It can be someone else or you. While your customer is with you, you have a lot of control over who will close—the most control you will ever have. After you've left your customer, you have very little control, if any. *So while your customer is with you is the best time to close.* Remember that closing is the name of the canvassing game. And though you must make a contact and a presentation, you should be thinking "close, close, close" all along. By doing so, you are gradually closing the entire time you're with your customer. And that's good.

Somebody will close the sale

In spite of the importance of closing, it is crucial that you *make* your contact. If you don't, you may not have a chance to move on to the close. Do the contact well, and you may breeze through to the actual close. That's how important the initial contact is.

Guerrilla tips about the contact

If your contact comes from a cold call and your prospect is a complete stranger, take steps to make that prospect a new acquaintance. If your contact comes from a lead—a recommendation from a friend, an answer to an ad you ran, or some other reason to make you believe the prospect can be converted into a customer—refer to that relationship, that bond between you. It will help break the barriers that much faster. You are no longer a complete stranger. Now you are, at the very least, an acquaintance of an acquaintance. Here are some tactics that canvassing pros use:

- Greet your prospect warmly and sincerely, using eye contact.
- Allow your prospect some time to get acclimated to being with you, some time to talk. Don't come on too strong. But don't waste your prospect's time, either.
- Engage in casual conversation at first—especially about any-

thing pertinent to your prospect. Make it friendly and not one-sided. Be a good listener, but also let the prospect know that your time is precious. You are there to sell, not to talk.

- Ask relevant questions. Listen carefully to the answers.
- Qualify the prospect. Determine whether or not this is the specific person to whom you should be talking, the person with the authority to give you the go-ahead, to buy. Try to learn, during the contact, what to emphasize in your presentation. Try to learn of your prospect's attitude toward your type of offering. Focus on his or her fears, expectations, and feelings so that you can tailor your presentation to them.
- Learn something about the person to whom your contact is directed so that he or she will feel like a person rather than a prospect. Make your prospect like you: people enjoy doing business with people they like. But don't be phony. The best possible thing you can do is to make your prospect *feel unique*—proving that you recognize his or her individuality and needs.
- Be brief, friendly, outgoing, and truly inquisitive. But be yourself.
- If you're in a retail environment, one of the best questions to initiate healthy contact is "Mind if I ask what brings you into our store today?"
- Even though you are selling, don't think of yourself as a salesperson but as a partner to your prospect. This healthy mindset improves both your perspective and your chances of closing. Realize that you have an opportunity to *educate* your prospects to *succeed* at whatever they wish to succeed at. As soon as possible, learn what it is that your prospect wishes to succeed at, then show how what you are selling can make that success achievable.

Nonverbal communication

Important elements of your contact are your smile, your attire, your posture, and your willingness to listen and look directly into the prospect's eyes. Your nonverbal communication is as important as your verbal communication. The impression you make comes as much from what you don't say as from what you do say.

It is often during the contact that the sale is cinched. This happens if your contact has truly opened up communications and you have convinced your prospect that you are honestly interested in helping him or her. During a successful contact, each party will have made a friend—and thereby paved the way to a sale, and hopefully to continuing sales. The contact may be the shortest of the three phases of a canvass. But it does establish the basis for the presentation and the close.

When making your presentation, keep in mind that you are not talking by accident. You are there because of intent on your part. If your prospect is still with you and has not ended the canvass, there is intent on his or her part, too. And the intent is to buy. Either you will buy a story about why a sale cannot be made, or your prospect will buy what you're selling. It truly is up to you. Don't forget that people do enjoy being sold to. They do like being persuaded by honest enthusiasm to buy. But they don't like being pressured. Here are some tips to make your presentations flow smoothly:

Guerrilla tips about the presentation

- List all the benefits of doing business with you, one by one. The more benefits a prospect knows about, the more likely a prospect will buy. When compiling your list of benefits, invite your employees and at least one customer. Don't take the benefits that you offer for granted—customers need to *hear* about them.
- Emphasize the *unique* advantages of buying from you. You should be able to rattle these off with ease. It is upon these competitive advantages that you should base your marketing. Don't knock your competition, whatever you do, but don't hesitate to make comparisons between you and that unworthy lout—just as long as they're true.
- If your prospect has no experience with what you are selling, stress the advantages of your *type* of offering, then of your specific offering. If you're selling security devices, talk of the value of owning them, then of the value of owning yours.
- Tailor your presentation to information learned during your contact—and before. I hope you learned a lot before making any contact. Homework pays off tremendously to guerrillas.
- People do not like to be pioneers because they know darned well that pioneers get arrows in the back of their necks, so mention the acceptance of your products or services by others—especially people in their community. If you can mention names and be specific, by all means do so. The more specific you are, the more closes you'll make. But don't be tedious. You can't bore a prospect into buying.

- When you know enough about your prospect, you can present your product or service from his or her point of view. This **Pay close attention** ability will increase your number of closes dramatically. Emphasize what your product or service can do for your *prospect*, not what they can do for the general population.

- Keep an eagle eye on your prospect's eyes, teeth, and hands. If the prospect is looking around, rather than at you, you've got to say something to regain attention. If your prospect is not smiling, you are being too serious. Say something to earn a smile. Most important, smile yourself. That will get your prospect to smile. If your prospect is wringing his or her hands, your prospect is bored. Say something to ease the boredom and spark more interest.

- A sales point made to the eye is 68 percent more effective than one made to the ear. So show as much as you can: photos, drawings, a circular, a product, your sales video, *anything*. Just be sure it relates to your presentation.

- Sell the benefit along with the feature. If the feature is solar power, for instance, the benefit is economy. If the feature is new computer software, the benefit is probably speed or power or profitability.

- Mention your past successes so the prospect will feel that the **Pride goeth before a sale** key to success is in your hands and there is little chance of a rip-off.

- Be *proud* of your prices, your benefits, your offering. Convey your pride with facial expressions, tone of voice, selection of words. Feel the pride and let it come shining through. There are 250,000 commonly used words in the English language, but there are 600,000 nonverbal methods of communication: stance, facial expression, hand gestures, eyebrow position, and 599,996 others. Learn them and use them. They're completely free—another example of pure guerrilla marketing. No cost. High payoff.

- Throughout your presentation, remain convinced that your prospect *will* buy from you. This optimism will be sensed by the prospect and can positively affect the close.

Despite the importance I have attached to the contact and the presentation, I still reiterate that all the marbles are in the close. Effective salespeople and canvassers are effective closers. Aim to be a dynamite closer and your income will reflect this. To close effectively, try to close immediately rather than in a week or so. Keep these points in mind:

Guerrilla tips about the close

- Always assume that your prospective customer is going to do what you want. Close with a leading question such as, "Will it be better for you to take delivery this week or next week?" "Do you want it in gray or brown?"
- Summarize your main points and confidently end with a closing line such as, "Everything seems to be in order. Why don't I write up your order now?"
- Ask the customer to make some kind of decision, then close on it. Typical points that must be agreed upon are delivery date, size of order, method of payment. A good closing is: "I can perform this service for you tomorrow, the eighth, or the fifteenth. The eighth would be best for me. Which would be best for you?" Attempt the close as soon as possible by easing your prospect into it. If that doesn't work, try again, then again. Continue trying. If you don't, your prospect will spend his or her hard-earned money elsewhere—and with someone else. Count on that. Remember: people *like* to be sold to and *need* to have the deal closed. They won't make the close themselves. So you are performing a service when you sell and close. Always be on the alert for signs that the time is right to close. The prospect will hardly ever tell you when the time has come. You must look for hints in the prospect's words *and* actions. A mere shifting of weight from one foot to another may be a signal to close.
- Try to give your prospect a good reason to close *immediately*. It may be that you won't be back in the neighborhood for a long time, or that the prospect will wish to use your product or service as soon as possible, or that prices are expected to rise, or that you have the inventory available now but might not have it later.
- Let your prospect know of the success of your product or service with people *like* the prospect, with people *recently*, with people in the community—with people *with whom the prospect can easily relate*.
- Be specific with names, dates, costs, times, and benefits. Evasiveness in any area works against you.

Why wait?

- If the prospect likes what you say but won't close now, ask, "Why wait?" The prospect may then voice an objection. And you may close by saying, "That's great, and I understand." Then you can solve the objection and close on it. In fact, one of the easiest ways to close is to search for an objection, then solve the problem and close on it. If you have not yet completed your presentation but feel the time may be right to close, attempt to close on the most important sales point you have yet to state. Always remember that a person knows what you want him or her to do, that there is a reason for your meeting, and that your offering does have merit. If you remember these points, it will be easier for you to close. When a prospect says, "Let me think it over," they mean no.

- If you don't close just after your presentation, you will most likely lose the sale. Few prospects have the guts to tell you they will definitely not buy from you. They search for excuses. So do everything you can to move them into a position where they will buy from you. If you don't, a better salesperson will.
- Tie the close in with the contact. Try to close on a personal note. Say something like, "I think you'll feel more secure now with this new security system, and that's important. Shall I have your smoke alarm installed tomorrow or the next day?"

Lucky canvassers

Some canvassers are lucky—those who talk only to people who are honest-to-goodness leads, who have actually demonstrated an interest in the product or service. But most canvassers have to make cold calls. Brrr! A pundit once observed, "Throughout history, the most common debilitating human ailment has been cold feet."

Hot tips on cold calling

Guerrillas, however, aren't troubled by this ailment. They thrive on cold calls. They need no introduction, referral, or appointment. They know that the key to success is to *make the most of the short time they have to attract their prospect's attention.* Here are six hot tips on cold calling:

1. *Do your homework.* Learn as much as possible about the company that you'll visit. The more you know, the better you can tailor your presentation to the prospect.
2. *Start at the top.* Ask for and speak with the person in charge, the one who can say yes. Do what you must to find out this person's name and title before you begin. Anything you can learn will prove to be very helpful to you.
3. *Be brief.* Don't waste anyone's time. Keep your message concise. Brevity in cold calling primes you for success.

4. *Get to the point.* Tell if your offering does the job faster, easier, lasts longer, saves time, saves energy, or whatever. Zero in quickly on the prime benefits of your product or service.

5. *Give references.* Give names of satisfied customers, names that your prospect will recognize and respect. If she doesn't know the name, she may know the company.

6. *Close the sale.* Make an appointment. Schedule a full presentation or a demonstration. Before you begin, know exactly what you wish to achieve, and close on that objective.

Ask for the order

Whatever you do, *ask for the order.* If you don't feel comfortable with ABC, "always be closing," you should learn to feel comfortable with ATC, which means, "always *think* closing." If you think closing, your thoughts will carry over to your prospect. And you'll close more as a result. Eventually, you may want to exercise your powers of selling on larger groups of people. One way to do this is to write personal letters. In Chapter 10, we examine the art of creating personal letters.

10

Personal Letters:
Inexpensive and Effective

The writing of personal letters—not direct mailings of large quantities of letters and brochures, but simple, personal letters—is one of the most effective, easy, inexpensive, and overlooked methods of marketing. The large corporations certainly don't use this type of communication, for it doesn't reach enough people to enrich their coffers. However, it's just the ticket for many an individual businessperson. If you can write clear English, spell properly, and keep your message brief, you should develop enough business through this mode of marketing so that you need not employ many other methods. If you're a dismal grammarian, professional word processors can usually help you put your ideas into acceptable form on the printed page. Also, computer software corrects grammar, spelling, and word repetition.

The personal touch

The primary value of a personal letter is that it enables you to convey a truly personal feeling and reach a special place in the mind of the reader. You can relate specific thoughts in personal letters that are simply not practical in any other medium, except for certain kinds of telephone marketing.

For example, you could write, "Ms. Forman, your gardenias and carnations look wonderful this year. However, your roses look as though they can use a bit of help. I can provide that help and bring your roses back to glowing health." This is much more personal than to write, "Dear Home Gardener, perhaps your garden isn't as beautiful this year as usual. We offer a full range of garden supplies and expertise to aid you."

In a personal letter you can, should, and must include as much personal data as possible. Word processors make it easy.

Type the person's name, of course, in your personal letter. You want to write about the person's life, business, car, home, or, if you're in the gardening business, the person's garden. By doing so, you are whispering into someone's ear rather than shouting

Whispering instead of shouting

through a distant megaphone. Naturally, you can't mention personal things unless you know the person. Therefore, you need to do your homework and learn about your prospective customers — their working and living habits, their hopes and goals, and their *problems.* In your customer questionnaires, ask about people's problems — this will help you learn important things about the person.

The ability to solve problems will be a growth industry in the twenty-first century, indeed, forever. Businesses devoted to success are devoted to obtaining information about their prospects. You can get much of this information from your on-line or off-line questionnaire or through personal observation. Include your findings in your personal letter; you'll be dazzled by its effect.

Doubling the effectiveness

After you send your personal letter, you can *double* its effectiveness if you do one of two things — or preferably both: write another personal letter within two weeks; and call the prospect on the telephone.

Your repeat letter can be brief — for the most part, it's a reminder of your original letter. However, it should provide new information and give more reasons to do business with you.

When you make the follow-up telephone call, refer to your letters. Ask if the person read them. Take advantage of the fact that your letter has broken the "stranger barrier." You are now on speaking terms with your prospect. Use the phone to develop a relationship. The stronger that relationship, the likelier the person is to do business with you. This relationship will intensify if your letter includes a number of specific *personal* references — it demonstrates that you have not sent a clever mass-mailed flier.

These days, people are literally bombarded with advertising pieces in the mail. Make your letter stand out by making it part of a three- or four-letter campaign. Multiple mailing campaigns are more expensive than single letters, but they are incredibly effective. Many studies confirm that people patronize businesses with which they are familiar. One of the most enlightening studies was conducted to ascertain the factors that influence a buyer's purchase decision. Five thousand respondents indicated that confidence ranked first, quality second, selection third, service fourth, and price fifth. Don't be surprised by the fifth ranking — price ranked ninth in the '80s. Price will always be of primary importance to a minority of people (17 percent at the time of the last survey).

New research conducted on the retail level indicates, however, that buying attitudes change during a recession. During the economic downturn in the early '90s, the biggest purchase motivation was price (quality the second, and environmental safety third). In another study of retail customers, price was first, selection second, quality third, location fourth, and service fifth. Confidence was not included as a factor in these surveys. But you must understand that people will *not* buy the lowest-priced item if they don't trust it.

The truth is that the reasons people buy a product vary from industry to industry, from age group to age group, from target market to target market, from circumstance to circumstance. The leading appeal to a mother buying baby food differs from the appeal to that same mother buying a sports car.

If you don't have a clear idea of the leading appeal to your potential customers, forget personal letters altogether. You'll gain the greatest benefit from your personal letter if you know the leading appeal and as much personal data as possible. You've got to know what you want your personal letter to accomplish before **Multiple** you write it. And what might that be? It could be an order, a **mailings** request for more data, a meeting.

By sending out multiple mailings of personal letters, you build customer confidence through familiarity, paving your way to a relationship and a sale. Only an entrepreneur with a carefully **Personalized is** targeted market can afford this luxury. A large company has too **not personal** many prospects to engage in personal-letter campaigns.

There is a difference between a personal letter and a personalized letter. The latter is a rather impersonal letter with a person's name in the salutation and within the body of the letter, along with some personal references. The personalization is accomplished by means of a word processor. A personal letter, on the other hand, is extremely personal. It is directed to one person and contains so many specific personal references and so much personal information that it cannot possibly be meant for anyone but the person to whom it is addressed. It is signed in ink—smearable, fountain-pen ink. It has a P.S., possibly handwritten. Naturally, it has a greater impact on the reader than a mere personalized letter.

Fortunately, it is now possible to generate computer-printed personalized letters that look, act, and feel like a personal letter. Just make the changes on the word processor, print it, and sign it by hand—and write the P.S. by hand.

A goal of your personal mailing is to make it *unnecessary for your prospect to respond.* Your letter might have an E-mail address or standard mail address or phone number, but it should not ask for a written reply or a phone call. It should not include a means for responding. However, it should whet the reader's appetite. It should tell the reader that you will telephone within a week to set up an appointment or firm up a sale.

The personal letter accomplishes several things: it forces the reader to think about your offer—because it tells the reader that you'll be talking with him or her about it soon; and it separates you from the writers who leave everything to the discretion of the reader and require the reader to take action. You ask the reader to wait for *you* to take action and provide the missing information. *And your letter prepares the reader for your phone call.* When you do call, you will not be a stranger but an expected caller.

This luxury to withhold a response mechanism in your letters cannot be practiced by big firms: it is inefficient on a large scale. It is the essence of guerrilla marketing, however, because it gives you an edge over the mass marketers. The personal letter goes to a unique extreme to gain attention.

The tone of your letter should incorporate business matters and personal feelings and should appeal to the reader's self-image. If written to the president of a company, for example, your letter should mention the responsibilities of a president, the importance of the job, and the problems encountered. Your letter should be well written, employing a relatively sophisticated vocabulary.

How long should a typical personal letter be? One page. Be sure to convey all the information you feel you must convey, but be as brief as possible. A good rule is to make your personal letter short unless it *must* be long. When I say short, I mean one full page of warm, personal, motivating, enticing copy. Because it is a personal letter, it need not have a brochure or circular enclosed— although it may. But be warned: if you add an enclosure, you lose the effect of an honest-to-goodness personal letter. Auntie Myrna never enclosed a brochure or a coupon, did she?

Your letter should give the reader relevant information—data that he or she might otherwise not have known. Occasionally I will remind a prospective advertising client of an upcoming event or a promotion that worked well for another client. A gardener might alert a prospect to a coming season that is right for the planting of certain species. A tutor might talk of advances in education. *Give something to the reader rather than merely asking*

for something or selling something. Impress a reader with your intelligence, insight, or personality. The prospect might use your **The letter** information with no acknowledgment of you, but the rewards are **is not about** usually worth the risks.
you
It is crucial to remember that the letter should *not* be about you. It should be about the reader. It should be in the reader's terms, about the reader's life or business. The letter should be loaded with potential benefits for the reader. The greater the number of benefits, the better. Remember the opera *Aida.* This is a memory crutch to remind you to get *attention* first, then *interest* the reader, then create a *desire,* then make a call to *action.* It may be simpler for you to remember to secure the reader's attention first, then state the benefits of doing business with you, and finally explain the specific action the reader must take — make a phone call, write a letter, read page 15 of the Sunday paper, expect a phone call, or visit a Web site. Tell the reader exactly what you **Personal letter** want him or her to do.
wisdom
From a purely technical standpoint, I offer these gems of personal-letter wisdom:

- Keep your letter to one page.
- Make your paragraphs short — five or six lines each.
- Indent your paragraphs.
- Do not overuse underlining, capital letters, or writing in margins.
- Do everything you can to keep the letter from looking like a printed piece.
- Sign your letter in a different-colored ink than it is typed in.
- Include a P.S. It should contain your most important point with a sense of urgency.

The potent P.S.   Studies reveal that when people receive personal, and even printed, letters, they read the salutation first and the P.S. next. Therefore, your P.S. should include your most attractive benefit, your invitation to action, or anything that inspires a feeling of urgency. There is an art to writing a P.S. — don't sell such a brief comment short. I recommend that your personal letters include a handwritten P.S. message because it proves beyond doubt that you have created a one-of-a-kind letter, that it wasn't sent to thousands of people. In our age of technology, personal touches stand tall.

Ten sage suggestions for your P.S.:

1. Motivate the prospect to take action. Tell that person to place his order now. Waiting is fatal to your cause.
2. Reinforce your offer. Make it the same as you made in the body of your letter but make it more urgently, more cogently.
3. Emphasize or introduce a premium or a bonus. The power of freebies cannot be overestimated.
4. Introduce a surprise benefit. It might be just enough to get that prospect off the fence and onto your customer list.
5. Emphasize the price or terms of your offer. If that financial enticement is the heart of your offer, be sure to restate it in your P.A.
6. Stress the tax deductibility of the purchase. If this additional justification to buy is true, here's a good place to mention it.
7. Highlight your guarantee. Present it with pride and excitement, remembering that to your prospects, it removes all element of risk.
8. Tell how many customers you've satisfied in the past. Be specific so that readers will realize that buying from you is the normal thing to do.
9. If you're asking readers to call a toll-free number, repeat it in the P.S. to make it as easy as possible to respond to your offer.
10. Stress an element of urgency. Tell them the date the offer expires, the limited quantities available, the reasons now is the time to order.

What to say when you say P.S.

As with a great advertisement, a great personal letter should tell the reader what you are about to say, what you want to say, and, lastly, should summarize what you just said. This may seem repetitious, but it's *practical* in these days of mailboxes filled with direct mail.

I have written myriad personal letters. Five in ten probably get ignored completely. One in ten probably results in business. The business from that one, however, is usually so profitable that I can easily overlook the nine rejections. Ten percent is an excellent response rate compared with the 2 percent aimed for by many mass mailings.

To give you insight into how I create a personal letter, I provide one here, to which I clipped a crisp one-dollar bill. I mailed it twelve times, with zero business to me, then a thirteenth time, which resulted in enough business to keep me grinning for months. The idea is nearly two decades old, yet versions of it

The letter with the crisp dollar bill

continue to gain an impressive response. When I used the tactic of adding a million-dollar check (unsigned) instead of a buck, the letter pulled equally well. The gimmick is strong because it ties in with the letter's promise.

November 6, 1981

H. H. Thomas
Pacific Telephone & Telegraph
1313 53rd Street
Berkeley, CA 94705

Dear Mr. Thomas:

The dollar bill attached here symbolizes the thousands of dollars Pacific Telephone & Telegraph may be wasting by not utilizing the services of a prime quality freelance writer.

During this year alone, I have accomplished writing projects for Visa, Crocker Bank, Pacific Plan, Gallo, Bank of America, the University of California, and the Public Broadcasting System. Although these companies do not ordinarily work with free-lancers, they did work with me.

In each case, the projects were completed successfully. In each case, I was given more assignments. There must be a reason why.

If you want to provide Pacific Telephone & Telegraph with the best freelance writing available for any type of project—or if you have a seemingly impossible deadline—I hope you will give me a call.

I have enclosed a description of my background—just to inform you that I have won major writing awards in al the media and that I have served as a Vice-President and Creative Director at J. Walter Thompson, America's largest advertising agency. I guarantee you, however, that I am far more interested in winning sales than winning awards.

By your company settling for mere competent writing, or by having your writing assignments handled by traditional sources, you just might be wasting Pacific Telephone and Telegraph's money. A good number of the *Fortune* 500 companies have already figured that out.

Now, I look forward to hearing from you.

Very truly yours,
Jay Levinson

P.S. If you are not the person who assigns work to free-lancers, I would appreciate it if you would pass this letter (and this dollar) on to the person who does. Thank you very much.

It usually helps if you include a unique or informal enclosure with your letter. A newspaper article, a trade magazine article (especially in your prospect's trade), or a copy of your prospect's ad or a competitive ad helps a great deal, because the reader probably wants to read such material and will appreciate your sending it. In my case, the one-dollar enclosure served to separate my letter from the many others sent to the addressee. I'll bet many of them spent more than a dollar on a brochure. And I figure I'm the only one whose mailing piece was printed by the U.S. Treasury.

What to enclose with your letter

Would this letter be effective today? Judging by the way it has worked so far, it will be effective well into the twenty-first century. But I would make one change if there was a recession or economic downturn. After the fourth paragraph, I would write a separate paragraph, motivated by the recession: "My fees are not low. But in a recession, you can't afford to take chances with less than the highest possible quality."

Timing

Timing is very important. Be careful you don't mail when everyone else is mailing. Try to time your mailing to coincide with a particular season or the advent of a new competitor, or when you hear word that your prospect may be in trouble and in the market for whatever it is you're offering. Marketing during a recession is very different from marketing during boom times. Guerrillas are sensitive to the economy because they know it is also on the minds of their prospects and customers.

Marketing in a recession

During the bleak days of a troubled economy:

1. Market more to your customers and less to your prospects and the universe in general. Rely on, love, and make enticing offers to the people who have already learned to trust you — your customers.
2. Use the telephone as a follow-up weapon. We're talking relationships here, and if you've got one on paper, widen it to include the telephone, a potent weapon in tough times. When the going gets tough, the tough make phone calls.
3. Eliminate any perceived risk of buying from you. Do it with a guarantee, a warranty, a deep commitment to service. Let the customer know that *the sale is not over until the customer is completely satisfied.* Guerrillas use this tactic to assuage skittish prospects.
4. Keep an eagle eye out for new profit centers, fusion marketing opportunities, cooperative ventures. Because others are also

suffering through the dismal economy, there's a good chance they'll be willing to go along with your idea for a collaborative effort.

5. Instead of shrinking your offerings, go against the grain and expand them. Do what you can to increase the size of your purchases, your selection of profit-producing items, the services you offer. Never forget that geometric growth comes from larger transactions, repeat business, and referral customers. Be geometric as often as possible.

6. Let your customers know that you are fully aware of the state of the nation economically and that you are basing your prices and offerings upon it, making your business a more sensible place to patronize than ever before.

7. Tap the enormous referral power of your customers, knowing that your warm and careful follow-up to them will make them want to help you by giving you three, four, or five names of likely prospects.

Who should be reading your letter?

It's important to mail your letter to the person who ought to be reading it. Find out who that is by studying the appropriate directories on the Internet or, better still, by phoning all the companies to which you hope to mail. When in doubt, mail your letter to the company president, who will either *be* the person you want to reach or will see to it that the right person does read your letter. It's worth a call to the company's phone operator to find out the president's name and the correct spelling. If you aren't willing to take the time to do that, you probably aren't meant to be a guerrilla. Take the time to attend to tiny details. You can be sure that if the president asks a subordinate to read something, it will get read.

With a word processor and laser printer you can send out several thousand letters or more, all of which will appear to be personal letters, for all can be personalized with appropriate comments. But keep in mind that these are *not* personal letters unless they are written to sound personal and you take the time to learn personal details. Only a letter that is full of personal references is really a personal letter. It has nothing to do with technology and everything to do with psychology.

Personal letters can be sent out in smaller numbers. They will give you, the entrepreneur, a big advantage over the huge corporation. Take advantage of this valuable tool. If you do so, you are practicing guerrilla marketing with maximum skill.

Once you have a customer, do all you can to intensify the relationship. Do not treat all customers and prospects equally. Consider a menswear chain with a database of 47,000 names. Never include more than 3,000 pieces in a mailing. Who receives the mail? Says the owner, "Only the people appropriate to mail to." When he received trousers of a specific style, he mailed only to those customers to whom he was certain they'd appeal. He enjoyed a 30 percent response rate.

Does it take extra time? Yes. Does it take extra energy? Yes. Does it take an extra dollop of imagination? Yes. Does it take extra money? No. But it earns high profits for you. And that's what makes it guerrilla marketing.

Do not treat all customers equally

11

Telephone Marketing: Dialing for Dollars

Among the many forms of marketing is telephone marketing. In 1982, telephone marketing surpassed direct mail in revenues spent, and the gap has been widening ever since. In 1997, well over half of all goods and services sold were sold by phone. Telephone marketing is used both by the big guys and by budding entrepreneurs. It costs roughly one-third the rate of direct mail, with some experts pegging it at about $10 per call that gets through. Telemarketing employs more than 9 million people, compared to 175,000 back in 1983, when guerrilla marketing was invented.

There's no question that telephone marketing has emerged as a prime marketing force, especially for business-to-business marketing, except for many of the telecommunications companies, who market to individuals, with special intensity, it seems, during the dinner hours.

Three ways to telemarket

Currently, there are three ways you can engage in telephone marketing. The first is individual phone calls, made by you or a member of your company. The second is mass telemarketing, which is carried out by firms specializing in it or by dedicated telemarketing departments and is directed at thousands of potential customers at a time. The third is by computer. Computerized calling machines actually call prospects, deliver tape-recorded sales pitches, and even pause during their messages so that prospects can answer questions and place orders. This method may be a bit impersonal, and many consider it an invasion of privacy, but it's commonly practiced. And for many a company, it works. Machines aren't hurt by rejection. A 1 or 2 percent response rate can be very cost-effective.

A telephone call takes less time than a canvass, is more personal than a letter, costs less than both (unless it's long-distance), and provides you with fairly close personal contact with your prospect. It's difficult to say no to a person's face. It's less difficult to say no to a person's voice, and it's least difficult to say no to a person's letter.

Guerrillas use telemarketing to make their ads and other marketing efforts work harder. They know that 7 percent of people hang up on all telemarketers, that 42 percent hang up on some telemarketers, and that 51 percent listen to all telemarketers. Bless that teensy majority. Even though most say no, each one should be appreciated for the clarity of their answer and for not wasting your time.

What happens to telemarketers

Experienced telemarketers realize that many calls are screened by secretaries or assistants, and they know they must view the screener not as an enemy, but as an ally. Screeners are given information, treated with respect, and informed of the results you are offering, not merely your product or service. When you enlist the screener as a resource, you'll find that the door to the boss's office more readily opens.

What kinds of companies telemarket?

What kind of companies use telemarketing? Mainly they are businesses that sell to other businesses. Often, though, they are businesses trying to sell directly to a cunsumer, trying to sell anything from storm doors to automobile windshields to photographic services to chimney sweeps. The businesses that succeed plan the entire phone call: the objective, the words spoken, the mood and tone, and the follow-up. Calls to individuals and families account for less than 10 percent of telemarketing revenues, while more than 80 percent of revenues—and 90 percent of jobs—come from calls to businesses. Telemarketing produces 45 percent of all business-to-business direct marketing purchases. Direct mail produces 26 percent.

Before calling a number, savvy telemarketers ask themselves what they know about the prospect, what they need to know in order for the prospect to take the action desired, what information might be obtained from a screener, what to say in case voice-mail technology answers the call, what their opening statement will be, what questions they'll ask, and how they'll *end* the call (no matter what happens).

As with advertising, telephone marketing should be part of an overall marketing program. And it should be a continuing effort. One phone call isn't enough. If a member of your company makes the phone calls, certain incentive policies should be instituted. For instance, you should always pay your designated callers both by the completed call and by the completed sale. Even if you use a salaried employee, add incentive bonuses to the salary. Give an even higher incentive for first-time sales to new customers.

How guerrillas talk

Regardless of who makes the calls, proper voice training is a good idea. Talk clearly. Use short sentences. Talk loudly, but not directly into the mouthpiece; talking across the mouthpiece gives the most effective voice transmission. Your voice should project authority and warmth while instilling trust. Your message should be stated as concisely as possible. Whatever you do, don't read from a script. However, research shows that it's always a good idea to *memorize* a script, changing any words that feel "uncomfortable." The script must be so well memorized that the words sound as though you know them by heart, as natural as the Pledge of Allegiance. Find words and phrases that come naturally to you. Leave space for the person on the other end to respond. Guerrillas are in full control of their telemarketing and do not recite awkward speeches to their prospects.

Memorized scripts are the best

Studies in varied industries consistently reveal that a memorized telemarketing presentation always produces better results than the same presentation from an outline. It may be more humanistic to let the caller use his or her own words, but few callers have the ability to summon the right ones. Gone are the days when it was recommended that callers use an outline, or "thought flow." However, the more naturally conversant you sound, the more sales you'll make. And that takes practice. Naturally, much of what you say will be in response to what the person being called says, but the best telemarketers are in full control of the call. They stay in control by asking questions, responding to the answers, and then asking more questions, directing the conversation toward the customer's needs.

Streamline that outline

If you are more comfortable using an outline to structure your phone presentations, be sure to heed the following guidelines. If the outline is longer than one page, you should try to streamline it. An outline does create a structure for your thoughts and ideas, and it keeps the call on track when the person at the other end redirects it. If you do work from an outline—against my recommendation—it's a good idea to write a script of a phone call. After you write the script, you should do three things: (1) Record it. See what it sounds like. After all, you'll be using "ear" words that are heard, rather than "eye" words that are seen. There's a big, big difference. Words that callers unconsciously love to hear are: profits, sales, dollars, revenues, income, cash flow, savings, time, productivity, morale, motivation, output, attitude, image, victories, market share, and competitive edge. (2) Make sure the recorded script sounds like a conversation and not like an ad. Leave room for the person being called to talk. (3) Make it a point not to restate the script but to rephrase it. State the same selling points. Present them in the same order. Use words with which you are comfortable. Your telephone outline should be able to accommodate several situations. After all, if your prospect decides to buy just after you've started, you should be prepared to close the sale and end the conversation.

Notice how your friends, and probably even you yourself, assume different voice personalities when speaking on the phone. This is subtle, but it's there. Try to eliminate that telephone personality and bring out your most conversational qualities by actually practicing on the phone—talking to a tape recorder or to a friend. If you're going to do a good amount of telephone marketing, engage in role-playing, with you as the customer and a friend or associate as you. Then switch roles. Role-playing gives you a lot of insight into your offering and your message. Repeat this until you are completely satisfied with your presentation. **Your telephone personality**

Many telephone solicitations crumble when objections are made. These objections are really opportunities in disguise. Many successful telephone salespeople (and nontelephone salespeople) are able to close sales when handling objections. In fact, "close on the objection" is a sales credo for many pro sellers. One way to handle an objection is to rephrase it. By doing so, you may be able to dissipate it. "We're already buying from someone else," says the person at the other end. "Oh, you're completely satisfied with the price, quality, and service you're currently receiving and feel there's no room for improvement?" By rephrasing the objection, you not only defuse it but create an opportunity for yourself. **The value of objections**

When calling a potential customer, try to establish a real relationship with that person. You may never speak to him or her again, but you should try to create a bond. Do so with a couple of personal questions or observations. Ask the person about a non-job-related subject. Relate as a human being before you relate as a salesperson. You probably have some interests in common. Meet on that common ground if possible. **Find the common ground**

Make no mistake: your purpose in making the phone call is to

A script that worked

make a sale. So go for it. A good opening that has worked for many guerrillas is straightforward: "This is _____ with _____. We specialize in working with businesses, helping them to _____. Depending on what you're using in the area of _____, we might have something that could potentially help you to _____."

Another good way to open is to explain exactly why you're calling. "Hello, Mr. Coopersmith, my information shows me that you're driving a 1976 Buick. I'm calling because our company installs new automobile windshields on older cars and we're going to be in your neighborhood during the afternoon of Tuesday, November second."

As with the standard canvass or sales presentation, think in terms of contact, presentation, and close. Remember, your contact should be brief and warm. Your presentation should be concise yet loaded with references to benefits. And your close should be clear and definite. Don't pussyfoot. There is nothing wrong in most instances with asking for the sale. Just don't do it in such a way that a yes or no answer can be given. Close by saying something like, "What will be the most convenient way for you to pay for this, check or credit card?"

A guerrilla telemarketing script

The following script is from a telephone marketing program that was used in conjunction with a direct-mail program. This makes for a potent combination. These days, as direct mail increases rapidly, it makes sense to follow up a mailing with a phone call. For guerrillas, it's almost mandatory with big-ticket sales. In this instance, the mailing was followed two weeks later by a phone call. A week later, another call was made. The program worked. Direct mail alone would not have worked.

> Hello, Mr. _____? This is _____. I'm calling for the Wilford Hotel in Los Angeles. Have you ever been to the Wilford? _____ When was the last time you were in Los Angeles? _____ Recently, we sent you an invitation. Did you receive it? _____ Are you the person who makes out-of-town meeting arrangements for your firm, or is it someone else? _____ Do you plan to take us up on our special offer now, or do you plan to request more information? _____
>
> As you may recall, we are offering special prices and complimentary services to companies that hold meetings at the Wilford between April first and June thirtieth. Will your company be holding a meeting in Los Angeles during that time? _____ Did you like the special offer we made to you? Do you have any questions about it? Do you usually have meetings in hotels such as the Wil-

ford? _____ How many people attend the meetings? _____
Where do you ordinarily meet? _____ I think you might be interested in holding a meeting at the Wilford. Don't forget, during the
period from April first to June thirtieth, we're offering:

- Special room rates
- Complimentary meeting room
- Complimentary wine with dinner
- One free room for every fifteen booked
- A complimentary coffee break daily
- Discounts on audiovisual equipment
- Preregistration for your people
- A suite for the meeting planner

Doesn't this sound good? _____ You get all these benefits with a
minimum of only fifteen guest rooms.

Is there anything else we might offer you? _____ When do you
plan to hold your next meeting? _____ When would be the best
time to arrange a reservation for your group at the Wilford? _____
Would you like to make the arrangements right now or later? _____
When? _____ Is there any other person at your company that you
suggest I contact? _____ Thanks very much for taking this time to
speak with me. Good-bye.

Asking as much as talking

As you can see, a good phone script calls for lots of questions,
so that the person will feel he or she is part of the process and
won't feel "talked at." What you say on the phone should be part
of your overall marketing and creative plans, so measure your
scripts against your marketing strategies.

An unfortunate aspect of telemarketing is that most calls are
poorly scripted. It takes talent to create a good call. That means
more than a way with words. A guerrilla telemarketing script helps
telemarketers overcome employee turnover, despondent moods,
lack of enthusiasm, and rejection daze. It keeps callers on track
and ensures that prospects receive accurate data—all the while
allowing for natural telephone conversation. It even raises and
answers objections.

Most scripts fail because they don't give enough credence to
the very important human element, and because telemarketing is
now regarded as suspicious by an increasingly sophisticated public. Be sure your scripts are tight, yet loaded with warmth. Difficult
to do? You bet it is.

Be sure your script has tons of humanity built into it, with
room for give-and-take. Let the telemarketer add his or her own

Relax words and phrases to the script. The more comfortable the tele-marketer, the more relaxed the prospect. Relaxed prospects are good to have.

Keep your script one page long, single-spaced. Paragraph one introduces the caller and the company. Paragraph two gives the reason for the call or makes the offer. Paragraph three highlights the benefits of the offer. Paragraphs four and five close the sale or set the stage for the next step—possibly a personal appointment.

Your script should contain a good reason for your call. You have fifteen to twenty seconds to gain or lose your prospect's attention, so don't waste one second or one word. Guerrilla scripts contain about four interest-creating comments and flow directly to the benefits. They build rapport immediately with questions.

Get set to be Good scripts have systems to handle objections to the sale and
rejected to close the sale. You'll need a system to test and improve your script. More about this later.

You must be prepared for massive amounts of rejection when you embark on a telephone marketing program. For this reason, employee turnover in telephone marketing firms is tremendous. On the other hand, telephone marketing is so instantly effective for some companies that they set up what are known as boiler-room operations. In these operations, several people gather in one large room, which is often partitioned. Each has a phone; each can see the others. Each person makes call after call, working to get as many sales in as short a time as possible. When a sale is made, a signal is given, such as an upraised fist. The other phoners give a reciprocal signal to indicate that they recognize the success. This seems to give a lift to the group morale and helps the tele-
The boiler phone salespeople deal with the horribly high number of rejec-
room tions. It also seems to nourish enthusiasm.

You can set up your own boiler-room operation. Or you can hire one. Many telephone marketing firms exist—more now than ever, because just two decades ago none existed. These firms are permanent boiler-room operations. They operate from their own facilities, using their own scripts, tailored for your needs, and their own telephone sales pros. They charge by the hour and by the call. And many companies find them well worth the expense. If you consider establishing a boiler-room setup, first look into the economics of hiring an outside firm with a going operation. These firms can put their facilities to work for you or they can set up an operation for you, training your people to be masters at telephone selling.

One of the great advantages of telephone marketing is that you can obtain an instant response to your offer. You can deal with objections and overcome them. You can, by using a boiler-room operation, talk to literally thousands of people per day. In doing so, you can categorize the people you have called as customers, near customers, and noncustomers. In rare instances, you can accomplish all of your marketing by phone. Some companies do.

An advantage of telemarketing

It's not difficult to see why such marketing works far better for businesses selling to other businesses than it does for companies selling directly to consumers. This is because consumers at home have little time for business, but businesspeople in their place of business do have a bit of time for business matters, even those that come by phone. High-ticket sales are one of the reasons for telemarketing success in business-to-business transactions, whereas with individual consumers, profits tend to be far lower, making telemarketing to them less cost-efficient.

Be sure that you don't expect too much from your telemarketing campaign. A financial organization mailed a letter to its prospects, offering a free gift to those who requested a brochure. Telemarketing to the brochure requesters netted many personal appointments. It was during these appointments that sales were closed. Although sales may be closed on the phone, telemarketing is merely a crucial cog in a big machine.

When you telemarket, you must know which benefits turn on your prospective customers. Give prime emphasis to the benefits you feel have the most impact. Be sure you are speaking with the right person. Make a specific offer—preferably a special offer that is not available to all people at all times. And know how you'll handle objections because they'll be as common as busy signals and answering devices.

The more you call, the more you'll close

The more people you call, the more sales you'll close. Of every 20 people you *call*, you'll probably make contact with only about 5 on your first try. The others will be busy, sick, away, on the phone, or otherwise indisposed. Of every 20 people you *reach*, you may close only 1 sale on the phone. You'll have to make about 100 calls to close 1 sale. It may sound like a lot, but to a true telephone marketing pro, it means that a mere 1,000 phone calls will result in 10 sales. The top telemarketers cherish every no they get because they realize that the 99 are worth the 1 sale. Figuring an average of 3 minutes per call (some will take up to 10 minutes, but most will take less than 1 minute), this means that 50 hours of calling will result in 10 sales.

This also means that you'll either spend one hard workweek on the phone, or you'll hire someone to be on that phone for you. If your profit per sale is great enough, you should give serious consideration to this kind of marketing. If 10 sales aren't nearly enough, perhaps you should think about using other marketing methods. For some entrepreneurs, 10 sales in 1 week mean joy, wealth, and fulfillment. If you believe that telephone marketing makes sense for your offering, use it and take advantage before your competitors discover its powerful capabilities.

Four hours of rejection is enough

If you have an in-house calling department, let them call for no more than four hours a day. The rejection rate is extremely high, and I know that so much rejection dampens enthusiasm, sometimes permanently.

Look at the cost/return feasibility before starting a telemarketing campaign of your own. Only 3 percent of people called sit through a computerized telemarketing call, while 33 percent sit through a call from a live human being. A mere 4 percent of people reached by telemarketing actually place an order.

Getting your telemarketing act together

To help you get your act together, find out what's new in telemarketing by contacting AT&T and your own local telephone company, both of which conduct regular telemarketing seminars. Both groups will tell you to test, to test, and to test. What they are referring to are your scripts, your callers, and your target markets.

If you are pleased with the results of your telemarketing—and you will be if you combine it with other guerrilla marketing methods—remember that it can always be improved. That's why guerrillas never stop testing their scripts. They will constantly experiment with new words, phrases, and ideas. As a result, their response rates continue to rise.

In this chapter we discuss only one aspect of telemarketing—outbound telemarketing. We don't discuss inbound telemarketing—which means the taking of incoming calls—because it involves proper telephone demeanor and is in the domain of large businesses rather than small guerrilla businesses.

Toll-free numbers

A toll-free number can increase your response rate by 30 to 700 percent, and the cost to offer one continues to get lower. If you deal with local prospects and customers only, do not establish a toll-free number, for people like to deal with local companies. It's the confidence factor again. If you feel you must have a toll-free number, we warn that if it spells out a word, people probably won't write it down because they figure they'll remember it. The truth is, they won't! That's why the toll-free phone number for the free catalog offered by Guerrilla Marketing International is 1-800-748-6444. I provide this number when I give talks on guerrilla marketing, and people write it down. If I said a word instead of these numbers, people would probably trust their memories, and we'd get fewer calls.

Telemarketing is a superb mini-marketing weapon, already doubling as a maxi-marketing weapon. I encourage you to give it a try, especially if you're selling to businesses. In 1997, the average telephone transaction—contact to closed sale—was higher than $380 per call when one business telemarketed to another. Maybe you can improve on that figure. This guerrilla sure hopes so.

12

Circulars and Brochures:
How, Where, and When

Let's get this straight at the outset: there isn't much difference between circular and a flier, but a brochure is a different kind of animal. To me, circulars and fliers are short and single-minded; a brochure is longer and more detailed than either. My off-line and on-line dictionaries don't shed much more light on the subject, so we'll have to live with my distinctions.

Distribution

There are several ways to distribute circulars and brochures. They may be mailed alone or as part of a mailing package; placed in mailboxes; slipped under doors or windshield wipers; handed out at street corners, at trade shows, and wherever lots of prospects congregate; given to prospects and/or customers; placed in racks that say "take one" or on counters for general distribution; posted on community bulletin boards; and placed in hotel rooms.

If you're going to distribute many pieces, make them circulars, because circulars are less expensive per piece. If you are distributing relatively few pieces, you might opt for the more expensive brochures.

Form and content

The simplest form of circular is a single sheet of paper, printed on one side. Printing on both sides makes matters and format a tad more complex. Printing on both sides of two pieces of paper—each folded in half—makes a booklet, which I call a brochure if it is loaded with information, printed or visual. If it isn't, it's not really a brochure, but a folded circular. Some brochures run as long as twenty-four pages.

A circular is considered by many astute guerrillas to be the purest of weapons. It gets instant action if used properly. It is astonishingly inexpensive, especially if produced on your own computer. It lets you use color in a sea of black and white. And it's the essence of simplicity and flexibility if you do it right. This is what your circular should do:

- Make a clear and persuasive offer
- Have an element of urgency
- Get right to the point
- Tell the prospect what to do next
- Tie in with your current identity

One equals four

When planning to produce such materials, remember that when you fold a sheet of paper in two, you have a total of four pages (two on each side). So generally you must think in terms of four-page units. Brochures are ordinarily four or eight or twelve pages. Some brochures have panels that fold rather than pages that turn. Usually, these are six-panel brochures—three panels on each side. If you start with a standard 8×11 piece of paper, folding it twice makes it ready to become a six-panel brochure and the ideal size for a standard #10 envelope.

The format isn't nearly as important as the content. And the content must be factual information, enlivened with a touch of style and romance. Unlike ads, which must flag a person's attention, a brochure or circular already has that attention. Its primary job is to inform with the intention of selling. Most brochures, and some circulars, display artwork to keep the piece visually interesting. The purpose is to explain, inform, and sell.

When writing a circular, think first of the basic idea you wish to express. Then try to marry a picture (art or photograph) to a set of words. After you've stated your idea as briefly as possible, try to explain more fully what you are offering. *Always* be sure to include relevant information: your address and phone number. A circular is a headline. No need to attract attention; you've already got it. If you don't state your offer in a way that can be understood at a glance, I'm not too hopeful about your success. There's no need to list all of your benefits—list your greatest benefit. My first boss and marketing idol, Howard Gossage, said, "You don't have to wound a charging tiger all over to stop him; one well-placed shot ought to do the job."

What's the big idea?

I know an entrepreneurial-minded contractor who calls himself Super Handyman. He markets his services well, and he decided to improve business by distributing a circular or a brochure. This is how he proceeded. He first used a circular to see how this marketing vehicle would work for him. If it worked well, he might upgrade it to a brochure. On the circular, he included a drawing of a man (himself as Superman) doing five tasks at the same time

Super Handyman's circular

in front of a house. Above the drawing, he listed his company name, which, incidentally, made a dandy headline for his circular: IT'S SUPER HANDYMAN! Beneath that headline and picture, he briefly stated his offering:

He builds sun decks and patios.
He installs skylights and hot tubs.
He paints and puts up wallpaper.
He does masonry and electrical work.
He also designs and makes building plans.
SUPER HANDYMAN DOES IT ALL!
Call him at 555-5656 any time, any day.
All work guaranteed. Contractor's License #54-45673.

Not very fancy, but quite explicit. The cost for Super Handyman to write this circular was nil. An art student drew the illustration for $50, and the cost to produce about 5,000 of the circulars, including paper, was another $100. It would have cost less if Super Handyman had a computer on which to create the circular, but he didn't. So he spent about $150, which comes to three cents per circular. If printing costs had been higher—and they are higher now—he would have spent less than a nickel per circular. He didn't want to pay for color, but he was able to get a colorful circular by the ingenious use of colored ink on a colored paper stock—dark blue ink on light tan stock.

Super Handyman then distributed his circulars by several methods: he mailed 1,000; he placed 1,000 on auto windshields (he hired a high school student to do some of this for him); he distributed 1,000 at a home show in his area; he handed out 1,000 at a local flea market; and he kept 1,000 to give to satisfied customers to pass on to their friends and neighbors. The enterprising handyman also asked each of his customers where they had heard of him. When they said, "I saw your flier," he asked where they had seen it. By doing so he learned which of the five methods of circular distribution was most effective. That's guerrilla marketing! Not expensive, but very effective. One job could recoup for Super Handyman his entire marketing budget for circulars. And since 5,000 circulars were distributed, you have to believe that he found more than one job.

Super Handyman's brochure

Perhaps he will decide to distribute a brochure someday. To

plan a successful brochure, he'd ask himself what the brochure is specifically supposed to do for him. Get leads? Close sales? Generate phone calls? Web site visits? People won't take the time to figure it out for themselves, so Super Handyman has to do it for them.

My guess is that he'd think in terms of photography, so that he could show actual pictures of work he has accomplished. And because he has such a comprehensive offering, he'd figure that an eight-page brochure was needed to do the trick. He'd use a simple $8\frac{1}{2} \times 5\frac{1}{2}$ size, which is half the size of a standard $8\frac{1}{2} \times 11$ sheet of paper. Unless the brochure was full-color—a good idea because color increases retention rate by 57 percent and proclivity to buy by 41 percent—all type and photos would be in black ink. The paper stock, either glossy or not, would be white or a light color.

Give them a reason to read it all

He'd plan to use the same drawing on the cover that he used on his circular. After all, if it worked once, it ought to work again. And it makes good economic sense. His cover would show his drawing, list his company name (which fortunately doubles as a headline and a brochure title), and maybe, but not definitely, list the other copy points from his circular. Let's say he does list them, since he wants to impart as much information as possible. *Repetition in marketing is far more of a good thing than a bad thing.* And guerrillas realize that the real purpose of the cover is to give people a reason to read the rest of your brochure. The cover should go a long way toward answering the prospect's most important question: "What's in it for me?"

His second page might list pertinent information about Super Handyman. It would list his experience, his training, the jobs he has accomplished, his skills and offerings. It might even include a photo of him. The purpose of this page? To build his credibility. As a guerrilla, he knows that the more credible he is, the better results he will derive from his other marketing.

Page three might show photos of a sun deck and a patio, and would give a description, about five sentences long, of the handyman's capabilities in this area. Page four would show photos of a skylight and a hot tub that he installed. Again, five or six sentences would indicate his expertise. Page five would show photos of a room that Super Handyman painted and another room that he papered. It would also include a bit of copy attesting to his talent at painting and papering. Page six could feature photos of houses with masonry and electrical work he accomplished. One would be an exterior shot and the other an interior shot. Again, copy would describe the work accomplished. Each of these pages should repeat the short copy lines from the cover. For example, the seventh page, carrying a photograph of a gorgeous room addition that he designed and built, would carry the headline, "Super Handyman also makes building plans and building designs." A few sentences of copy would follow the photo. The purpose of the brochure is to *inform*.

The purpose of a brochure

Finally, his eighth page, the back cover, would provide the name of his company, his phone number, fax number, Web site, E-mail address, his contractor's license number, and a copy of the best photo from the interior of the brochure. Such a brochure might cost him as much as one dollar per unit. It's worth it, considering his profit per sale. He runs a relatively simple business, so his brochure is focused. If he had other special offerings, such as stained glass windows or hot tubs, he'd create separate brochures for those talents.

A solar-heating company for which I created a brochure had a problem. They realized that a brochure would help their business, but the technology in their industry was changing so rapidly that they were reluctant to commit themselves to producing one. Solution: I created an eight-page brochure with a pocket inside the back cover. Within the eight pages, the brochure addressed all of the aspects of solar technology that were not changing: its economy, cleanliness, responsibility to the environment, its acceptance and success in all parts of the world. In the pocket the company inserts separate sheets that describe specific equipment as technology marches forward. These are replaced at will. Price lists, also replaceable at a whim, are inserted there as well. This enables the company to have flexibility with its brochure.

The flexible brochure

Let's look at another example. A jewelry-making firm in San Francisco manufactured beautiful but very expensive jewelry. To add an element of value, it produced a lavish brochure—full color, glossy, and photographed in the most glamorous parts of San Francisco. Each two-page spread contained one gorgeous photo of the San Francisco area and one photo of an item of jewelry. This lent an air of value to each piece of jewelry that could not have been created with a single photo. It connected the jewelry store with San Francisco, where tourism is the largest industry. A brochure was just the ticket.

One of my clients sent a photographer on a dream assignment: to visit Mexico and shoot photos of a wide variety of villas and condominiums that my client was renting to people for vacation use. These photos were later made the basis for a colorful brochure. Without the photos, the brochure could only have dealt with villa and condo vacations in a theoretical sense. The photos brought the theory to vibrant life. The brochure helped the company quadruple its sales. Without a vehicle to show the many villas and condos, complete with beaches, pools, balconies, lush living rooms, and spacious bedrooms, the company could not have made its point. Less than a brochure could not have done the job.

A brochure success story

Still another company was able to grow from tiny to tremendous merely by the proper use of a brochure. The company owned the patent on a new product that replaced the old-fashioned blowtorch. But it couldn't communicate all of the advantages of its product with ads or letters or phone calls. Personal demonstrations were impractical because of logistics problems. A brochure was the answer. It was incredibly detailed, listing all of the advantages of the product and all of the famous-name companies using it, and showing several exciting shots of the product in use. The brochure included a pageful of testimonials from satisfied users, and it described the technical data in such detail that even the most nitpicking engineer would be impressed. In addition, it was very handsome. This inspired confidence in the company. To this day, the company's primary marketing tools are its Web site and that brochure.

Many companies have a story that does not translate well in advertising but becomes brilliantly clear when the details, both verbal and graphic, are communicated in a brochure. You can afford to spend a great deal of your marketing budget producing a knockout brochure. The cost, including everything, runs anywhere from $500 to $50,000. But don't let the $50,000 figure dazzle you. That's only $4,166.67 per month, much less than many companies spend on media advertising alone. Perhaps you won't even need the mass media — perhaps a brochure will do the trick for you.

Until now you've read only the bad news about circulars and brochures. Here's the good news: they are more inexpensive to create and produce than ever before. Easy-to-use computer software is the reason. It lets guerrillas like Super Handyman produce circulars and brochures at a fraction of what they used to cost. The figure of from $500 to $50,000, if you own a computer and current

Good news about circulars and brochures

software, is more like $50 to $500 these days, an enormous difference, which is why guerrillas are so quick to embrace today's simplified technology.

Make no mistake: there is *no* room these days for a *trace* of amateurishness, sloppiness, smudges, poor grammar, misspelled words, typos, contradictions, or omissions. Use your computer's spellchecker and then hire a good proofreader to check anything you intend to expose to the public. Better that one friend or associate catch your goofs than five thousand prospects.

At the end of your brochure, be sure to tell people exactly what they are supposed to do—whether they should call you, visit you, visit your Web site, fax you, or E-mail you. Tell them exactly what you want them to do now that they know about you. Guerrillas assume nothing and test everything.

Although some businesses benefit almost every time they give away their brochure, there are instances in which you shouldn't give one away. If you have a store and distribute brochures to your potential customers, you are giving them an excuse not to buy. They can tell you that they want to look over your brochure before buying. I advise my clients, except those selling very expensive items, *not* to give their brochures to shoppers but to give them only to people who have purchased or to those who are on their way out. But do ask if they want one. Don't waste weapons.

I also advise people who run newspaper or magazine ads that convey a lot of information to consider using those ads as brochures. Reprint them and add front and rear covers by printing on the back of the folded-in-half advertisement. Often the magazine will do this for you for peanuts.

If you don't have the budget for large ads, consider running small ads offering your free brochure. I know a man who earns his entire income (a six-figure income, I might add) by running tiny ads in myriad publications, offering his free brochure in each ad. Those who request the brochure are serious prospects: they took the time to write for the brochure. They are interested in what he's offering. My friend's brochure does his entire selling job for him. It describes his offer, gives the details, and asks for the order. His ads and his brochures are his only marketing tools, and he is very successful as a one-man show. This demonstrates how important a brochure can be.

Guerrillas consider their brochures to be part of a dance called the two-step. Step one is running a lot of little ads that say one salient thing about their companies and then have the magic line: "Call or write for our *free* brochure." You must give people a choice between calling or writing because half of them won't call and the other half won't write. And you should highlight the absence of cost, because "free" is the most powerful word in the language of marketing.

When people call or write requesting your free brochure, should you send it to them all by itself? Of course not. Because people are bombarded with an estimated 2,700 marketing messages every day, contacting you for your brochures signifies a mighty powerful *act of intent* on their part. Acknowledge that fact by sending, along with your free brochure, a brief note thanking them for taking the time to request it. Sign that note in ink before mailing the brochure. Follow up with a card or letter within ten days (a week is even better), taking the sale to the next level. If you do this, you can expect between 25 and 33 percent of brochure-requesters to become paying customers. Brochures should be given only to people who really want them. Circulars and business cards can go to anybody.

2,700 marketing messages every day

A mighty important point: when printing your business cards, think of them as mini-brochures. On them, print your name, address, phone number, logo, fax number, E-mail address, Web site, and theme line, of course. Also include brief body copy—as much as you can fit. Some clever entrepreneurs hand out double-size business cards, folded in half. The outside of the cards has the standard business-card information. The inside has a headline, beneath which are listed several features and benefits, products and services. These cards look like business cards but work like brochures. And brochures work well.

Mini-brochures

To see what a twenty-first-century business card will look like, make a simple phone call to InfoCard at 512-327-3385 and request a sample. It will plant healthy ideas in your mind.

If anything does a brochure's job better than a brochure, it is an *electronic brochure*—a five- to nine-minute version of a printed brochure. The cost of duplicating videos is under $1.50 and falling. The cost of producing videos is $100 to $10,000 per minute. The lower cost is if you do it yourself—not recommended. The higher number is for letting a first-rate video production company handle it. Guerrillas find a happy medium somewhere between the two.

Electronic brochures

A *video brochure*—and about 86 percent of Americans have

The video brochure

access to a VCR—will give more of an impression of worth and value than a printed version. Prospects will view it, then probably view it again with one or more people. They may give it to a friend or an associate. The purpose of such a brochure is that of a printed one—to use words, pictures, music, emotions, intellect, demonstration, and believability to create a desire to buy your product or service. However, don't pretend that you're now in show business. Guerrillas don't fall into that trap.

Guerrillas do not send video brochures to people on a mailing list, such as huge corporations can and a few automobile manufacturers have done. One car maker sent a video introducing the local dealer's name at the beginning, starring the car with glitzy cinematography in the middle, then ending with the recipient's name *superimposed across the video image*—it was the first of **By request** many personalized video brochures. Guerrillas like the idea of **only** personalization and are wowed by the potency of video information. Still, they send their video brochures only to people who *request them.*

People learn of videos through magazines, direct mailings, trade shows, and other modes of communication. When they request one, it should be sent free, with no obligation. Whatever you do, send a personal letter along with it, just as you would with a printed brochure. Follow up within ten days via a phone call or letter. A request for a video should be seen as the first step in buying. Be sure to follow up—don't lose the momentum you've created.

The audio You may not require visual input to tell your business story; **brochure** perhaps you can do it with words. Put your words onto tape and offer an *audio brochure.* Approximately 97 percent of Americans have access to an audiocassette player. A growing number of Americans commute for longer than thirty minutes each day. Instead of listening to the radio, they'll probably listen to your five- to fifteen-minute tape. They know it's a way to learn while saving time.

Create a video brochure according to a strategy, just as you'd create a printed brochure. Say as much as you can *visually.* Realize that your visuals will communicate more powerfully than your verbiage, so keep the visual excitement to a maximum. Be sure the visuals pertain to your company and aren't merely special visual effects substituting for a solid idea.

A video brochure is jazzy and more dynamic than a printed

piece, but its purpose is to make a sale, either all by itself, in concert with a sales rep who is present during the viewing of the tape, or in tandem with a direct-mail letter, card, or a phone call. In numbers there is strength. In visuals there is strength. As wonderful as your video brochure may be, it is only as powerful as your idea.

Electronic and printed brochures are expensive, so don't say anything you'll want to amend within a year.

Follow up on everyone who requests any kind of brochure. Guerrillas rarely send brochures to anyone who doesn't actually request them. And when they do send brochures, they always include a brief note, signed in ink by them, identifying themselves as the president or owner of the company, thanking the person for requesting the brochure. They also send a follow-up note to these people within one week of mailing their brochure. Anyone who takes the time to ask for a brochure is really a torrid prospect asking for all the details. When's the last time you requested a brochure and received a note from the head of the company? Probably never. And that's why you will stand out so much when you do it.

Always include a note

Converting the curious

Guerrillas go all out to convert curious prospects into paying customers. They do it with classy, professional, and inexpensive brochures, intensive, caring follow-up, and personalized service. Now it's your turn!

13

Classified Advertising Hints: Making Small Beautiful

When you think of classified advertising, you probably think in terms of finding a job, looking for a car, selling a sofa, buying a boat, or locating a house or apartment. Think again. Classified advertising can also be used to support a business. And many a flourishing enterprise exists primarily on the pulling power of classified ads.

On a random weekday, my local newspaper featured classified ads for a ticket-selling firm, a number of attorneys, an advertising medium, a pregnancy consultation center, a credit association, a fortune teller, a job-finding service, several books, a game arcade, a psychic adviser, a rent-a-mailbox firm, a ghostwriter, several introduction services, a group of escort services, two full columns of massage businesses, one and a half columns of firms offering loans, unique telegram companies, hairstylists, barbers, moving companies, auto transport firms, travel agencies, calligraphers, gobs of home-service entrepreneurs, tropical fish stores, pawnbrokers, coin and stamp dealers, antique dealers, auctioneers, TV dealers, computer equipment stores, Internet consultants, musical-instrument stores, a horse ranch, boat dealers, a flying school, two résumé-writing services, loads of schools, tutors, employment agencies, auto and truck dealers, motorcycle dealers, hotels, rooming houses, bed and breakfast inns, rest homes, guest houses, Realtors, business brokers, motels, and mobile-home deal-

Do your own homework

ers. And this was a weekday paper—not a Sunday paper. I wouldn't even attempt to list the entrepreneurial enterprises using the Sunday classified section. Do your own homework and see for yourself—in your own community. Better do that homework on a regular basis because the classified section is a living, growing thing that changes pretty darned fast—to the delight of the burgeoning number of small-business owners who profit from it.

If all of these entrepreneurs and/or businesses use the classified section, it makes sense for you to consider it. Many of these advertisers have had ads in the classified section for more than fifteen years. And I know that they wouldn't spend their money there if they weren't getting handsome returns.

In my files, I have magazines that run far more classified ads than are in the newspaper just mentioned. And I'm sure you know of newspapers—many of them—that consist of nothing but classified ads. Obviously, classified ads work as a marketing medium. And if you can see any advantage for your company in using this medium, a bit of investigation and investment on your part is worthwhile.

$12.5 billion worth of classified ads

In 1995, $12.5 billion of the $34.1 billion spent on newspaper ads went into classified advertising. Among the fastest-growing segments of classified ads are those conveniently appearing on-line. Generally, there are four places you can run classified ads: in magazines, in daily newspapers, in classified-ad newspapers, and on-line. If your offering requires proximity to your customers, forget the magazines. And if your offering is national in character, forget the newspapers. There is little likelihood that you'll want to run classified ads in both local newspapers and national magazines—unless the papers you select are in localities spread throughout the country, and you want to combine that advertising with national magazine advertising.

Four places to run classified ads

You are probably noticing that more and more magazines are offering classified advertising. They know that many of the new small businesses just plain can't afford a display ad, and they have this deep longing for revenue. So the magazines offer classified advertising sections for entrepreneurs. Look deeply into this, for the cost is relatively low to get into a major magazine and because the classified section is generally at the back of the magazine.

Guerrilla hint: because 61 percent of Americans read magazines from the back to the front, your economical classified ad will have a decent shot at being read. It's a glorious place to do step one of the two-step.

As you may have heard, it doesn't cost an arm and leg to run a classified ad. And you'll usually be offered a frequency discount. This means that if your five-line classified ad costs you $20 to run one time, it will cost only, say, $18 per insertion if you run it three times, and only $15 per insertion if you run it five times. The more frequently you run it, the lower your cost per insertion. This is

How much it costs

called a frequency discount. Classified ad charges are based on the number of words, the number of lines, or the number of inches. It depends on the publication. The cost of the ad is also based on the circulation of the publication—both in quantity and quality.

Many people read the classified ads each day. Some read them to find specific bargains. Others read them merely to browse via the newspaper. And still others find them the most fascinating part of the newspaper. Check them yourself. See which ads draw your attention. Note which classified-ad categories catch your attention. By reading through the ads, you'll get a sense of whether or not your business can profit from this method of marketing. You'll also begin to learn, by osmosis, what to say in a classified ad and what not to say. Although classified ads are short, fraught with abbreviations, and devoid of illustrations, they aren't as simple as they may seem.

On-line classified ads are a relatively new phenomenon even though they're the oldest and most widely used forms of on-line advertising. Many on-line services allow you to run your classified ad for free, and some offer video and audio capabilities, which means your prospects can listen to a symphony as they read about your consulting service. They can also listen to rock and roll as they take an on-line tour through your facilities—all courtesy of classified advertising, twenty-first century. One such service, Classifind Network at www.classifind.com, provides a searchable database index and up to two hundred descriptive words to help the right buyer find the right ad. Their multimedia advertising rates are far less than the cost of most one-column-inch print ads. I'm talking about an investment of less than ten bucks a month. It's guerrilla marketing with sight, sound, action, technology, interactivity—but with an extraordinarily low cost.

Classified ads of all kinds reach people who are *already shopping*. They're easy to create and run, can commence very shortly after you decide to run them, are simple to test, and have paid rich dividends to entrepreneurs for centuries. If you decide to use the classified-ad section, there are a few concepts that you should keep in mind.

For one thing, keep your headline short. You must have a headline, printed in capital letters. Don't use abbreviations unless you are sure that people will understand them. While living in England, my wife and I searched for an apartment by scanning the classified ads. Many said that the rental included CCF&F. We were thrown by that. Do you know what it means? Later, we

Learning by reading

On-line classified ads

Writing strong ads

learned that it stands for "carpets, curtains, fixtures, and fittings." We also found that most Britishers know that.

Don't use esoteric terms in your ads unless you're sure that most of your readers (99 percent) know the meaning. Write in short sentences. Try to sound more like a human being than a want ad. And include your phone number and address—more than once I've seen an ad with no phone number or address.

Many publications have employees who can help you word your want ads. I suggest that you use them as guides, but don't always follow their advice. If they were brilliant writers, they'd probably be paid for their writing. If you are a good writer, write your own classified-ad copy. If not, go to a pro. Don't rely on the person who takes the ads to write your copy.

Choose very carefully

Word your ad in such a way that it contrasts with other ads in the same section. And choose that section very, very carefully. Some newspapers have categories that don't appear in other papers, such as attorneys, announcements, Christmas items, and computers. Advertise in the proper category. Make that plural. You may want to place your ad in more than one category.

Strange as it may seem, classified ads often outdraw display ads. So don't think that just because an ad has no picture and doesn't cost much it's not going to be effective. Many companies run display ads and classified ads in the same newspapers on the same day. They claim that the ads reach different classes of consumers.

A money-making ad

I earned about $500 per month for at least a dozen years working about half an hour per month. I did it with a classified ad. I ran the same ad, with minor changes in wording, for twelve years. After I'd been working for a few years as a freelance writer, I'd learned quite a few important things about freelancing—things nobody had ever told me, things that weren't written in books. So I wrote a book and published it myself. I called the book *Secrets of Successful Free-Lancing*. And although it had but forty-three pages, I priced it at $10. The reason I charged $10 was because I sincerely felt the book was worth it. The book cost me about $1 to print, including type and binding. Advertising ran about $3.33 per book. So I figured that I made $5.67 per book. Here's a sample of the classified ad I ran:

I EARN MORE AS A FREELANCER THAN I DID AS VP/CREA-TIVE DIRECTOR AT J. WALTER THOMPSON. I loved my JWT days. But I love now more. I live where I want. I work only 3 days a week. I work from my home and take lots of vacations. To do the same, read my incisive book, *Secrets of Successful Free-Lancing*. Send $10 to Prosper Press, 123 Alto Street, San Rafael, CA 94902. $11 refund if you're not completely satisfied.

Note that my ad used standard language rather than want-ad language. When I've run other classified ads using "people talk," I've also had good results. A regularly worded ad appearing in a sea of want-ad-worded ads tends to stand out.

The cost of the ad was $36 for one inch in the publication in which it originally appeared. And the entire ad fit in one inch in the classified section. For every dollar I invested in the ad, I aver- **The biggest** aged $3 in sales, $2.50 in profits. It cost fifty cents to mail it, enve- **challenge** lope included.

For me, the biggest challenge was to find enough places to run the ad. After all, everybody isn't a prospect for a book on freelancing. I ran the ad in three advertising trade magazines, two art-director publications, two writers' magazines, the *Wall Street Journal*, and four opportunity magazines. Some of these publica-tions drew a great response every time I ran the ad—and I ran it every three months. Others didn't pull well for me, so I withdrew them from my schedule. By sticking with the four publications that worked, I was able to bring in around $500 per month in profits—after paying for the ads, the books, and the mailing. I had all the orders mailed directly to a mail-order-fulfillment house that mailed out the books on the day orders were received, put the names of the people who ordered into a computer, and sent me the checks weekly—coded so that I knew which publications were working best.

People in the mail-order book business report that a 5 percent request rate for refunds is about par for the course. My requests for refunds were 1.2 percent. And don't forget, I offered an $11 refund for a forty-three-page $10 book.

The half-hour per month I spent on this business was used to keep tallies on the pulling power of the various magazines and to fill out deposit slips for my bank. And $500 per half-hour isn't anything to complain about. And just think—my only method of marketing was classified advertising.

That book is no longer available by that title because I ex-panded it to help others. It is available in two versions: *Earning Money Without a Job* and *555 Ways to Earn Extra Money*. (In fact, it was the response to those books that prompted me to write *Guerrilla Marketing* in the first place.) If financial independence and the freedom to enjoy it sound good to you, I unabashedly call your attention to *The Way of the Guerrilla: Achieving Success and Balance as an Entrepreneur in the 21st Century,* published by Houghton Mifflin. Enough about me and my books. Back to you and your marketing.

Some on-line guerrillas use classified ads solely to direct viewers to their Web sites. Many other marketers use the classified ads only to check out the pulling power of products, claims, prices, copy, headlines, and appeals. It's an inexpensive way to gain valuable information. Once you have a proven winner, you can then put forth your message in display ads if you wish. But remember, classified ads sometimes pull better than display ads.

A friend who advertised his books in *Psychology Today* found that classified ads, at 25 percent of the price of display ads, pulled considerably better than display ads. The kind of classified ad he ran is called a *classified display ad.* It's an ad that appears in the classified section but has a box around it and features dark, large display type. It costs more than regular classifieds, less than regular display ads, and depending on the offering, pulls better than both in many instances.

Classified display ads

In your classified ad, don't use too many adjectives, but do use a lot of facts. Aim to be as clear in your message as you can. Remember that your classified ad is really your sales presentation. Don't hold back on features if your offering has features to boast about. You may end up spending several dollars more because your ad is longer, but if it brings you sales, this will easily outweigh the extra cost. *The cost of all advertising is measured not in dollars but in response.*

When thinking about classified advertising, think first in terms of clarity and then in terms of reader interest. You must capture your readers' attention. Do it with a catchy word such as GHOSTWRITING! or with a headline such as NEED EXTRA MONEY? You have but a *fleeting* instant to gain attention. Get it with your short headline. The rest of your copy should follow directly from the headline. The GHOSTWRITING headline might be followed with this sentence: "A professional writer will write, rewrite, or edit your letter, essay, manuscript, or advertisement so that it sings." The NEED EXTRA MONEY? headline might be followed by copy that begins: "Obtaining the extra cash you need is not as hard as you think." If I needed money, I'd read on. Wouldn't you?

Talk to one person at a time
The idea in your classified ad is to maintain the momentum created by the headline. Write copy as though you are talking to one human being and not to a mass audience. Although you should mention as many features and benefits in your ad as you can afford, practice the selective withholding of information. Merely by omitting certain facts, you may generate phone calls, visits, or other types of desired responses. The information you withhold may be the price, the location, or some other data the reader needs to complete the picture. Just be careful not to withhold enough information so that you attract a horde of unqualified prospects.

A good exercise for classified-ad writing is to write your ad as though it were to be a display ad in a newspaper. Cut copy to make the ad shorter and shorter. Finally, you will be left with the pure facts. But remember *quality*. Pepper your facts with adjectives. "I can paint your house so that it gleams like the day it was built" sounds more appealing than "House painting at reasonable prices."

Though classified ads need not be as short as possible, they must nonetheless motivate your prospective customers. They must create a desire to buy. One advertising genius who specializes in classified ads claims that the key to success in the classifieds is simplicity and tight copy. If you think that is easy to achieve, you are wrong. It's tough to be simple, tough to be brief. The writing of classified ads is a very special art. The ads must be well written or else they will not inspire confidence. Just because they're short does not mean they can be shabby.

Study the winners
To gain insight into writing successful classified ads, look through current newspapers and magazines, studying the classifieds. Then look at one-year-old issues of the same newspapers and magazines. Check to see which ads are in both the new and the year-old publications. Those must be winners, or the people running them would not be repeating them. By studying them, you can learn what it is that makes them so successful. Is it the headline? the offer? the price? the copy? Apply whatever you learn to your own business. You can't compare today's on-line classified ads with those of a year ago, but you can browse through the free and the paid on-line classified ad sections to see who is advertising what. If you regularly surf on-line, you can spot the winners as the losers drop from sight and vanish.

The guerrilla Charles Rubin, coauthor of *Guerrilla Marketing Online,* tells us that on-line classified ads age quickly. If you're running a classified ad on an on-line service, you'll notice that most ad classifications have a few hundred ads, arranged chronologically from top to bottom in each category. This means that the latest ads submitted for publication are at the top of the list. The ad you post which appears on the first screenful of ads today may be three or four screens down the list tomorrow. To avoid getting lost, *resubmit your ad every day* to maintain its position near the top. You may have to use different titles for your ad to post it more than once. Still, most shoppers won't browse down more than three screens to view older ads.

Resubmit your on-line ad every day

Many large businesses that run high-powered advertising and marketing programs, making use of TV, radio, magazines, and other publicity, still use the classified section. They recognize that there are some people who read classified ads when looking for, say, antiques or certain automobiles. Classified ads are *not* small potatoes. There are advertising consultants who *specialize* in classified ads. You give them your ad copy and they return it to you, improved, and with a list of publications in which it is likely to elicit a response. If you will market a product or service nationally, consider newspapers in multiple markets as well as national magazines.

If our friend Super Handyman were to run a classified ad in a local newspaper, he'd probably run it in the "home services" section, and it might say:

WANT A SUN DECK? PATIO? SKYLIGHT? HOT TUB? Let Super Handyman do it! Super Handyman can give you those things plus masonry work, electrical work, and building plans. Free estimates. Call 555-5656. All work is fully guaranteed.

I know a person with an offering similar to Super Handyman's who ran such an ad. After it appeared only six times, he had to withdraw it because he couldn't handle all the work. I wish you the same success.

Remember that classified ads in newspapers allow you to home in on a local audience. Classified ads in magazines allow you to home in on a more widespread audience. Classified ads on-line allow you to do both—proving once again the potential of on-line marketing. And all classified ads allow you to test your strategy, your message, and the advertising media you are trying

Testing the waters

out. They're glorious places to say that magic sentence: "Call or write for our FREE brochure."

If you feel that classified advertising might be your marketing mainstay, I heartily recommend that you call Agnes Franz at 602-778-6788. Her newsletter, *Classified Communication,* is devoted to classified advertising and how to make it work. She demonstrates that classified advertising is important advertising even though it comes in short paragraphs consisting of short sentences. Franz will explain to you the directories that list all the magazines that accept classified advertising, and if she can, she'll recommend a few that have proven themselves in action.

Although classified ads are small and inexpensive, they *are* effective. A true guerrilla marketer tries to find ways to put the power of classified ads to work. Hardly any other medium enables you to talk to honest-to-goodness prospects and not only browsers. There's a huge difference between the two.

14
Signs: Big and Little

Think of signs in two ways: those that appeal to people *outside* your place of business and those that appeal to people *within* your place of business. The first category consists of billboards, which we'll discuss in another chapter, small signs on bulletin boards, which are discussed in this chapter, window signs, store signs, banners, signs on trees, and poster-type signs. Category two is made up of interior signs, commonly called point-of-purchase (POP) or point-of-sale signs.

Whichever you use, or if you use both, be certain that your signs tie in as directly as possible with your advertising. The dictum, as stated by the late, great advertising pro Leo Burnett: "Plan the sale when you plan the ad." The dictum, as stated by Jay Conrad Levinson: "Signs trigger impulse purchases; guerrillas are trigger-happy."

Signs trigger impulse purchases

Your ads will have made an unconscious impression on your potential customers, and your signs will awaken the memory of that advertising and motivate a sale. Many people will patronize your business because of your ads. Your signs must be consistent with your advertising message and identity or those people will be confused. If the signs are in keeping with your overall creative strategy, consumers' momentum to buy will be increased. The Point-of-Purchase Advertising Institute tells us that in 1996, 76 percent of all purchase decisions were made right at the place of purchase. They cannot help but smirk when they report that all 22 industry categories that they studied in 1996 increased their in-store sign spending, with an industry average increase of 5.1 percent. In real money, that means 22 product categories—from tobacco to fresh foods to jewelry to professional services—invested a bit less than $4 billion in in-store signs.

A vague notion of buying

People enter a store with a vague notion of buying but no brand preference. They don't solidify their decision until they are *in* the store. And what do you suppose influences their decision? In many cases, a package. In many other cases, a sign.

Signs have exceptional power in the realm of malls, hyper-markets (a galaxy of malls), shopping centers, warehouses, super-markets—large spaces where many businesses are competing for the eye and business of passersby. Many smart retailers have used their signs and their decor to tie in with the times. The idea is to match confidence in the offering—accomplished with mass marketing—with a reason to make an impulsive purchase. This is, in part, accomplished by the use of a sign. Make that match and—bingo!—you've made a sale.

How many words on a sign?

Most exterior signs are there to remind, to create a tiny impulse, to implant inclinations a wee bit deeper, to sharpen an identity, to state a very brief message. As a rule, exterior signs should be no more than six words long. Some successful signs have more than six words, but not many. Probably the most successful of all have just one to three words.

Sign language

Now, since we're talking about the power of words—few words—let's examine some of the strongest words in the English language. Many are used in headlines; many are used in signs. Almost all are used in advertising.

Psychologists at Yale University tell us that the most persuasive words in the English language are:

you	results	love	new
money	health	discovery	safety
save	easy	proven	guarantee

To that list, I would hasten to add:

free	why	sale	announcing
yes	how	now	benefits
fast	secrets	power	solution

Now that you know these words, I'll bet you can come up with some dandy signs.

Frequently, motorists make abrupt decisions (and right turns) when they pass windows with huge banners proclaiming SALE! or FREE GIFTS! or SAVE FIFTY PERCENT! As you probably know, it doesn't take many words to convince some people that they ought to buy from you right now.

Many famous businesses were built with signs and signs alone. I instantly call to mind Burma-Shave (for which I had the privilege of writing two signs that were actually published, or shall I say "road-sided"), Harold's Club in Reno, and Wall Drug Store of South Dakota. These are nationally known businesses. Many locally famous concerns marketed their wares the same way. You can be sure that the Burma-Shave people, Harold, and Mr. Wall were all pioneer guerrillas, for they blazed trails that led directly to the bank. They also incensed coming generations of environmentalists who claimed the signs were encroaching on the beauty of America. Lady Bird Johnson spearheaded this movement, and it will never die. Be aware of it, and don't put up exterior signs that will be picketed by planet-savers. As a guerrilla marketer, you must stay in touch with trends, and I, for one, am heartened by the nation's growing concern with the environment, as indicated by new marketing strategies, use of recyclable materials, and production measures to guide our species toward cosmic sanity.

Pioneer guerrillas

Mike Lavin, a true "green guerrilla," searched for a unique way to promote his Berkeley business. A healthy combination of environmentalist and capitalist, Mike was able to have his cake and eat it, too, by erecting, in a field, a large sign frame with no sign inside the frame. Beneath his see-through creation was smaller sign that said "SCENERY COURTESY OF BERKELEY DESIGN SHOP." His store, at the same location in Berkeley for more than twenty-five years, is now called European Mattress Works, but he still relies on signs to serve as silent salespeople, on and off the premises.

Silent salespeople

Other exterior signs that usually work well are those that say such things as VOTE FOR LEVINSON, GARAGE SALE, FLEA MARKET, PARK HERE, and GAS FOR LESS. Perhaps the most profitable investment a retail business owner can make is in a red neon sign that says OPEN. Not a lot of creativity in the copy for those signs, to be sure. Nonetheless, they work. Failure to make a sign investment early on may mean making a sign investment later on, putting your money into a GOING OUT OF BUSINESS sign.

Almost (but not quite) as important as the wording of the sign is the overall look of the sign. By this I mean the picture or pictures, the lettering style, the colors, and the design of the sign. A powerful graphic lends more power to the words. A sign that says FRESH DONUTS can be made doubly effective if it shows donuts growing in a meadow like flowers. If the sign says DELICIOUS DONUTS, it can be more motivating if it shows a picture of a

Effective sign graphics

grinning little girl holding a donut with a giant bite taken from it or a closeup of a donut in the process of being dunked.

It usually makes sense to use very light lettering against very dark background colors or very dark lettering against very light colors. One type of lettering is easier to read than more than one type. The words on the sign should be as large as possible while leaving room for the picture.

Although your sign should be expected only to remind and not to make an actual sale, go for the jugular and try like crazy to make the sale from the sign. Large advertisers with humongous marketing budgets can use signs to remind only, but guerrillas have to get more mileage from their money. Although we know that signs remind, it *is* possible to sell *some* people with a sign, so go for the sale with the sign.

The clutter factor

Consider also the "clutter factor." Are there many other signs nearby? If so, make sure *your* sign stands out. If not, you can approach the creation of your sign with a different mindset. In England, when designing an outdoor sign campaign for a product that promised economy, we took the clutter factor into account and introduced black and white signs that contrasted with the surrounding sea of color signs. Our black and white beauties not only won awards but, more important, won customers. Had we used color with the same words and pictures, we would not have enjoyed such a high level of success. Our uniqueness, which tied in directly with our promise of economy, helped us stand out and make our point. Calvin Klein uses the same technique on television—black and white in a color environment.

A powerful visual image should be created if you are going to use many signs. The Marlboro cowboy comes to mind immediately. Because you want your sign to be instantly identifiable with you, a graphic identity is highly recommended. The look should be unusual, connected with your company's identity, and suitable for being maintained over a long period of time. Consistency. Remember?

The only punctuation mark with which you need be concerned is the exclamation mark. It lends a tone of excitement. Question marks, while of use in print advertising, take too much reflection time to be utilized on signs. Stay away from them unless you have a good reason to break that rule. Commas and periods usually are not necessary with six-word messages. And long words are to be avoided whenever possible.

In order to make a sale with a visual image plus five or six words, you'll need a great deal of thought and creativity. As with all other marketing devices, a great sign starts with a great idea. If you lack the idea, your words and pictures won't work. However, if you have the right words and the right pictures, along with the right idea and the right location, a sale can be made.

Guerrillas must fight their battles with every single available weapon. Small signs on bulletin boards have proven to be extremely effective weapons for many an entrepreneur. I'm talking about signs on cars as small as 3 inches by 5 inches. Even business cards. A sign need not be big to attract customers. Little signs do the job, too.

Small signs and big results

What kinds of businesses and individuals might avail themselves of this medium? Tutors, gardeners, plumbers, typists, writers, baby-sitters, house sitters, movers, accountants, room renters, music teachers, nurses, answering services, pet groomers, cleaning people, painters, astrologers, mechanics, printers, seamstresses, decorators, Web site designers, dog walkers, tree pruners, entertainers. And a whole lot more!

If your business has any prospects who have occasion to see bulletin boards, perhaps you should use small signs on bulletin boards to promote your business. You'll find such bulletin boards on campuses and in libraries, cafeterias, dormitories, company rest rooms, offices, supermarkets, Laundromats, locker rooms, bookstores, pet stores, sporting goods stores, barbershops, hair-styling salons, toy stores, and sundry other locations. Most major cities have hundreds of such locations; many small towns have as many as five or ten. Guerrillas post signs in places where there is high visibility and no cost:

Where guerrillas post signs

- In front of their own business
- In front of neighboring businesses
- Subway stations
- School offices
- Senior recreational facilities and retirement homes
- College dormitories—in the community area, hallways, and bathrooms
- Fraternities and sororities
- Churches
- Other local community clubs and organizations
- Apartment buildings—in laundry rooms

- Community activity centers
- Grocery stores
- Shopping malls
- Car washes
- Condominium complex party centers
- Hotel and motel lobbies
- Utility poles
- Military cafeterias and recreation centers
- Counters of public places
- Meeting convention centers and rooms
- Construction walls
- Libraries
- Union halls
- Chambers of commerce
- Medical or professional offices
- Roller rinks and bowling alleys
- Waiting rooms at auto repair and tire shops
- Liquor and convenience stores
- Company bulletin boards of friends and family
- Tourist information centers
- Highway rest stops
- Banks
- Factories
- Their cars—featuring a compelling sign, parked in a conspicuous place
- On the fences outside a construction site

Limitless options

The point here is that guerrillas are not very limited in their options. You can either post the signs yourself or you can hire companies that specialize in posting the signs for you. In the San Francisco Bay Area, where I live, a local company called the Thumb Tack Bugle provides this service. In 1981, it serviced eighty locations; now it services more than eight hundred locations in the Bay Area. Their chief rival is the Daily Staple, a company that was spawned by the obvious success of sign-posting. The point is—this is a growing medium, and guerrillas must be aware of it because of its efficiency and low cost.

In most instances, your sign must be replaced on a regular basis (monthly or weekly). But sometimes it can stay in place for years. In a few cases, you'll have to pay a tiny fee to post your sign, but often this method of marketing is free (if you do your own posting). The companies that post for you promise to place your sign on a guaranteed number of boards—a large number, I might add—and they'll also replace it on a regular basis. Unless you have the time to check your signs, look into these posting services. You can find them listed in your Yellow Pages under "signs" or "bulletin boards." If signs do work for you, consider hiring one of these companies to handle the work for you so you can concentrate on earning money.

A crucial point is to keep the lettering on your sign very CLEAR. Fancy lettering is out of the question. Typewriter type is fine. Other than the typeface in your handy computer, clear, handsome hand lettering is probably best. If you haven't the proper calligraphic skills, ask a pro or a friend with immense talent to letter your sign for you. Remember to keep your copy short and to the point. Incidentally, it's fine to make copies of your signs. One original plus a slew of copies and enough thumbtacks, and you have the marketing tools to become a success. Once again, technology is your ally, because a wide variety of simple software makes it easy to create signs.

No fancy lettering please

If Super Handyman posted bulletin-board signs throughout his area, they'd be very similar in wording to his circular. In fact, a sign for him might say:

Super Handyman's signs

IT'S SUPER HANDYMAN!
He builds super sun decks and patios,
installs skylights and hot tubs,
does masonry and electrical work,
and designs building plans.

Call Super Handyman at 555-5656 anytime, any day.
All work guaranteed. Contractor's License #54-45673.

Super Handyman probably wouldn't need a 3 x 5 sign. Instead, he could post his circular. Circulars double as small signs.

Amazingly, there are some businesses that need only promote via this wonderfully inexpensive method of marketing. Perhaps you can be one of them. Although guerrilla marketers should use as many marketing methods as they can, they should save marketing money when they can do so intelligently. If you promote your business with 3 x 5 cards, you truly save money. In fact, if you do the lettering, the writing, and the posting, it's free.

Creating your own signs

If you own and operate a computer, you're now wondering if you can use desktop publishing to help you produce and design signs. The answer is that you certainly can—and should—if you have the proper software, skills, and taste. If you do, you can use your desktop publishing prowess to produce newsletters, direct mail, brochures, and a host of other marketing tools. The technology is becoming easy to use. People are used to a higher quality of production in the marketing materials they are exposed to.

The creative genius within you

The opportunities for a business with desktop publishing capabilities are endless. There's a creative genius lurking within you! Desktop publishing can set it free. You don't have to draw things, merely select from things already drawn—a huge variety of dazzling graphics, just waiting for you to select, point, and click. Just be sure you devote your time to the areas where it can most help your business. If that includes desktop publishing, great. If you love it, but should be doing something else, delegate it to someone else. A hallmark of the guerrilla is in the intelligent apportionment of time.

Ornate graphics are generally not necessary when marketing with small signs, though borders, typography, and little illustrations enliven most signs. If you post on a regular basis, it's a good idea to change the wording—but not the basic message—of your sign periodically. It's also a good idea to use different-colored paper so that your sign stands out from the rest. But be careful that your paper color does not impair the clarity of your ink color. Green ink on green paper makes for a very green but very unreadable sign. If you use green paper, make it light green—and make your ink a very dark color. Don't forget: your major purpose is to motivate prospective customers, and if they can't read your message, they can't be motivated.

Pinpointing your best sign locations

I suggest that you visit a few places where signs are posted in your region and notice the clever ways people are using this unique marketing method. A guerrilla marketer seriously considers such a method when developing an overall marketing plan. A true guerrilla doesn't think it at all silly to combine radio advertising, newspaper advertising, and bulletin-board advertising in his or her marketing strategy. Would General Motors consider such a tactic? Is the Pope Buddhist?

Be sure to make your headlines large. Make plenty of signs. In fact, it's a good idea to make about ten at a time and staple them together. Tack the whole packet to a bulletin board and carefully letter the words "Take One" atop your signs. People can read your sign, and the serious prospects can take one home with them for future reference—and then pass it along to someone who is looking for a product or service exactly like yours.

If you place signs on ten different bulletin boards, do the same kind of research you would if you were testing any other type of marketing. Ask your customers, "Where did you learn of my business?" When they tell you that they saw your sign, ask, "Where did you see it?" This way, you'll be able to pinpoint your best sign-posting locations. The more you can home in on your most productive marketing methods—including such subtleties as wording, sign color, sign location, and lettering style—the more successful you'll be.

It won't hurt for you to call some of the people who have posted signs in your area and ask about their effectiveness. Ask how long they've been posting signs, where they post them, whether the one you saw was typical, which locations seem best, and what success stories they may have heard. People are surprisingly open with information like this, and many enjoy being singled out as experts.

Interior signs require far more creativity than exterior signs, and you are allowed to use far more words. In fact, you are encouraged to.

Point-of-purchase signs are considered by those who use them to be extremely effective because they create impulse sales. They also put forth extra selling energy and cross-merchandising opportunities. A person comes in to buy a pen, sees a sign that says briefcases are marked down, and buys a briefcase, too. That's cross-merchandising.

POP signs make it easier for customers to locate and select products. They serve as silent salespeople, as aids to the actual salespeople. They demonstrate product features. POP signs give customers product information, reinforce the ad campaign at the retail level, offer premiums and discounts, and actually generate sales all by themselves.

POP

Many manufacturers offer free point-of-purchase materials to their customers. If you purchase from a manufacturer, you should ask if POP materials are provided. If not, request some. Most manufacturers are happy to comply. They'll set you up with signs, brochures, display racks, window banners, display modules, counter cards, window cards, Plexiglas merchandisers, posters, display cases, stand-up signs, and more. Just ask.

The growth of in-store signs is causing the giant advertising agencies to change their attitudes toward this nonglamorous medium. They can't help but notice that during the 1990s, in-store **Couponing** media expenditures doubled, outgrowing more traditional vehicles such as television and print. The in-store sign industry is growing. And growing along with it is couponing, part of the in-store experience with Americans. Approximately 55 percent of all cereal is now bought with a coupon, compared with less than 20 percent back in 1987. But most ad agencies don't take in-store signs and couponing as seriously as they should. You, as a guerrilla, will not make the same mistake.

New video technologies are creating opportunities for in-store marketers. TV monitors are cropping up over product displays and store shelves, at checkout counters, and even on shopping carts. This very definitely is a happening medium, though it is not happening as rapidly as some experts predicted. As a guerrilla, you can get in on the new technologies while the big guys are waiting around to see how well they work. Many new marketing weapons are ideal for guerrillas because of their low cost, nontraditional nature, and ability to let guerrillas market like the big dudes (and dudettes) before the biggies even get started.

Where the money meets the merchandise In the 1980s, telephone marketing was an emerging marketing force, according to *Forbes* magazine. In the '90s, *Adweek* claimed that POP would be the emerging force. The money meets the merchandise in the supermarket aisles, they told us. Of course, it also meets and greets on the computer monitor. Still, the reason for POP advertising's popularity is its ability to connect mass media marketing with the consumer at the time of purchase. This makes it cost-effective. Some surveys indicate that in the near future, POP materials will make up 80 percent of many advertisers' budgets.

Plan the sale when you plan the ad As I mentioned earlier, the basic rule in creating any advertising is to plan the sale when you plan the ad. That means that you shouldn't think in terms of a person reading your ad or hearing your commercial. Instead, think of the person at the moment of purchase. Is your message designed to motivate the potential customer at that crucial moment? By nature, almost all POP marketing materials are. POP signs get to people when the getting is good. They are there. They are in a buying mood. They are thinking in terms of the type of merchandise or service you offer. POP advertising gives them many reasons to buy, or at least it should.

Many a smart guerrilla has run an ad, then blown it up into a five-foot-high poster, mounted it, and used it as a sign—inside the place of business, outside the place of business, and in the window. This is a way to market intelligently while saving lots of money, and it ensures that the interior signs will tie in with the ads.

What interior signs can do

Interior signs can be used to encourage customers to touch your offering, taste it, try it out, and compare it with the competition, and also to explain complex points by means of clear graphics. Remember that 76 percent of all buying decisions are made right in the place of business, but even half that number would be impressive. It should cause any guerrilla to take the use of signs very, very seriously.

The Institute points out that today decisions to buy are less casual than they once were, and that people need to be convinced right there, at the point of sale. If your business is in a location where your customers will come to browse or buy, the Institute says you should consider your aisles to be your "trenches"—where the true battle for customer dollars takes place. Since many battles are won or lost in the trenches, your point-of-purchase materials should be as potent as possible.

Promise instant rewards

While the other marketing methods and materials create in the customer a desire to buy, as well they should, point-of-purchase signs promise instant rewards. Americans love instant gratification. True guerrillas recognize that people patronize their businesses on purpose, not by accident. And they capitalize on the presence of prospects by using motivating, informative signs. Some have lengthy copy. Some have brief copy. Some go into detail about product features and benefits. Some contain lists of satisfied-customer testimonials. Some display ornate graphics, some point out advantages of related merchandise. Each is there to move as much merchandise or sell as many services as possible.

Walk the aisles

You might want to walk the aisles of successful businesses in your area to learn how they use point-of-purchase signs. To learn even more about point-of-purchase signs, drop a line, requesting free information, to POPAI, 60 East Forty-second Street, New York, NY 10165.

The other marketing primed the public for the sale. The sign generates the actual purchase decision. Whenever possible, signs should be employed to pull the trigger on the gun already cocked by aggressive guerrilla marketing.

15

The Yellow Pages:
Turn Them to Gold

If your business is off and running, you probably know quite a bit about the Yellow Pages. But if your business hasn't yet opened, it's a great idea to name it something that will appear as the first listing in its category in the Yellow Pages. For example, a new storage company called itself Abaco Storage. It advertised only in the Yellow Pages. Success came to the company that first year, and phone inquiries resulting from the first listing in the Yellow Pages were clearly responsible.

The first thing to decide is whether or not your business can benefit from Yellow Page marketing. Will people look in the Yellow Pages to find a product or service such as yours, as they do for storage companies? If you are a retailer, chances are that people will consult the Yellow Page phone directory and find out about you. But if you're an artist or a consultant, people will probably find out about you through other sources. Once you've decided you should be in the directory, determine which directory or directories. Will one be enough? Or, as is the case in large metropolitan areas, will you have to be in five or ten? The answer may be clearer after you've considered these findings by the Small Business Administration:

- The average independent store draws the majority of its customers from not more than a quarter of a mile away.
- The average chain store draws most of its customers from not more than three-quarters of a mile away.
- The average shopping center draws customers from as far away as four miles.

Some businesses draw customers from as far away as 100 miles—especially in wide-open areas such as North Dakota and

Iowa. Furniture stores attract business from an average distance of ten miles away. One of my enterprises, Guerrilla Marketing International, draws business from around the world. How about your enterprise? If you think you should run Yellow Page ads in a number of directories, decide whether the ads in other areas should be as large as or smaller than your primary area ad. Decide whether you should have an advertisement or a listing. Decide whether the listing should be in dark, bold type or in regular type. Choose the size, the colors you'll use, and whether you want to connect with the electronic portion of the Yellow Pages—a growing option.

My publishing business was listed in but one directory, in normal type. It wasn't the kind of business that attracts Yellow Pages searchers. But some of my clients have large Yellow Page ads in three directories, two with extra colors, small Yellow Page ads in five more directories, and bold-type listings in six other directories.

The cost for a large number of listings is assessed monthly, and it's steep. Find out the names of other companies in your business category and try to learn what percentage of their business each month comes from people who have located them through the Yellow Pages. I have some clients who obtain 6 percent of their business from people who first learned of them by consulting the Yellow Pages. Others obtain 50 percent of their business that way. And some received less than 1 percent of business from the Yellow Pages, yet wish to continue advertising there. I am not in agreement. The Yellow Pages should be an investment that pays off every time.

You must do the groundwork to see how, where, and whether you should make use of a strong Yellow Pages program. Now you know some questions to ask and answer. Here's another: in which categories in your Yellow Pages directory will you list yourself? For example, if you run a sleep shop in which you sell beds and bedroom furniture, should you list your shop under "furniture," "mattresses," or "beds"? Can you do with one listing, or do you need to pay for several? Answer: you'll probably have to list where people look. And they look in all three categories. One of life's necessary bummers.

A prime advantage of listing in the Yellow Pages is that you can appear as big as your biggest competitor, as large as the largest business of your type in town, and as well established as the oldest business of your type in town. Although directories differ from publisher to publisher (there are several), the largest space unit

Where do your customers come from?

One of life's bummers

A prime advantage

you can usually purchase is a full page. In some cities, the largest space unit you can purchase is a quarter of a page. Because these are also the largest ad spaces available to your competition, you can appear equal in size. Take advantage of this by running a more powerful ad than your competition. Often, the largest ads get placed first in the section, where customers will first see them.

Guerrillas have learned to control the page in their Yellow Pages directory—not by purchasing the largest ad, but by running two different dimension ads on the same page. This eliminates the possibility of anyone running a larger ad on that page.

Some bright entrepreneurs, who realize that a great deal of their business comes from people who consult the Yellow Pages, spend the majority of their marketing budgets on this medium. But here's a crucial truth: unless you dominate your section of the Yellow Pages—I mean run the only large ad and the only good ad—you should never, in your advertising on radio and/or television, direct people to your store or phone number by saying, "You'll find us in the Yellow Pages." By doing so, you are wasting your media dollars by leading people to your direct competitors. Believe me, many people innocently do this. They run a fine radio commercial and tell listeners to find them in the Yellow Pages. But nothing happens. Why? Because in the Yellow Pages, the listeners learn of several other places where they can buy the product or service being advertised.

Never direct them to the Yellow Pages

If you don't appear as the clear choice within your category of the Yellow Pages, don't recommend that people look there. Tell them, "You'll find us in the white pages of your phone directory." There, in the peace and quiet of the noncompetitive white pages, listeners and viewers can learn your phone number and your address, and they're not aimed in the direction of your competitors.

Now that that's understood, you'll need to view the Yellow Pages as a marketing vehicle, an advertising medium, an opportunity to sell. Many people think the Yellow Pages are merely a place to put their phone numbers in large type. Silly thinking! The

Readers are in a buying mood

Yellow Pages are an arena for attracting the business of active prospects, a place to confront prospects on a one-on-one basis. You are selling. Others are selling what you sell. The prospect is in a buying mood. Understand this opportunity and you'll be able to create Yellow Pages ads that translate into sales.

Many Yellow Pages directories are now offering the option to use color. If you're springing for a large ad, or even a small ad, go for it. Clients from around the country tell me it's worth the investment. Many directories also give you the option to participate in coupon promotions by placing coupons for discounts on your offering in the back of the directory. I recommend that you call some of the coupon placers and ask them outright if it's working—because you're considering it and you're not a competitor. Maybe it's a hidden gold mine. Maybe it's a disaster area. A guerrilla would check into it.

The electronic Yellow Pages

A guerrilla would also inquire about the electronic Yellow Pages. The way this works is that each ad contains a toll-free number that prospects can call for further information. You can update the information on a monthly basis. Contact your local Yellow Pages rep to see if the service is available to you and what kinds of results others are getting. Call the toll-free number of some of the advertisers and see if it's a forum for your message. Then call some of the advertisers. I realize that what I'm asking is not all that easy, but it's a lot easier than losing money by latching on to a misguided missile or missing out on a rich opportunity.

If you decide to run one large ad in the Yellow Pages directory for your locality, you may want to run smaller ads in outlying directories. You may need a large ad and a small ad, and maybe more. At any rate, it's too expensive to run Yellow Pages ads that are poorly written. And most of them are. By putting thought into the content of your ad, you can greatly increase your Yellow Pages response rate.

A 600 percent increase

I'm familiar with a local business that was attracting 2 percent of its sales with Yellow Pages ads. Two percent isn't all that good, but it does represent a fair sum of money at the end of the month, so the business couldn't eliminate that particular marketing tool. Instead, it changed its ad copy. That's all. The result was a 600 percent increase in business from Yellow Pages ads. The store then drew 12 percent of its sales from people who first learned of it through those pages of yellow.

What accounted for this dramatic increase? The owner of this store (the store carries a goodly selection of beds—by no means the largest in the area but big enough to enable her to promote her products seriously) understood the mindset of Yellow Pages readers. She realized that those people who consult the Yellow Pages are actively looking to find specific information. And she understood that one can usually motivate people more effectively by getting them to agree with what you are saying—to the point where they say yes to questions you are asking.

Ask the right questions

This store owner asked a question to which the person looking in the bed section of the Yellow Pages directory would always answer yes. The question was, "Looking for a bed?" Naturally, the answer was yes, and the reader read on. Whatever buttons the reader had regarding beds were intentionally pressed by the ad.

Get them to say yes

The advertiser didn't feel self-conscious about putting forth a lot of information. She also recognized the nature of the medium and actively sought the business of her prospective customers.

See the two-column-by-five-inch ad on page 158 as it appeared in the San Francisco Yellow Pages. Other advertisers in the same directory used the same space to list their names, phone numbers, and little else. If your offering is suitable for Yellow Pages advertising, you have a splendid opportunity.

The dos and don'ts

If you use the Yellow Pages, here are some tips:

- Do list a whole lot of facts about yourself.
- Do make your ad look and "feel" classier.
- Do treat it like a personal communication, not a cold listing.
- Do let folks know if you accept credit cards or can finance.
- Do gain the reader's attention with a strong headline.
- Do let people know all the reasons they should buy from you.
- Don't let the Yellow Pages people write your ad.
- Don't run small ads if your competitors run big ads.
- Don't allow your ad to look or sound boring.
- Don't forget to use handsome graphics to communicate.
- Don't list your business in too many directories.
- Don't treat your ad less lightly than a full-page magazine ad.
- Don't hold back on the data; people are looking in the Yellow Pages for information. Give them lots of information.
- Don't fail to include your Web site in your Yellow Pages ad; people can learn a lot more about you on-line than in any directory.

Never fall into the trap of thinking your Yellow Pages ad must dazzle the populace with beauty. Credibility, yes, but not necessarily beauty. If people want beauty, they go to national parks or art museums, certainly not to the Yellow Pages. They go there to learn, to get information, to assist them in making a purchase. The more information you provide, the more purchases browsers will make from your business.

A trap to avoid

More and more Yellow Pages advertisers are including a photograph of themselves. If you honestly look warm and friendly and can convey this with a professional photograph, and if a galaxy of competitors aren't using their photos, you might give it a shot—especially in a business where there is a lot of one-on-one contact. Generally, photos are better than artwork. Artwork is better than no artwork. In the Yellow Pages, *information* is best of all.

If there are several pages of Yellow Pages listings for your competitors, which is often the case, take heed of the chiropractic guerrilla who was in the same situation. There were five pages of ads where he wanted to run his. So he ran a smallish ad, clear yellow type reversed against a black background. The copy stated:

"FREE TELEPHONE CONSULTATION
ON HOW TO SELECT A CHIROPRACTOR"

Getting the lion's share

Then he provided his telephone number. Guess who got the lion's share of the calls and the tyrannosaurus rex's share of the business?

Consider your situation in the light of your competition. If all the gardeners are running yellow and black ads and you can run a green, red, and white ad, go for the colors—and the chance to stand out.

Lucky for you, the Yellow Pages are a misunderstood advertising medium. Specialized Yellow Pages advertising companies can help businesspeople take advantage of the opportunities offered. The Yellow Pages deserve your careful attention. However, there is absolutely no reason why you must advertise there. If in doubt, read the Yellow Pages where you live and see what your competitors think about the whole idea.

III
Maxi-Media Marketing

Maxi-media marketing refers to the mass-market media, such as newspapers, magazines, radio, TV, billboards, and direct mail. Mistakes cost dearly in this area. The competition may be able to outspend you dramatically. For instance, the average cost to produce a television commercial in 1997 was in the neighborhood of $210,000. Some neighborhood. And that's for a thirty-second live-action commercial. Add to that the cost of running the commercial, and running it often enough. But don't be put off by the high number. It's high because of the fast-food chains, beer, athletic shoe, automobile, and soft-drink companies that spend lavishly to create a desire for what they produce. But don't think of maxi-media marketing as expensive. That is not the case. Expensive marketing is marketing that does not work. If you run one radio commercial on one local radio station and it costs you only $10, but nobody hears it or acts on it, you have engaged in expensive marketing. But if you shell out $10,000 to run one week's worth of advertising on a large metropolitan area radio station and you realize a profit of $20,000 in that week, you've engaged in inexpensive marketing. Cost has nothing to do with it. Effectiveness does.

Expensive marketing

When a guerrilla marketer uses the mass media, he or she does what is necessary to make them effective, therefore inexpensive. A guerrilla is not intimidated by the mass media. Guerrillas must use the mass media with precision, carefully measure the results, and make the media part of an overall marketing plan. When guerrillas use the media, they must rely on intuition and business acumen. Maxi-media marketing is about two things: selling, and creating a powerful desire to buy. Also, maxi-media marketing enhances the success of mini-media marketing—response rates to simple circulars jump when radio advertising blazes the way for them, and telemarketing results improve when TV spots

A guerrilla is not intimidated

presell the market. Guerrillas wage and win marketing battles by using mini and maxi weapons. Maxi weapons make the other marketing weapons work more effectively, and maxi weapons are coming down in price.

A marvelous revolution

Since I first wrote this book, a marvelous revolution has taken place: maxi-marketing is now more affordable and more sensible for very small companies than ever before. Responding to the growing number of small businesses—which comprise 98 percent of all businesses—the advertising media have bent over backward to attract business, offering far lower prices than ever before. Magazines and newspapers are available on regional and zone editions, and radio stations offer extremely attractive package rates. Postcard decks make direct mail extremely affordable and attractive to right-thinking guerrillas. The maxi-media are within your reach and right up your alley because they allow you to advertise the way the big guys do *without* spending big.

Today, guerrillas compete in all arenas. Guerrillas take on the big players when it comes to attracting the attention—and the disposable income—of the American public.

Change favors guerrillas

Change favors guerrillas because guerrillas employ many weapons of marketing rather than a few: customers are now in many places rather than only a few. In 1982, a TV spot on the top-rated "Cosby" show would reach one in four households. In 1997, a TV spot on the top-rated show *Seinfeld* reached only one in *seven*. In 1975, the three major networks attracted 82 percent of the twenty-four-hour viewing audience. In 1995, it dropped to only 35 percent and is expected to be at 25 percent by 2005. And TV isn't the only maxi medium facing a shakeup. The hottest magazines of today are titles you hadn't heard of yesterday. And they'll be different still tomorrow. Guerrillas know that the media never stand still and that prospects are moving targets.

Embracing the technologies

Desktop publishing, laser printing, satellite TV, Web sites, the Internet, cellular telephones, fax machines, voice-mail, and electronic mail are now the arsenals of guerrilla *marketers*. Be aware of these technologies. Embrace them before the big corporations do. You're a guerrilla, lithe and agile. Large businesses may be bright and wealthy, but their marketers must maneuver through the molasses of bureaucracies, and meetings, committees, reams of memos, and layers of decision-making make them clumsy.

Be known for your quality, innovation, flexibility, and respon-

siveness to customer needs. Be known for epic service. The definition of service is *whatever the customer wants it to be*. If you have
trouble with this definition, you will lose customers to businesses
that do comprehend and live by it. Enter with confidence the
world of the maxi-media. There has never been a better time to be
a guerrilla. So get 'em while the getting's good.

**The definition
of service**

16

Newspapers: How to Use Them with Genius

Whether you use the mini-media, the maxi-media, both, or neither, you should be aware of the constant shifts in the U.S. marketplace. Due to the baby boom from 1946 to 1964, the median age in the United States is steadily rising, and people are living longer. In fact, *Newsweek* accurately predicted that in the 1990s geriatric social workers would be in high demand. In 1900, only 4 percent of Americans were older than eighty-five. Today, 11 percent of Americans are older than eighty-five—about 3.6 million people. According to the U.S. census, this is the fastest-growing age group in the American population.

We're older than we were

The population shift to the Sunbelt—Texas, Florida, Arizona, and California—will continue. Immigrants will account for 25 to 33 percent of our population, with Hispanics superseding blacks as the largest minority group. Ten percent of the population will be Hispanic. Minority groups will continue to move from cities to the suburbs. The Asian-American population will rapidly increase.

Which newspapers are for you?

Marketers must be aware of these trends as they begin to consider newspaper advertising and its place in their media mix. In most areas, a large number of newspapers are available. They all reach specific audiences. Which newspapers, which audiences, are best for you? There are metropolitan newspapers, national newspapers, local newspapers, shopper-oriented newspapers, classified-ad newspapers, campus newspapers, business newspapers, ethnic newspapers, and daily, weekly, and monthly newspapers. Your work is cut out for you: make your selection skillfully.

By far the major marketing method used by small business is newspaper advertising. Of course your type of business may not benefit from business advertising. But if you think it may, pay close attention.

Newspapers offer a high degree of flexibility in that you can decide to run an ad or make changes in it up to a couple of days before the ad is to run. Radio gives you even more flexibility in that regard, allowing you to make changes up to the day your spot is to run. A Web site provides a great deal of flexibility; and magazines and television marketing allow you the least leeway.

If you don't have a clear-cut favorite newspaper (defined as best targeted for your market and most appropriate for your ads) there is a test. Remember that there are most likely far more newspapers in your region than you ever imagined. Run an ad in as many of the newspapers in your area as you can—there may be as many as thirty. Use coupons in your ads. Have each coupon make a different offer, such as $5 off or a free book or a 15 percent discount or a free plant. In the ad, request that the customer bring the coupon when coming to your place of business, or mention the coupon when calling you.

A newspaper test

By measuring the responses, you'll soon see which newspapers work, which don't work, and which work best of all. You don't have to run ads in all thirty newspapers to learn which is the best paper. Maybe you'll only have to test in three or five or ten papers. But you are nuts unless you test. And be sure to determine what generated the customer's response—the offer or the newspaper. You can do this by means of a second test. Make a different offer in the most effective paper. If it still pulls well, you've got a horse to ride.

Don't forget, we're talking about advertising in terms of a conservative investment. So don't waste your money advertising in a paper that you happen to read or that your friends happen to recommend or that has a supersalesperson selling ad space. The paper you eventually select will be the one in which you advertise consistently. That paper is the one to which you will commit your marketing program, your regularly placed ad, your money, your hopes. Select with the highest care possible. The paper must have proven itself in your coupon test, and it should be the one read by prospective customers in your marketing area. A monthly paper is not preferable. Use it if you wish, but be sure that your major newspaper is at least a weekly, if not a daily, paper.

Make the paper prove itself

Marketing is part science and part art—and the art part is very subjective. The artistic end of marketing is not limited to words and pictures: it involves timing and media selection and ad size.

The importance of your ad's appearance is not to be underestimated. Far more people will see your ad than will see you or your place of business, so their opinion of your business will be shaped by your ad. Don't let the newspaper people design your ad and don't let them write the copy. If they do, it will look and sound like all of the other ads in the paper. Your competition is not only the others in your business, but everybody who advertises.

Your real competitors

You're vying for the reader's attention with banks, airlines, car companies, cigarette companies, soft-drink companies, and who knows what else. You must give your ad a distinct style. Hire a professional art director to establish the look for your ad. Later you can ask the paper to follow the design guidelines created by that art director. At first, however, you or a talented friend or a gifted art director should make your advertising identity follow your marketing plan—and do so in a unique manner. You won't win customers by boring them into buying. You've got to create a desire, and a good-looking ad helps immeasurably, even measurably if you do your tracking.

Create a desire

I must caution you that perhaps one in twenty-five newspapers has a first-class art department that can design ads with the best of the expensive graphics companies. Put another way, twenty-four out of twenty-five newspapers have art departments that can help you waste your marketing money by designing ordinary-looking ads. The same goes for copy. Newspapers will help write your copy—because they want you to advertise. Give your marketing money to charity instead. Or spend it on a great ad writer who can make your ad sing, motivate, and cause people to sit up and say, "I want that." If you have a winning ad, your marketing money can be safely invested in newspapers with the expectation of a high return.

Only one in twenty-five

Select the type used in your ad for readability and clarity. Don't use a type size that is smaller than the type used by the paper. (In fact, even type that size is too small.) Make it *easy* for the reader to read your ad. If you decide to reverse the type (a black background with the type appearing in white) be sure that the black ink doesn't spill over into the white letters, obliterating them. It happens every day. Don't let it happen to you. Newspapers are notorious for running ads that look faint and unreadable (as a result of their particular printing process). You or your art director should discuss your ad with people in the newspaper's production department to confirm that the ad will print well.

Make it easy for the reader

Then there's the matter of size. Of course, a full-page ad is probably best if you want to make an impact. But you won't want to pay for a weekly full-page ad, so you must make do with something smaller. What size can you comfortably afford?

Newspapers charge you by the line or by the inch. There are fourteen lines to the inch. If the newspaper charges, say, $1 per line, you are paying $14 per inch. If you want your ad to be fifteen inches high and three columns wide, you multiply $14 by fifteen, coming out with $210, then multiply that by three, for a total ad cost of $630. If you run an ad that size weekly, it will cost $2,709 per month. (I multiplied the $630 by 4.3 because that's the approximate number of weeks per month.) If the figure is too high, run a smaller ad—one you can afford. Some people can run a weekly ten-inch ad (two columns by five inches) all year every year and enjoy a 25 percent sales increase each year. Others want a greater increase, so they design a larger ad and run it two times a week. A lot depends on the cost of advertising in the particular paper.

Most full-size newspapers are twenty-two inches high. If you can afford it, run an ad that is twelve inches high or higher. That way, you'll be sure your ad is above the fold. Most full-size newspapers are six columns wide. So you can be certain of dominating the page with a four-column-by-twelve-inch ad.

That's a great tack, and if you use it you won't be wasting your money. But you can save a bit of money if you run a smaller ad with a powerful and unique border. An ad does not have to dominate a page to be seen. It merely has to interest the reader, create a desire, and then motivate the reader to do something you want him or her to do.

If you run your ad in a tabloid-size newspaper rather than a full-size newspaper, you can save money by running a smaller ad. A ten-inch ad may appear to be buried in a large newspaper, but it stands out in a tabloid. Many Sunday newspapers have tabloid-size sections, and you can save money by using them. But don't use them for that reason only—be sure that your prospects read that paper and that section.

There are guidelines that will help you decide whether to run large or small ads. Consider the advantages and disadvantages of small ads. Small ads don't:

- Impress as much as large ones
- Allow you to include long lists of names or lots of information

- Enable you to use color
- Provide enough space for photos or drawings
- Generate high-volume sales
- Allow you to have the position you want in the newspaper

What small ads do

But small ads do:

- Allow you to run several for the cost of one large ad
- Let you feature samples of your selection in each
- Let you run them in several publications for valid test results
- Allow you to offer free brochures, samples, or catalogs
- Enable you to compile a database from the leads you get from inquiries
- Serve as logical places to advertise single items or announce new ones
- Let you run in the middle of the classified section, where the serious shoppers look

What are the best days to run your ads? It differs with different towns and different businesses. Ask your local newspaper's space salesperson for a recommendation. Generally, Sunday is the day that the most people read the paper and spend the most time with it. But can your business succeed by running ads on days your doors are closed? Some businesses can. If yours can, give a nod to Sunday.

Guerrillas favor Sundays because there are more employment opportunity ads, which results in a higher readership of the newspaper—especially the classified section. People who are often on the road are usually home on Sundays and have more time to spend with their newspaper.

Monday is a pretty good day if your offering is directed to males because many males read the Monday papers carefully to learn about the sports events of the preceding weekend. Saturday is also a fairly good day because many advertisers shy away from it and you'll have less competition. Some papers make Wednesday or Thursday their food day, so the papers are loaded with food and grocery ads.

You'll have to observe the papers yourself, then ask the person who will be selling the ad space to you. That ad space comes a lot cheaper if you sign a contract for a given number of lines or inches per year. Ask about the discounts you can receive for volume usage. They are quite substantial—a fringe benefit of consistent advertising in the same paper.

It's usually best if your ad appears as far to the front as possible, on a right-hand page, above the fold of the paper. But few, if any, papers will guarantee placement unless you sign a giant contract. The main news section is also considered to be an optimum place for an ad because of high readership by a large cross-section of readers.

The best placement of your ads

Because of the nature of your product, you may want to run your ad in the business section, the sports section, or the entertainment section. Run your ad where competitors run theirs. If you have no competition, run your ad where services or merchandise similar to yours are being offered. Why? Because that's where readers are conditioned to look for offerings such as yours.

Incidentally, readers most likely will read your ad. Study after study reveals that newspaper readers read the ads almost as intensively as they read the stories. And due to the power of graphics, some ads attract more attention than the actual news stories. Use graphics in your ad (but go easy!). Generally, more than three or four pictures—whether art or photography—is too many. But that's a rule that is both useful to know and useful to break; I've broken it on purpose and with good cause more than once. I've also run very successful ads that have only one illustration or photo. Lack of an illustration or photo means the ad will be 27 percent less effective.

Readers read newspaper ads

Another rule to know in case you want to break it intentionally is that one of the great powers of print advertising is that it easily enables you to repeat your message three times—in the illustration or photo, in the headline, and in the copy. Illustrations that relate directly to the message work 32 percent better, unless they're a cliché.

Long copy works as well as short copy, and better in many cases when serious prospects are looking over your ad. Vague headlines reduce the effectiveness of an ad by 11 percent, while humor can add 10 percent. Celebrities add another 25 percent to the power of the ad, though it's not guaranteed. Recipes can add 20 percent and coupons 26 percent. If you also use TV, including just one frame from your commercial will boost the power of your newspaper ad by 42 percent. See? There is a lot of crossover value from one medium to the next.

Long copy or short copy

When selecting your newspaper, you certainly need to know

its circulation. And you also need to know if the paper's circulation is in your marketing area—otherwise you'll be paying for wasted circulation. When you hear a circulation figure, you can multiply it by three and learn how many people are actually reading the paper. When a family has a subscription to the paper and two adults and three kids read each issue, this is counted as only one subscriber. When a woman buys a copy of the paper to read on the bus on her way home and her husband reads it when she arrives home, that is counted as only one reader, according to circulation statistics. Newspaper circulation figures are one of the few marketing statistics that are understated.

Reprint your ad   If you have a truly good ad—one that states all the features and benefits of your offering—consider making multiple reprints. Use the reprints as circulars, customer handouts, mailing pieces, or interior signs. Their true cost was incurred when you originally produced the ad. Remember, you can enlarge the ad and make it a poster.

Many people newspaper-shop before they buy: that is, they scan the papers before purchasing a product. Keep this in mind when running your ads. If your product is aimed at a particular group of people, such as businesspeople, run your ad in a business paper rather than a metropolitan paper. If your offering is geared to discount hunters, run your ad in shopper-oriented papers. If it will appeal to college kids, advertise it in the campus paper.

A finished newspaper marketing plan usually calls for ads in a number of papers—some primary, others secondary. The combination you choose may be the key to your fortune. You want to obtain exceptional results from both primary and secondary newspapers. Exceptional results mean many sales. And many sales come from many inquiries, be they in the form of phone calls, visits to your place of business, or even letters.

To increase the number of inquiries you receive through newspaper advertising, *always* remember to consistently state your name and primary message throughout your ads. In addition, put these ideas into action:

- Mention your offer in your headline.
- Emphasize the word *free* and repeat it when possible.
- Restate your offer in a subhead.
- Run a picture of your product or service in action.
- Include testimonials when applicable.
- Do something to differentiate yourself from others who adver-

tise in the newspaper. That means all others—not just your direct competitors.

- Say something to add urgency to your offer. It can be a limited-time offer. It can be a limited-quantities offer. Get those sales *now*.

Ideas for successful newspaper ads

- Put a border around your ad if it's a small ad. Make the border unique.
- Be sure your ad contains a word or phrase set in huge type. Even a small ad can "act" big if you do so.
- Always include your address, specific location, phone number, and Web-site address. Make it easy for readers to find you or talk with you.
- Create a visual look that you can maintain every time you advertise. This clarifies your identity and increases consumer familiarity.
- Experiment with different ad sizes, shapes, days on which you run the ad, and newspaper sections.
- Consider freestanding inserts in your newspaper. These are increasingly popular and may be less expensive than you imagine.
- Try adding a color to your ad. Red, blue, and brown work well. You can't do this with tiny ads, but it may be worth trying with a large ad.

Add a color

- Test several types of ads and offers in different publications until you have the optimum ad, offer, and ad size. Then run the ad with confidence. It's very unusual to get everything right the first time.
- Be careful with new newspapers. Wait until they prove themselves. But once they do prove themselves, think of yourself as married to the newspaper—you're in it for the long haul.
- Do everything in your power to get your ad placed in the front section of the paper on a right-hand page above the fold. Merely asking isn't enough. You may have to pay personal visits. Be a squeaky wheel.
- Don't be afraid of using lengthy copy. Although lengthy copy is best suited for magazines, many successful newspaper advertisers employ it.
- Run your ad in the financial pages if you have a business offer, in the sports pages if you have a male-oriented offer, in the food pages for food products. The astrology page usually gets the best readership. In general, the main news section is the best location for ads.

- Study the ads run by your competitors. Study their offers. Make yours more cogent, more concise, sweeter, different, better.

Keep track
- Keep detailed records of the results of your ads. If you don't keep track of your experiments, you won't learn anything.
- Be sure your ad is in character with your intended market.
- Be sure your ad is in character with your product or service.
- Be sure your ad is in character with the newspaper in which you advertise.
- Use short words, short sentences, and short paragraphs.
- If you distribute a coupon, make sure that your address appears on the coupon and also next to the coupon so that if the coupon gets clipped, your name and address still appear.
- Use photos or illustrations that reproduce faithfully in newspapers.
- Always put the name of your company somewhere at the bottom of your ad. Don't expect people to get the name from the copy, the headline, the picture of the product, or the picture of the storefront. And it's a good idea to put your name in your headline. At least put it in the subhead.
- Include your Web-site address at the top of your ad. Place it prominently. Invite people to visit you there.
- Say something timely in your ad. Remember, people read papers for news. So your message should tie in with the news when it can.
- Ask all of your customers where they heard about you. If they don't mention the newspaper, ask them directly, "Did you see our newspaper ad?" Customer feedback is invaluable.
- Aim your ad to people who are in the market for your offering *right now.*
- If you don't plan to use newspapers to support your other marketing efforts, use them weekly or stay away from them altogether. Occasional use doesn't cut it.

These tips, your common sense, the quality of newspapers in your community, the newspaper production department, the newspaper representative calling on your business, and the presence or absence of your competitors in the newspaper should be prime considerations in your decision to advertise in newspapers as part of your guerrilla marketing mix. To many guerrillas around the world, a newspaper looks like a meal ticket!

17
Magazine Advertising

Whoever heard of a small-time entrepreneur advertising in well-known and respected national magazines? You have now. Magazine advertising has been the linchpin for many a successful small business. Remember, the single most important reason people patronize one business over another is confidence. And magazine advertisements breed confidence by instilling familiarity and giving credibility. A *properly produced magazine ad, preferably of the full-page variety, gives a small business more credibility than any other mass-marketing medium.*

You will not necessarily gain consumer confidence from a single exposure to your magazine ad. But if you run the ad once, you can use the reprints of that ad forever. One highly successful company ran a single regional ad in a single issue of *Time* magazine, then used reprints of the ad (reprints are available at a fraction of a cent each) in its window and on its counter for more than twenty-five years afterward. Reprints were also sent in direct mailings. His mailings in 1998 could even run a reprint that stated, "As seen in *Time* magazine"—heavy-duty name-dropping from an ad run once in 1973. That's getting mileage out of magazine advertising!

Reprints are forever

The magazine ad that you run in 1999 can bring home the bacon for you in 2024. The investment isn't very high. Several bright entrepreneurs have run an ad one time in a regional edition of a national magazine, then mailed out reprints in all direct mailings—each time gaining the confidence that prospects ordinarily placed in the magazine itself. This is the *point* of magazine advertising for small business. It gives them a great deal of credibility. And credibility creates confidence, which translates to sales. And profits. If people feel that *Time* magazine is reliable, credible, trustworthy, and solid, they'll feel the same way about the companies that advertise in *Time*. So if you wish to gain instant credibility, advertise in magazines that will give it to you.

Gaining credibility

I'm talking about running your ad in your regional edition *only*, and just one time. Not all magazines have regional editions. But those that do have regional editions can save you a fortune.

The number of publications offering these affordable methods of reaching target audiences is growing fast. It takes a media-buying service to keep up with the maxi-media's efforts to woo budgets from small businesses. That's one reason guerrillas use them.

Regional means affordable

Most people don't realize regional editions exist. When they see your full-page (or smaller if you engage in fusion marketing and split the cost of the page with one, two, or three others) ad in *Time* magazine, they'll be quite impressed that you are advertising in a respected national magazine. And they'll turn that state of being impressed into a state of confidence in your offering. Check your library for the latest issue of *Consumer Magazine and Agri-Media Rates and Data* (published monthly by Standard Rate and Data Service, Inc.—known as SRDS), and you'll learn which magazines have regional editions and how much they charge for advertising in them.

If you run a small display ad for a mail-order venture in a national publication, you should do as much testing as possible. An inexpensive method of testing is to avail yourself of the split runs offered by many magazines. By taking advantage of them, you can test two headlines. Send your two ads to the publication, being certain to code each ad for response so that you'll be able to tell which of the two headlines pulls better, and ask the publication to split-run the ads. One headline will run in half the magazines printed; the other headline will run in the other half.

Split-run testing

For example, a manufacturer of exercise equipment once ran a split-run ad with a coupon. One headline said, STRENGTHEN YOUR WRISTS FOR BETTER GOLF! The other said, STRENGTHEN YOUR WRISTS IN ONLY TWO MINUTES A DAY! The coupon in the first ad was addressed to Lion's Head, 7230 Paxton, Dept. G6A, Chicago, IL 60649. The coupon in the second ad was addressed to Lion's Head, 7230 Paxton, Dept. GOB, Chicago, IL 60649. Although the coupons looked alike, it was easy for the advertiser to tell that the appeal of two minutes a day was stronger than the appeal of better golf, even though the advertiser had guessed that the golf headline would attract the better response. How could the advertiser tell that his guess was wrong? Because the responses to Dept. GOB ran four times higher than those to Dept. G6A. Incidentally, the advertiser could also tell by referring to those responses that they came from *Golf* magazine (G) and that they were in answer to an ad run in June (6). The code indicated three points: the publication, the month in which it is run, and which of the two ads drew the best response.

Codes can also tell you the year, the ad size, and other information. Some publications allow you to do a triple-split run and not just a double, enabling you to test three headlines rather than two. If you can test three headlines, do it. Let your audience make your judgments for you when possible. After you count the coded responses, you'll know which headline is best. And the cost of the test itself will have been minimal. The magazine's split-run capability will have saved money for you while giving you valuable information. Now you can run the successful ad with boldness and confidence.

Coding tells you even more

Don't count yourself out of advertising in national publications because of the cost. You can cut down on that cost by establishing an in-house advertising agency, by purchasing remnant space or space in regional editions, and by purchasing a tiny space unit—say, one column by two inches. Or you can advertise in the classified section that is available in many national magazines. Also, many magazines offer enticing discounts to mail-order advertisers. And virtually all magazines offer impressive merchandising materials: easel-back cards, reprints, decals with the name of the magazine (for example, "as seen in *Time*"), and mailing folders. The magazine's advertising sales representative will be happy to tell you about all of the merchandising aids offered. Take advantage of them. They'll be useful at your place of business, in your window (if you have one), and in your other modes of advertising.

How to afford magazine advertising

Your business will be helped if you simply mention, "You've probably seen our ad in *Woman's Day* magazine." Materials can be used as enclosures in direct mailings, as enclosures with personal letters, as signs on bulletin boards, as counter cards, as display pieces at trade shows, exhibits, or fairs, and in a brochure or circular. The cost of these powerful guerrilla marketing aids is ridiculously low, sometimes even free. Use them to the fullest extent. Magazines can help you market your offering immediately and in the years ahead. It's the years ahead that will result in profitable business for you.

When the waterbed industry was in its infancy, growth was dramatically spurred when Chemelex, a manufacturer of waterbed heaters, ran full-page ads in *Time, Newsweek,* and *Sports Illustrated.* Chemelex then distributed reprints of the ads to retailers throughout the country. The retailers prominently displayed the ads throughout their showrooms, and the industry grew to the point where it turned from a hippie-image industry into a steady $2 billion per year furniture-image industry. One reason: the instant credibility gained by advertising in highly credible publications.

The advantages of magazine ads

Magazine advertising offers other attractive advantages. You can better target your market with magazines than with newspapers. Also, you can reach a specific circulation rather than a general circulation. You can reach people who have demonstrated an interest in skiing, gardening, do-it-yourselfing, snowmobiling—you name it. Little waste circulation. Everyone who sees your ad is a prospect. And one of the basic tenets of guerrilla marketing is to talk primarily to prospects and not to browsers.

Trade magazines

A good guerrilla marketer also considers advertising in magazines other than consumer magazines. There is a whole world of trade magazines out there. Almost every trade and profession has its own publication or, more likely, group of publications. Because you want to focus on prospects, consider advertising in some of these trade publications, because they are subscribed to and read cover-to-cover by many prospective customers. This is especially true if your product is at all business-oriented.

A plethora of publications

Research your options on-line or at the library. Visit MediaFinder at http://www.mediafinder.com/ and you'll gain access to on-line versions of directories containing more than 80,000 U.S. and Canadian magazines, newsletters, journals, newspapers, and directories. Locate *Business Publication Rates and Data,* another valuable directory published by SRDS. Try to find publications in which you might advertise your products or services. You'll find many, many magazines you've never heard of, and quite a few may be read by prospective buyers of what you sell. I've always been amazed at the amount of information in SRDS—as it's called in the ad biz. If you find magazines (newspapers are also listed) that interest you, send for sample copies. I predict that you'll be pleasantly surprised at the great number of marketing opportunities available in trade publications. You may find entrepreneurs with whom you can team up for greater sales. You may realize that you ought to be advertising in some of these publications. And you'll learn a lot of inside information about your type of business. Most likely, you'll want to subscribe to at least one trade magazine to keep abreast of new developments in your field.

Standard Rate and Data publishes a host of directories that may be of use in your business. If I ran a business school, I'd make it mandatory to spend a day looking through SRDS publications. Success-bound students would petition for more days. If you want to subscribe, write to Standard Rate and Data Service, 5201 Old Orchard Road, Skokie, Illinois 60077, or call them at 708-256-6067. Naturally, they're on-line at http://www.srds.com.

Another important advantage of advertising in magazines is you can use color much more effectively than you can in newspapers. If your offering is oriented to color—if you're marketing fabrics, for instance, consider advertising in magazines to show off the hues and tones.

Be a showoff

Magazines are better-suited to lengthy copy than any other medium: people buy magazines with the idea of spending time with them, unlike newspapers, which are read quickly for news. Magazines involve their readers, and your ads may do the same. Studies reveal that nonprospects screen themselves out voluntarily and that hot prospects read every single word. Use subheads. Figure on using three of them for an ad where 33 to 50 percent of the total space is devoted to text. If it's less than that, one or two subheads will do the trick. Write your subheads in upper- and lowercase letters and boldface type. Keep them short—people read them *before* they read your copy.

How to use subheads

It is primarily because of guerrilla marketers that magazines now publish so many regional editions. Now that you know this, look through your local issue of *Time, TV Guide,* or *Better Homes and Gardens.* How many regional advertisers are using those media? How many use color to show off their product? How many run long-copy ads? Which ones share the cost of a full-page even though they run different half-page ads? Most important, remember that in all likelihood these advertisers could never afford a national ad in the same magazine. But the growth of the entrepreneurial spirit in America has necessitated an increase in regional editions. Advertisers in these regional editions know that by advertising in a major magazine, they are putting themselves in the big leagues. Their ad might run on the page next to an ad for General Motors or Rolls-Royce or IBM. Not bad company for a guerrilla, no? Guerrilla marketing lets you play in the big leagues without first struggling in the minor leagues.

You and Rolls-Royce

Many major magazines have been available to minor advertisers for longer than thirty years. Guerrillas avail themselves of major magazine opportunities and of their merchandising aids as a key to successful marketing. This gives you credibility within your community; and it gives you respect in the minds of your sales staff, your suppliers, and even your competitors.

If you're a thinking entrepreneur, you'll use magazines in several ways. You'll advertise regularly in a magazine that hits your target audience right on the nose. You'll advertise only one time in a prestige magazine so as to use its merchandising aids. You'll use the classified sections of national magazines if you are in the mail-order business. And you'll use the display sections of national magazines if what you sell is too big for the classified sections or if your chosen magazine doesn't run classified ads.

It may be that you want to advertise in a national magazine because of the status, the huge circulation, and the easily identifiable audience, but don't have the money for a large ad. In that case, use a two-step process. You might also consider *marketing with your own magazine.* In a fusion marketing effort with three or four other companies with the same types of prospects, you can produce your own beautiful, glossy magazine, replete with elegant photos, stylish writing, and fancy paper stock.

Be respected

To make this magazine work for you and your marketing collaborators—who each have several full-page ads in the magazine and are the only advertisers—you must mail it to a carefully selected audience, consisting mostly of your customers and those of your fusion partners. Your identity will be impressively conveyed through the editorial material, the style, and the ads. The readers will develop a tighter bond with you, much tighter than if you had invested this money in mere advertising. The cost of this endeavor is high—nearly a dollar per reader. This figure is based upon 100,000 copies of the magazine, about $25,000 each for you and your three other fusion partners. The same reader that costs you one dollar by this advertising method costs you only half a cent for a full-color, full-page ad in a standard magazine. But that's like comparing apples with emeralds.

You have total control

With your own magazine, you have total control of the editorial environment, can run as many ads as you want, and can eliminate ads by competitors. Phooey on them. This idea is already being used by MCI, Federal Express, Philip Morris, Benetton, and others. Is it cheap? No way. Is it guerrilla-like? If you do it with fusion partners, yes. Guerrillas market with big ideas.

If you're practicing guerrilla marketing to the hilt, you will mention your national magazine advertisements in the other media you use: on the radio, in your direct-mail advertisements, on your signs, in your Yellow Pages ads, in your personal letters, in your telemarketing, at your Web site, in your E-mail signature—wherever you can. "As seen in *Fortune*" carries a lot of prestige.

Guerrillas excel at doing the *two-step*, the marketing dance I mentioned in Chapter 12. Step one is to have a magazine (or any publication) run a small display (or classified) ad that hits the high points of your offering, then tells readers to call or write for *free* information. When they respond, you can take step two: send them your brochure and a motivating sales letter. Follow up with still another letter if they do not order. Consider selling or renting their names to mailing-list brokers. These people buy and sell or rent names and addresses of many different types of consumers. Find them in your Yellow Pages under "mailing lists." The two-step process lets you tell your entire story but does not entail the high costs of large-space advertising. It also gives you a large number of salable names, and you can be sure these are valuable names for your own mailing list.

The two-step in action

This two-step process worked for an entrepreneur friend of mine after the running of a large ad failed. In the classified section of *Psychology Today*, he ran a classified display ad that informed readers that they could earn a legitimate college degree—B.A., M.A., or Ph.D.—from their homes. Then he wrote that they could secure free details about the offer by writing him. My friend later told me that he made a great deal of money with this two-step process, but that it was twice as much work as the one-step process that I was employing at the time. He employed someone to handle the detail work for him, and his two-step ads continue to run in *Psychology Today* and in thirty other publications. It's been over twenty-five years since the first ad ran.

If you come up with a winning magazine ad, you may be able to run it in a multitude of magazines. The result can be a multitude of profits. You can run your proven money-maker for years and years in a wide selection of publications. To a guerrilla, few marketing situations are as delightful.

But the prime reason for using magazines is the lasting value of the ad. I recall placing a full-page ad in *Newsweek* for a client. After the ad was run, the client asked each customer where he or she had heard of his company. At the end of one week, only five people claimed to have seen his ad in *Newsweek*, where it had run

The prime reason to use magazines

only one time. At the end of one month, that number climbed to eighteen people. And after a full year, a total of sixty-three customers said they had first heard of the company through its ad in *Newsweek*. And that's not even the impressive part! The really significant aspect of this story is that the entrepreneur blew up a reprint of the ad to the size of an enormous poster—five feet high—then mounted it and placed it outside his place of business. Thousands of customers patronized his business because of that poster.

Newsweek turned out to be his most effective advertising medium that year—and yet he placed but one ad there. To make matters more wonderful, the *Newsweek* page was purchased at less than half the going rate because it was remnant space. The magazine had sold three full-page ads to regional advertisers and had one page left over—a remnant. So my client was able to buy the space for a fraction of its original price.

If you're interested in advertising in any particular magazine, call the local representative of the magazine and say that you are definitely a candidate for any remnant space and that you should be phoned when it is available. You may wait a bit, but it will be well worth the wait. Do Coca-Cola and AT&T practice this tactic? No. Do successful guerrilla marketing people practice it? You bet their bank balance they do!

There are four thousand magazine titles right now. There will be two thousand new titles before 2005. Guerrillas pay close attention, knowing that some of those new titles hit their prospects in the middle of their purchase patterns.

What they don't know will hurt them

Most small-business owners never even consider advertising in magazines. That's because they don't know about regional editions, remnant space, in-house agency discounts, the two-step process, and valuable merchandising aids. Now that you do know about these lovely aspects of magazine advertising, give serious consideration to the medium.

18

Radio: It Costs a Lot Less
Than You Think

Unless you have a good friend who owns a radio station, most of your radio marketing will be of the paid, rather than free, variety, though remember, in 1996, over 50 percent of all media was obtained via barter, according to the head of one of the nation's largest media-buying services. It is possible to have stories or interviews about your product or service on the radio, and it may be that those will cost you nary a cent. In Chapter 26, we explain how to get free publicity on the radio and in other maxi-media. But as far as this chapter is concerned, you'll have to pay or trade for your radio marketing. For purposes of simplicity, let's talk paying.

Although newspapers are the primary marketing media for most small businesses, and direct mail has taken over second place, radio does come in a strong third. Radio advertising can be used effectively by a company with a limited budget. And radio can help improve your aim when you're trying to reach your target consumers. Radio helps you establish a close relationship with your prospects. Because of its intimate nature, it brings you even **Radio is** closer than newspapers do. The sound of an announcer's voice, **intimate** the type of musical background, the sound effects you use to punctuate and enhance your message—all of these are ammunition in your radio marketing arsenal. All can help win customers and sales for you.

Although it's true that you can, if you try, pay $500 or more for a single thirty-second radio commercial on a large commercial radio station, you can also, if you try, pay $5 for a single radio commercial on a smaller, less popular station. You'll certainly talk to more people with the $500 spot, but you will reach more than a few people with your $5 commercial.

Don't think, however, that you can spend $5 and be involved in radio marketing. But if you spend $5 for five spots per day ($25) and you run your spots four days a week ($100) three weeks out of four, you may say that for $300 a month you are adequately covering the listener profile in the community that the particular radio station covers.

The fickle radio listener

Because radio listeners often change stations, you should run radio spots on more than one station. This is a rule to know and to break. But know it. One station does not a radio campaign make.

How many stations?

How many stations do you need? Well, you may really need only one. But you'll probably need three or four or five. It may also be that you have the type of offering that lends itself so well to radio that you'll need no other ad media and can dive headlong into advertising on ten stations. Some of my clients have. One of the advantages to being on so many stations is that by carefully tracking your audience response—that is, learning which stations are bringing in the business—you can eliminate the losers and narrow your radio marketing down to proven winners. You can also use the coupon-type testing we explored in the chapter on newspapers. That means you pick, say, five stations and run commercials on all five. In each commercial, make a different offer—a discount, a free gift, a 50 percent reduction—and ask listeners to mention the offer when they contact you. By keeping assiduous track of the offers mentioned by your customers, you'll know which stations to drop (maybe all of them) and which to continue with (maybe all of them).

Unless you really keep track of all of your media responses, you are not a guerrilla. If you run your ads and keep selecting media on

Guerrillas and lemmings

blind faith, you are closer to a lemming. You've got to make your marketing as scientific as possible. This is one of those rare instances where you can measure the effectiveness of your media scientifically. Avail yourself of it.

If you have salespeople, ask them to track responses. If you're the person taking orders from customers, then you must track

Questions to ask

responses. Ask the customers, "Where did you hear of us first?" If they say radio, ask "Which station?" If they name a station that you don't use, ask, "Which stations do you ordinarily listen to?" If that doesn't net a solid response, prompt the customer, naming a few stations (one of which you use). It's a drag to do this, but it's a bigger drag to waste marketing money and bankrupt a business. Do everything you can to learn which stations are pulling in customers and which are not. After you've been marketing seriously for a year or three, you can cut down on your media tracking, though I don't suggest that you do. If you start learning for sure which stations pull best, you may feel that you need no longer ask. But until you're certain, you must ask. Because stations and people change, keep track consistently.

There are many types of radio stations: rock and roll, rap, middle of the road, country, public, all news, talk show, drama, Spanish language, religious, black, top 40, bubble-gum rock, jazz, oldies, intellectual, avant-garde, local interest, farm-oriented, progressive rock, reggae. Public radio and community radio do not run commercials, but they do make public service announcements for free. Which stations do your prospective customers listen to? Although it's possible to divide radio stations into twenty-three categories, as I've just done, it's advisable to divide them into two categories—background stations and foreground stations.

What kinds of stations?

Some radio stations play *background* programming. That means they play music that is generally a background sound. People talk, converse, work, play, iron, cook, and do myriad other things with background radio sounds. The music does not get in the way, does not command attention, does not distract. Unfortunately, because people are not actively listening, the commercials are also in the background. Sure, when a person is driving home with the radio on, all alone, the commercials—and the music—move up from the background. But in general, all music stations are background radio stations. And many music lovers have CD players or cassette decks in their cars, not to mention their homes.

Background and foreground programming

Sports, religion, all news, and talk stations are *foreground* radio stations. They are in the foreground of people's consciousness. They command attention. They are poor stations to have on when conversing, when working, and in situations that require your concentration. As a result, the commercials that these stations broadcast are likely to attract more active listeners. These people pay closer attention to commercials because they are actively listening to the radio. This is not to say that foreground radio is better than background radio for advertising. But be aware of the difference.

Active listeners are the best

There are other differences as well. Talk radio is hosted by "personalities." Disc jockeys at music radio stations say what music has just been aired and what music is about to air. Sometimes this is on tape. Talk radio involves listener rapport, more informal chatter, and more personal asides.

Here's a guerrilla tactic that works gloriously well on foreground stations when it is appropriate. Suppose you have a new company that sells, say, computer instruction. Invite a talk radio personality to take a few lessons. Then buy time on that personality's station. Rather than give him a 60- or 30-second script for your commercial, which you might ordinarily do, give him an outline—and invite him to ad-lib as much as he wants. The result is usually a sincere commercial, far longer than the commercial for which you have contracted, that has loads of credibility. If your product or service is worth raving about, you can count on most personalities to give it their all. You have to pay only for a sixty-second spot but you may end up with a three-minute spot at no extra cost.

A guerrilla radio tactic

That is about the only instance in which I'd advise you to put your message into the hands of the radio station. In virtually all other instances, I suggest that you provide recorded commercials, which you can tape at an independent facility or at the station itself. Do *not* furnish scripts to the station. Although some of their announcers may read them well, other announcers may make mincemeat out of them, may read them with no conviction and no enthusiasm. Murphy's law has a way of asserting itself at radio stations: if the commercial can be messed up, it will be. Protect yourself by supplying finished tapes only—unless you can get a personality to breathe true life into your script.

Who writes your commercial?

Just as it is bad business to let a newspaper write your newspaper ad copy, it is also a grave error to let a radio station write your radio ad copy. Most stations will be all too willing to volunteer. Don't let them. If you do, your commercial will sound just like everyone else's commercials. One of the most asinine methods of saving money is to let the station write your advertising.

If the station offers to produce your spot, that's a different story. Check out their equipment. It's probably all right. Listen to their announcers. If you trust their equipment—as measured by the sound of finished commercials produced on it—and you like one or more of their announcers, allow the station to voice and produce the commercial on tape for you. Generally there is no charge or a low charge for this service. In most cases, but not all cases, it's worth the price.

The top ten radio formats

The following were the top ten radio formats in the United States in 1996:

- Country
- News/Talk/Sports/Business

- Adult contemporary
- Oldies
- Religion-Music
- Rock
- Adult standards
- Religion-Talk
- Spanish
- Soft adult contemporary

Country accounts for 25.3 percent of all radio; the News/Talk/Sports/Business format is a distant second with 11.7 percent.

Whichever format you select as the home base for your radio marketing program, should you run 30-second spots or 60-second spots? A 30-second spot is usually far more than 50 percent of the cost of a 60-second spot. In most instances, what you can say in 60 seconds can also be expressed in 30 seconds. So go with the shorter spots even though they are not great values. In the long run, they'll give you more bang for your budget. If, however, you have a complex product or service, you'll have to run a full 60-second spot. Some advertisers achieve superb results with 2-minute commercials. Take as long as you must to state your message, but make it 30 seconds in length if possible.

Thirties and sixties

A long-time radio pro once told me that if he had to cut 33 percent of his radio advertising budget, but could spend that 33 percent on a music track for his commercials, he'd gladly do it. He believes that the presence of music lends a powerful emotional overtone to the commercial. I agree. Music can convey what words frequently cannot, and music can be obtained inexpensively. You can rent it from the station's rights-free music library. You can have a music track made by hungry musicians who will record a track for very little money, appreciating the exposure they will receive. Or you can purchase an expensive music track—made expressly for you or taken from a hot record—and use it so much that the amortized cost is mere peanuts.

Music hath charms

I know an entrepreneur who made a deal with a composer who had recently released a record album. The entrepreneur, upon learning that the particular music he liked would cost $3,000, said that he'd pay the composer $100 per month for a full year. If, at the end of that period, he was still in business and wanted the music, he would then pay $3,000 in addition to the rental fees he had paid. If he hadn't been successful, he would

The entrepreneur and the composer

merely be out the rental fees, and the composer would still have the music. It sounded like a fair deal for both parties, so the composer agreed. At the end of one year, the composer did receive $3,000 in addition to the $1,200 he earned for renting his music. His total gain was $4,200. The entrepreneur, who at the time could barely afford the $100 rental, could later easily afford the $3,000. Everyone came out a winner.

If you have to use announcers and musicians who are members of the various unions (Screen Actors' Guild and/or American Federation of Television and Radio Actors), be wary. Union costs and paperwork are overwhelming, and you might be better off to avoid unions. I work with unions only when I absolutely must, and when I do, I see that all the paperwork is handled by an independent party. Unions and guerrillas mix like gasoline and water.

Sound effects

As music adds new dimensions to your selling message, so do sound effects. Use them when you can; radio stations (and most production facilities) have libraries of them and rent them at nominal costs. Just be careful you don't get carried away with their use.

Three citical seconds

You have but three seconds to catch and hold the attention of the listener. Be interesting during those first three seconds and say what you have to say, lest the listener's attention stray. Be sure you use "ear" words rather than "eye" words. Whatever you do, repeat your main selling point. Also, repeat your company name as many times as you possibly can.

Interviewing the president

A good idea for a radio commercial: put the president of the company into a recording booth and interview him or her. The interview should last for thirty minutes or longer. Then use small sections of the interview as ingredients—sound bites—in future commercials. Sound bites are ideas expressed simply and briefly. The concept was spawned for the political process by public relations pros, who are called "spin doctors" by the media. This is based upon their ability to give the proper "spin," or public perception, to the activities of the firms they represent. Spin doctors can create the perception that an oil company is a group of ardent environmentalists. The 1998 movie *Wag the Dog* was an accurate if exaggerated demonstration of the power and skill of spin doctors as they manipulate public opinion from Washington. But our government isn't the only one to employ spin doctors. They have long been functioning in the capitals of nations around the world.

As a guerrilla, you can be your own spin doctor. Select your
own sound bites from the interview for your marketing. It's important to remember that trust is the key—you never want to be
perceived as a spin doctor; you only want to put the right "spin" on
your marketing. Your use of selected interview sound bites must
come across as different, believable, and best of all, allow the
president of the company (you?) to go out on a limb publicly—a
good idea.

**Be your own
spin doctor**

The following script won Radio Commercial of the Year hon-
ors in Chicago, and it *successfully* sold dog food. It is a sixty-second
spot and cost very little to produce.

Announcer:	Ladies and gentlemen! The makers of Perk dog food—the rich, meaty, energy-giving, delicious dog food—now bring you one minute of rich, energy-giving, delicious . . . *silence.*
Sound:	*(Five seconds of silence)*
Man:	*(Whisper)* Aren't you going to say anything about the big Perk sale?
Announcer:	*(Whisper)* Shhh! This is supposed to be silence!
Sound:	*(Four seconds of silence)*
Man:	*(Whisper)* Won't you even remind people that if they buy three cans of Perk dog food during the sale, they get five cents off?
Announcer:	*(Whisper)* Quiet!
Sound:	*(Four seconds of silence)*
Man:	*(Whisper)* But this is important! Aren't you—
Announcer:	*(Whisper)* Will you be quiet!!
Man:	*(Whisper)* Yes, but—
Announcer:	*(Whisper)* I mean now!
Man:	*(Whisper)* Yes, but the big Perk sale! You've got to say something about how now is the time to stock up on Perk because people can get five cents off when they buy three cans!
Announcer:	*(Whisper)* I m not going to say a word! Now quiet!
Man:	*(Whisper)* Then I'm going to say something—
Announcer:	*(Loud whisper)* Keep away from that microphone!
Man:	*(Loud whisper)* Listen, everyone . . . *(Louder)* Perk is having a big sale, and—
Sound:	*(Scuffing and fighting sounds. Man yells "Oof!")*

It's a humorous commercial, and the humor worked to gain attention.

In a more serious vein (and more economical because it requires the service of only one announcer), the following straightforward spot might be broadcast, in 30 seconds, for a service-oriented entrepreneur:

> *Male voice:*   (*Over music*) If you dislike the inconvenience of driving your car to a mechanic, you'll like the convenience of having the Mobile Mechanic drive to your car and fix it while you're relaxing at home. If you're not happy with the price of having your car tuned up at a garage, you'll be very happy with the bargain price of having your car tuned up at home by the Mobile Mechanic. Keep your car in top shape, conveniently and economically. Call the Mobile Mechanic. Find him in the white pages of your local phone directory. The Mobile Mechanic. Call him.

Speed talk

Radio hints for guerrillas

Although most announcers can easily fit 70 words into a 30-second spot, studies indicate that people listen more attentively if the announcer talks faster and crams more words into a short space. Columbia University conducted the study, which gave speed-talk a shot in the arm. A few radio hints for guerrillas:

- Save money by running ads three weeks out of every four.
- Concentrate your spots during a few days of the week, such as Wednesday through Sunday.
- The best time to run radio advertising is during afternoon drive time, when people are heading home. They're in more of a buying mood than in the morning, when work is on their minds.
- When listening to the radio commercials you've produced, listen to them on a car-radio-type speaker, not on a fancy high-fidelity speaker like the ones production studios use. Many an advertiser, dazzled after hearing his commercial on an expensive speaker system, has become depressed when hearing what the commercials sound like on a typical car stereo system.
- Consider radio rate cards to be pure fiction. They are highly negotiable.

- Study the audiences of all the radio stations in your marketing area. Then match your typical prospect with the appropriate stations. It's not difficult.
- If you want to reach teenagers, advertise on the radio, not in the newspaper.
- Mention your Web site in your radio commercial. You only have a minute or less to convince them to buy from you on the radio, but you have unlimited time on-line.

One of radio's surprises is its power as a direct-response medium. Many companies spend 25 seconds delivering their sales pitch and 5 seconds providing their toll-free number. Because companies are advertising on radio and realize people can't write the number on a piece of paper, they spell a word with their phone number. Response rates are equivalent to those on TV, and the cost is usually much lower. The influx of car phones can't be a hindrance to the use of radio for direct marketing. But please don't make a call while you're heading in my direction on the highway.

If you plan to use radio for your direct response offer, repeat your phone number at least three times. Use a high-quality voice. Take advantage of the intimacy of radio. Air your spot on weekends and during evenings, and figure on receiving responses within three to four days. Change your copy immediately if you get a poor response, and change your product if new and improved copy doesn't help. Before you change your product, however, be absolutely certain that your offering matches the tastes of the listening audience. **Direct-response radio**

Unless you simply cannot see your way to using radio, do give it a try. You'll appreciate its flexibility, its ability to allow you to make last-minute changes, and the opportunity to home in on your prospects on the basis of station format, time of day, and day of the week. I have a client, very successful, who owns a furniture store. Although he uses many marketing media—newspapers, Yellow Pages, billboards, point-of-purchase signs, and direct mail— he spends 90 percent of his marketing money on radio advertising. With such a high concentration of dollars in only one medium, does he qualify as a true guerrilla? He sure does! He has learned through the years that radio reaches his exact audience and motivates them to come into his store. He runs his commercials on anywhere from 6 to 10 stations, and he often runs the same commercial 15 times in a day. What's more, he's never off the radio, **Last-minute changes** **Never off the radio** using it 52 weeks per year. Because he learned to use this medium to the benefit of his bottom line, he is a true guerrilla marketer. After experimenting with all kinds of marketing mixes, he finally decided that radio was the medium for him. He uses it with music. He uses it consistently. And he makes so much money that he lives a luxurious life in Hawaii while his business, located in the Midwest, continues to flourish. Although many factors are responsible for his success, he gives most of the credit to radio advertising. He is living proof that you can prosper in style as a one-medium guerrilla.

19

Television: How to Use It, How Not to Abuse It

Television is the most effective of all marketing vehicles, the undisputed heavyweight champion, though on-line marketing is becoming a contender for the title and should hold it before long. But television is also the most elusive and easiest to misuse. It is elusive because it is not as simple as it seems, because it requires many talents, because it is not normally associated with small businesspeople, and because it is dominated by giants who give entrepreneurs a mistaken impression of how it should be used. You cannot use TV as Nike, Coca-Cola, and McDonald's use it unless you have their money.

Television is easy to misuse because it does seem straightforward, because almost anyone can afford to run one or two television commercials, because it is readily available, because there are more TV options than ever, because it is the medium that strokes the entrepreneur's ego the most tantalizingly, and because it requires a whole new discipline. Television is not, as some believe, radio with pictures.

Television is merging with computers in the form of Web TV–type products, which enable you to view the Internet and E-mail on your TV screen. Of all the activities being displaced by computer use, watching TV comes in first, though currently, the average American spends 19 hours a week watching the tube, more than the citizens of any other nation. Japan comes in next, followed by the Czech Republic, Portugal, and Greece. In case you're wondering, Norwegians watch the least TV. Globally, people watch 2.7 hours of TV per day and have an average of 12 channels to choose from. They like, in order, movies, news, and comedy. They don't like, in order, soap operas, kids' programs, and religious shows. North Americans receive an average of 27 channels; Russians receive an average of 4.

Television has changed in many ways, all of them favoring guerrillas. Advertising costs have plummeted to the point where a 30-second prime-time commercial costs $20 or less, even in major markets. (This is not for network programming.)

Targeting ability has improved: you can run commercials in specific city neighborhoods, in selected suburbs, right in your community. Also, satellite and cable TV allow you to pick TV channels that hit your audience smack-dab in the middle of their viewing patterns. With a dish called an uplink, satellite TV is broadcast upward to one of 30 communication satellites. The satellite then sends the TV signals back to earth. They are picked up by the 2 percent of Americans who have conventional home satellite dishes and the 4 percent who subscribe to direct broadcast satellite services. Add to that the many cable stations that transmit satellite broadcasts to umpteen million more homes. You probably know that many communities today receive more than 70 TV channels. But to give you an idea of the choices of today's TV viewer equipped with a satellite dish, consider the selections available on the communication satellites now in orbit. Each satellite

can broadcast on 24 transponders, or channels (although few use all 24). Our choices are bountiful—249 channels are listed in the January 3rd, 1998, issue of *Satellite TV Week*, and that number grows each month. And I haven't even mentioned the 5 Ku-band satellites and their 71 transponders.

Whether your interest is education, international news, movies, adult programming, network TV, kids, business, animals, game shows, romance, history, information, shopping, religion, sports, travel, or weather, chances are that it's on satellite. Because satellite dishes are sold in different sizes, the cost of ownership is quite low, attracting more viewers and making the television medium more enticing to guerrillas.

Satellite-dish owners have a mean household income of $78,400; 86.7 percent own their own house, but that percentage is dropping due to the availability of smaller, apartment-size dishes, and 42 percent live in areas where cable is also available. The favorite fare of dishheads: movies.

Cable stations select their programming from both local sources and all these satellite options. Penetration of cable in the United States is up to 67 percent for wired systems and 73 percent for those who access CNN, ESPN, and others directly with their satellite dish. Some cable systems have only five choices; others have more than 70. The number is growing. And one of the fastest growth areas is in home shopping channels.

As TV technology, cable systems, satellites in orbit, and video-cassette ownership—now approaching 85 percent—have changed, so have viewing patterns. Of the ten prime uses of TV sets, three do not allow commercials: rented tapes, video games, and the TV as a monitor for a computer. PBS, the third most popular use of TV, is not a good station on which to market, though you shouldn't overlook it if your target audience watches it. If you sponsor a PBS program, you'll create as much awareness as you would with a commercial on CBS.

When you were a kid, network TV ruled the roost. Today it's hanging in there, but it's not enjoying a growth spurt. Cable and satellite TV are growing at a much healthier rate.

Another new option now available is the increasingly ad-friendly Public Broadcasting System. Many local affiliates now accept sponsorships that look and feel—and sell—much like standard TV commercials. One guerrilla, Jerry Baker of Garden-Care, participates in PBS fundraisers by giving gardening advice during pledge breaks. The stations then offer his books and videos as premiums for donations. His success on PBS has been translated to QVC, one of the shopping channels, where he sells thousands of videos each time he appears. If you can't give gardening advice, perhaps you can give something to your local PBS station that they can auction at a fundraising drive.

The TV marketing is becoming fragmented, just as is happening with all media, and the Internet seems to be the only place where all the fragments can and do come together. In 1997, the Nielson Share of Viewing Report disclosed that during a typical day, 32 percent of viewers watch cable TV, 26 percent watch network TV, 19 percent watch local or other TV, 13 percent watch syndicated TV, 6 percent watch pay cable TV, and 3 percent watch PBS. Not like it used to be when everybody seemed to watch network TV and nothing else. **What folks watch**

TV viewers are now more sophisticated than ever. They've been around the block when it comes to TV advertising spots, and they have opinions about the spots that you should know: 31 percent find TV advertising spots to be misleading; 24.3 percent find them offensive; 17 percent think they are informative; 15.9 percent think they are entertaining. **The sophisticated viewer**

If you're planning to test TV for advertising to your market, give cable serious consideration. Cable TV is growing, and it's becoming more and more affordable. But don't be deceived by the low cost. For the tiny sum of money it costs, expect it to deliver a tiny audience. Experts say it's best suited for marketers with small trading areas where other media alternatives charge you for a lot of waste coverage—meaning that they reach people not in your trading area.

Affordable cable TV

None the less, now small-business owners can advertise on TV, on any satellite-delivered cable show, for prices even the smallest can afford. The twenty-dollar figure I mentioned was on the high side for cable. Most slots are considerably less than that. Think single digits. You can advertise on prime time, cherry-pick the subscriber neighborhoods and suburbs in which your spots appear, pick stations such as CNN, ESPN, MTV, the Nashville Network, Arts and Entertainment, the Discovery Channel, and loads more—*for not much more than the cost of a radio commercial.* Never before has TV been more available and desirable to owners of small businesses. Guerrillas in droves are, at this very moment, discovering the awesome power of TV, and I suggest that you do the very same.

You might want to look into interconnects, companies that serve as middlemen between the cable companies and small-business owners who want to go on TV but can't afford standard spot advertising or network TV. Ask your media-buying service how to get in touch with your local interconnect company. The major media-buying services may not be interested in handling your business if you have a small budget, but if you speak to a local TV sales manager, you can often get the names of local freelance media buyers. Many good ones are working from home these days, including many new moms who can do everything that a media-buying service can.

Awesome power, teensy prices

Television is effective only if you use it enough. And enough is a lot. Enough is expensive. How much is enough? Many experts say you can measure how much enough is by understanding rating points. A GRP, or Gross Rating Point, is calculated on the basis of 1 percent of the TV households in the TV marketing area. If 1 million TV sets are in the area, one rating point equals 10,000 TV households. The cost of TV advertising is determined by the size of each GRP in the marketing area, and advertisers pay for a given number of GRPs when they buy advertising time. The experts advise, and I agree, that you should not consider TV advertising unless you can afford to pay for 150 GRPs per month. Those can come in the form of 75 GRPs per week every other week, or 50 GRPs for three weeks out of four, or even 150 GRPs for one week per month. How much a single rating point costs in your area depends upon the size of the area, the competitive situation, and the time of year. Points tend to cost more around Christmas shopping time—October through late December. They tend to cost less during the summer, when reruns are being shown. Rating points in small towns cost far less than rating points in big cities.

The price ranges from about $4 per GRP in a small city such as Helena, Montana, to about $2,000 per GRP in a big city like New York or Los Angeles.

Can you start small in TV and then build up? Only if you start out by buying 150 GRPs for one month and have the funds and emotional endurance to tough it out for a minimum of three months. If you can't do that, don't fool around with TV. If you can afford to pay for the proper number of rating points—and you can if you live in a low-cost TV marketing area such as those found in many rural sections of the United States, or if you are well funded—you'll find that TV can do many things the other media cannot. Television allows you to demonstrate, to act, to dance, to sing, to put on playlets, to show cause and effect, to create a lively identity, to be dramatic, to reach large numbers of people, to home in on your specific audience, to prove your points visually and verbally—all at the same time. Not only can you provide your Web-site address, you can show your Web site. No other medium provides so many advantages to the advertiser at one time.

Of the various times you can advertise on the tube, steer clear of prime time—the 8:00 P.M. to 11:00 P.M. period (unless you're going to economize by advertising on cable channels). You can realize better values—more viewers per dollar—by using fringe time (the time before and after prime time), especially on local affiliates of the big networks. You might also look into daytime TV, which attracts many women viewers. The audience size is smaller and so is the cost. The time period past midnight, when few people are watching, is very inexpensive and can prove a springboard to success. Some postmidnight shows have ratings so low they are unmeasurable. This means, happily, that air time is inexpensive.

When to advertise

If you truly want to advertise on television, learn which shows your prospects watch, then run commercials on those shows.

Many of the shows are available on cable. For example, when the solar energy industry was in its infancy, aggressive marketing people soon learned that the same people who watch *Star Trek* tend to buy solar energy units. They also learned that men who watch science-fiction movies, not sports, have a proclivity toward solar power. Some solar energy companies went to the bank as a result of that fascinating information. Even though *Star Trek* was in its tenth series of reruns, it still proved to be a marvelous and inexpensive vehicle for solar heating marketers. Talk shows, which frequently attract an older audience, were determined to be poison for solar energy sellers. Their product simply did not appeal to seniors—at least it didn't at first. Today, solar energy is more acceptable as an alternative source of power, and media coverage of solar applications is generous, appealing to the increasing number of environmentally aware citizens. Is that your electric car I hear (barely) pulling into my driveway?

TV rate cards   To get the most out of TV, keep in mind that TV rate cards, like radio rate cards, are established as the basis for negotiation and are not to be taken as gospel. In fact, if you're going to go on to television, you should consider retaining a media-buying service to make your plans and buys for you. They'll charge about 7.5 percent of the total for their services, but they'll save you more than that. Many small businesspeople make their own buys, thinking they are getting good deals. But the media-buying services, which purchase millions of dollars' worth of TV time monthly, get bargains that would shock the small businessperson.

Another warning about buying your TV directly: TV salespeople have a powerful way of putting the egos of their commercial clients to work for them. Some convince an advertiser that he or she would be a terrific spokesperson. The advertiser, enjoying the strokes to his or her ego, then goes on TV and presents the commercial in person. Sometimes, but rarely, this is effective. Generally the advertiser loses as many sales as he or she gains. Frequently the advertiser becomes a laughingstock but continues to present the ads because his or her TV salespeople wouldn't dream of risking their sales by telling the truth. Don't let your ego get in the way of your TV marketing when it comes to buying the time or presenting the information. If you've watched enough TV, I'm sure you get the gist of what I'm saying.

A guerrilla I know used to offer to buy any unsold TV time from 6 A.M. through midnight from a TV channel. He purchased the time at far below market rates. You can afford prime time on a network affiliate if that station is willing to sell the prime-time slots at the same cost per rating point as after-midnight time slots.

I strongly suggest that you look into cable TV and satellite TV. It just may be that you can afford to market your offerings on television because of the new cable availabilities. Instead of going on TV and reaching the 90 percent of the audience who are out of your marketing area, you can telecast only to people within your marketing area. As cable TV (and satellite TV) are making television advertising more and more affordable to more small businesses, the networks are losing their shirts to cable—billions of dollars each year. And TV is still in a state of flux—all favoring the guerrilla. So be one! And get yourself onto the tube.

Actually, test TV for yourself. Put an offer into your commercial so that you can track the results. Perhaps you'll offer a free brochure. Maybe a special discount for people mentioning the commercial. Possibly a sweepstakes. Run your spots on different stations, cable and broadcast, and use a different phone number for each channel, enabling you to track easily. You might hire a 7-day, 24-hour telemarketing service to take your phone calls and report the results for each station.

Also, VCR sales are skyrocketing—nearly 90 percent of Americans have access to one now, compared with 45 percent in 1984—letting audiences view postmidnight programming anytime the next day. Satellite TV is also booming now that the prices have dropped. Stay tuned. These are very interesting times from the standpoint of television. My wife recently wanted to see a movie on the dish, but we weren't receiving the particular satellite beaming the movie. I called a satellite company, and within five minutes I did get that satellite—and we watched the movie! Who says movies-on-demand aren't an option? In reality, they are just making their presence known, another dark cloud over the video rental biz.

Many guerrillas have discovered the joys of direct response television, allowing people to order immediately after viewing the commercial. They do this because you furnish a toll-free number and accept most credit cards. Products that move well with direct-response TV are cooking and kitchen appliances, books and videos covering a wide range of topics, health and beauty aids, cosmetics, exercise equipment, and CDs and tapes. I'm sure many items can be added to that list. Recently, I ordered a buckwheat

Direct-response TV

husk–filled pillow because of a direct-response TV spot that caught my fancy—and just at a time I was contemplating the purchase of a new pillow. I'm always floored when guerrilla marketing works on me. But it does!

A soul-satisfying aspect of direct-response TV is the brief wait before knowing if you have a hit or a miss. Usually, within a week, you can tell if you've got a winner, and then you begin narrowing down the factors as to what channels work best, what time slots, what days of the week, how often, what times of the year, and how long it will continue serving as a cash cow. You might run it six months and wait two months.

Your CPO

The yardstick by which you measure your success or failure is your CPO, which stands for cost per order. If you can gain $2.00 in sales for every $1.00 invested in TV, your cost per order is $1.00, and I'm hoping your profit is healthy. If you earn $2,000 in sales for an investment of $1,000 in TV time, don't forget your investments in producing the commercial and the cost of your product. The money left over after those are deducted is your profit. If you don't have money left over, you need a lower CPO, often possible by changing your pricing.

Here are guideposts for guerrillas who opt for direct-response TV:

Guerrilla guideposts to direct-response TV

- *Your product must have a 500 percent markup.* Your sales-to-cost ratio should be five to one. Don't kid yourself into choosing a lower ratio.
- *Your product must have mass-market appeal.* If it's of interest to the general public instead of one specific group, you're in good shape. The burgeoning numbers of targeted TV channels are enabling marketers to pinpoint smaller groups.
- *Your product should have middle-class appeal.* In direct response, the blue-collar product will generally sell more than a white-collar or upscale product.
- *Your product should be unique.* If your product is a new idea, it will do better than an improved version of an existing product. A "me-too" product will not be successful unless it's a unique "me-too" product. A CD of '60s music is unique in a market offering CDs of '70s, '80s and '90s music.
- *You should have testimonials for your product.* Your product will move faster if real people are shown or quoted as saying wonderful things about it. If it's music, you don't need testimonials, only more music.

- *Your product is easy to demonstrate.* If it takes a long time to demonstrate, your chances for success are diminished. The best medium in which to demonstrate your product or service is television.
- *Your product is in the correct category.* These categories are proven by direct-response TV—housewares, books, videos, health and beauty aids, music CDs.
- *Your sales are emotionally motivated.* The strongest sales come when the product sale is motivated by fear (burglary), greed (make money), glamour (how to be more attractive), or sex (be loved).
- *You take the time to make the sale properly.* Often, that means 90 seconds or 2 minutes, and it means showing your toll-free number and the credit cards you accept for at least 20 seconds, while repeating your number at least three times.
- *Your commercial has a celebrity presenter.* Guerrillas try to spare this expense, but they know recognizable faces improve sales.
- *Your price is right.* The best prices seem to fall between $19.95 and $49.95. Guerrillas are assiduous price testers.

One of the most lovable parts of direct-response TV is the low cost of failure and the high payoff for success. If your venture fails on cable TV in Boulder, Colorado, it won't hurt you too much. But if it succeeds, many cable stations out there will want to run your spot. If you can make an offer that makes a profit for you, try making it on television.

Direct-response advertisers avoid cable like the plague unless they can buy their spots on a "per inquiry" or "per sale" basis, which means they pay nothing up front and pay only based upon how many inquiries or sales they make as a result of the TV spot.

If you do decide to invest in television marketing, there are many methods by which you can cut down drastically on the cost of producing TV commercials, which in 1996 ran over $200,000 for a 30-second spot. Truth is, you can turn out a very good 30-second spot for about $1,000. And even that figure can be reduced as you increase your TV savvy.

First of all, let your TV station provide all the *production* assistance. Not the writing. Let *them* put up the equipment and furnish the camerapeople, the lighting experts, the director, the all-important editor. Don't let them write the spot. If you do, it will look like all their other homegrown TV commercials. Instead,

Production assistance

either you or a talented individual you coerce, barter with, or hire should write a tight script. The left side of the sheet of paper upon which the script is written is reserved for video instructions. There, describe every single action the viewers will see, numbering each one. The right side of the script paper is for the audio portion. These are the sounds the viewers will hear. Again, number each audio section, matching it up with the appropriate video section so that the audio and video make a team.

Storyboards   If necessary, and it usually is not necessary, make a storyboard. A storyboard is a pictorial representation of your script. It consists of perhaps ten "frames," or pictures. Each frame contains a picture of what the viewers will see, a description of what will be happening, and the message that will be heard while the action is taking place. Storyboards tend to be taken too literally, however, and do not allow you the leeway to make changes during production. Those little changes are often the difference between an ordinary and an extraordinary commercial. Most (but not all) people have the imagination to understand a commercial from a script alone. If the people you are working with don't, you just may have to resort to a storyboard. Artists charge from $10 to $500 per frame, so you can see how storyboards make costs rise.

While working in major ad agencies, I had to prepare a storyboard for every commercial I wrote. And I know that I wrote more than a thousand. Many art directors enjoyed gainful employment because of my active typewriter and the traditions of advertising agencies, which called for storyboards. Since I've been working on my own, I have written well over a thousand commercials. Only five or six required storyboards. Yet the commercials were no less successful than those I made using storyboards.

Intense preproduction   You can also save money by scheduling preproduction meetings with all who will be involved in the production of your commercial. Meet with the actors, actresses, director, lighting person, prop person, and anyone else involved. Make sure everyone knows what is expected and understands the script. Make sure the timing is on the button. Leave not one detail unexplored. Then hold at least one tightly timed rehearsal. Have the people involved go through the motions before the cameras are running. By doing so, you can produce two commercials in the time usually necessary to produce one. You'll even be able to fit three commercials into the same production time, if you're good enough. When you are paying $1000 per day for equipment and crew, that comes to $333.33 per commercial when you do three commercials at once. A far cry from the average cost of $197,000. That $333.33 figure was true in the 1980s and remains true in the '90s. It will be very close to that figure for the first decade of the twenty-first century. All it takes is shopping around plus the attitude of a guerrilla.

To keep the cost down, which is one characteristic of a guerrilla, avoid expensive union talent and crew whenever possible (in some union cities such as Los Angeles and San Francisco, this is not easily done). Get everything right by planning rehearsals and preproduction meetings, and plan the editing when you plan the spot. Editing videotape can be very expensive, so plan your shooting so that little editing will be necessary. Experts say that the commercial is really made in the editing room. So make it a point to be there watching—and commenting—when the editing takes place. It's an important process of guerrilla learning.

The use of film or tape usually won't make a great difference in your final cost. Film allows you to use more special effects, has more of a magical quality because it has less "presence" than tape, and allows for less expensive editing. But with film you have no instant feedback. If someone goofed, you won't know it till the film is processed. With tape, you can replay what you have shot immediately, and if anything is wrong, you can redo it. No processing is necessary. As to which is better, there is no correct answer. Both can be ideal, depending upon the circumstances. But if you are planning to have the station help with production, better plan on videotape. Stations don't usually film for you. That's OK; guerrillas seem to opt for tape.

What makes a great TV commercial? Well, Procter & Gamble, one of the most sophisticated advertisers in the United States, frequently uses "slice of life" commercials, which are little playlets, the type that seem boring and commonplace. But with the big bucks P&G puts behind them, they work extremely well. And many companies have made a bundle copying this format. So don't knock them if you are considering TV as a marketing vehicle. You can learn plenty from P&G. I certainly did.

What makes a great commercial?

There are a few guidelines that will help you regardless of the type of commercial you wish to produce:

Remember that television is a *visual medium with audio enhancement*. Many ill-informed advertisers look upon it as the opposite. A guerrilla marketer knows that a great TV commercial *starts with a great idea.* Try to express that idea visually, then add the words, music, and sound effects to make it clearer and stronger. Try viewing your commercial with no sound. If it's a winner, it will make its point with pictures only.

Again, go with 30-second spots rather than 60-second spots, and if you are using TV for direct response, such as for ordering by toll-free number, try two-minute spots. They're very effective. Say that phone number at least three times. And show it as much as you can.

Say the phone number three times

Keep in mind that, as with radio, you have three seconds to attract the viewers' attention. If you haven't hooked them right up front, you've probably lost them. So say what you have to say in a captivating manner at the outset. Say it again, in different words, in the middle of your spot. Say it a final time, again in different words (or maybe even in the same words), at the end. Don't fall into the trap of making your commercial more interesting than your product. Don't allow anyone to remember your commercial without remembering your name. There are bushels of sob stories about commercials that won all sorts of awards while the products they were promoting died horrible deaths. You want sales—not awards, praise, or laughs.

People who hate advertising

These days, many TV commercials, to my mind, are created by people who hate advertising and are ashamed of it. This explains why many TV spots are visually dazzling but give no clue as to who is advertising. You've got to pay close attention to see who you should purchase from, and guerrillas know that people don't pay close attention to TV commercials. My wife calls this the "By the Way" school of advertising, as in, "Let us entertain you and amuse you, enthrall you, and delight you. By the way, we're also hoping you'll buy our beer."

TV spots, the researchers tell us, offend more than print ads. Studies show 15 percent of people condemning TV and only 7 percent badmouthing print. A huge 41 percent say TV talk shows are a menace to society and 42 percent of Americans believe that TV talks down to them.

Communicate to their eyes

When you can, *show your product or service in action.* People's memories improve 68 percent when they have a visual element to recall. So say what you have to say verbally and visually, especially visually.

The following 30-second commercial won first prize at the Venice TV Film Festival. The advertiser then had to withdraw it from the air because he could not keep up with the demand for his product. The idea conveyed in the commercial is that this particular cookie, known as "Sports" and manufactured by a company called Carr's, has more chocolate on it than any similar cookie. Simple enough? Here's the script:

VIDEO	AUDIO
1. *Open with two slapstick characters facing the camera. One is tall and one is short. Tall one speaks:*	1. *(Tall man)* Good evening. Sidney and I would like to prove that Carr's Sports have the most chocolate—by showing you two ways to make chocolate cookies.
2. *Short man smiles when his name is mentioned, but loses the smile when he hears that he is a cookie.*	2. Imagine Sidney here is a cookie.
3. *Tall man lifts huge container marked "chocolate" and pours real chocolate fluid onto short man.*	3. Now take your cookie. Cover it with chocolate.
4. *Camera tilts down to show pool of chocolate at short man's feet.*	4. Effective, but not much stays on. Carr's makes Sports a better way.
5. *Cut to the two men. Tall man now carries short man, holds him above a tub marked chocolate. Tall man then drops short man into the tub.*	5. Pop the cookie in chocolate.
6. *Cut to short man's head surfacing from the chocolate. As it surfaces, more chocolate is poured on it.*	6. Top it up, and when it is set . . .
7. *Dissolve to short man, now encased in chocolate. He is lying down. Tall man stands proudly above him.*	7. You have your cookie with all your chocolate on it.
8. *Tall man molds out a Carr's Sports package as camera zooms to closeup of it.*	8. That's how Carr's makes Sports.

9. *Hand sets package down next to short man, still encased in chocolate. Man looks at package.*

9. Carr's Sports—the bar of chocolate with the cookie in the middle. Right, Sidney?

State the premise up front

The commercial, which cost about $1,500 total to produce, states the premise *up front*. In the beginning the two characters are whimsical, so the viewer's attention is caught. The commercial is very funny. But the product is always the star. All the talk is about the product. The theme is chocolate. And the viewer makes a clear connection between Carr's Sports and chocolate, which was the basic idea all along. Viewers are told in frame one that the product has the most chocolate. In frame seven, the point is made again. In frame nine, it's made one more time. Even if there were no words, viewers would know what the commercial is about and understand the connection made between Sports and chocolate.

93 instead of 65

The commercial uses no music, has 93 words instead of the pedestrian 65, and employs humor to make its point. Humor, often referred to as the most dangerous weapon in advertising because it is so frequently misused, works well here, selling a product that retailed at the time for about 75 cents. And the spot makes full use of television's ability to demonstrate product advantages. Best of all, the commercial is so much fun to watch that viewers could watch it several times without becoming bored with it. They must also have remembered the name of the product, in view of the sales that resulted.

This goes to show that you don't need a huge budget and a fancy jingle to make a successful commercial. As a marketing man, I am far more proud of the sales than of the awards won by this commercial.

Because so many people, estimated now at 93 percent, have remote controls with both their TV sets and their VCRs, there's a great chance (estimated at 70 percent) that your commercial will get "zapped"—fast-forwarded or muted. Does this steer guerrillas away from television? No.

Overcoming zapping

Instead, guerrillas take heed of this ugly reality by working with it, not against it. They make their TV commercials remote-proof by telling their stories visually, using words and music, but not really requiring them because their pictures make their point. They show their names—often throughout the commercials—by superimposing them in the lower corner of the screen, à la CNN.

Notice how many networks have climbed aboard that particular bandwagon, finally realizing the visuality of their medium.

TV guerrillas show their commercials enough times to their target audiences that they begin to see the results of this powerful guerrilla marketing after a few months. A few months? Why not instantly? Because TV, as high potency as it is, does not bring about instant results unless you are having a limited-time sale, making a limited-time offer, or using TV as a direct-response medium, providing viewers with a toll-free number and enough information to make the decision to buy from you.

You're going to be a happy guerrilla if you *lower your expectations for TV in the short run*. Over time, TV will work its miracles for you. Only they won't be miracles. They'll be the result of your patience combined with your knowledge that no medium does as much to sell your offering as television. Don't think that you can make TV prove itself to you with limited funds. As low-cost as a spot may be, you still must have a decent-size war chest to use it. One expert for whom I have a lot of respect counsels his clients that if they can't stand to lose their TV investment, they should try something else. But if you can test it and make it work for you, you'll be one very happy guerrilla.

Do keep in mind that you must have a great product or service for TV to do its job for you. The next century appears to be shaping up as a century that responds most to the basics. The hot buttons will be the functionally elegant, the plain and simple, the healthy and sensible, the politically correct, the environmentally responsible, what is good for America, and what is solidly positioned as mid-price.

The hot buttons

Once you have offerings that live up to these consumer demands, TV can be most effective for you, the guerrilla. That's when to use and not to abuse TV.

20

Outdoor Advertising:
What It Can and Cannot Do

Outdoor advertising consists of billboards, bus ads, taxi signs, painted walls, and outdoor signs. I guess it also included skywriting since that never occurs indoors. Still, let's deal with billboards first. Rare is the entrepreneur who can survive on billboard advertising alone—although it can be done. We have already chronicled the successes of Harold's Club, Wall Drugs, and Burma-Shave, but these enterprises really used outdoor signs, not billboards. Billboard advertising—and to use the term *advertising* is somewhat of an overstatement— is really reminder advertising for the most part. It works best when combined with advertising through other media.

An important ingredient

Each year, an Iowa entrepreneur runs a month-long, one-cent-sale promotion on the radio and in newspapers. He also supports the radio and newspaper advertising for a month each year with billboards. His sales rise an average of 18 percent. With billboards alone, this would never happen. But the billboards add an important ingredient to his marketing mix. He uses them only once a year to promote his furniture business. They work wonderfully.

Billboard advertising doesn't have to be strictly reminder advertising. In some instances it can lead directly to sales. In regard to this, let me tell you the two most important words you can use on a billboard. They aren't at all like the high-motivation words we discussed several pages back—not that obvious. The two magic words that can spell instant success for you if used on a billboard are *next exit*. If you can use them on your billboard, they may do a great job of marketing for you. For example, a new store in the San Francisco Bay Area could afford only one billboard. That billboard, fortunately, was able to display the words *next exit*. Success came rapidly and overwhelmingly. Of course, the store had to do

Two magic words

everything else right to succeed, and it did. But the billboard gets the prime credit. If you can't use these two words, these three also work well: *two miles ahead.*

Most of the time, you cannot lease only one billboard. You will usually have to rent ten or twenty billboards at once. Some are in winning locations; some are sure-fire losing locations. You must take the bad with the good. However, through cogent arguing or a loophole in the billboard firm's policies, you may be able to lease just one beautifully located billboard. If ever you can, do it. Otherwise, be careful. Consider using billboards if you have a restaurant, tourist attraction, garage, gas station, motel, or hotel. Be wary of billboard advertising if your business doesn't have instant appeal to motorists. If you have a car wash that really is at the next exit, a billboard might just be the ticket. If you own a computer-education firm, forget it. A billboard can, however, help you maintain your identity if your identity is established.

When to use billboards

Marlboro maintains its cowboy identity with billboards. Words aren't necessary. If you're thinking about using billboards simply as reminders and haven't invested a lot in your identity, as Marlboro has, scratch the idea from your marketing plan.

To ascertain whether a billboard might work for you, find out how many cars pass the billboard site each day. This is known in the business as the traffic count. Billboard firms have the data at their fingertips. What type of traffic passes by? Trucks won't be able to patronize your car wash. On the other hand, homeward-bound affluent suburbanites may be interested in your take-home restaurant.

When planning a billboard, keep the rules for outdoor signs in mind. Rarely use more than six words. Remember that people are probably driving around fifty-five miles per hour or are negotiating in traffic when they glance, if they glance at all, at your billboard. Keep it simple for them. Give them one large graphic upon which they can concentrate. Be sure the type is clear and the words are large. If the traffic count remains more or less the same at night, be sure your board is illuminated. That costs more than a nonilluminated board but may be worth the extra bucks.

Six words only

Billboard companies are open to price negotiation, although they may not appreciate my putting that in print. They are also amenable to location negotiation. Once I wanted a specific location and was told that in order to get it, I'd have to rent nine other billboards—all in dismal locations. I said I wasn't interested. A couple of weeks later, I was offered the billboard along with only four other locations, also dismal. Again, I said no. Finally, I received a call from the sales rep saying I could have the one location I wanted, but the price would be significantly higher than originally quoted. It would have been a good deal, and I wished I could have said yes. But by this time, my client's monies had been committed. So we all lost out. Too bad the rep hadn't made me the same offer in the beginning. I could have used "next exit" on the billboard and had one more success story to report here.

Three other ways billboards work
In addition to attracting direct sales on occasion, billboards help guerrillas in three other instances: when you are new to an area and want to make your presence known; when you want to tie in with a unique advertising campaign or promotion; and when you have an idea that translates ideally onto a billboard, and you can rent just one board. An example of the third instance is a roadside cider stand that sells cherry cider grown from trees visible from the highway. A gutsy entrepreneur might display a billboard with the entire center section cut out so that motorists can see right through the billboard to the cherry trees. A simple line of copy at the top (or bottom) might say, Cherry Cider from These Trees—Next Exit. I know it's seven words long, but it's all right to break the rules occasionally, just as long as you know them and have a good reason for breaking them when you do.

Producing your billboard
One of the more attractive aspects of billboard advertising is that if you supply the design, the billboard company will produce the billboard for you. That means the company will handle blowing the artwork up to a size that will fit on the billboard. Billboard sizes are measured in sheets, with one sheet approximating the size of a large poster. The usual size is a 24-sheet. Whatever you do, make sure your billboard fits in with the rest of your advertising campaign. The Iowa man was able to present his message in six words on his immensely successful billboard only because the message had been explained more fully elsewhere. A guerrilla uses billboards like darts. A guerrilla either says "next exit," "two miles," or "five minutes ahead," ties his or her billboard in directly with a strong campaign, or uses a single billboard with surgical precision. No guerrilla uses a "next exit" billboard for the usual one month or three months. After testing the merits of a billboard, a guerrilla signs a one-year, three-year, or five-year contract for such a board. A guerrilla contracts with a billboard company to erect a billboard in a place where "next exit" can be used, if one

does not yet exist there. And a guerrilla still realizes that a great billboard isn't much more than a great reminder.

I would suggest that you avoid the use of billboards unless there is a compelling reason to use them. Drive around your community and carefully note the local companies that use billboards. Then talk to the owners of those companies and find out if the billboards work. Unless you are in a business that competes with theirs, you'll probably get a straight answer.

Sometimes a guerrilla can get several fellow guerrillas to collaborate on a billboard. This brings the cost of the board down considerably and puts it within range of many an entrepreneur. If two or three companies share a board, the cost may be low enough to enable each of them to use the board on a full-time basis, as part of their overall marketing plan.

Bringing down the cost of the board

Call the billboard representatives in your area and listen to their sales pitches. Perhaps they can enlighten you as to special opportunities, new boards to be erected, chances to go in on billboards with other companies. Maybe you won't be persuaded to use even a small billboard in your marketing plan. But you've nothing to lose by talking with them. So do it. Better yet, listen to them. If you have a well-known theme, billboards might be for you. As with many other marketing media, it may be worth your while to test their efficacy. Different towns respond in different ways to billboards. Maybe you live in a town that gets motivated by billboards. Los Angeles seems to be the billboard capital of the universe, with a multitude of ornate moving billboards in high-traffic locations—all heralding movies, stars, shows—but never Preparation H. Maybe you are located near a street that is ideal for a billboard. If that's the case, I recommend testing. If you test a billboard for a month or two and nothing happens, you're not out all that much money. But if you never give it a try, and then your biggest competitor tries billboards and goes to glory with them, you'll kick yourself from now till Sunday.

Billboard marketing is, almost without exception, *share-of-mind* advertising. Share-of-mind advertising is advertising that attempts to win sales down the road by implanting a thought or establishing an identity. It tries to win for you a constantly increasing share of the minds of the people in your marketing area. It does not normally prove effective in a hurry, cannot be translated into results, and is only profitable in the long run, if ever. *Share-of-market* advertising, on the other hand, is advertising that attempts

Share-of-mind advertising

to win instant sales. It tries to win for you a constantly increasing share of whatever market your offering belongs to. Share-of-market advertising is the kind of advertising that is the most effective, the most instantly translated into results, and the most profitable in the short run. Most entrepreneurs are a bit too concerned with cash to worry about shares of minds. They want increased shares of markets, and they want them right now. So consider using billboards, but don't expect to attract highly motivated prospects through them.

You can expect about the same, perhaps a little more, from bus signs, both interior and exterior, and interior or exterior taxi signs. These may be employed as part of a marketing plan that calls for the use of signs in targeted urban areas. These moving signs are seen by many people, many of whom may be serious prospects. Taxi signs are seen by people throughout the metropoli-

Buses and taxis

tan area. Bus signs are usually seen by the same people—bus riders and people who live along the route. Of course buses don't always travel the same routes taxis do. But this should be kept in mind if you're thinking about using both bus signs and taxi signs.

A client of mine enjoyed a great deal of success attracting temporary office workers with signs placed inside buses. The client was an agency that provided these workers to large employers, and the signs were designed to appeal to both the workers and the employers. If your product or service is located near a bus line, you should consider placing signs on that particular bus line—on the exterior of the buses. Such signs will not serve as a complete marketing plan, but they can be an effective part of one.

If you know where your prospects go, you can better determine a good location for outdoor advertising, whether it be placed on a billboard, a bus, a painted wall, or a sign on a barn. For example, if you sell a new type of tanning oil and a paintable wall is available near a sunbathers' beach, grab it. If you market agricultural products or services and a paintable roof is available on a well-traveled country road, rent the space and paint it with your message. Give serious thought to placing a sign outside your own place of business. A good sign often results in good business. A poor sign invites disaster.

A bad billboard

What makes a bad outdoor sign? Lack of clarity. Lack of uniqueness. Fancy lettering. Bland colors. Tiny words. Improper placement. Little connection with your other marketing. What makes a good outdoor sign? Readability. Warmth. Good location.

Uniqueness. An identity that matches that of your business. Clarity from afar, from moving vehicles, on dark nights. Good colors. Clear and unmistakable connection with your other marketing. Make certain that your sign communicates what your business is all about. For instance, "Moore's" tells us a lot less than "Moore's Stationery." To gain community acceptance, try to have your sign designed in such a manner that it fits in with the character of the community. Garish signs may be dandy in some locations and horrid in others. A large neon sign, like you'd see in Las Vegas, would win nothing but enemies for the advertiser in my community. Conservative signs may be just the ticket on some streets but a ticket to doom on others. Be sensitive to the tastes of your community.

A neon money-maker

Always be on the lookout for potential sign locations. I know a guerrilla marketer who could not secure a billboard near his place of business. But he was able to persuade the owner of a drive-in located within one mile of his business to sell him space on the back of the drive-in screen. It's no accident that the back of the drive-in screen faced a heavily traveled freeway.

If you're using a few billboards now, consider that when you begin to advertise in other media, your sales should rise anywhere from 25 to 250 percent. Of companies who augmented their billboards with other marketing, 83 percent said media advertising raised sales, while 79 percent claimed promotions should get the credit.

Successful guerrilla marketers tell me that one of the most important signs they have, though hardly a billboard, is the neon one that says OPEN. Some remind me that the high cost of neon signs prevents a few business owners from using them, necessitating instead the eventual expense of a GOING OUT OF BUSINESS sign.

Don't allow yourself to be hemmed in by a small imagination. But remember that advertising seen by speeding motorists has less impact than advertising seen by relaxed prospects—the type that might take the time to read a direct mailing from you.

21

Direct-Mail Marketing:
Pinpointing Your Prospects

Attention all guerrillas! Direct marketing is where it's at. Direct marketing is the name of your game. Direct marketing has a built-in mirror that reflects the true effectiveness of your advertising message. All other forms of marketing have much to be said for them, but direct marketing has more. All other forms of marketing can help you immensely, but direct marketing can help you more.

Gallup reports that direct mail was the most common communications medium used in the United States during 1997 and 66 percent of companies seem to agree. Direct mail generates 5 percent of U.S. company revenues. Of all sales revenue devoted to marketing, 22 percent is invested in direct marketing.

Direct marketing refers to direct-mail, mail-order, or coupon advertising, to telephone marketing, direct-response TV, postcard decks, door-to-door salespeople, home shopping TV shows, Web sites, or any method of marketing that attempts to make a sale right then and there. It doesn't require a middleman. It doesn't require a store. It requires only a seller and a buyer. And because of that, much unnecessary game-playing is removed form the marketing process, leaving only accountable results. Let me repeat that word: *accountable*. When you run a radio commercial or a newspaper ad, you do all in your power to make sure that it works, but you don't really know if it does. But when you engage in direct-mail advertising, you'll know clearly whether or not your mailing worked. If it worked, you'll know how well it worked. And if it failed, you'll know how dismally it failed.

Accountability is all

Direct mail doesn't always make the sale all by itself, but it obtains crucial leads that result in sales. A huge 89 percent of marketing directors use it to generate leads, while 48 percent use it to generate sales.

Along with its all-important accountability, consider some of the other advantages of direct mail over other advertising media:

1. You can achieve more accurately measured results.
2. You can be as expansive or concise as you wish.
3. You can zero in on almost any target audience.
4. You can personalize your marketing like crazy.
5. You can expect the highest of all response rates.
6. You can use unlimited opportunities for testing.
7. You can enjoy repeat sales to proven customers.
8. You can compete with, even beat, the giants.

Direct-mail advantages

Along with those eight advantages come eight rules of thumb:

Eight rules of thumb

1. The most important element is the right list.
2. Make it easy for the recipient to take action.
3. Letters almost always outpull mailing packages with no letters.
4. The best buyers are those who have bought by mail before, a rapidly growing number.
5. Do anything to get your envelope opened. (A list of hints is given later in this chapter.)
6. Keeping good records is paramount.
7. Testimonials improve response rates.
8. Remember that *nothing is as simple as it seems.*

In true guerrilla fashion, I also offer you eight tips for gaining the response rate you want with direct mail:

How guerrillas boost response rates

1. Ask for the order in the headline of your brochure.
2. Always tell the person what to do next.
3. Blue is a dandy second color, but red with black is generally the best-pulling direct-mail combination.
4. Don't overuse red; use it primarily for highlights.
5. Experts say the four most important elements in direct mail are the list, the offer, the copy, and the graphics. Guerrillas pay close attention to each.
6. The fastest-growing segment of the direct-mail industry is nontraditional mailers—those who haven't used direct mail in the past.
7. Direct-mail success comes with the cumulative effect of repeat mailings. Make them repetitive, yet different from one another.
8. Direct-mail spending by consumers has quadrupled since 1980 and tailed off a bit, but there's no end in sight for direct

marketing. Direct mail isn't growing as rapidly as telephone marketing and selling via the Internet. They are growing at a record pace.

**The normal
response rate**

Guerrillas realize that when it comes to determining the normal percentage of return on direct mail, *there is none*. You'll have to determine your own, then go about improving it—the name of the game in direct mail.

Right now, about 40 percent of direct mail is from national advertisers, 25 percent from local advertisers, 20 percent from mail-order firms. The average U.S. household receives an average of 104 pieces of direct mail each week. To a guerrilla, this means a slimmer chance than ever for a great response rate and a more acute need than ever for true creativity in their mailings. More money is spent on direct mail than on magazines, radio, or TV. More than 112 million Americans responded to direct-mail pitches in 1996; one in six Americans purchased six or more items via this maxi-medium; older people want less mail, while younger folks want more; and nonprofit groups use direct mail to raise up to 90 percent of their funds. Finally, keep in mind that with postal rates rising, amateurs are being forced away from direct mail, leaving a lush new universe for guerrillas.

**The least
expensive
method**

Those same guerrillas are grateful that direct mail is the least expensive method of marketing—on a per-sale basis. The overall cost may be high, but if it works for you, it is inexpensive marketing. There are many books, many articles, many chapters devoted to enlightening marketers on the intricacies of direct-mail marketing. Read them.

To a guerrilla, marketing is part art and part science. Direct mail is more science than art. This is not to downplay the art of creating a successful direct-mail package. But let's focus on the science, the things we already know. For instance, we know that the three most important things to do if you are to succeed at

**Test, test,
then test**

direct marketing are to test, test, and test. If you know that and do that, you are on the right road. If you play it by ear, you will probably fall on your ear. Direct marketing is growing faster than any other type of marketing. More and more people trust it. More and more people enjoy the convenience of being able to shop and buy by mail. More and more people want to be spared the lack of parking places, high fuel costs, irritable sales clerks, and crowded stores. They turn, therefore, to companies that make their products or services available through direct mail. In 1996, 96 percent of Americans purchased something by mail. They obviously appreciate the convenience and the saving of time. With a mailing, you *have a good chance of getting through to people*. Studies reveal that 60 percent of people say of direct mail, "I usually read or scan it"; 31 percent say, "I read some of it, don't read some of it"; 9 percent say, "I don't read any of it." The bottom line: you have a shot at reaching 91 percent of your audience. That's a healthy number.

Current estimates say that people get twenty direct mailings each day. They also inform us that only 50 percent of direct mail gets through to the boss; the other 50 percent is handled by assistants—the gatekeepers of industry. Guerrillas know how gatekeepers make their decisions. Those protectors of the boss's time want to know if it's a credible offer from a credible firm, if the subject matter is relevant to their boss and the company, and if the mailing is personal or business. **Gatekeepers**

Guerrillas know to shorten their copy when writing to high-level executives (two or three paragraphs maximum). They also make sure a high-level executive signs any letters directed to other top execs. The title "account executive" really doesn't cut it anymore. Sometimes, they send their mailing in a box because it is just too tempting to ignore. And when they absolutely positively want their mailing to get through to the recipient, they pop for the cost of Federal Express or UPS.

More on the science of direct mail is embodied in the *60-30-10 Rule*. Sixty percent of your direct-mail program depends upon your using the right list of people; 30 percent depends upon your making the right offer; 10 percent depends upon your creative package. You can make it creative if you take to heart these three tips: **The 60-30-10 rule**

- Brightly colored envelopes grab attention. Although red and blue are time-honored direct-mail colors, the nineties are proving that yellow, orange, and pink merit consideration, too. But white is always a safe, good bet.
- Oversized addressing stimulates the unconscious pleasure people gain from seeing their name in print. The larger, the better.
- A white #10 (business-size) envelope with a first-class stamp and no return address is especially intriguing and gets rave

notices when it comes to response rates. Look into it (that's a guerrilla hint to test it).

There are many reasons to do a direct mailing. And when you think of mailing, don't always think of mass mailing. Guerrillas write letters to:

Why you should write letters

- Follow up on a salesperson's call
- Set up an appointment
- Apologize for something you may have done wrong
- Compliment someone for something
- Recognize an anniversary of almost anything
- Celebrate holidays—Christmas, Hanukkah, Thanksgiving, Valentine's Day, Passover, Easter, Independence Day, and Yom Kippur, for instance
- Solidify telephone contact
- Thank someone for seeing your demo or hearing your presentation
- Thank someone for making a purchase
- Thank someone for their time even if they turned down your offer
- Thank someone for giving you a referral
- Welcome someone to anything at which they're new
- Applaud someone for a job well done
- Reiterate how much you've enjoyed working with someone
- Congratulate someone on a promotion or new job
- Mention you saw the person in the news (enclose the clipping)
- Congratulate someone on a special achievement
- Thank a person for doing a favor
- Thank someone for exceptional service
- Let a person know you appreciate their product or service
- Thank a person for their time or effort
- Express regrets if they are merited
- Thank someone for inviting you to something
- Tell somebody you hope they get well
- Express condolences
- Congratulate someone on a new baby, marriage, or new home
- Recognize a person's birthday
- Announce a new product or service
- Give advance notice of a discount

- Sell something. If you send letters about the topics listed above, this letter will be more warmly received.

The complete honesty that results from direct-mail marketing is invaluable. Because it is so accountable, it lets you know if you have done a good job making your offer, pricing your merchandise, constructing your mailing package, writing your copy, timing your mailing, selecting your mailing list. Soon after you have accomplished your mailing, you learn whether it worked or failed. That's what I mean by accountability. In the past few years, more of my work has been in the area of direct response. This is because companies are moving rapidly into direct-response marketing; they are learning that the feedback is instant and accurate when they employ this marketing vehicle.

Instant and accurate feedback

Before studying the secrets imparted in these pages, you must honestly ask yourself whether or not your product or service lends itself to direct marketing. If you have a product or service, are trying to select a product or service or to market through direct-mail or mail-order marketing, you should first consider several factors.

Checklist for direct marketers

- Is there a perceived need for the product or service?
- Is it practical?
- Is it unique?
- Is the price right for your customers or prospects?
- Is it a good value?
- Is the markup sufficient to assure a profit?
- Is the market large enough?
- Does the product or service have broad appeal?
- Are there specific smaller segments of your list that have a strong desire for your product or service?
- Is it new? Will your customers perceive it as being new?
- Can it be photographed or illustrated interestingly?
- Are there sufficient unusual selling features to make your copy sizzle?
- Is it economical to ship? Is it fragile? Odd-shaped? Heavy? Bulky?
- Can it be personalized?
- Are there any legal problems to overcome?
- Is it safe to use?
- Is the supplier reputable?

- Will backup merchandise be available for fast shipment on reorders?
- Might returns be too huge?
- Will refurbishing or returned merchandise be practical?
- Is it, or can it be, packaged attractively?
- Are usage instructions clear?
- How does it compare with competitive products or services?
- Will it have exclusivity?
- Will it lend itself to repeat business?
- Is it consumable, so that there will be repeat orders?
- Is it faddish? Too short-lived?
- Is it too seasonal for direct-mail selling?
- Can an add-on to the product make it more distinctive and salable?
- Will the number of stock-keeping units—various sizes and colors—create problems?
- Does it lend itself to multiple pricing?
- Is it too readily available in stores?
- Is it like an old, hot item, so that its success is guaranteed?
- Is it doomed because similar items have failed?
- Does your mother, wife, brother, husband, girlfriend, boy-friend, sister, or kid like it?
- Is direct mail the way to go with it?
- Does it meet an unfilled niche in the marketplace?

These questions were posed by Len Carlson, who for thirty years has sold about 10,000 different items from a direct-marketing company called Sunset House. They were listed in *Advertising Age,* in an article written by Bob Stone, president of Stone and Adler, a direct-response firm in Chicago.

Ask yourself these hard questions and come up with answers that please you. If you can't, you should discard the idea of direct mail for your particular product or service or make some major changes in your offering. If as few as five of your answers to these thirty-seven questions are not the right ones, you may be veering in the wrong direction. This checklist can serve as a handy guide to direct-marketing success. It will save you from spending money unwisely.

Only after you are satisfied that you ought to proceed into the world of direct marketing should you take the next step—which is to understand the relationship of direct-response advertising to

Direct is different from indirect

non-direct-response advertising. Rather than giving you my words about that relationship, I would like to quote from a speech made to the Direct Mail/Marketing Association's 65th Annual Convention by David Ogilvy—the head of a major advertising agency that has offices. Keep in mind that David Ogilvy's agency is a standard agency, not a direct-response agency, although it now has a branch called Ogilvy and Mather Direct. These are some statements from Mr. Ogilvy's speech:

- "In the advertising community there are two worlds. Your world of direct-response advertising and that other world—the world of general advertising. These two worlds are on a collision course. **What David Ogilvy says**
- "You direct-response people know what kind of advertising works and what doesn't work. You know to a dollar.
- "You know that two-minute commercials are more cost-effective than thirty-second commercials.
- "You know that fringe time on television sells more than prime time. In print advertising, you know that long copy sells more than short copy.
- "You know that headlines and copy about the product and its benefits sell more than cute headlines and poetic copy. You know to a dollar.
- "The general advertisers and their agencies know almost nothing for sure, because they cannot measure the results of their advertising. They worship at the altar of creativity. Which means originality—the most dangerous word in the lexicon of advertising.
- "They opine that thirty-second commercials are more cost-effective than two-minute commercials. You know they're wrong.
- "In print advertising, they opine that short copy sells more than long copy. You know they are wrong.
- "They indulge in entertainment. You know they are wrong. You know to a dollar. They don't.
- "Nobody should be allowed to create advertising until he has served his apprenticeship in direct response. That experience will keep his feet on the ground for the rest of his life. The trouble with many copywriters in ordinary agencies is that they don't think in terms of selling. They have never written direct response. They have never tasted blood.

- "Until recently, direct response was the Cinderella of the advertising world. Then came the computer and the credit card. Direct marketing exploded. You guys are coming into your own. Your opportunities are colossal. . . .
- "Ladies and gentlemen, how I envy you. Your timing is perfect. You have come into the direct-response business at the right time. You are onto a good thing. For forty years I have been a voice crying in the wilderness, trying to get my fellow advertising practitioners to take direct response seriously. Today my first love is coming into its own. You face a golden future."

David Ogilvy's speech was considered so important that he was the keynote speaker, and yet his entire speech was delivered on videotape. Goes to show that it's the content that counts. And the words just revealed to you are loaded with meaning. Heed them. I hope you realize the enormity of Mr. Ogilvy's truth: if you don't know about direct-response marketing, you don't know about marketing.

According to technical experts in the field, direct marketing is not a fancy term for mail order. It is an interactive system of marketing that uses one or more advertising media to effect a measurable response and/or transaction at any location. We have the magazine *Direct Marketing* to thank for this definition.

The same publication reminds us that marketing is all the activities involved in moving goods and services from seller to buyer. Then *Direct Marketing* makes a crucial distinction. It says that direct marketing has the same broad function as standard marketing but also requires the maintenance of a database. This database records the names of customers, prospects, and former customers. It serves as a vehicle for storing, then measuring, the results of direct-response advertising. It also provides a way to store, then measure, purchasing performance. And finally, it is a way to continue direct communication by mail and/or telephone.

Targeting prospects directly

Risk-wary advertisers are shying away from the mass market media, choosing instead to target their prospects directly. These advertisers might have invested 50 cents a person to reach a general audience in the past, but in the 1990s, they're putting up $1 for someone whose demographic and economic profile indicates they're predisposed to making a purchase. From Waldenbooks' Preferred Reader Program to Liz Claiborne's store-based computers to Hyatt Hotels' Gold Passport program to Prodigy's on-line buying to the myriad of frequent-flier programs, retailers and advertisers are hoarding information on exactly who their customers are, what they bought, and what they are likely to buy in the future.

Scads of information pulled from scanners, coupons, and even a check-cashing card pinpoint exactly where a person lives, how many people they live with, how much they learn, what they drive, read, and eat, even what kind of toilet paper they use. Every right-thinking guerrilla is building a database because so few markets are growing. Companies are desperate to hold on to their current customers.

Looking into the future, *Direct Marketing* reminds us to consider interactive TV as an up-and-coming selling device. This device, already in use in test markets and in the many home shopping shows now on TV, lets shoppers see items on TV, then order them immediately. Eventually, interactive TV will be a major vehicle employed by large users of direct marketing, but the Internet will be the biggest. Whatever you are offering, even if you never go on the Net, you should consider direct marketing.

Interactive TV

The value to you is potentially enormous: you can home in on your prospects with amazing accuracy. You can be selective in regard to age, race, sex, occupation, buying habits, money spent on past direct-mail purchases, education, special interests, family composition, religion, marital status, and geographic location ranging from state to county to town to ZIP code to block. Expensive? Yes. But it's the real cost to build lifetime customer loyalty.

The astonishing growth of on-line commerce proves beyond doubt that people will happily shop from their easy chairs. Video shopping networks are already with us, as you gleaned from the chapter on television. In 1996, video home shopping sales topped $3 billion. Literally hundreds of millions of people watch Home Shopping Network, Cable Value Network, QVC Network, and a host of others. And those numbers are growing, along with the mailing lists compiled by the home shopping networks.

Home shopping networks

If you have the soul of a guerrilla, you will have been compiling your own mailing list from the day your business began. The list should naturally start with your own customers. From there, expand it to include people who have recently moved into your area and those who have recently been married or divorced or become parents. Eliminate people who have moved away—a full 21 percent of Americans, nearly one in five, moved in 1996.

Your customer mailing list

You might engage in a simple direct mailing of postcards to

customers, informing them of a sale you'll have the next week. They will appreciate the early notification and might show their gratitude by purchasing from you. You might also engage in a full-scale direct mailing, using what is known as the "classic package," which consists of an outer envelope, a direct-mail letter, a brochure, an order form, a return envelope (maybe post-paid, maybe not), and other marketing materials.

The process begins

The process begins when you decide exactly what it is you wish to offer. How will you structure your offer? Then you must select your mailing list. If you don't have names already, you can purchase them from a list broker (look under "mailing lists" in your Yellow Pages). Buy a clean, fresh list. The broker (and the price) can give you clues on this. You *must* know all the costs involved: postage, printing, writing the mailing, artwork, paper, personalization (individualizing each letter by name and address, rather than saying "Dear friend" or the like), and repeat mailing costs. Your gross sales, minus these costs and your production, handling, and shipping costs, will constitute your profits. Be sure you make financial projections and know your break-even point. According to Lynn Peterson, a former direct-mail executive in the direct-response arm of a major advertising agency, the three biggest secrets that can be disclosed to a direct marketer are:

Secrets and errors

1. Pick your list with the utmost care.
2. Structure your offer in such a way that it is extremely difficult to refuse.
3. Plan your projections so that you earn a profit.

Ms. Peterson was also asked to describe the three biggest errors made by direct marketers. Never one to be inconsistent, she said they were:

1. Failure to pick the right list or lists.
2. Failure to structure an offer properly.
3. Failure to plan projections with enough foresight.

Guerrilla direct-mail gems

Along with her insights into making direct mail a moneymaker for your company, I offer these gems:

- Printing your most important sentences in a second color will increase sales enough to warrant the extra money. Be sure you choose a bright, pleasing color.

- Restate your main offer on your response form. The repetition will motivate the reader.
- Illustrations or photos incorporated in your letter will also improve your response rate. Just be sure that the graphic element adds to the offer or the promise.
- The worst months for direct mail are June, March, and May. The best are January, February, and October. January through March is best for business direct mail.
- Guerrillas juice up their offers—and response rates—with free gifts for ordering, a photo of the free gift on the envelope, or a free trial of their product or service. Something free always aids in marketing.

  Juicing up your offer

- If your mailing list hasn't been updated in two years, you've got to figure that 20 percent of it is probably decayed or out of date. Assume that 10 percent of addresses go bad every year.
- Always do a few intensive hours of research before you write even the first word of your letter. Ask some current customers what they like about doing business with you and begin your letter with those benefits.
- Find a new and appealing way to bundle your products or services. Offer special payment terms or a unique guarantee. One guerrilla offers a five-year guarantee in a field where others offer a one-year guarantee. It pays off handsomely in his response rates and doesn't come back to haunt him.
- Think short. Use short words, short sentences, and short paragraphs. James Michener, among others, said that the job of the writer is to use ordinary words to convey extraordinary ideas. People won't read a letter that is not easy to read. Life is tough enough without your letter contributing to the complexity.

  Ordinary words to convey extraordinary ideas

- Count the number of "you's" and "your's" in the letter. It should have at least twice as many "you's" and "your's" than "I's" and "me's." A ratio of four to one is even better.
- In your letter, write about your customers' dreams and problems. List the solutions you can provide to those problems and benefits that you offer.
- Don't mail your letter right after you write it. Let it sit a day or two. Then rewrite it. Make it shorter, simpler, more clear, and more compelling. Show it to customers. If they say, "Wonderful letter," thank them politely. If they say, "Where can I get one of these?" you know you've got a winner.

  Don't mail it right away

- Be brutally honest with yourself in determining whether you vividly state what it is you are offering and how a reader can accept your offer. Some guerrillas show their letter to a child because kids can often see the obvious before adults can.

- Send a test mailing and measure the results. A few dozen or a few hundred letters will give you a good feeling for the response you can expect. You'll get it—or not get it—in a hurry. If the mailing earned more profits for you than you would have earned if you spent your time and money in other ways, smile widely and accept my congratulations.

These are not the old days   In the old days, a direct-mail campaign meant a letter. Today it means a letter, two or three or five follow-up letters, perhaps a follow-up phone call or two, and finally, one more direct-mail letter. Many entrepreneurs engage in weekly or monthly direct mailings.

There are a multitude of decisions for you to make when you embark upon a mailing, so it is crucial that you know the right questions to ask. In addition to deciding about your mailing list, your offer, and your financial projections, you'll have to decide whether to mail first class or third class. Will you personalize your mailing? Will you have a toll-free number available for ordering? Which credit cards will you accept? Will you need to alter your pricing because you'll be selling direct? This seemingly simple subject becomes more complex as you learn more about it.

The envelope for a direct mailing merits a chapter of its own. Executives should not be sent envelopes with address labels. For maximum response, their names must be typed on the envelope. And for selling stationery, feminine products, or political candidates or causes, a handwritten envelope provides a wonderfully personal tone. Envelopes can be standard size (#10) or oversize (6 inches by 9 inches), manila, covered with gorgeous art, foil-lined, or window-type. They can have a return address, or, to pique curiosity, omit the return address.

One of the best devices you can use on an envelope is a "teaser"—a copyline that compels the recipient to open the envelope. Examples of successful teasers are: "FREE! A microcalculator for you!"; "Want to get your hands on $10,000 extra cash?"; and "The most astonishing offer of the year. Details inside."

As you can see, there are myriad ways to get a person to open an envelope. And that is the purpose of the envelope—to interest the recipient so that he or she will open it and read the contents.

Guerrillas know that people read the addressee name first, then they look at the teaser copy, and finally they read to see who sent it. Was it the Office of the President? The Awards Committee? The IRS? If it has the name of the person's bank, it usually gets opened. No teaser is needed. I doubt if the IRS needs one either.

When planning your envelope, determine the needs and wants of your target audience. Remember that you can use the *back* of the envelope; 75 percent of the people holding it will read it. Figure that you have three seconds to get them to open it. Say something *enticing* to *motivate* that action. Examples:

Getting them to open the envelope

- Free gift enclosed
- Money-saving offer inside
- Wealth-building secrets for the '90s
- Private information for your eyes only
- Did you know you can double your profits?
- What every business like yours needs to know . . .
- How to add new profits for only six cents a day
- See inside for exciting details on (virtually anything)
- Read what's in store for you—this week only!

The idea of teaser copy is not to be cute, clever, or fancy. The job is to be provocative, to entice the recipient into opening the envelope. Yes, it's only an envelope, but guerrillas know that it's often the key to a successful or a failed mailing.

The teaser

Naturally, people are quick to open priority and express mail. But it costs a lot to send—unless you're a guerrilla. Envelopes that *look* like priority and express envelopes and that are approved by the U.S. Postal Service are available to be sent first-class or bulk rate. To get a free sample, call Response Mail Express at 800-795-2773. If it's important to you to get your envelope opened, you'll call that number.

Some guerrillas call attention to their mailings by printing them on pieces of wood, jewelry boxes, CD cases, brown bags, greeting cards, pieces of plastic, or paint cans! Others include something bulky in their envelopes: an audiotape, a coin, a piece of gum, a magnetic business card, a balloon. However, when all is said, done, and mailed, you must get the order with the letter you've written when your envelope is opened.

What to say on the envelope

Include a P.S. in your letter. The P.S. is read with regularity (more often than is body copy). Many direct mailings now include

Always end with a P.S.

what are known as lift letters—little notes that might say some-thing like, "Read this only if you have decided not to respond to this offer." Inside is one more attempt to make the sale, probably a handwritten message called a "buck slip," signed by the company president.

There are seven reasons to add a P.S.:

1. *Motivate the prospect to take action.* Do all you can to over-come procrastination and get the person to order this very moment.
2. *Reinforce your offer.* Make the same offer you made in your letter, but do it more cogently and urgently. If you have a solid offer, this is the safest use of a P.S.
3. *Emphasize or introduce a premium or bonus.* This might get folks off the fence and right onto your customer list. People love freebies.
4. *Emphasize the price or terms of your offer.* If your price or payment plans are the heart of your offer, dramatize it in your P.S.
5. *Introduce a surprise benefit.* This might be just the ticket to move people from apathy to enthusiasm. It's also a place to restate the primary benefit you offer and why it's so darned important.
6. *Stress the tax deductibility of the purchase.* Everybody loves a good deduction, so if your product or service cost is honestly deductible, say it in the P.S.
7. *Highlight your guarantee.* Don't take it for granted, but in-stead, present it with excitement and enthusiasm.

Guarantee what you sell   Guarantee what you are selling, because you are not as "in touch" with customers as you would be with a store-sold product or service, and they will want the reassurance of a guarantee. You've got to do all you can to remove any possible perception of risk.

The most effective direct-mail efforts allow people to buy with credit cards. "Bill me" also works well as a rule. An element of urgency, such as "offer expires in one week," increases the re-sponse even more. Guerrillas always put a time limit on their direct-mail offers.

Whatever you do, make your offer clear, repeat it several times, keep your message as short as possible, and ask for the order.

Don't pussyfoot around. Ask people to do exactly what you wish them to do. Then ask them again.

I also recommend toll-free phone numbers, which can triple the response rate or even better. Every day, three-quarters of a million Americans order $225 *million* worth of merchandise by phone!

Let them order by phone

When you create a direct-mail ad with a coupon, make the coupon a miniature version of your ad, complete with headline, benefit, and offer. In short, make it a brief summary of the advertisement. Some direct-mail pros write their coupons or response devices before they write their ads. This is called "working backward," and guerrillas see the wisdom in it. Working backward helps you immensely when you write the letter or brochure because it helps you remember what you want the recipient to do.

If you're up and running with direct mail, you know the importance of delivering orders within one week of receiving the order (and less time than that for phone, fax, and on-line orders). Answer all customer inquiries within one week (again, faster if they used a speedy technology). Guerrillas never offer merchandise that isn't in stock and on-hand for instant delivery. They want profits, not enemies. And they also have on hand the information that customers need. Every order is treated like a rush order. Most guerrillas are able to handle calls without putting people on hold. I recently received a postcard informing me of a special rate if I resubscribed to a magazine. I called the 800 number to sign up and was put on hold. I tossed the postcard and hung up the phone.

Don't let them order what you can't ship now

Where should your mail-order ad appear in a publication? The best place, although relatively expensive, is the back page of a newspaper or magazine—where response can be as much as 150 percent greater than from the same ad inside the publication.

When you consider direct marketing, always consider including an insert with your bill. People certainly open bills, so that means they'll probably see your insert. And you'll get a free ride because the bill is paying the postage for the insert. Another type of insert is the freestanding type that often appears in newspapers or magazines. These are known to be *effective*. Check with your newspaper or magazine rep to find out about their services with regard to inserts.

Including an insert

What's even more effective than a direct mail letter? A direct-mail postcard—because people don't get to make the decision as to whether or not to open the envelope and because you can make

More effective than a direct-mail letter

the offer so concise that they don't get to make the decision as to whether or not to read the copy. Other reasons that guerrillas like postcard mailings is because they're nearly one-third lower in cost than letter mailings and because their computers can churn them out in a manner some people find akin to printing money. They're great for saying thank you, reminding customers of their next appointment, and announcing a killer discount, new product, or valuable service. Consider using oversized (six-inch-by-nine-inch) postcards as well as high-impact full-color postcards. They should convey your identity and your attitude.

Freeman Gosden, Jr., president of Smith-Hennings-Gosden in Los Angeles, has come up with a direct-mail marketer's checklist. He offers these points for consideration:

Points that guerrillas consider

- Look at the mail as your reader will.
- Keep your primary objective foremost in your mind.
- Does the number-one benefit hit you between the eyes?
- Does the number-two benefit follow close behind?
- Does the message of the mailing package flow?
- Does the outside envelope encourage you to open it—now?
- Is the letter the first thing you see upon opening?
- Does the letter discuss the reader's needs, product benefits, features, endorsements, and ways to respond?
- Do graphics support the copy?
- Does the reply card tell the whole offer?
- Is there a reason to act now?
- Is it easy to reply?
- Would you respond?

Twenty tips that can help you

Dare I add more tips to help you succeed? Take heed of these twenty pointers and see the difference in your response rate:

1. Decide exactly to whom you should be mailing. Do this first and do it right because if you do it wrong, nothing else will go as you wish.
2. Decide which specific action you want your recipient to take.
3. Create an outer envelope that will get opened.
4. Come up with an offer your prospects can't possibly ignore.
5. Write a first line and a P.S. that compel your prospect to read your letter.
6. Describe your offer in the most enticing terms possible.

7. Explain the results your offer will deliver, focusing on the main benefit.
8. Explain why your offer makes so much sense to your prospect.
9. Give your prospect other key benefits of accepting your offer.
10. Show that you know who your prospect is.
11. Describe the key features of what you are offering.
12. Make it irresistible to take action right now.
13. Tell your prospects the exact steps to take.
14. Set measurable goals for yourself.
15. Make a plan for your follow-up—either by mail or by phone.
16. Track your results precisely.
17. Improve your results by increasing what's working and eliminating what's not.
18. Consider bolstering your mailing with E-mailing, faxing, or with overnight mail.
19. Identify new markets that you can tap.
20. Increase your sales and profits by improving all your copy.

I'm certainly not suggesting that you give your prospects your home phone number. I do know a guerrilla who includes hers on her business cards—and she encloses a card in every piece of mail she sends. She sends a personal letter to 25 customers each week and a warm and friendly form letter to 1,500 customers each month.

Catalogs are a different ballgame—part of direct mail, to be **Catalogs**
sure, but a very different part. As your business grows, you may want to send a catalog to spur your direct marketing. When you do decide to market with a catalog, be absolutely certain that your catalog has the right positioning, the right merchandise selection, the right kind of merchandise, the right graphics, the right use of color, the right size (thirty-two pages is considered optimum), the right headlines, the right subheads, the right copy, the right sales stimulators, and the right order forms. Formulate your projections correctly. Other than this, direct marketing with catalogs is a piece of cake.

In 1996, the nation's 10,000 catalogs reaped sales of $74.6 billion, a 7 percent gain over 1995 but less than the double-digit gains of the early 1990s. The slackening in rapid growth was due to the high cost of paper and postage, neither of which is expected to drop shortly. Be sure you factor in all the numbers when you decide to publish and distribute a catalog.

If you run a mail-order business, your catalog will be the heart of your business—it will be a mighty contributor to your bottom line. The success of your mail-order catalog will depend on customers with which you've already had one or more satisfactory transactions. Those customers, when they receive your catalog, will trust you and will have confidence in your offerings.

Be prepared to invest

Be prepared to invest in your catalog. A friend of mine who ran a successful mail-order company ($2 million in sales, with $500,000 in marketing expenses) spent 50 percent of his marketing money on direct mail, 30 percent on catalogs, and 20 percent on mail-order ads. Did he believe in catalogs? You bet! He changed his marketing budget so as to spend 15 percent of his marketing money on mail-order ads, 20 percent on direct mail, and 65 percent on catalogs. He learned that his catalogs were the most important selling tools he had. In fact, he used to say he was in the catalog business rather than the mail-order business. My friend became a millionaire in the business, so take heed.

How to think about your catalog

Think of your catalog as a specialized form of direct mail. It's a store on paper—a complete presentation of your merchandise. The items within your catalog should reflect the interests of your audience and should be similar in nature.

To print a catalog you should have about 25,000 customers. That's a lot. But if you want to earn a whale of a lot of money, you'll have to start developing a customer list that long. The big money—the truly large sums—will come to you when you send those customers your catalog. What if you don't have 25,000 customers? Create an inexpensive catalog, perhaps a mini-catalog of eight pages with black and white photos.

Once designed, a catalog can be printed for 5,000 customers or 5 million customers. However, the amount of work required to prepare the catalog for the printer makes it cost-ineffective unless you print 25,000 copies. It's only a rule of thumb, but it's a good one.

Catalog costs

If your catalog describes approximately 100 items, the cost of your art direction, copywriting, photography, type, graphic design, and production will run about $8,000. Your printer will charge about $2,000 as a make-ready (preparation for print) fee. The cost of the printing (in black and white plus one color) for an 8 × 11 format on regular paper, sixteen pages, will run about 20 cents per catalog. Postage will run another 20 cents. So the 25,000 catalogs will cost about $20,000 by the time they're in the mail—

about 80 cents each. Assuming you have a gross profit margin of 55 percent, you must sell at least $1.25 of merchandise per catalog mailed. You must sell $31,250 worth of goods just to break even. That's not easy. But if it's your first catalog, it's fine to break even. It builds business. The next year, when you have 50,000 customers, your catalog work will mostly have been accomplished. You can pick up most artwork and copy from the first catalog, and your in-the-mail costs will be substantially reduced. You should make an impressive profit on your catalog the second year, more the third year, and still more each succeeding year. As with all kinds of guerrilla marketing, you must be patient. Consider your expenditures as an investment, and remain committed to your catalog marketing program.

What if you want to supplement your own list of customers? If you purchase outside lists, even exceptional ones, don't figure on a return that is more than 85 percent of that realized from your own list. Test other lists *carefully* before plunging in. And whatever you do, mail your catalog before Christmas. People want to buy at that time, and you've blown an important opportunity if you don't mail then. Everybody mails their catalogs at that time, but they do so because people are *buying* before the holidays. The infamous bank robber Willie Sutton said, when asked why he robbed banks, "Because that's where the money is." Holiday time is *when* the money is.

Supplementing your mailing list

A few more pointers about catalogs. Work with your printer to determine the optimum number of pages, the paper stock, the format, and the print run. Naturally, your printer must be experienced in catalog production. Find one that is. Also, don't produce full-color catalogs until you can mail 200,000 or more of them. Use the front and back covers, along with your order form, to sell merchandise. They are very effective. Stay away from group-item shots—display your merchandise item by item. Don't try to be artistic; instead, be clear. If you hire models, your costs will increase. If you sell clothing, it's almost impossible to avoid using models, but avoid it if you can. Also, it's not a good idea to mix photos with illustrations. Choose between the two and stay with your choice.

Catalog pointers for guerrillas

Your copy should be simple, straightforward, and concise. Provide the *facts* and the *benefits*. Describe the features. It's better to answer any questions that may come rather than to be too brief. If you can write the copy yourself, do so.

Bind in an order form

By all means, bind an order form into your catalog. And offer some merchandise on that order form. Bribe people to order more than they ordinarily would. For instance, tell them that if they order $25 or more in merchandise, they will receive a free gift, and if they order $50 or more, they will receive a better free gift. And promise them a doozie of a gift if they order $100 or more. Try it. People love free gifts. Don't you? On your order form, also include a brief letter to your customers. Make it warm, personal, and not too long. Be sure to include your toll-free number on every single page of your catalog.

The Sharper Image is very sharp

Richard Thalheimer of the Sharper Image does a wonderful job, not only with his warm, personal letter, but also with the copy and graphics in his catalog. Happily, it gets better ever year, so Richard is getting smarter or delegating more wisely. Fortune's Almanac is beautifully written, as are others—L. L. Bean, the J. Peterman Company, Hammacher Schlemmer, and Seventh Generation come to mind.

Guerrillas need to establish a successful mail-order marketing plan, and it's most important to *give people what they want*.

What do people like about catalogs?

What people like about catalogs

1. 36 percent say *convenience is* what they like most.
2. 19 percent give the nod to *more variety*.
3. 17 percent like *low prices* (hard to find in my Tiffany catalog, and it's quite a successful one; has been for a long time).
4. 6 percent say they go for the high quality offered.
5. 22 percent list the inevitable "other" or list nothing.

After the 78 percent who have good things to say about catalogs finish reading or ordering from them, what do they do with them? Forty-two percent save them; 41 percent toss them; 10 percent pass them on; 7 percent say "it depends."

If you're thinking of mailing a catalog, follow these guerrilla guidelines:

Guerrilla guidelines

- Set specific objectives on what the catalog should do for your business.
- Define your audience so that you know who will receive your catalog; that helps in creating and producing it.
- Preplan all the elements of your catalog before going into production: products, prices, fulfillment, and more.

- Make all the hard decisions up front: which products to include, which to exclude, how production will be handled.
- If possible, group your offerings into clearly defined groups so that the catalog is not a hodgepodge.
- Make a rough outline of the contents of your catalog, including everything you wish to have in it—everything.
- Determine the exact format you want: size, typeface, color or black and white, paper stock, binding.
- Make a layout that is organized, logical, and pleasing to the eye of your target audience. Think of their eyes only.
- Plan, write, and perfect the copy. Then set up a timetable and stick with it.

As you can tell, the business of producing and mailing catalogs is complex. But after the first year, it is exceptionally profitable—if you do it right. If you think you might ever offer a catalog, start putting your name on as many catalog mailing lists as possible. Then you can expect your mailbox to be filled with informative examples every day but Sunday. Mine is.

Exceptional profits if you do it right

Keep in mind that the number of Americans ordering at least one thing from a catalog is fast approaching 97 percent, and the percentage continues to grow. There must be a reason.

American catalog companies are now being counseled that if their catalogs draw 1 or 2 percent in the United States, they can draw between 10 and 20 percent in new markets where competing catalogs aren't around and catalog glut is no problem. If this helps you think more globally or give more serious consideration to putting a catalog up on the Internet, you're thinking like a guerrilla.

Going global with a catalog

Even if it isn't practical for you to use catalogs, I hope you will try direct mail if it is at all feasible for your business. If you do, you will get a head start by using the major marketing method of the future.

Try a small number of mailings first. Test always. Learn from each test. In truth, if you break even while testing, you are doing fine. The goal is to come up with a formula that can be repeated and expanded. If you ever obtain a publicity story about your business, consider enclosing reprints of it in a mailing.

In my own experience as an entrepreneur and as a direct-response specialist, I have found that envelopes with teaser lines get a better response than those without. I have found that short letters work better than long letters, that long brochures work better than short brochures, that postcards often make superb mailers all by themselves. I have learned that it is worth the time to check out many lists before selecting one, and that one's own customer list is a gold mine when it comes to direct mail. I know that a single mailing isn't nearly as effective as a mailing with one, two, or more follow-ups, and that a mailing with a phone follow-up is frequently best of all.

A guerrilla will either realize that direct marketing is not the way for his or her business to proceed, or will use direct marketing with intelligence, reading books about it, talking with direct-marketing pros, and making it his or her most cost-effective marketing method. Strange as it may seem, the majority of people like to receive mailings from businesses; so don't feel self-conscious, and put the U.S. Postal Service to work for you.

If you've got this feeling that all direct marketing is going to be changed by the Internet, you're thinking the right way. In fact, to alert you to more valuable information about direct mail, I call your attention to Direct Mail World on the Internet at www.dmworld.com and to Direct Mail News at dmnews.com. I rest my case.

IV
Nonmedia Marketing

N ow that you know you can market your products and services
through mini-media and maxi-media, you should also know
that you can succeed without using media at all. You can invite **No media**
groups to your place of business to hear speakers. You can put on **at all**
programs for these groups if they won't come to you. You can stage
exhibits at fairs. You can display your offerings in model homes or
auto showrooms or restaurants or other nonmedia places where
groups of people will see them. You can participate in your local
Welcome Wagon, which helps newcomers to the community and
enlightens them as to products and services available. You can talk
with fellow merchants and entrepreneurs and arrange to exchange
information, assistance, and ideas with them when possible. You
can hold sales training sessions for your own people. You can ask
the manufacturers that supply you for their aid in marketing. You
can develop incentive plans to spur your people to greater heights.
You can hold open houses and parties. You can create dazzling
window displays.

Coming up are even more ways that successful entrepreneurs
can promote their businesses without using the media—at least
not directly. Some of these methods ought to become part of your
marketing plan if you are serious about success. They are hard to
develop. They require painstaking detail work. They are far more
complex than they appear. But they are worth your time and
effort, and for many a guerrilla they pay off handsomely.

Is it possible to succeed using only nonmedia marketing? Yes.
But it is easier to succeed with a combination of mini-media, **Succeed with a**
maxi-media, and nonmedia marketing. There are far more non- **combination**
media marketing opportunities available to you than there are
media opportunities. *Use as many as you can use properly.*

The way you answer the phone has a powerful influence over
how people will feel about your company. Either an untrained,

**The way
you answer
the phone**

unfriendly voice will turn off a potential or, worse yet, a current customer—or a warm, welcoming voice will make the caller want to do business with a company such as yours. Is this media? No. Is this marketing? It is. So are the neatness of your premises, the smiles prospects receive upon entering, the respect for their time displayed when they place an order or make a request. If you know the name of your customer and use it, that's personalized marketing on a face-to-face basis. Guerrillas know the importance of eye contact in nonmedia marketing such as trade shows and of greeting people who visit their business.

**A prime example
of nonmedia
marketing**

Let me give you a prime example of nonmedia marketing that is so unusual it doesn't fit into any chapter. Although it's unique, it is the spirit of common sense. This guerrilla marketing technique helps you obtain the names of prime prospects, a noble endeavor. To do it, guerrillas invest in high school students on bicycles. The roofing guerrilla pays a student $1 for the address of each home in the community that needs a new roof. The gardening guerrilla pays $1 for the address of each home that could do with some quality gardening. The paving guerrilla pays for the address of each home that needs work on its driveway.

These guerrillas know that they will get only about thirty to fifty new addresses a month, not a lot. But at each address is at least one human being who needs a new roof or a manicured garden or a smooth driveway. And that person is probably soothed by the fact that you're a local business. Guerrillas get the names of these people from the phone directory, then write to them in a highly personalized way, pointing out the problem and offering a solution. The tactic of securing these names of honest-to-goodness prospects involves no media. Then guerrillas use the mini-medium of a personal letter to make everything happen (as is so often the case). I predict that you will get a lot of mileage from the nonmedia weapons you employ—in the form of PR, reprints of PR, and a warm, cozy relationship with your entire community, if not the entire planet.

**Linear growth is
not effective
enough**

Nonmedia marketing incorporates what may be the single most important concept in guerrilla marketing—the idea of *geometric growth*. Most companies attempt to grow in a linear fashion—that is, by adding new customers all the time. That's a nice thing to do, but it's pretty expensive. Linear growth is not nearly cost-effective enough for guerrillas.

Sure, they attempt to add new customers on a constant basis, growing linearly as they do. They also generate business by an intense devotion to *follow-up*, realizing that 68 percent of business lost in America is lost due to lack of follow-up. They know it costs only one sixth as much to sell something to an existing customer as to sell the same thing to a new person, and so they follow up conscientiously and optimistically. This follow-up helps them grow more than linearly.

In addition, they *raise the size of their transactions*. If a person decides to buy one of what they sell, the guerrillas make it attractive to buy three instead of one, or perhaps one year's worth. This increases their profits once again because the cost of marketing those extra purchases is close to nil. Finally, guerrillas are very serious about obtaining *customer referrals*. They know darned well that their greatest source of new customers is old customers and all they have to do is ask. They let current customers know how important referrals are to their business, usually rewarding customers for names that end up on their customer list. They write two letters each year to current customers, asking for the names of people who might benefit from being added to their customer list. Since they only ask for three, four, or five names and enclose a postpaid envelope, and because they take such good care of customers, the names of potential buyers are given generously. I know of one chiropractor who asks this question whenever he receives a call for an appointment: "Is this appointment for you or for your whole family?"

Increase the size of their transactions

There are many ways of obtaining referral names. Guerrillas employ several of these methods at the same time. By growing due to adding new customers, following up with existing customers, enlarging the size of each transaction, and mining current customers for referral names, these guerrillas grow geometrically. It's an inexpensive way to succeed with marketing—and it does succeed, almost every time.

In fact, the primary difference between a guerrilla and a nonguerrilla is that the nonguerrilla thinks marketing is over once the sale has been made. But the guerrilla knows that after the sale has been completed, that's when the real marketing begins. The idea is to have long-term relationships with that customer and the people that customer knows. That won't happen if you quit marketing once you've made the sale.

Guerrillas and nonguerrillas

Because I know that most business lost in America is lost not due to poor quality or poor service, but because customers are totally ignored after the sale, I want to put the importance of geometric growth into numerical terms so that it will hit home deeper with you.

Suppose you earn a $100 profit every time you make a sale. That's great. If you're not a guerrilla, you pocket the $100 and that customer is history, a person you'll never see again. So each customer represents $100 in profits to you.

If you're a guerrilla, you still earn the $100, but you send a thank-you note to the customer, expressing gratitude for the business, within forty-eight hours. When's the last time you received a thank-you note from a business within forty-eight hours? Maybe once (but probably never), and that's why your customer will remember you. Within thirty days, you send another note to the customer, this time asking if he or she has any questions and is completely satisfied. Notice that you're not trying to make a sale. Your customer will notice that, too, and as a result, you'll be on your way to making a friend—which is a lot better than a customer.

Within ninety days, you send the customer a mailer or make a phone call, informing him of a product or service available at a discount, something that may relate to his previous purchase. Naturally, you add the customer's name to your newsletter subscriber list, and within six months you send a customer questionnaire, asking lots of questions so that you can become the nation's leading expert on your own customers. Because you take good care of customers, your questionnaire will probably be completed, providing you with invaluable information. Within nine months of that first sale, the customer receives another notice of a product or service that's new or discounted—something that you offer or perhaps an offering from one of your fusion marketing partners. Within ten months, the customer receives a letter asking for the names and addresses of three people who might appreciate being added to your mailing list. And within a year, the customer gets an anniversary card, commemorating the one-year anniversary of their being your customer.

As a result of all this warm, inexpensive follow-up, instead of making one purchase from you during the year, the customer makes three purchases. In addition to giving you the names of potential customers that you request, your customer refers your business to at least four people during the course of a year. And instead of a one-time transaction, your relationship with your customer—

and the referral customers—lasts around twenty years. That one customer is worth about $400,000 in profits to you—*if you understand the power of follow-up*. That same person is worth $100 in profits if you don't. That's a $399,900 difference—one that guerrillas do not pass up.

The cost of this nonmedia method of marketing—geometric growth through follow-up, larger sales, and referral business—is negligible compared with maxi-media mass marketing. But the necessity is dire if you're to be a guerrilla bound for success. When people think of marketing, they generally think maxi-media marketing and sometimes mini-media marketing. One of my purposes on this planet is to get you to think of nonmedia marketing, and then to practice it with devotion.

I know I don't have to say this because you know it deep in your heart, but I'll say it anyhow because it's so important: two nonmedia marketing weapons rank up there just as high as follow-up. They are:

1. *Service*. Defined as "anything the customer wants it to be."
2. *Attention to details*. This may seem insignificant to you, but it is crucial to customers and prospects.

Nonmedia marketing also includes your own attitudes. Your willingness to abide by guerrilla marketing principles indicates the right spirit of *competitiveness*. Your belief in the benefits of your product or service is manifested in the *enthusiasm* that spreads from you to your employees to your customers. These attitudes are nonmedia marketing in that they influence people, but don't cost you a cent for media. Combine them with media and with nonmedia, and get ready to soar.

22

Advertising Specialties and Samples: If You've Got It, Flaunt It

Advertising specialties are items on which the imprinted name (and sometimes the address, phone number, Web site, and theme line) of the advertiser appears. Examples of advertising specialties are ballpoint pens, scratch pads, mousepads, briefcases, calendars, key chains, paper-clip holders, caps, T-shirts, pins, screen-savers, playing cards, shopping bags, belt buckles, decals, banners, lighters, coffee mugs, license-plate frames, fanny packs, and lots more.

Consider these specialties to be the equivalent of billboards. That means they are great for reminder advertising. They are usually terrible as your only marketing medium. They do, however, put your name in front of your prospective customers. And your prospects don't even have to leave home or their office to see them. As part of a marketing mix, that's a very good thing. As you well know by now, familiarity is one of the keys to success. And there is no question that ad specialties breed increased awareness.

Yet that's just the tip of the advertising specialty iceberg. Those free gifts—and that's the whole idea—to give them away gratis—can be used to leverage many a sale, and our nation abounds with billionaires who realized the power of something free. As a Fuller Brush man while in college, I was amazed at how free samples worked like magic as door openers. Procter & Gamble is famed for its generosity with free samples.

Everyone loves free gifts Advertising specialties make your prospects and customers feel good about you, especially if the specialty items are valuable. I remember that a businessman buddy of mine was ecstatic upon receiving a digital clock–pen. He spoke with reverence of the supplier who gave it to him, and he continues to show his loyalty to the firm. A specialty item with a high perceived value does breed a sense of unconscious obligation, to be sure. If you can purchase a breakthrough type of inexpensive product for your deserv-

ing prospects *and customers,* by all means give it serious consideration. There are no particular industries or businesses that benefit
more than others by this marketing medium. But if, for example,
you come across a unique and advanced measuring device, and
your prime prospects are contractors and carpenters, you'd be well
advised to give it a shot. Be proud to put your name on such a gift.
Guerrillas never put their names on anything shoddy, anything
that will break easily, anything that doesn't make them proud to
give it away.

Be proud to use sampling, too, if you sincerely believe that by
providing exposure to your product or service you will win loyal
customers. Choose sampling over advertising specialties every
time, if it comes to making a choice. Both involve giving something away. Both win friends and create favorable associations. But
sampling accomplishes these things by means of freebies that are
more pertinent than advertising-specialty items, valuable as they
may be.

Give away a sample

I strongly suggest that you examine the use of ad specialties if
they seem to lend themselves to your type of business. If, for
example, you are a mobile auto mechanic, it's a dandy idea to give
your customers and prospects key chains (for their car keys) with
your name and number on them. On the other hand, if you are a
computer consultant, handing out key chains makes no sense
whatsoever. But handing out small guides to software makes a lot
of sense. So do mousepads and screen-savers.

You can gain a wealth of information from the following tactic. Consider your line of merchandise or services very carefully,
then look in the Yellow Pages under "Advertising Specialties" and
pick out the best ad—judging it by the amount of information it
gives and its credibility. Call the rep listed in that ad and ask him
or her to pay you a visit. While still on the phone, tell the rep who
is your target audience and ask the rep to recommend specialties
that have worked for others in your line. Ask also about new ad
specialty items that haven't yet been tried, especially high-tech
products that come from Asian manufacturers. Each year, a plethora of new items come onto the market, and a good rep regularly
alerts his clients to the new ones. When the rep pays you a visit,
take the time to look through his or her pleasantly cumbersome
catalog of available specialties, and perhaps you'll get ten ideas
that hadn't occurred to the rep.

Selecting the best ad specialties

You might ask the rep to tell you about upcoming specialties, gift ideas, and specialties that you might recommend to your clients. You might decide that none of the specialties are for you. But at least you'll know a lot more about what is available, what certain specialties cost, and what use other companies have made of this method of nonmedia marketing. Perhaps you won't want to use a specialty now but will want to use one sometime in the future.

Do people really pay much attention to the stuff that is given away as advertising specialties? Depends upon the stuff. Let's take calendars, since they were among the first of the freebies. An impressive 72 percent of people look at a calendar five or more times a day. That adds up to 1,800 calendar consultations per year. But guerrillas know that 1,800 is a tiny number compared the number of advertising impressions obtained by the 40 percent of people who glance at their calendar *ten times a day.*

Marketing daily with calendars

I must admit to a prejudice toward calendars as an advertising specialty. I'm not talking about ordinary calendars. I'm referring to gorgeous calendars that most people will happily hang in their homes or offices, then look at almost every day. I have such calendars in my own home, and I have patronized the companies that gave them away. (I'm not really sure whether my business was instigated by the calendars; probably not, but one can't be too sure of one's unconscious thought processes.) And I have recommended the use of handsome calendars to my clients. They have used them and continued to use them.

One of the reasons I like calendars as ad specialties is that people tend to look at them a lot, as you now know. One of the reasons I do not like, say, playing cards, is that people tend not to look at them a lot, and when they do, they look at the side without your name and logo.

If you do decide you want to distribute calendars, you've got to make that decision in the summer, at the very latest, so that the right calendars with the right inscriptions can be in your hands at the right time—probably in early November.

Put your name on their scratch pad

You might also consider scratch pads. Imprinted scratch pads have become very effective lead-generating gimmicks for salespeople, I'm told. What you do is pay a printer to stick a photo, your name, address, phone number, and theme line on a sheet of paper, then print up a bunch of sheets that are made into scratch pads—or Post-its—each sheet of the pad an ad for you. Next, distribute those pads—free, naturally—to your prospects. Either hand them out or mail them. People tend to keep such pads by their phones or on their desks. They use them to write notes to themselves. Every time they look at one of the scraps of paper, they see the name of your offering. Of course even the hottest offer will not motivate them to pick up the phone and order whatever you are selling unless they need it. But when they do need what you have to offer, chances are your name will come to mind first. And that's a big help to any guerrilla.

As with other types of marketing, the key here is repetition. Because it takes times to become known in a community, it's important to keep circulating new scratch pads.

The key is repetition

I know of a real estate salesman in southern California who estimates that he earns between $15,000 and $20,000 in commissions per year from listings generated by his scratch pads. He sounds like a real guerrilla in that he obviously tracks his sales leads like crazy, and then even translates them into dollar figures.

There are no hard and fast rules as to who should use ad specialties, when they should be used, or how they can be used best. But your ad specialty rep probably has many tips for you. You should consider advertising specialties, like calendars and rulers, ballpoint pens, or scratch pads.

The cost of an individual advertising specialty is tiny. But the volume in which you must order each specialty is not tiny. I once gave away felt-tip pens for a business I was running. The cost of each pen was less than a dollar. But I had to order 300 pens before the manufacturers would put my name on them. At the time $300 sounded like a lot.

A client of mine who is very successful at fundraising for public schools gives away pens with his name, company name, and phone number on them. His costs are even lower than mine were, because he orders so many pens. His pens, by the way, are neither felt-tip nor ball-point. Because he's a real guerrilla, he gives away a new type of pen. People perceive it to be a breakthrough product, and they associate him with innovation.

His company achieved tremendous profitability by using advertising specialties as a key ingredient in its marketing mix. Prospects were sent a letter or postcard with a color picture of a free gift such as a microcalculator or a quartz desk clock—both available for under $2. The teaser said "A free gift for you!" and the recipient, being of the human race, would open the envelope and learn that merely by requesting more information, the gift would be given without obligation. From this point on, the company gave

Free gifts as door openers

the gift, paid a personal call, telemarketed, sent another letter, made a phone call or two or three, and prospered to a point where it was one of the hundred fastest-growing companies in America. All because of advertising specialties? Of course not. But they did a bang-up job of getting that door open, never an easy task.

In regard to the copy on your ad specialty, don't make the mistake of leaving it off entirely. I suggest that you include your name, address, phone number, Web site, theme line, and as much copy as will tastefully fit on the item. Not much will fit on a key chain or a pen. A bit more will fit on a calendar. But use restraint and remember that people won't hang a calendar if it looks like an ad. Nonetheless, it is possible to convey more information than the usual name and address. A guerrilla markets at every opportunity. Still, I caution you to use good taste more than hard sell.

A final hint: talk to people who give away ad specialties themselves. Ask if they consider them effective. Ask them to recommend a good rep. Ask about cost-effectiveness and how long they've been using ad specialties.

I'm knocked out at each year's crop of new advertising specialties. Several are exciting and economical inventions. Clock-pens, solar calculators, solar wristwatches, Lucite-framed quartz desk clocks for a buck—don't let any winners pass you by. If there is any potential reason for you to invest in this low-cost marketing method, see to it that you find out about the new specialties each year. They can't help you all by themselves—but they won't hurt you either, unless they break on day one.

If you're considering using advertising specialties as a guerrilla marketing tool, you should have an idea of what your target market might want in the way of a free gift. *Business and Incentive Strategies* magazine reported on a survey conducted to see what sorts of incentive items people most like to receive from their employers for special performance. Say what you will about **The quality of** stereotypes, but when merchandise incentives were offered, men **your offering** preferred electrical gadgets while women chose clothing. For merchandise incentives worth over $1,000, men went for big-screen TVs while women selected a new wardrobe. In travel incentives, women's top choices for vacation activities were relaxation, sightseeing, and culture. Men opted for relaxation, sports/outdoor activity, and sightseeing. For an overseas travel destination, both men and women picked Australia and New Zealand as their top choice. For domestic trips, women wanted to visit the

Pacific Northwest while men were attracted to the links and beaches of the Southwest. The favorite incentive for both men and women (as if you didn't know) was money—preferred by 51 percent of the men and 56 percent of the women. One thing about crisp, green American cash: you don't have to question its quality.

The more thought you give to your advertising specialty, the better and more valuable it can prove to you. As you probably know, at trade shows, you are given much information and quite a few freebies in bags supplied by the exhibitors. Most of these are placed in the "official" bag of the trade show, for which tabs run as high as $50,000. So some companies, such as Iomega Corporation, display at trade shows and give away bigger, better bags into which all of the other trade show bags are placed. For a fraction of the cost of the "official" bag, one company makes the most of a platinum opportunity to talk to prospects who are in a buying mood.

If you're giving out free samples, the quality of your offering is as or more important than with a free gift. Sampling can help you all by itself if the quality's there. And it can kill you if your product or service is at all shoddy. Guerrilla marketing can hasten the failure of your business by letting more people know faster about the faults of your offering.

Insights into incentives

I consider sampling to be the most effective marketing method. Of course I am assuming that you have an excellent product or service. If your product is wonderful, sampling will help it take off in a hurry. You've got to have the ability to service the people you sell, and you've got to offer true quality. But if you do, sampling works wonders. It sure has influenced the computer software world. And the computer browser market.

The most effective marketing method

One of my marketing idols, Procter & Gamble, spends a fortune on sampling. So do other large, successful, sophisticated marketing concerns. But that does not rule out guerrillas. In fact, before this chapter ends, you'll know of six instances where sampling helped businesspeople realize healthy profits.

You'll have to examine your offering to see if it lends itself to sampling. Most offerings can be sampled. The first one that comes to mind is a car. You certainly won't want to give away a sample car. But almost all auto dealers offer free test rides. That's a sample. And it succeeds. Usually, and especially when you are offering a service, your sampling must be offered to one person at a time.

A test drive is a sample

But if you are offering a product, perhaps you can give away several of your items as free samples.

At my current address, I've received in my mailbox free samples of toothpaste, detergent, shampoo, cigarettes, and chewing gum. I continue to use the toothpaste. And we buy the new detergent. I doubt if any other marketing method would have persuaded me to switch brands so quickly. In time, more sampling will probably woo me from the brands I currently use. Like most Americans, I'm a fickle consumer, though I drove my Buick GS-400 convertible 338,000 miles with the same engine and transmission. (When it had 300,000 miles on it, I took a photo of it, with its fancy new gold paint job, and sent it to Buick, along with a letter thanking them for making such a grand car; a month later I received a two-line form letter signed by a machine. I'm ashamed of such an unguerrilla-like response from the city of my birth.)

Naturally, it costs a bundle to give away free samples. But if you can look upon the cost as a conservative investment, you might be tempted to engage in sampling rather than radio advertising. It's worth thinking about. I cannot think of a more guerrilla-spirited marketing method. It is the essence of honesty, since it

That's the spirit! forces you to offer quality, and people will appreciate you for it. What's more, your competition probably doesn't do it. Not for the lazy or unimaginative, it is an optimum marketing vehicle for guerrillas.

Examples of samples Now here are the six examples I promised you on how sampling works: in the early days of waterbeds, people considered the beds to be a fad, a mere offshoot of the counterculture. To overcome sales resistance to the new product, a retailer offered a free thirty-night sleeping trial: he would deliver and install the beds, then make a phone call thirty days later to see if his prospects wanted him to pick up the beds or were willing to pay for them. Ninety-three percent of the people were willing to pay for the beds. Sampling paid off.

Another entrepreneur was launching a newsletter. He advertised in magazines. He engaged in direct mail. Both got mediocre results. Then he mailed free sample copies to prospects. Instant success. Sampling came through. Incidentally, it cost him a total of $500 to try the sampling; he realized $7,000 in profits from the attempt.

A third guerrilla was marketing a large-screen television set of his own design. Very few people took the time to visit the showroom in which it was displayed. So he took out ads offering free home trials. Soon he had to discontinue the ads because the response was so great. And even better than the response to his trial offer was the fact that 90 percent of the respondents purchased from him after sampling. That is the main idea, you know.

A fourth guerrilla, an office manager who baked chocolate chip cookies and sold them at flea markets on weekends (earning more doing that than through her office-manager salary), engaged in sampling. She baked two sizes of cookies. The tiny ones were free samples; the large ones were $1 each. She gave away the small ones—one per customer. More than half the customers were then tempted by the enchanting flavor and crispy goodness of the sample to purchase one or more of the $1 variety. One more case of sampling that worked.

Thus far, I've told you about two samples of merchandise that were loaned rather than given away (waterbeds and large-screen TVs) and two samples that were given away permanently (newsletters and cookies). What you can learn from this is that it does not take a giant company to engage in sampling, and sampling can be employed even if your product is too large or too expensive to give away. Free sampling can provide instant results that are not achievable through any other marketing method.

If it is at all possible to allow your prospects to sample your offering, let them. Are you a consultant? Offer a free one-hour consultation, a sampling of your work. We'll talk about free consultations in the next chapter. The large-screen-TV entrepreneur had to make his sampling come alive through advertising. His ads called attention to his sampling. Certain sampling methods depend on other methods of marketing, and some sampling can work on its own.

Let them sample if you can

My fifth guerrilla sampler, a person who washed windows for commercial establishments, frequently washed the windows of his prospects for free. This demonstrated his proficiency, his speed, his method of working. It also netted him several large customers. And it didn't require any advertising to get started.

Sometimes I see ads in marketing publications for writers who offer to write for free—just to prove how good they are. If they are indeed good, this advertising-then-sampling combination nets them quite a lot of business. Hardly anyone turns down something that is offered free. It seems that I'm seeing more and more ads of that type these days. It may be that the economy is tough as nails, but it also may be that people are catching on to the effectiveness of this method of marketing.

Example six also involves a person who offered a service. He offered to come to my residence weekly and wash my car, and promised to wash my car that night for free, to show how good he was. I could see the results of his work the next day, realize how convenient his service was, and then when he came back, sign up for it. Was I ever tempted to say no to his offer? Of course not. In fact, he made it nearly impossible to say no. The next morning, my car was gleaming. The next evening, he knocked on my door and asked if I wanted the same service every week. That man had **Why my car** earned himself a steady customer with one free sample. It prob-**is so clean** ably took him fifteen minutes to wash my car. But it demonstrated to me how good he was, how convenient he was, and what a nice fellow he was. That his price was definitely not competitive didn't even enter my mind.

By giving me a sample of his great service, the car washer caused me to think positive thoughts about his offering. So I was won over quite easily. I wonder if he could have ever obtained my business through other methods. Let's see. He could have talked me into buying from him by canvassing. And in a way, his initial contact with me was a canvass. He might also have signed me up through telephone marketing, but I'm not so sure I would have signed. It certainly wouldn't have been as easy a sale as the sampling was, since he couldn't have proven his worth over the phone. A personal letter might have impressed me, but it wouldn't have given the opportunity for give and take that the personal contact did. It also wouldn't have let him prove his point. I would have read his circular or brochure with interest. But since I had never had a car washer who paid house calls, I might not have given the matter serious thought. And a sign, a classified ad, or a listing in the Yellow Pages would certainly not have won my business.

None of the maxi-media marketing methods would have worked as well. Newspapers, magazines, radio, TV, billboards, direct mail—I doubt if any of them would have made me an instant customer. Certainly if he had put his name on an advertising specialty, I would not have signed up so quickly. But sampling did the trick for him. And it might do the trick for you—in a hurry.

Such sampling of services is very expensive if you place a price tag on your time, and believe that terrible lie about time being money (time is far more valuable than money; stop kidding yourself), but very inexpensive if you think of out-of-pocket expenses only. Sampling is quite different from other methods of marketing, including ad specialties, because it does not depend upon repetition. One great sample will do it all. Before you purchased this book, perhaps you looked through a few pages. Maybe you looked at the table of contents. If so, that was sampling on the part of the bookstore. And it worked. I bet sampling will work for you, too. Use it if you possibly can.

One great sample will do it all

23

Free Seminars, Consultations, and Demonstrations: Show and Sell

I do recommend free seminars, consultations, and demonstrations. As you can see, guerrillas give things away! To give and to receive are two sides of the same coin.

**Two sides of
the same coin**

The coin is called business. Guerrillas have learned (though they may have always suspected it in their bones) that the more they give, the more they receive. They are extremely imaginative about what they can give, shifting their generosity into high gear and seeing the world through the eyes of their customers. That's where to start when determining what to give away.

Gifts are given in the form of desk items and computer and personal trinkets. Guerrillas are also quick to give extra service, extra attention, extra value. Because we're in the middle of the information age, we can give away information.

The information they provide will benefit their customers, help them succeed at whatever they are striving for. The information will make their target market smarter and therefore richer and happier.

**Giving away
information**

Guerrillas give away their information in many forms. Some give talks at local clubs and organizations; some give free seminars and clinics. Some give free consultations and demonstrations; others host on-line conferences. Some guerrillas give tours of their facilities or the facilities of satisfied customers. And still others give valuable data in the form of columns or articles in publications read by their target audience.

Many guerrillas empower their generosity with technology. They use technology to help them in their quest to edify, educate, and enlighten their prospects and customers. They write articles for the Internet and are able to locate many Web-site operators who are thrilled to get such worthy information at no cost. They create Web sites that brim with crucial content, that bring prospects back for more of the same.

These kinds of guerrillas sponsor forums, host conferences, sponsor chat sessions for their prospects and customers. They produce diskettes and CD-ROMs, audios and videos to help their prospects see the light. Because they realize how technology can help them disseminate information and that information is a powerful marketing ally, they let their minds wander freely through the available possibilities.

Help prospects see the light

They can produce newsletters on a regular basis. They can create information-laden brochures. They can give away information in the form of self-published booklets and pamphlets, catalogs and bulletins, even by daily E-mail communiqués and mousepads and screen-savers (such as those offered at my Web site at www.gmarketing.com).

When a high-rise apartment building was erected in a Los Angeles neighborhood already teeming with similar high-rise buildings, the owners knew that they had to be creative in their generosity in order to rent their apartments. After all, the average occupancy rate in the neighborhood was a paltry 71 percent.

In less than a year, their occupancy rate reached 100 percent and has remained there since. How did they do it? By offering "free auto grooming." What the heck is that? I'll answer by saying that they paid some guy to wash the tenants' cars once a week. The salary they paid him was easily covered by the enormous difference between 71 and 100 percent occupancy.

Free auto grooming

I tell you this not to get you to wash your prospects' cars but to implore you to be creative in your generosity. Ask yourself what your prospects might want. In many cases, what they want and need — what separates them from success — is information. And it's information that you can provide. Are you the only company that can provide it? If so, wonderful!

Be creative in your generosity

Determine the best way to serve up that information. Perhaps you should do so with a meeting at which you enlist the hearts and minds of your prospects with technology, a multimedia presentation.

I attended a presentation that made such an impact that nearly a third of the audience signed up to invest. It felt like show biz, but it was sell biz, designed to look like an entertainment extravaganza! It's amazing that music and exciting graphics can be combined with content, thanks to computer technology.

Felt like show biz but really was sell biz

There is little doubt that your mission statement is devoted to what you can get and what you can earn. If you're a guerrilla, it will also include what you can give. These days, you can give a lot.

I have a client whose business is computer education. His classes are unique, effective, and impressive. But standard marketing methods didn't attract many customers, so he decided to hold a free seminar on computers for people who knew nothing about them. He placed an ad, and more than five hundred people showed up for the seminar.

Had he teamed up with a great salesperson, he might have sold his program to as many as 50 percent of the people attending. But he'd never dreamed so many people would show up, so the number of people he sold on his series of lessons was closer to 5 percent. Next time he holds a free seminar, he'll be better prepared to close his sales. In fact, he might even hire a professional salesperson.

Many people who give paid seminars or courses for a living advertise free seminars with ads in the business sections of newspapers. One speed-reading school advertised its free seminars with television commercials. An income tax expert markets his free seminars by means of publicity stories coupled with radio commercials on talk-oriented stations. Many entrepreneurs earn a great deal of money with paid seminars and courses. But they cannot attract large numbers of people to paid seminars and **Attracting and** courses merely through newspaper ads, so they attract them to free **then converting** seminars, then convert them to paying customers.

As one guerrilla to another, I sincerely recommend the same tactic to you. I recommend, if it is feasible for your type of product or service, that you advertise in the newspaper that you are holding a free seminar on the topic most closely connected with your product or service. Get as many customers to come to your free seminar as you can. They may purchase your products or they may sign up for your service. If you hold a decent seminar, they will.

When I say seminar, I really mean lecture. Give your audience valuable information and demonstrate your expertise or your **Forty-five** product's efficacy for, say, the first forty-five minutes, using visual **plus fifteen** support if you can. It's easier these days than ever to put on multimedia presentations. Then spend the next fifteen minutes selling whatever it is you wish to sell. What I am talking about is a fifteen-minute, straight-from-the-heart commercial—delivered by you or by someone you hire. The entire process takes one hour. After that, sign up the prospects. Unlike professional seminar leaders, you probably won't be signing them up for a paid seminar (unless selling information is your business). But you will be allowing them to buy your offering. And they'll want it because your message, your demonstration, your enthusiasm, and your proven expertise will have created within them a desire to purchase from you.

There is no question that an in-person commercial is better than a radio or TV commercial. Certainly a fifteen-minute selling opportunity will pan out better than a thirty-second selling opportunity. For this reason, seminars and demonstrations are being utilized more and more to market products and services.

A lecture, consultation, or demonstration is very much like a sample. Your prospects get to see for themselves what you have to offer. They probably get to touch it, if it's a product, and they get to ask questions, whether it's a product or a service. They get to learn more about your offering this way than they do by standard marketing methods. And just as sampling convinces many people that they should buy a good product, so can your seminar or consultation.

A seminar is a sample

Before I write one more word, I should emphasize that a free seminar/consultation/demonstration amounts to marketing in a vacuum unless two other factors are present. First, your free imparting of information must be advertised so that you'll have a large group of prospects. Advertise in the newspaper, on the radio, or on TV. Use direct mail and telemarketing. Post signs. Go for the free publicity that is readily available when you're offering a free seminar. Tell the truth in your ads as to the contents of the seminar, and try to attract honest prospects, not just warm bodies. Second, be sure that either you or an associate can sell your offering to those prospects after the seminar is over. My client was a brilliant lecturer. People listened intently to his every word. They enjoyed looking at him and listening to him. As a lecturer, he was first-rate. As a salesman, though, he was eighth-rate: he hadn't an inkling of how to close. He had no instinct for blood. He didn't have a personality that could take advantage of the momentum he created in his lecture. Unfortunately he signed up only 5 percent of the audience rather than the potential 50 percent.

Two key factors

If possible, demonstrate your product or service at your seminar. Although your offering is free, people *are* giving up their time; they are traveling to attend your seminar. And they have expectations, based upon your ad. You must give them value in exchange. You must live up to their expectations and move beyond them. You must treat them as if they have paid to hear you. You should make sure that even if they do not buy from you, they still feel that their time was well spent. Perhaps they'll buy from you later.

Where should you conduct your seminar? At your place of business, if possible. Just rent the chairs you'll need. Perhaps you'll conduct it outdoors, if you are demonstrating gardening skills or the like. Perhaps you'll conduct it in a gym, if you want to show and sell exercise equipment. Eventually, you'll be able to hold it on the premises of a "partner" with whom you have a *fusion marketing arrangement*—a collaboration of marketing talent, money, and ideas. (Read more about the fascinating topic of strategic alliances in *Guerrilla Marketing Excellence*.) Most seminars are held in motels or hotels where seminar facilities are readily available. Such facilities provide a lectern, a microphone, a blackboard, chairs, and coffee, water, and restrooms. It is also advisable to offer free parking. If you have a store, hold a free seminar there—that will work best. Your prospects can learn where you are and what you sell. For instance, a decorating seminar in your furniture showroom is a natural.

People appreciate useful information. They appreciate it all the more when it is free. When you conduct a seminar or workshop, when you give a lecture, when you demonstrate a product or service, when you consult with a prospect about that person's business, you prove your expertise. You establish yourself as an authority. You gain credibility. Even if people do not buy from you right then and there, they very well may buy from you later.

There is a tactic that some very successful (and high-pressure) businesses employ to get the maximum number of people to buy right then and there at the seminar location. They establish three "sales points" on the way to the exit. At the end of the free seminar, the speaker tells the customers that they can either sign up for the paid seminar at a particular table or with specific representatives located throughout the room. Four reps are usually present to work with the potential customers. Prospects who do not buy must pass the three sales points before leaving the room. At each they are given a different sales pitch, each stronger than the one before. Some people sign up in the main room, others at the first sales point, and still others at the second sales point. Another group signs up at the third sales point. Only a tiny group—who have world-class sales resistance—leave the building without putting their hands to their wallets. Sounds a bit pressured for this guerrilla.

This practice was common among certain consciousness-raising groups. It is the most pressured of all possible sells, and it's not easy to resist. As you can see, it takes several reps to make the seminar a success. But it does work. And if you care about profits more than you care about social propriety, you might employ it. Keep in mind, however, that guerrillas do have a social conscience.

Free seminars, even without triple-teamed closes, can be a bonanza for you, and you should try to market with them if you possibly can. It may be that your business just doesn't lend itself to seminars. If you operate a window-washing business, a carwashing business, or a mail-order publishing business, perhaps seminars are not for you. But if you run an income-tax preparation, instructional, or retail furniture business, perhaps they are.

Think about the field in which you operate. Can you give a lecture for forty-five minutes on any aspect of it? Which aspect? How will this tie in with your offering? Do you have the showmanship to lecture for forty-five minutes and hold the attention of your audience, or should you delegate that task to someone else? Do you have the salesmanship to close sales right then and there, or should that, too, be the job of an associate? What will you be selling at the seminar? Will it be products? services? books? lessons? a paid seminar? products or services of a fusion marketing partner?

As with sampling, if feasible try to offer one free seminar to market your business. It can be a lot of fun. And it can be extremely profitable, with a lower cost per sale than advertising in any newspaper or on any radio station. It will give you both immediate and long-term benefits. You'll get to mention in future marketing that you have lectured in your field, led seminars in your area of expertise. Giving free seminars is a very innovative way to market.

Fun and profits

Giving a seminar that's not at your own place of business will run you about $50 to $200 for the room, plus whatever it costs to buy coffee or juice for your guests. If you will keep them for only an hour, you need not provide refreshments, but if you plan to go longer than that, it's a good idea to have them. Some morning seminars also offer free donuts. Even donuts are weapons in the arsenal of a practitioner of guerrilla marketing! Guerrillas know the dynamic power of small details.

Seminar costs

To the cost of the room and refreshments, add the price of the ads you'll be running and any seminar materials you'll be handing out. After your seminar and sales pitch are completed, you can add up your receipts, then divide them by the total cost of the room, the ads, the refreshments, and the materials. That will give you your cost per sale. If it is low enough, continue to market this way. In fact, it doesn't have to be low. Even if you sell ten people a $1,000 product that costs you $100 and it runs $1,000 for your room and ads and handouts, you will have earned $10,000 while spending $2,000—a cost per sale of $80. This is a high cost, but it's minuscule when compared to your $900 profit on a $1,000 product. This is why so many free seminars are being offered these days. Also, you want the opportunity to talk to honest-to-goodness prospects, people who have already shown that they will expend time and effort to learn more about your field.

Demonstrations   Demonstrations can be given not only at seminars, but also in homes, at parties (be sure you consider party-plan marketing for your business), in stores, at fairs and shows, in parks, at beaches, or almost anywhere. People are attracted to small crowds, and a free demonstration will almost certainly attract a small crowd. At a free demonstration, which is much shorter than a seminar—no more than five minutes—be prepared to sell and take orders immediately afterward. Folks who give seminars and demonstrations often have cohorts all set to accept customers' credit cards, checks, and cash. The person giving the demo or seminar is usually too busy answering questions to take orders, so get that base covered.

A free demonstration need not be marketed in the same way as a seminar—simply showing up at a high-traffic location or placing a few well-conceived signs may do the trick. Of course, it's fine to advertise and distribute circulars, although they may not be necessary. It *will* be necessary to provide the showmanship and salesmanship.

Can you demonstrate your product or service effectively? Answer honestly. If you can say yes, by all means give it your best shot. Rarely will you be afforded so golden an opportunity.

A few moments ago I mentioned the idea of giving your free seminar or demo in a party situation. More and more items every year are being marketed through party-plan marketing. Here's how it works: a person becomes a party-plan representative for a company. Let's say it's an art gallery, since so many of them engage in this kind of marketing. No, wait—let's say it's your business. You throw a party for all of your friends and close acquaintances, just as Tupperware party-planners have been doing for decades, and very successfully.

At the party, serve coffee and pastries, or maybe little sandwiches. You also give a well-planned sales spiel about whatever you are selling. You offer examples, conduct a brief seminar, distribute samples, or give a demonstration to the assembled throng. The lighting is optimum. Music selected especially for the occasion may be playing in the background. Your enthusiasm is bubbly and contagious. You're obviously proud of your offerings. Your friends start to like them, too. And the prices! They sound so low. A buying frenzy starts. Fifteen of your offerings are sold. They sell for an average of $100 each. But you purchased them for $25 each, including everything, from your supplier.

Each $100 sale results in a $75 profit. You should feel proud of yourself. You earned $1,125 for the night and spent only $50 for refreshments—a $1,075 profit. And that's just the start. Now you tell your friends that they can do the same. The word spreads. The parties spread. Soon they're being held in several towns. Naturally, you get the lion's share of sales from the parties thrown by the people you've signed up. You're raking in the bucks. Your buddies, along with strangers who are enthused about what you sell, are raking in the bucks. Your suppliers are doing very well, thank you. You are very, very happy that you engaged in party-plan marketing.

Guerrillas are party animals

Can you? Here are the types of companies that do already: exercise-machine companies, art galleries, kitchen-equipment companies (such as Tupperware), women's clothing manufacturers, vitamin manufacturers, X-rated product companies (the burgeoning "pleasure" industry), cosmetics manufacturers, computer companies, and lingerie manufacturers. The list is not shrinking.

Who throws parties now

Such parties are ideal places for demonstrations. And the people attending are already *conditioned* to buy. You can't beat that kind of situation if you're a practicing guerrilla. Of all the places at which free seminars or demonstrations can be held, parties certainly rank up there near the top.

The main disadvantage of free seminars, consultations, and demonstrations (except for parties) is that you must travel. You can't always hold free demos and seminars in the same area over again. You've got to hit the road and talk to fresh prospects. But you can make these free sessions part of your marketing plan and give one or two per year. A guerrilla would find some way to utilize them. Will you?

Have seminar, will travel

I know that you'll want to open the door to long and lasting

Opening the
door to lasting
relationships

relationships. That's why I want you to know of one of the world's great door openers. It's a free consultation. When you offer it—by letter, phone, advertisement, or Web site—it carries no pressure and requires little time. "Want a free sales presentation?" "Uh, no thanks." "Want a free thirty-minute consultation?" "Hmm, that sounds good. When can we set it up?"

Free consul-
tations are
samples

A free consultation is a lot like a free sample in that it's a sample of how good you are. It's also like a free seminar at which you get to develop a personal, one-on-one relationship. It's even similar to a demonstration because it allows you to demonstrate how you can help your prospects. The offer of a free consultation is easy to accept, and the rules guerrillas follow are only five in number:

Five consulting
rules to follow

1. You are not allowed to make a sales presentation. You offered a free consultation and that's what you've got to deliver.
2. You must offer to leave after thirty minutes if it's a thirty-minute consultation that you offered. Your prospect may ask you to stay and continue your consultation, and if you'd like to, fine. But you are honor-bound to offer to depart when you said you would. You prove in a consultation your professionalism, your ability to listen, your ability to help your prospect, your reliability, your enthusiasm, and your maturity in a potential buyer-seller relationship.
3. Your job in a free consultation is to prove how valuable you can be to your client. Do it with sincere, valuable help. Don't worry about giving things away for free—that's the whole idea.
4. Ask questions and listen carefully to the answers, responding to them the best way that you can. The idea is not to hold things back but give freely. If what you give is valuable enough, you'll be amply repaid.
5. Follow up within forty-eight hours. I know you're busy and may have other free consultations set up, but no matter what, you should thank the person for his time and restate the high points of the consultation. If you're not willing to follow up, you may be wasting your time during the consultation.

If you can demonstrate while you consult, such as the Web designer I know who uses his laptop computer to show computer-illiterate prospects how simple it is for them to have a site on the Internet, you can sign up customers in droves. They are learning and seeing at the same time, all in the safety and comfort of their own office.

Think of your business as an ice cream store and your free consultation, demonstration, or seminar as a free sample of your ice cream. If it's truly delicious, your prospect will want more—and want it in a hurry.

You're an ice cream store

24

Trade Shows, Exhibits, Fairs: Making a Public Spectacle

Some wildly successful entrepreneurs employ only one major method of marketing: they display and sell their wares at trade shows, exhibits, and fairs. They realize that many serious prospects will attend these gatherings, so they put all their efforts into exhibiting and selling their merchandise (they usually sell products rather than services). This is not to say that their show booths are their only marketing vehicles. But they are their primary ones. And in a few instances, this is the only way a person needs to market. I don't like telling this to you for fear it might encourage a lax attitude, but it is the truth.

Trade shows and circulars only

The marketing plan of many a guerrilla consists of appearances at four major shows or fairs, plus circulars or brochures to be distributed at the shows. Nothing else. Nothing else is needed.

I once attended a large national furniture show with a client who owned a chain of furniture stores. He very much wanted to be one of the first people through the doors at the three-day event. When I asked him why, he told me that he would first breeze through the show, making notes and looking at all the exhibits. Then he would quickly return to the displays that had caught his attention and order a full year's worth of items, making certain to get agreements that he would be the exclusive outlet for each item.

Sure enough, it took him, with me hot on his heels, a mere thirty minutes to walk the miles of aisles. Then he spent the next two hours dickering with the manufacturers or distributors that tickled his fancy. At the end of two and a half hours he was delighted, having signed up for a year's worth of purchases, all with exclusive arrangements. And just as happy—maybe even happier—were the entrepreneurs who had attracted his attention with their merchandise, displays, salesmanship, and readiness to grant concessions. I well recall the look on one man's face when he realized that in only ten minutes he had sold half a million dollars' worth of goods. Fifty thou per minute is a luscious sales rate.

The $50,000 minute

I suggest that you browse through a copy of *Tradeshow and Convention Guide* at your library, or order a copy from Budd Publications, P.O. Box 7, New York, NY 10004, to learn of a multitude of shows at which you can display your offerings. The shows are worth your time.

If you opt for this method of marketing, I not only suggest but urge you to read *Guerrilla Trade Show Selling: New Unconventional Weapons and Tactics to Meet More People, Get More Leads and Close More Sales*, by yours truly, Mark S. A. Smith, and Orvel Ray Wilson.

There are a couple of ways to display what you sell at trade shows. One way, the standard way, is to rent a booth for several hundred dollars, set up a display, and give it your best. Another way, guerrilla-like in character, and a fine method of testing the efficacy of trade shows as a nonmedia marketing medium for you, is to visit a show, find a display booth that offers merchandise compatible with yours, and strike up a deal with the exhibitor whereby you share a portion of the next booth the exhibitor rents. That means you pay part of the rental fee, assume part of the sales responsibility, and allow your items to be displayed and sold along with those of your new compatriot.

Two ways to display

When you visit one or two shows, you will learn of products that compete with or complement yours. You'll also discover products that knock your socks off—products with which you would love to become associated, and possibly could, as a fusion marketing partner. You'll learn the right way to display goods and the wrong way. You'll pick up some dandy ideas for brochures, signs, and demonstrations. You'll learn a heck of a lot from the mistakes of others—people who have great merchandise but don't know how to market it. And you'll meet people who may be able to help you distribute what you sell.

Be a visitor

Let's look at a case in point. A man-and-wife team who marketed greeting cards all by themselves by calling on stationery stores were soon alerted to the existence of stationery shows at which greeting cards are displayed. There, they were told, they could display their own cards and make sales, they could team up with other card manufacturers, and better yet they could meet distributors who could distribute their cards throughout the country. The two budding entrepreneurs went to the show, looked at others' cards and displays, and met several representatives who offered to distribute their cards. Because they were greenhorns at the business, they were delighted, and they signed on with several of the reps.

Two kinds of reps

Their business grew in the next year. But in talking with a few fellow card sellers, they learned that there are basically two kinds of reps one meets at shows: ordinary reps and Rolls-Royce reps. Ordinary reps conduct an ordinary amount of sales activity and achieve ordinary distribution in ordinary stores. These, alas, were the kinds of reps the man and wife had signed up. Rolls-Royce reps, however, can move prodigious numbers of greeting cards by distributing only in high-volume stores and expending a great deal of selling energy.

The following year, the man and wife went to the stationery shows and signed up with only Rolls-Royce reps. By doing so, the couple increased their sales fivefold over the year before, propelling themselves into a deliriously wonderful tax bracket. If you are looking for national distribution of your goods, do look for Rolls-Royce reps at major trade shows.

Market with more than your display

While displaying your products in your own booth—something you'll most likely want to do when you begin to take large orders—you can engage in four other types of marketing at the same time:

1. Hand out circulars. I suggest that you hire someone, preferably a gorgeous woman (or a gorgeous man, if women are your prime prospects), to distribute your circulars while walking through the show. The cost to hire the person will be about $75, and for that, she or he will pass out as many as 5,000 circulars—all inviting people to visit your booth. If you do that, you will instantly rise above most of the other exhibitors, since they will not be practicing such a guerrilla-like tactic. You'll also attract more prospects.

2. Give away brochures. Because brochures are more costly than circulars, you won't want to give as many away. But by disseminating them at your booth only, you'll be able to narrow the distribution down to serious prospects only. And your brochures will do heavy-duty work for you. Many people attend shows and exhibits merely to collect brochures. Then they study the brochures and place their orders on the basis of the information

they've gleaned. So this is a chance to make your brochure a powerful sales tool. Be sure to get the names and addresses of the people to whom you give brochures. Just ask for their card.

3. Demonstrate your goods to real prospects who are in a buying mood. You can demonstrate your offerings to large groups of people. And since your competitors will probably be at the show too, you'll have a good opportunity to prove the advantages of your product.

4. Offer free samples. Rarely will you be afforded the chance to give samples to so many potential customers. If it's possible to let people sample your merchandise, a show or exhibit is the place to do it.

Entrepreneurs avail themselves of the opportunities at shows with 100 percent effort—they concentrate their marketing energies and dollars on shows. Of all sources of purchasing information that businesspeople rate "extremely useful," trade shows are at the top of the list, mentioned by 91 percent of respondents. Also, trade shows aid and abet your other marketing efforts. A typical direct-mail campaign nets about 13 percent readership and a 2 percent response rate, which is considered good by nonguerillas. That same direct-mail campaign, if based on contacts made at a trade show, generates 45 percent readership and a 20 percent response rate, which is considered quite acceptable by guerrillas.

Trade shows are at the top of the list

Why do guerrillas exhibit at trade shows? Our *Guerrilla Trade Show Selling* books lists fifteen reasons:

1. To sell what you offer to visitors
2. To sell what you offer to other exhibitors
3. To get leads for your sales force to follow up
4. To network and troubleshoot with other professionals
5. To establish your industry positioning
6. To meet with existing customers
7. To visit with people whom you otherwise wouldn't see
8. To introduce new products to the market
9. To do market research
10. To find new dealers, representatives, and distributors
11. To find new employees
12. To conduct business meetings
13. To scope out the competition
14. To get smart
15. To gain media exposure

Why guerrillas exhibit at shows

Here are ten more reasons:

16. To generate thousands of qualified leads
17. To build rapport with customers and prospects
18. To increase your name awareness
19. To penetrate new markets in a brief time
20. To present your business in a new perspective
21. To increase contact with your suppliers
22. To find names for your mailing list
23. To make friends
24. To immerse yourself in your own industry
25. To separate yourself from the competition

The show begins before the doors open

Guerrillas are well aware that a trade show begins long before the doors open. They begin trade show promotion by identifying and contacting their key prospects and then inviting them, along with good customers, to their show booth. Guerrillas send both the invitations supplied by the show organizers and personalized invitations. Guerrillas are acutely aware of the power of personalization.

They promote their attendance at trade shows with ads in trade magazines, faxes, E-mail, personal letters, and telephone calls. Because they're guerrillas, they learn of the hotels at which attendees are staying and then place fliers and invitations under the hotel room doors.

Follow-up

A major guerrilla secret to successful trade shows is follow-up. As interactive as trade shows are, the most crucial interactivity often takes place after the show—follow-up leads to success.

Today, 75 percent of the people who attend trade shows know exactly what they want to see, whom they want to see, and how much time they'll spend at the exhibit. I hate to tell you this, but 90 percent of the literature they collect at the shows gets tossed before the attendee goes home. And more gets tossed at home.

Send literature after the show

That's why many guerrillas send their literature *after* the show.

Pay close attention to this next guerrilla secret. It frequently means the difference between astonishing success and depressing failure. Let me make it obvious right here and now: your main purpose in having a booth at a trade show, fair, or exhibit is *to sell your product.*

Yes, it is important to display, to demonstrate, to educate, to get names for your mailing list. But you really want to *sell*. You need to take orders right there at your booth. You must have a person there who is dedicated to selling. You should aim for a large volume of sales at the show itself, in spite of the brochures you will distribute. Don't forget the furniture store entrepreneur I wrote about earlier: he visited the shows to look and then to buy. He didn't care about brochures. He wanted to place his orders at the show.

If you don't sell a lot of what you want to sell at a show, you may have failed in this marketing effort. If you have not sold a large volume, you have not taken advantage of the glorious opportunity afforded you by such shows. I recall two competitors at a national show. Both had attractive displays, both gave imaginative demonstrations, and both handed out compelling brochures. But the first company assumed that the show was a place to display—and it made no sales. The second company, a small, young partnership, figured that the show was a place to sell—so it made $4.5 million in sales in a three-day period. I've made my point.

Two guerrilla tactics. Recognize that there are prospects and there are large, hot prospects. If you've done your crucial pre–trade show homework, studied the trade magazines, and talked with industry insiders, you'll know the big fish. These hot prospects deserve to be invited to your hospitality suite at a hotel near the trade show. In it, intensify your personal bond with these people. Don't sell. Make your friendship closer.

The second tactic is mandatory for companies that didn't sell well at the show. *Follow up within ten days on the prospects you met. Five days is even better.* Write them, call them, and keep the memory of your offerings fresh in their minds. Without follow-up, you're probably just wasting your time at a trade show because people forget trade shows lightning fast. And you know how important your time is—far more important than money. If you run out of money, any guerrilla can find ways to generate more. But if you run out of time, no guerrilla tactic can alter that reality.

Follow up within ten days

Many craftspeople sell all the crafts they make at one or two yearly shows. They spend most of the year making their items, then spend a few weeks—at two three-week shows—selling them. Often, no other marketing is necessary for them. Generally, to succeed at marketing in a show, exhibit, or fair, you need a combination of marketing tools: a professional-looking and beckoning display; a supply of informative brochures; a larger supply of enticing circulars to be passed out at the show; a method of demonstrating, sampling, or showing off your goods; and at least two high-energy salespeople. If you have all of those, you are a guerrilla and you have primed yourself to succeed.

Your exhibit at the trade show should be as professional as you can afford to make it. New technology in audiovisual presentations makes it possible for you to stage a continuous multimedia extravaganza—including slides, film, videotape, and music. Lighting can be combined with this multimedia display to literally spotlight your products as they are being featured in your
Dancing visual images multimedia show. As the visual images dance before the eyes of your prospects, and as music soothes their conscious minds and gains access to their unconscious, the tape-recorded voice of a master motivater tells your audience that they should buy from you, that they should trust you, that they should give their money to you. And there you can be, order pad at the ready, all set to sign, seal, and deliver.

The best possible scenario That's the best possible scenario for a trade-show exhibit. If you can't afford it, then work down, step by step, including as much as you can.

In most big-city Yellow Page directories are several columns of "Display Designers and Producers." These businesses offer such lovelies as modular exhibit systems. They will construct or they will rent; they'll also store your exhibit while you're not using it. They'll make a miniature model of your exhibit for you to approve before they build the real thing—or ten real things. They craft handsome exhibit displays of wood, plastic, cardboard, or metal and they make displays of any size, wired and ready to go.

I'm always impressed and educated when I walk through a
The display warehouse display warehouse. I discover great ideas for future displays. I get a good fix on current prices, both for renting and for purchasing. Because the technology is moving so rapidly, it's a good idea to make a yearly visit to one of your area's largest display companies. Ask to see the best they have. And remember—you may be able to afford it if you go in with a few other compatible companies. Case in point: at a bedding trade show, the best exhibit was a multimedia display using holograms and laser technology. It was paid for by three different companies, each manufacturing a single component of the whole bed. Each of these three compatible companies got a first-class reputation for 33 percent of the first-class price.

Of course, you can build your own display if you have the

time, talent, and equipment. But do me a favor: before you do so, look at what is available to you now. That's what your competitors will probably use. Can you do better? Can you keep abreast of new developments?

Just as important as an award-winning display are the people who man—or woman—your booth at the trade show. They should be talented in several areas. Here are a few tips:

Trade-show success tips

1. Staff your booth with *enough* people. Not doing so can be fatal. I recall a show booth that was manned by two marvelous company reps. They were backed by a beautiful display. At one point, one of the reps was having lunch and the other was visiting another booth. The only person left was a lackadaisical fellow who didn't really understand the company's business and was really hired to be a gofer. Naturally, that was when two of the biggest customers in the industry visited the booth. They couldn't get answers to their questions, couldn't get an explanation of a new product being introduced, so they moved on and gave their business to someone else. Don't blow your opportunities. Be sure that a top-rate person is always at the booth. To do that may require at least two, and if you can arrange it, even three, top-rate people to attend the show and attend to the exhibit. One of those people must always be on hand to answer questions and take orders.

2. Be sure the people staffing your booth are *personable, extroverted,* and *friendly.* You don't want an introverted genius up there on your stage. Some people serve best from within the inner sanctum of the company. Others are made for the road. The truth you must know is that 85 percent of your success will come from the abilities of your trade show staff. Your staff should understand exactly what you hope to accomplish and should have *no* fear of rejection.

Personable, extroverted, and friendly

3. Do what is necessary to staff your booth with *knowledgeable salespeople.* Your staff should be comprised of naturally upbeat people who comprehend the precious nature of time, who know how to give and get information, and who know how to obtain commitments. Of course, they must be exceptionally good listeners and dynamite qualifiers.

4. Hire people who have a *high energy level* and won't burn out. Trade shows are exhausting. They are astonishingly intense for the staff. It's hard to stand up and be bright and charming for one full day, much less three days in a row. Give your staff frequent breaks to help them maintain their energy level. It's been estimated that the average human being is fully aware only 2 percent of the time and in a state of semiawareness 98 percent of the time. Trade show staffers must be fully aware at all times—this requires inexhaustible energy.

Stay relatively sober

5. Carefully select people with the *proper social graces* to represent you at trade shows. Trade shows invariably involve parties. I've seen enough people become embarrassingly drunk at such parties to realize that their energies on the exhibit floor were ruined by their antics on the sixteenth floor.

At trade shows, glorious things can happen for your company. It is possible—and I know of at least three instances in which this

Gigantic orders

happened—to make one contact who will place an order so large that it will put you on easy street for at least a year. A woman who invented a paper-towel dispenser printed her circulars on paper towels, then gave them away at her booth—dispensed from the dispenser she had invented. One buyer placed an order with her for 250,000 units. Was this due to her unique way of supplying information? Maybe yes, maybe no. But she wouldn't have made a sale that size had she not been at the show. And she may not have attracted attention had she not developed such a unique way of sampling, demonstrating, and providing information.

There are more trade shows today than ever before. That means you've got to know which to attend, which to exhibit at. Except for the big national trade shows, most people attending a trade show come from a 100-mile radius. They come to buy, to see what's new, to investigate the competition, to spot trends, and to find new tools and services that can help their companies profit. When you attend a trade show, heed this advice:

How to attend a trade show

- Know just what you want to accomplish.
- See the entire show. Profits hide in esoteric places; small companies with exciting products are often in inexpensive locations on the fringes of a show.
- Prioritize by visiting the important exhibits first.
- Bring a sturdy, lightweight case in which to carry show materials.
- Wear comfortable shoes and take breaks to lighten your load. A trade show is not as exhausting as a full-court basketball game, but many attendees will tell you that it comes close.

Several enlightening statistics about trade shows: 80 percent of attendees are the actual decision-makers; 90 percent of attendees have not been seen by your sales force during this past year; 90 percent of attendees plan on making a purchase in the coming year.

If you're an exhibitor, recognize that the show begins long before the show. Preshow promotion is a crucial marketing weapon. Your job is to get your prospect's attention and explain how you'll help the prospect profit. Truisms about shows:

Preshow promotion

- Select the right shows, guiding your selection with past experience, quality of the sponsor's past shows, who the audience is, and who the other exhibitors are.
- Guerrilla rule of thumb on show selection: the more valuable the show is to your prospects, the more valuable it will be to you.
- Important criteria to consider are location, timing, convention center, on-site services, and your display.
- Guerrillas are definitely party animals! They will ring up the most sales with a party for sizzling prospects in their hotel hospitality suite.
- Play favorites by inviting your customers and most likely potential prospects to your hospitality suite. This is not an equal-opportunity suite; it is a golden-opportunity suite where you can make friends. Remember that friends are quite easily transformed into customers. Guerrillas do *not* befriend people simply to make the sale—it's too crass, and life is too short to waste on phony friendships. Unless the chemistry truly exists between you and the prospect, it's better not to invite the person to your suite.

Guerrillas play favorites

- Know for certain whether you want to penetrate your existing market or expand into a new market; know if you're going for sales or leads.
- Don't send any trade-show reps who will wish to go home so that they can get down to "real" work. The real work is at the *show.*
- Be absolutely certain that your booth reflects your marketing identity and your current marketing theme.
- People don't like to walk into a booth where they feel trapped. Be sure your booth has an open feel.
- Include a hands-on demonstration or something that people can handle. Studies show that folks love to touch things.
- Research reveals that location has *little* to do with the amount of traffic at your booth. Believe it.

Let them touch things

- Keep things easy to understand; a few large pictures are better than many small ones. It is crucial that your company name is highly visible.
- Know all your costs. These include rent, displays, electricity, carpeting, furniture, transportation, lodging, food, entertaining—hey, that's a lot! Keep track or you may end up kidding yourself.

What determines your profitability
- The profitability of a show is determined primarily by the quality of your people and how they work a booth. Be sure they take breaks every four hours and see the entire show as early as possible to gain a feel for the competition.
- Quickly separate the serious prospects from the browsers. Don't spend too much time even with the serious prospects; there are many others to meet.

Don't sit down
- Don't have chairs in the booth. Visitors won't disturb seated staffers. If you must have a chair and table setup, put it in a quiet corner. Don't give away too much literature. People get overloaded. Save your best weapons for major prospects during follow-up. With qualified leads and notes made at the show, follow-up will be effective. *Start with a thank-you note within one week, or you may be completely forgotten.* What a waste of time, energy, and money! Don't let it happen.

A few guerrilla tactics that have worked for others before the show will also work for you. As usual, they require generosity, one of the key characteristics of a guerrilla:

Epsom salts and footpads
- Send prospects a small packet of Epson salts and an offer of free footpads at your booth.
- Send an invitation to pick up a free product from your booth.
- Send a photo or drawing of your booth so that your visitors can easily spot you.
- Send a map of the exhibit hall marked to show your booth, the rest rooms, the foot stands, pay phones, and all the exits.
- Send an entry form for a contest to be entered at your booth.
- Send a show schedule with a time to visit your display.

Your business simply may not be appropriate for such public gatherings. However, if it is at all possible to use this marketing tool, do so. At such events it's more of a virtue than a vice to make a public spectacle of yourself.

25

Miscellaneous Marketing Tools: Services, Searchlights, Contests, Newsletters, On-line Marketing, and Other Guerrilla Media

New marketing weapons are developed every few months. Some are ingenious; some are ridiculous; some are life-changing. All are worth examining. Simply because a marketing device is new doesn't mean it isn't worth consideration. One of the most interesting moments in my career in big advertising agencies occurred when I was working in England. We had persuaded a manufacturer (the largest in the country) of anti-acne products to experiment with television advertising. This was in 1968, hardly the Dark Ages.

After a three-month test, during which sales went through the roof, we prepared a plan calling for the year-round use of television. When we presented it to the client, he told us he didn't plan to include television in his marketing program. We wanted to know why, since our test had been enormously successful. "Because frankly, gentlemen," the client countered, "I am not convinced that television is here to stay." I'm afraid some people feel this way about the Internet.

I suppose you can take the same attitude when examining new methods of marketing. But even if a method is hot for only one year, a guerrilla should avail himself or herself of it during that year. It doesn't have to be "here to stay" in order to help your business. Any help you can find should be gratefully accepted.

Be wary of fads — but not too wary

Perhaps you've heard of moped advertising, a new marketing medium. For this type of marketing, you pay a company and provide them with a sign that advertises your product or service. Then one of their employees, usually clad in a bikini, drives a moped

Moped marketing

into high-traffic areas where your sign can be seen by large numbers of people. If you are marketing sunglasses, tanning oil, or soft drinks, it makes sense to employ this medium at beaches. Mopeds can go where buses and cars cannot—they can go to parks, ballgames, and parades—wherever lots of people congregate. I don't know whether moped advertising is here to stay, but it certainly is if "here" is southern California beaches.

There are also less obvious marketing tools. Matchbooks, for one. Package inserts, too, though they are really part of direct marketing. Searchlights are successfully used by many a retailer. If you live in a community that frowns upon their use, though, you'd better steer clear of them. Bench advertising is an option in certain towns (but not many). Might it be right for you? What about T-shirt advertising? Many small businesses see impressive results from commercials run in movie theaters and drive-ins. The cost is very low. Will this medium influence your prospects? If they are moviegoers, maybe so.

Bumper stickers, blimps, and buttons

In addition to these marketing tools, you can use bumper stickers to broadcast your message. Baseball hats with the name of an advertiser are ubiquitous in the United States, not to mention across the waters as well. Maybe you'll market with buttons as many political candidates do (though half of them lose). And then there are decals, imprinted sun visors, or skywriting. You can use banners that are towed by airplanes. Let's not forget blimps, once a mainstay for Goodyear, now flying high for many other marketers. Less popular is the use of A-frames, known as sandwich boards. Worn by people parading in front of groups of people, they can display your benefits or announce special offers. As a guerrilla, you have an obligation to seriously consider these off-the-wall marketing devices, and to consider on-line marketing as well.

Rent a picket

There are also several companies that will market your services with picket advertising. One is called Rent-a-Picket; another is called Positive Picketing. You pay them a set amount and their employees parade in front of your place of business carrying picket-type signs that say wonderful things about you. It's unique, all right, and it may be here to stay. For you, it might be worthwhile. As a practicing guerrilla, you can stage this marketing event by yourself, working with your own employees. If you use any picket marketing, be sure to contact the media. Because the medium is such a hoot, I'll bet you can get free media coverage—in the newspapers and possibly on television.

Such advertising methods—searchlights, skywriting, pickets, computer diskettes, and the rest—are similar to the concept of billboard advertising. They are reminder advertising. They keep your name in the public eye and they call attention to your prime attributes. They probably can't do the job all by themselves, but one or more will make up a smart marketing plan. And computer diskettes can do a whale of a selling job for you, as they have for others.

Technology has arrived on the marketing scene and is a boon to guerrillas in at least twenty-five areas. With technology, guerrillas can:

1. Produce fresh and up-to-the-moment customer mailing lists
2. Create extensive and thorough customer lists
3. Gain access to important competitive information
4. Desktop-publish a newsletter or catalog
5. Create fliers and brochures inexpensively
6. Use accurate automation in direct mailings
7. Use computer graphics—for print and video
8. Tap into on-line information services
9. Engage in quick and valuable research
10. Create a video about your offering
11. Unleash an electronic publicity campaign
12. Make a presentation with a CD-ROM
13. Prepare a multi-media presentation
14. Create a first-class proposal
15. Use automatic-responding software for fast service
16. Use video-conferencing for long-distance clients
17. Gain access to zillions of on-line classified sections
18. Use voice-mail
19. Accomplish multiple tasks using a cordless hands-free phone
20. Offer fax-on-demand to time-conscious customers
21. Create an interactive Web site
22. Engage in fax broadcasting
23. Use E-mail
24. Create a computerized order-tracking system
25. Encourage employees to telecommute

How technology helps guerrillas

All of these technologies, and many more, are chronicled in detail in *Guerrilla Marketing with Technology: Unleashing the Full Potential of Your Small Business*, which I published in 1997. I hate to sound like a walking commercial, but I'd hate it more if you failed to learn that technology can immensely empower your marketing.

You can expect technology to greatly influence guerrilla marketing in the new high-tech century. You'll learn of new, empowering technology on a regular basis. A recent newspaper article **Smart** described a "smart phone"—a single unit with a cellular phone, a **phones** computer screen, and a keyboard. It can be used to make phone calls, send and receive E-mail, surf the Web, and record addresses, dates, and other calendar information. Today it retails for $999 with a $24.95 usage fee. By the time you read this, it will be relatively old-fashioned and the costs will be lower. Count on it.

If you're frightened by technology (and fear of technology can be fatal to a business), take heart that many techno-geniuses share your fear and confusion. For example, Marc Andreessen, co-founder of Netscape, admitted recently on a TV talk show that his home PC crashes regularly, that he can't get his printer or CD-ROM drive to work yet, and that he hasn't figured out how to program his VCR.

All the miscellaneous weapons of marketing aren't high-tech. If you have a place of business where you occasionally run promo- **Low-tech can** tions, a searchlight to call attention to a late-night sale may work as **be cool, too** an attention-getter for you. I know of a waterbed retailer who once filled a waterbed mattress with helium and tied it to a rope. Then he set it out to float over his store, where it could be seen for miles. Many drivers slowed down and noticed the store. The store owner said that the stunt enabled him to sell his average monthly volume in one day and to double it within one week. Crazy, but it worked.

The concept of unique pricing is yet another guerrilla marketing weapon. The latest studies indicate that price is the major consideration of between 15 and 35 percent of the population— that means between 65 and 85 percent of people concentrate on factors other than price. Many companies act as though 100 percent of the population is price-obsessed. This delusion nibbles away at their profits and attracts only the most disloyal of all customers.

Unusual Still, unusual prices do attract attention. I'm not talking about **prices** one-cent sales or two-for-one sales, but instead creative price promotions such as the dentist who offered his clients and prospects a complete basic dental exam and cleaning for "whatever you think it's worth." Most patients paid the regular rate. Some paid less than that. As a result of this promotion, many people who had avoided a dental exam made an appointment and then became loyal patients. The dentist's office was booked solid during and after this promotion while building powerful word-of-mouth marketing.

Word-of-mouth will come to companies automatically if they use a broad array of marketing weapons over a long period of time. However, some guerrillas, as patient as they are, try to interrupt the process of obtaining positive word of mouth. One way to do this is to distribute brochures that are printed specifically for first-time purchasers. A phenomenon called the "moment of maximum satisfaction" is the thirty-day time period following the purchase date. During this period, a purchaser is most likely to spread the word about her purchase, conveying her enthusiasm and yours to all who will listen. If you hand such a person your new customer brochure, *you are putting the right words in the right mouths at the right time.* Small wonder your word-of-mouth will pick up.

Speeding up the word-of-mouth process

Another way to obtain healthy word-of-mouth marketing is to ask this question: Who else do your customers patronize? Then, do a favor for those people. Example: a restaurant opened in my community and asked that question. The answer turned out to be: hairstylists. So the restaurant distributed coupons good for two free dinners to all the styling salon owners within a two-mile radius of the restaurant. The salon owners would eat their free meals, then talk up the restaurant in their salons, generating loads of business for the restaurant. By recognizing that the salon was the nerve center of the community, the restaurant was able to succeed without spending one cent for advertising.

The question to ask

And so it is with many unusual marketing methods. As a small entrepreneur, you can take more chances than many well-established large companies. Take advantage of your smallness. Experiment. Make up your own advertising implements. If you make ten signs, you can hire ten high school students to affix the signs to their bikes and then ride the bikes to where your prospects might be. Would this work for you?

Taking advantage of your smallness

Perhaps you could arrange to have a truck with bells drive through neighborhoods, alerting the community to your offerings. Ice cream companies do this. Political candidates do this. It's worth it if you think it could work and if it won't offend the neighbors.

Many entrepreneurs use their voice-mail to market their services. When people call during the hours the businesses are closed, they receive new information about products and services or the latest sale. Other enterprising business owners offer to create free placemats for restaurants, highlighting the guerrilla's business name and address, along with concise copy.

Spare time as a marketing weapon

One of the more valuable miscellaneous marketing weapons is spare time. Guerrillas use it to write thank-you notes to customers, send greeting cards, clip articles of interest to key customers and then mail them, call ex-customers to see why they left, give advance notice to good customers about sales and promotions, and to pay attention to tiny details that are anything but tiny to customers—such as sending a note to customers congratulating them on accomplishments by them or their family. A buddy of mine received a thank-you note from Crystal Fresh Bottled Water. It was hand-signed by Jeanette, Lee, Joyce, Diane, Jered, Nancy, Chet, Time, Walk, Raye, Shelly, and Dan. Hard to forget such a card. Obviously, the people at Crystal Fresh Bottled Water do not waste their spare time.

Neatness counts

Neatness is also a marketing tool, because if your premises are neat, customers will assume that's the way you run your business, and if the premises are sloppy, people will figure you treat your customers the same way. The external appearance of a retail store exerts a powerful influence as well. In fact, 40 percent of a retailer's overall identity resides in that appearance. For every 200 people per month who drive or walk past a store, five to eight actually walk in. That means about 195 of 200 people get their impression of a store based solely on what they see as they pass it. It also underscores the importance of signage, window displays, architecture, and exterior paint jobs.

Unique ways to market

There are thousands of unique ways to market, all awaiting your discovery. A bakery prints its newsletter on the flip side of its bread labels, which are inserted into the plastic bag, along with the bread. An appliance store offers a five-year warranty on reliable products, costing hardly anything and boosting sales appreciably. A coffeeshop chain improved its profits with a coffee-of-the-month program at the same time a mail-order flower company reported receiving 40 percent of its revenues from its flower-of-the-month program. Such ideas help smooth out the seasonality of many businesses. A gourmet grocery saw its profits soar after it offered cooking classes. The classes, at $20 each, broke even, but they brought in $600 per customer in postclass sales. A furniture company sends lottery tickets in its direct mailings, stamping "Lottery ticket enclosed" on the envelope. The message inside promised a follow-up call and the winning number. A full 70 percent of callers listened to the pitch. A home furnishings store sends a Polaroid picture of big-ticket items. Result? Closing rates have risen 25 percent.

Speaking of photographs as a marketing weapon, a brewery sent digital color photos to 370 newspapers, along with a PR story. The cost was $725, but the photo and story were picked up by 36 newspapers. This payed for the cost of coverage.

In the next year and every year thereafter, two or three fascinating ad vehicles will be invented. TV cable interconnects for low-cost prime time come to mind. So do shopping cart video monitors, classified advertising TV channels, classified on-line ad sections, and the ubiquitous home shopping networks. Marketing to people on telephone hold was a novel idea once, and today it's standard for many a guerrilla company. To see how it works, ask for a free brochure and demo tape by calling 1-800-466-4653. Keep your eyes peeled. If you honestly feel that a new ad vehicle can help you—not as a gimmick but as a sales tool—give it a try. For example, if you're marketing a rock concert and you know of a beach where lots of potential concert-goers hang out, market your concert on a banner pulled by an airplane. It shouldn't be tough to find a plane owner who offers such a service.

Keep your eyes peeled for new weapons

Publish an annual report, especially if you're not a public company. It's a unique and rather wonderful way of communicating with your customers and prospects. It will get inordinately high readership because no small companies publish annual reports—everybody knows that. Or at least they didn't until guerrilla marketing became so necessary.

Annual reports aren't only for biggies

Market by providing extra services such as child care and baby-sitting services. Several exercise centers, for example, have increased their clientele by offering well-supervised services free of charge.

A videotape brochure will cut the cost of a sales call. The 7 percent response rate to video marketing is quite attractive compared with the 2 percent expected of most direct mailings.

You might plan to regularly publish a newsletter, as many companies do. Here are some guidelines for publishing a successful newsletter:

Guidelines for successful newsletters

- Remember that newsletters should motivate prospects to buy while helping them in general.
- Provide valuable, timely, brief information.
- Make your newsletter easy to read and easy to look at.
- Give a host of fabulous ideas; be known as an important source.
- Let a professional designer create a great-looking format for your newsletter or use new computer software to do it yourself.
- Don't let your designer create a costly, elaborate format.
- Don't publish on a random basis. You want your newsletter to be habit-forming.
- Don't send to people who never respond to any of your offers.
- Don't offer outdated, untimely, complicated information.
- Don't make your newsletter too long; they're popular because they don't take much time to read.
- Don't forget that people buy *solutions to their problems*. Newsletters, thanks to desktop publishing and a realization of the importance of time, are now easier and more sensible to add to your arsenal than ever before.

Marketing with a 900 number

Should you market with a 900 number? First off, realize that most people now associate 900 phone numbers with scams and porn. They also know they'll be hit with a dialing fee and they don't really want to pay it. That's why some companies look askance at 900 numbers. But Procter & Gamble ran a sweepstakes with a 900 number, costing 75 cents a call. Of the quarter of a million people who entered, only 24,000 used the 900 number, and P&G has no immediate plans to use a 900 number for its next promotion. Still, if you want to market this way, know these nine facts:

1. Callers with a 900 number will be fewer than with a free 800 number, but will be more qualified.
2. A 900 number is terrible for obtaining leads but marvelous for generating hot prospects.
3. A 900 line can help build a qualified base of prospects if you offer something other than your main offering. Example by a large guerrilla: Kimberly-Clark offered parents a 900 number that played a personalized lullaby. Now they gain revenues from the more than 100,000 calls they received.

4. Your 900-number callers can be categorized by forty different demographic and psychographic clusters. The 900 service offering this information is called Prizm 900. Ask your local phone company about it.

5. When supplying prospects with data, offer to fax it to callers who use your 900 number. Many, needing your data and needing it this instant, will gladly pay the $5 toll for the call.

6. A 900 number can generate revenues without sales when used to give people an edge in sweepstakes and an extra incentive, such as a special discount, for purchasing. Notice that I did say *revenue without sales.*

7. Samples can be distributed to very qualified people if they can request the samples only by calling your 900 number.

8. Memberships and subscriptions can easily be sold through a 900 number.

9. Fundraisers obtain money from small contributors by using a 900 number.

Contests and sweepstakes

Also consider contests and sweepstakes. These definitely do attract people, even though they may not be attracted to your primary offering. Those who enter do become involved with you, and involvement can lead to sales. Just remember that the purposes of contests and sweepstakes are (1) to get names for your mailing list, (2) to separate you from the ranks of strangers, and (3) to entice people to enter your store in order to enter the contest. Be sure you place the entry boxes in the rear of the store so that entrants can scope out your other offerings while they try to win that free trip to Hawaii.

Certainly you have seen ads or received mail that screams "You have been selected," or "Fabulous Sweepstakes," or "You may have already won $1,000,000," or "Be a winner." Some sweepstakes experts believe that although people may not have money for food, they do have money for sweepstakes. In fact, the experts say, "When times get bad, sweepstakes get good."

Sponsors spend hundreds of millions on prizes, plus even more advertising the sweepstakes. The number of contests and sweepstakes in America is growing steadily, about 33 percent each year. Contests and sweepstakes used to be shunned as legally and morally dubious. But they have now become a mainstay of American marketing. For that reason, they are worth considering. If you do get involved, be sure you do everything on the up-and-

Once shunned but now a mainstay

up. Check with your lawyer to be sure you aren't conducting an illegal lottery by asking people to guess the number of coins in a bottle.

If you want to attract foot traffic to a particular location, run a contest that requires people to come to your place of business to enter and to return to learn if they have won. Smart marketers know that everyone should win something. Whatever it is, it should be substantial enough so that they don't resent you and associate your offering with their loss. The best prize of all—better than cruises, convertibles, and round-the-world trips—is cash. No surprise there!

The gambling instinct

People like to gamble; even charities are jumping onto the contest bandwagon. So let your imagination run rampant. I know a retailer who filled a gigantic container with goldfish. Then he advertised his contest: "Guess the number of goldfish in the container and win $1,000!" His traffic count (and his sales) rose so dramatically that the $1,000 prize didn't even put a minor dent in his budget. Because he was a guerrilla, he gave twenty-five-cent plants to everyone who entered—after the prizewinner was announced. Again, people came in to collect their prizes, and while they were there, well, they purchased something else. Are you surprised?

Different communities have different laws regarding contests. I'm sure you've seen the disclaimer "Void where prohibited by law" appended to many sweepstakes entry forms. So don't leap into this type of marketing without first consulting the local authorities.

Contests always attract attention. What you want to do is attract the attention of *prospects*, and not just people. Because people want not only to make money but also to save money, try marketing with price-off coupons. If you're a retailer, use creative tags on your merchandise. Perhaps each tag can offer a different percentage discount. Then you can advertise a "Mystery Tag Sale." It's not a completely new idea, merely a variation on an old one. But it can, and does, work.

Giving "spiffs," or special commissions, to salespeople who surpass a certain goal or sell a specific item is also an effective method of marketing. Can you put it to work to increase your own sales?

How much is that doggie in the window?

Exciting, ever-changing window displays can also be effective. You're in luck if you can use them. And even if you don't have your own display window, you may be able to strike up a deal with someone who does, another person for your growing list of fusion marketing partners. Just imagine the difference between a store that has a window display and one that doesn't. Enormous!

I know of a fancy hairstyling salon that kept a poster in its window advertising a nearby clothing boutique. The boutique displayed a poster for the salon. Both gained extra sales as a result. The cost? Nil. The only price was the few seconds it took for someone to come up with the idea. As you know, guerrillas are all too happy to invest time instead of money when it comes to marketing.

Maybe you can market and *save* time. Who does that? Users of cellular telephones, that's who. Does that mean all guerrillas need one? Here's a test to help you answer this:

Do you need a cellular phone?

- Including commuting, do you spend two or more hours per day in your car for work?
- Do you conduct at least 20 percent of your business by phone?
- Do you often have unproductive time on the road?
- Are you often in locations where you are unable to be reached on the phone by others?
- Do you make frequent stops at pay phones to make calls during the day—and sometimes have to search for a pay phone?
- Have you ever lost business because you failed to get phone messages in time or didn't return a call promptly enough?
- Does your business require that customers be able to get information to you whenever necessary?
- Do you frequently need to reschedule appointments or inform people if you're running late?
- Are you often driving alone, and could it benefit your firm if you had an in-car meeting with someone?
- Do you ever get ideas while driving that you'd like to put into effect immediately?

If you answered yes to only two of these questions, you should look into a car phone. If you answered yes to four or more of the questions, experts say your car phone might pay for itself. I resisted buying a car phone for years. Now I wonder what the dickens I ever did without it.

All of the miscellaneous marketing methods are valuable to one entrepreneur or another. They very often make the difference between a profit and a loss. But they rarely can serve as the foundation for a marketing program. They should be used as adjuncts to a solid mass-media program. You've got to prevent your public from becoming callous to your marketing, and these miscellaneous marketing tools do the trick.

Although many miscellaneous marketing tools remain forever miscellaneous—that is, never enter the marketing mainstream—they are not to be ignored. Guerrillas look under every rock, peer around every corner, examine every opportunity. You never can tell when you might make a flurry of sales from a moped sign displayed before thousands of prospects in a park on a sunny day.

Guerrillas look under every rock

Postcard decks

A decade ago, nobody heard of postcard decks—those decks of twenty or thirty postcards encased in clear plastic, addressing the same topic—business, psychology, kids, whatever—and mailed to a specific target audience. I receive postcard decks centered on business offerings. My wife receives them focused upon psychology products—books, tapes, seminars, and directories. Each postcard has a different advertiser's name on one side and room for a stamp (no need to make these postpaid). The other side has a time-limited offer: a discount, freebie, or two-for-one deal. Postcard decks are today the second-fastest-growing marketing tool—only on-line marketing is growing more rapidly. The cost is very low and the response rate is in the 20 percent range. In 1997, more than 75 percent of advertisers who used postcard decks repeated the tactic. You can be sure they wouldn't have tried it a second time if it hadn't worked the first. Postcard decks gloriously build the selling momentum. To learn more about them, call 800-323-2751.

Always keep your eyes—and your mind—open to new media by studying the marketing publications. *Adweek* is my favorite; I recommend subscribing. Call 800-722-6658.

Hot items and markets

What are the hot new products of the times? Perhaps you can turn them into a marketing tool or offer them as an incentive or gift. In the '90s, the hot items and markets are:

Rain-forest goods	Persons suffer-	Big-screen TVs
Portable phones	ing from	White appliances
Doggie day-care	depression	Beach volleyball
Beach umbrellas	Early retirees	Supersize
Sports drinks	Environmentally	bookstores
Vegetarians	friendly items	Condoms

Catalogs/Catalog	Birkenstocks	Stepfamilies
shoppers	Nannies	Micro-TVs
Minivans	Men's hats	Sports-utility
Snowboards	Army families	vehicles
Rollerblades	Internet users/the	Compact discs
Airbags in cars	Internet	Wireless
Slow food	Mountain bikes	technologies
Liquid diets	Hair loss	
Living wills	Latchkey kids	

Other new products may be called to your attention on a regular basis with a subscription to *Product Alert*, a twice-monthly briefing on new packaged goods, or its companion publications, *International Product Alert, Lookout Nonfoods*, and Category Report—covering five product categories. Get more details by contacting Marketing Intelligence Service Ltd., at its toll-free number, 800-836-5710. Be warned, some of the subscription rates run $1,000.

As these publications alert you to new products, *Adweek, Advertising Age, Inc., Entrepreneur*, the *Wall Street Journal*, and perhaps even your local newspaper regularly inform you of new media—from ads in elevators to electronic bulletin boards accessed by your computer.

And keep in mind that once upon a time, newspapers, magazines, radio, and direct mail were miscellaneous media.

For guerrillas with deep computer expertise but not deep pockets, digital media technology offers cost-effective options. **Guerrilla media** These exciting new marketing tools allow you to support your basic message, focus more sharply on your niche markets, open doors to new markets, and reach higher percentages of your existing customer base. With these media, you can create world-class marketing materials with the finest production values.

Lou CasaBianca, president of New Media (415-456-1914) and a leader in the field of new guerrilla media, has long encouraged entrepreneurs to use their computers to design and print business cards, stationery, packages, brochures, circulars, direct mailings, newsletters, and media ads. Off-the-shelf software can put all these tools at your disposal. And database software can help you monitor and respond to trends and to changes in your customer base.

Computer-driven voice-mail devices can help you get the

most out of telemarketing media such as 800 and 900 phone services. They can also be very valuable when combined with product demos, seminars, trade-show exhibits, and the more advanced media, such as video discs, cable TV, desktop publishing, multimedia presentations, and infomercials. The proliferation of audiocassette players and VCRs makes the new media available to virtually every potential customer, and the growing use of computers widens your audience.

Get your feet wet, but don't drown

I encourage guerrillas to get their feet wet in the area of computer-based production, although I warn them to tread carefully in this area. Guerrilla production can be complex and technically demanding. You'll have to create it in-house, hire a consultant, or retain a company to handle the task for you. Beware of companies that are using outmoded equipment and technology. With the right equipment and expertise, you can produce most marketing materials in-house more cost-efficiently than by paying an outside vendor.

How do you start with these new technologies? By talking with a good consultant who will demystify the new media options for you and advise you on the *appropriate* combination of guerrilla media for your company. Note that italicized word. *Overkill is not necessary.* You don't need complicated or overly high-tech media components, merely the ones that can do the right job for you for the least money with the fastest turnaround.

The newest and smallest companies can certainly exploit guerrilla media techniques to the maximum. Remember, though, that these tools are the means to an end—not an end in themselves. Your goal is to establish a more profitable marketing communication system.

A profitable marketing communication system

Guerrillas take advantage of the technological options that are presently at their disposal or that are fast approaching. These technologies include personal computers, modems, fax machines, electronic bulletin boards, and interactive compact discs. Entrepreneurs who have technophobia will be left in the dust of the computer-literate guerrillas. Yesterday people *asked* if you have a fax machine. Today they *assume* you do. The costs of these guerrilla media devices are minuscule compared to the potential return. In little time you'll realize that they've added to your personal productivity, not to mention your company's profitability.

To gain further insight into guerrilla media, you can subscribe to *Marketing with Technology News* (phone: 212-222-1765;

fax: 212-678-6357). This newsletter is published once a month by fax. It covers fax broadcasting, fax-on-demand, videotext, FM subcarriers, cellular communications, audiotext, and the latest breakthroughs in marketing technology, including a marketer's resource catalog.

Fax marketing is based on the idea that less is more. People are inundated with information and have time to only glance at it—and the sooner it arrives the better. Speed is omnipotent. Fax marketing also helps guerrillas combat rising postal rates by aligning marketers with declining phone rates. I don't, however, recommend unsolicited faxes or "junk faxes," as a nonadoring public has christened them.

Fax marketing

Now that you have opened your mind to marketing with fax machines, open it more to consider voice-mail as a weapon of guerrilla marketing. To gain specific information about voice-mail in your part of the world, contact your telephone company. My phone company in California offers a voice-mail package that includes call forwarding, a message-waiting indicator, and a special dial tone that tells you when you have a message, and the message-receiving capability twenty-four hours a day, seven days a week. Callers are transferred automatically to voice-mail when the phone is busy or unanswered, and they receive a personal greeting with your own voice (or anyone's voice, for that matter). They can leave a detailed message for you to review any time and retrieve from virtually any touch-tone phone. You can use the system to send a message to one person or to a group with a single phone call. You can also add paging notification and call transferring to an attendant.

Guerrilla voice-mail

The phone company will manage your voice-mail system and handle all additions, deletions, and mailbox options: length of message, number of messages, messages to save, length of greeting, and paging notification. You can have a single mailbox—personal message center—or many mailboxes, one for each person in your employ if you want.

Costs for this guerrilla medium are lower than you might imagine, and the phone company owns the equipment. You don't have to purchase anything; you simply pay a monthly fee.

Your prospects and customers are getting used to voice-mail and appreciating its ability to get through to you even when you're not around. As with many new technologies, people seemed to resent voice-mail when it was first introduced. Today people don't mind it as much. And owners of small businesses wonder how the heck they got around without it.

Guerrillas today are converting their computers from passive tools into proactive assistants. The selections of your computer, software, and media peripherals will be among the most important decisions you'll make in building your guerrilla media capability. The technology of all these components will improve with time. The prices will drop. The power will increase. The design will become more handsome. If you don't act now, you cannot enjoy the income that they may provide. *It is not a good idea to wait.* I purchased my own computer gadgetry fifteen years ago. Had I waited until prices dropped and technology improved, I would have made my purchase yesterday and missed the bundle of money my computer enabled me to make during that decade. Buy now and upgrade later. All the pros will tell you this.

From passive to proactive

The emerging guerrilla media mentioned here can give you the clout of a *Fortune* 500 company, can target your message in a broad spectrum of media, and can reach a diversity of markets. At this moment, these are referred to as new media. But I remember when stereo music, microwave ovens, cordless phones, and quartz watches were considered new. Guerrillas have a knack for spotting the necessities from among the passing novelties. We must overcome any insidious signs of technophobia to ensure the success of our companies.

Overcome your technophobia

Now I'll tell you about on-line marketing. I waited this long because the field is changing so darned rapidly. Actually, I've already put what I know between the covers of two books that I coauthored with Charles Rubin. *Guerrilla Marketing Online: Second Edition—The Entrepreneur's Guide to Earning Profits on the Internet* and *Guerrilla Marketing Online Weapons: 100 Low-Cost, High-Impact Weapons for Online Profits and Prosperity*, both published by Houghton Mifflin, are filled with crucial information about marketing on-line.

On-line marketing

There are many statistics about the current state of on-line marketing and many more predictions about the future of on-line marketing. Both the stats and the predictions are suspect because the Internet is changing so fast. It's like describing a puff of smoke. It's one thing one moment and something else the next moment. However, I'll pin down for you those things which will probably never change.

The Internet is a marketing medium. It is one of many and

hardly ever the only one you should be using. It is not a means and an end all by itself, but simply another marketing weapon. It's a high-powered, interactive, comprehensive, and increasingly popular weapon.

To understand the popularity of the Internet, consider these numbers, which attest to the Internet's influence on business in 1997:

- Percentage of employers who think the Web has raised productivity: 48   **Internet facts**
- Approximate number of page views at Yahoo, one of the many Internet search engines, expressed in millions per day: 38
- Percentage of U.S. public schools connected to the Internet in 1994: 35
- Percentage of U.S. public schools connected to the Internet in 1996: 65
- Total number of issued U.S. patents mentioning the word "Internet": 170
- Percentage of commercial Web sites that attract advertising revenue: 16
- Percentage of people who remember a banner ad from a Web site: 12
- Percentage of people who remember a TV commercial: 10
- Percentage of CIOs (Chief Information Officers) planning to increase their company's Internet spending significantly in 1998: 31
- Number of Internet service providers in the United States and Canada listed in February of 1996: 1,447. Number listed in August of 1997: 4,133
- Number of Internet users worldwide as of the end of 1997: 100 million
- Number of users expected by the end of 2000: 200 million
- Percentage of increase in PC sales from Christmas of 1996 to Christmas of 1997: 100
- Number of documents on-line at the end of 1997, in millions: 100
- Number of documents expected to be on-line by the end of 2000, in millions: 800. It's unlikely that existing information systems will be able to cope intelligently with this volume of information, so big changes are coming.
- Amount of venture capital investment in Internet companies

during the second quarter of 1997, expressed in millions of dollars: $561.5

- Number of companies receiving all that money: 111
- Number of Americans who now consider the Internet indispensable, expressed in millions: 20
- By the year 2000, estimated percentage of Internet commerce related to travel: 41
- Number of E-mail messages sent in 1997, expressed in trillions: 2.7
- Number of E-mail messages that will be sent in 2000, in trillions: 6.9
- Number of people who subscribed to on-line services as of the end of November 1997, in millions: 25.3. Biggest on-line service: America Online (with over 10 million subscribers at this moment)
- Percentage of people on-line who use the Internet: 80; Percentage who use it for commerce: 8
- Christmas sales on-line for the holiday season of 1997: $1.1 billion (twice as much was predicted in January of 1997)
- Total on-line sales for 1997: $2.6 billion, which is big but still a mere 1 percent of total retail sales
- First year in which PC sales outpaced TV sales: 1996
- How often a new person joins the Internet community: every 1.89 seconds
- Number of Web sites active as of April of 1996: 1,002,612
- Number of new Web sites added each day: 400
- Amount invested in Internet advertising in 1995: $40 million
- Amount that will be invested in 2000: $4.5 billion
- Predicted amount that will be spent on-line in 2001: $220 billion
- Fastest-growing segment of the Internet population: people aged 55 and older
- Percentage of females on-line: 48
- Percentage who are college graduates: 48
- Percentage who are married with kids: 41
- By the year 2000, number of homes on-line in North America: 38.2. In Europe: 16.5 million. In Asia: 10 million. The Scandinavian countries and the Netherlands presently have a higher proportion of homes on-line than the United States.

I could go on indefinitely. Instead, I'll direct you to a rich source of Internet facts. Visit Nua's Internet Surveys at www.nua.

ie/choice. I'll also direct you to a valuable source of sources. Visit Internet InfoScavenger at www.infoscavenger.com. The E-mail address is scavenger@mailback.com. And I'd be remiss if I didn't direct you to our own site, which offers several hundred pages of valuable guerrilla marketing information: the Guerrilla Marketing Online site is located at www.gmarketing.com.

I want you to know what guerrillas mean when they talk about marketing on-line. They use seven avenues of marketing:

1. Send E-mail to people who *want* to receive it. Many do. Guerrillas do not engage in junk E-mailing, known as "spamming," because they feel that it litters cyberspace and intrudes in a nonintrusive medium. Guerrillas do have software, called auto responders, which enable them to automatically send E-mail to people who request it. The most popular use of the Internet currently is E-mail. By the start of 2000, there will be 140 million Americans using E-mail, and that's only in the United States, hardly the most populous nation. Compare the cost of a postage stamp with the cost of E-mail, which is on the verge of being free. Compare the time it takes to drop a letter in a mailbox with the time it takes to click a mouse. E-mail is spreading from businesses to families, friends, and on-line buddies. *An inability to type in the twentieth century is equivalent to the inability to read in the twentieth century.*

   Seven avenues of on-line marketing

2. Host chat sessions with people who are interested in the topic of your business. You can get feedback, prove your authority and credibility, and most important, establish relationships with people around the world and those in your own community.

3. Participate in on-line forums and newsgroups where you can post messages, respond to questions, and without being too pushy about it, herald your company as a source of excellent products and/or information.

4. Post classified ads in the many sections in which you can do so at no cost or low cost. You might combine audio and video with your on-line verbiage. Check out www.classifind.com to see for yourself. If you choose this avenue, post your ad *daily*. The newest ads appear at the tops of the listings.

5. Write articles. Articles are published on many on-line services. Prove your expertise and include your phone number and E-mail address. The more you give away on-line, the more you'll get.

6. Host conferences on-line—again, using an on-line service. Here, you get into interactive conversations with large groups of people, all of whom attend the conference to learn about what you have to say. Don't make your message too commercial, or they'll click you off. Word of mouse spreads incredibly fast.

7. Avail yourself of the World Wide Web. Many people think that the Web is the only way to market on-line and I'm here to say that it is one of many. It is wonderfully interactive and a place where people come to learn about you, where they can contact you and give you their names.

Some marketing experts believe that the most profound influence of Web retailing is the rupturing of a fundamental principle of real estate: *location*. Retailers must adapt to consumers who are no longer confined to ZIP codes or trade areas. Experts predict that consumers will use the Web at first to make airline, hotel, and car reservations, then car purchases, and then real estate browsing. It took forty years for the zipper to be recognized after it was invented, patented, and demonstrated. The Internet is fast becoming a component of our daily lives, with a far more comprehensive influence than the zipper!

The current cost of a retailing transaction is $15.00 in a store, $5.00 with a toll-free number, and $0.35 using the Internet. In 1995 only 10 percent of Web users purchased items on the Web. In 1996, 39 percent made purchases on the Web.

The Internet is convenient   Another reason for the influx of the Internet is convenience. On-line shoppers go on-line in their pajamas. Late in 1997, figures from America Online showed that 40 percent of on-line shopping takes place between 10 P.M. and 10 A.M., when stores are typically closed. Obviously, shoppers are increasingly turning to the Internet as a relaxing alternative to pounding the pavement.

Web marketing in 1997, according to *Advertising Age*, was handled by a Web specialist 54 percent of the time, in-house 27 percent, by an interactive ad agency 18 percent, by a PR agency 17 percent, and by a direct marketing agency 12 percent. My suggestion: look for a free brochure from a company that specializes in getting small companies on-line at a low cost. One such company is SupportWorks: phone, 800-318-2558; Web site, www.supportworks.com. Their E-mail address is info@supportworks.com.

When going on-line, guerrillas abide by *the rule of thirds*, which dictates that they invest one third of their on-line budget in designing and posting their site, one third in attracting people to their site, and one third in improving their site once they've learned the cyber ropes. They also are fully aware of *the rule of twice,* which dictates that it will cost twice as much as predicted to remain truly competitive on-line as technologies advance and evolve.

Let me boil down my Internet advice to three cogent points.

- You must know *marketing* to market on-line successfully.
- The keys to success are content, speed, change, and personalization.
- The moment you decide to market on-line, determine a plan to promote your Web site off-line as well as on-line.

Internet advice

Before moving on to real space, I'll give you a crash course in cyberspace, courtesy of Roger Parker, author of *Web Content and Design.* He says, and I agree, that you must place equal emphasis on eight elements in order to establish a successful Web site.

Establish a Web site

1. *Planning.* What do you want your site to do for you? How will it reach that goal?
2. *Content.* People will visit your site and return regularly if your content is intelligent, organized, and well presented.
3. *Design.* This refers to the look of your site. Will people be turned on or off by the graphics?
4. *Involvement.* Refers to interactivity. What do you want people to do while they visit your site and afterward?
5. *Production.* How will your site be created and posted on the Net?
6. *Follow-up.* You cannot ignore people or make them wait after they've contacted you.
7. *Promotion.* Let people know, on-line and off-line, about your site. Know your way around the search engines.
8. *Maintenance.* Unlike a TV spot, which can be finished, a Web site is a work in progress, and it must be nurtured as if it were an infant.

You must market on-line. In fact, it's so intriguing and instructive that many guerrillas spend at least one hour a week in the weekly surf—surfing the Net for fabulous ideas and horrendous

The weekly surf

Get out of that canoe

errors. On-line marketing works fabulously for those who make it part of a well-rounded guerrilla marketing program. Now I'll abide by an important rule of marketing on-line—*be concise*—and close this chapter by urging you to get your feet wet as soon as you can. The Internet is coming in like a monster tidal wave, and if you're in a canoe, you're facing major trouble.

26

Public Relations:
Instant Credibility

Public relations means exactly what it says. But it is also accurate to say that it means publicity—free stories and news about you and/or your company in newspapers, magazines, newsletters, and house organs, on radio and TV, and in any other types of media.

Here's what is good about publicity: it's free. It's believable. It gives you and your company credibility and stature. It helps establish the identity of your business. It gives you authority. It's read by a large number of people. It's remembered.

What's good about PR?

Many entrepreneurs feel that there is no such thing as bad publicity, that as long as you get your name out there before the public, it's a fine thing. But guerrillas know that bad publicity leads to negative word-of-mouth marketing, which spreads faster than wildfire. Bad publicity is bad. Good publicity is great.

There are even some bad things about good publicity, though I only mean bad in a relative sense. You have no control over publicity. You have no say-so as to when it runs. You have no control over how it is presented. It is rarely repeated. You cannot buy it. You cannot ensure its accuracy.

What's bad about PR?

On balance, however, publicity is an excellent weapon in any well-stocked marketing arsenal. And any marketing plan that fails to include some effort at public relations is a marketing plan that isn't going all out.

Public relations offers, as an unstated but valuable benefit, decades of staying power. Reprints of positive publicity can be framed, made parts of brochures, included in ads, put onto flip-charts, and leaned upon for precious credibility. The day the story appears is a heartwarming one, but the marketing power abounds in the following years. Try to use reprints of the story to empower your marketing.

PR power

When I was advertising my self-published book *Earning*

Money Without a Job in various magazines and national newspapers, I spent about $1,000 per ad. Each ad netted approximately $3,000 in sales. The book was not available in bookstores and could be purchased only through my mail-order ad. Then a reporter from the *San Francisco Chronicle* purchased a copy of my book. Because I lived in the vicinity, and because he took a liking to the book, he called and asked me if he could come to my home and interview me, and also asked if he could bring along a photographer. I extended a warm welcome to him and his camera-bearing associate.

The interview lasted about an hour and included a brief photo session. A few days later, an article about me and my book appeared in the main news section of the newspaper. Accompanying it was a photo of me. Well into the article was the address to which the $10 purchase price (now it's less) could be sent. Within a week, I received over $10,000 worth of orders! The article had not solicited orders, did not really try to sell the book, and mentioned the address and selling price in a place where only serious readers of the article would find them. More than $10,000 in sales, and the marketing didn't cost me one penny.

As wonderful as I felt about the results, I felt frustrated at not being able to repeat the process. I sent the article to other newspapers, letting them know I was available for interviews. I continued to advertise the book, achieving a fair degree of success. But never again have I been able to earn so much money with so little effort. I did make reprints of the article and then included them in mailings and press kits. Although I know of similar stories, and indeed have arranged and taken part in them, the value of PR has never been as sweet.

Because my book provided honest information on earning a good living without having to hold down a job, the reporter believed that my book was newsworthy. And this is probably the single most important factor in obtaining free publicity: provide news worth publicizing.

A fascinating P.S. to my PR tale is in regard to the reporter who interviewed me, Mel Ziegler. He took the concepts of my book to heart, quit his job at the *Chronicle*, and opened a store, the **Banana Republic is born** first of an empire, called Banana Republic. His business hit it monstrously big with its line of safari clothes—then a harbinger of fashion. Ziegler hired professional writers to describe his offerings in a catalog, which was beautifully written and designed. But, alas, what appeared to be a trend was instead a fad, and Banana Republic discontinued its safari-oriented merchandise, added mainstream clothing lines, and was then purchased by the mainstream clothing giant the Gap. The Gap is tuned in with regard to styles, prices, marketing, and selection. Because of its demonstrated genius at merchandising exactly what its target audience wants, I predict bigger and better, although less exotic, things for Banana Republic. I don't think Mel Ziegler minds one bit.

Before you read another word, understand this: *the media need you more than you need them.* They need news. They hunger for news. Their unquenchable need for news is what drives them. If you have news or can make news or can create news, you are exactly what the media are looking for.

Marcia Yudkin, who knows a thing or six about publicity, has put them into a neat book, *6 Steps to Free Publicity.* In one of the solar system's most ambitious attempts at simplifying her commonsense steps, I alert you to them here:

1. Find a news angle for your headline.
2. Present the basic facts for the angle of your headline in the first paragraph of your press release.
3. Gather or create a lively, fascinating quote that elaborates on the basic facts for the second paragraph of your release.
4. Elaborate still further on the basic facts in your third paragraph.
5. End your release with the nitty-gritty details about prices, addresses, dates, phone numbers, registration data if any. Keep this to one paragraph.
6. Send it out or hand it to your buddies who work for the media. It helps immensely if you have a specific editor or producer whom you can refer to by name. Your library has several directories with the names you want. So does Marcia's book.

Six steps to free publicity

How to generate news

How do you generate something newsy for the news media? Announce something new about your business or group. Describe what's unique and unusual about your business. Tell of an upcoming event. Write of the connection between your offering and what's in the news right now. Announce the results of a survey or research poll you conducted or even one you read about. Tell the community who won your essay contest. Tie in with a holiday or anniversary, especially a city event. Write of the connection between your business and a current trend. Make a controversial claim or at least, a very surprising claim. Make a humorous announcement. Write an eye-catching headline and you're off to the races for free publicity, appearances on talk shows, profits for a minimal investment.

If you want to, you can pay for public relations. You can hire a PR person, pay him or her a monthly or project fee—anywhere from $500 to $25,000 per month—and let that person do what is necessary to secure free publicity. PR people are experts at it: they have the contacts, the experience, the insights. They've made all the errors, learned from them, and are usually well worth their fees. But because you are a guerrilla, I want you to know how to do what PR people do. Then you can get the publicity and you won't have to pay anyone a dime.

Publicity contacts is where it's at

Moment of truth: the way to succeed at public relations is to have *publicity contacts*—people at the media whom you know on a first-name basis. It's one thing to mail a proper press kit to the proper managing editor at a publication. It's another thing to call Nancy at the paper and say, "Nancy, let's have lunch tomorrow. I have some information that will definitely interest your readers and I want you to have it first. I'll pop for the lunch."

Nancy, because she enjoys free lunches, but primarily because she knows and trusts you, has lunch with you. Never forget how hungry the news media are for news. If you have real news, they'll listen. So Nancy listens. The next day, there's a story about your product or service or company in her newspaper. When you pay a PR pro a steep fee, you're paying for a gob of Nancys, and those publicity contacts are usually well worth the price.

Make no mistake: a public relations pro works very hard and intelligently. So you'll have to put in the same kind of effort and intelligence. To gain free publicity, you must have three things: the imagination to generate real news that is worth publicizing; the influential contacts to whom you can offer your news for publication or broadcast; and the persistence to follow through and get the coverage you want.

Believe me, I was lucky when I received the free publicity for my book. I had done nary a thing to get it, didn't use much imagination, had no contacts, wasn't persistent. But I reaped rich rewards. Unfortunately, life does not usually work that way. You've got to knock yourself out to get the "free" publicity that helps so many companies. Instead of paying for the publicity with money, you pay with work: phone calls, writing, time, and determination. But all that effort will be worth your time. People who expend it say that PR really stands for profit.

If you do something worthy, you should get credit for it publicly. If you contribute money to charity, that's good—and it is a basis for PR. If you donate merchandise, that too can result in a publicity story. Be sure you let the local media know of your altruism. And find newsy ways of being altruistic.

Good PR

One of the most important public relations tools is the annual report. As a rule, entrepreneurs don't publish one. Why? It need not conform to the usual annual report sent to shareholders. It need not talk money. It can be a report that contains information valuable to your customers. When you do publish such an annual report, send copies to the media. Let them enjoy your creativity. Nudge them to give that creativity some "ink." And by all means, send your annual report to your prospects.

The guerrilla annual report

When you give a speech on a topic related to your business— and I recommend that you give them when you can—see to it that there is press coverage. After all, you are speaking because you are an authority on your topic. If the public learns that, they'll possibly reward your expertise with their patronage.

I recently went to a restaurant that was jammed. I hadn't seen any advertising for the restaurant, so I asked some friends there how they had heard of it. They told me they had been invited to an opening-week party—all the food they could eat. The restaurateur must have lost his shirt that week. But he gained it back—with a matching wardrobe and more—in the following weeks. Most likely, he wrote the free food off as a marketing expense—that's what it was.

Members of the press are frequently invited to "press parties." At these parties, cocktails or beverages and a meal or hors d'oeuvres are served, and frequently a presentation is made. It's a short one, but effective and hard-selling. The purpose is to woo the press, wine them and dine them, and then win their hearts with a dramatic presentation of the facts. Naturally, the facts are about a new business or a new direction for an old business. It's no surprise that the press coverage following these parties is tremendous. Guerrillas hold their press parties at unique places such as ferryboats, railroad cars traveling to interesting destinations, penthouses, haunted houses, parks, baseball diamonds, and art galleries.

Press parties

Press conferences

If you have a relatively momentous announcement to make, hold a press conference. Attract the press by letting them know you will tell them something newsworthy. Be sure, however, that you live up to that promise. You'll have to answer hard questions.

When a crisis develops in your community, do what you can to alleviate the problem and gain free publicity at the same time. When a flood hit the area in which I live, an enterprising businessman furnished free hamburgers to the volunteer relief workers.

Free hamburgers

He must have given away six hundred burgers. But his business was written up in five newspapers, mentioned on three radio stations, and shown on television. Well worth the 600 burgers. This is not taking advantage of an unpleasant situation as much as it is

Being "publicity aware"

being "publicity aware." A guerrilla smells opportunities every time. Example: an accident in a snowstorm closed Vail Pass in Colorado, and traffic was backed up for many blizzardy miles. Snowbound motorists were astounded when a deliveryperson from the local Domino's brought hot pizzas to their cars. Did this result in new customers and free publicity? You bet!

A major-league PR pro once told me that nearly 80 percent of the news is "planted"—sent to the media by publicity firms and lobbying groups. Sometimes planted news deals with political topics; sometimes it deals with industrial topics; and sometimes it deals with products or people. That PR pro repeated what insiders know—newspapers are hungry for real news. If you can furnish it, they'll gladly publish it. But telling a newspaper that you are having a sale is not news. Informing a radio station that you have

The hook

started a business is not news. News needs a slant to it, a hook that will interest people. If I wrote a publicity release saying that I had written a new book called *Earning Money Without a Job*, that would not really be news. But if my release stated that now there is a new way to combat unemployment, it would be news. And that might be a reason for a newspaper to write about my book.

Writing a publicity release

You communicate your news by writing a publicity release. Address your release to as specific a department as you can— Sports, Entertainment, Business, Food, or Technology—and use the name of the editor of that department. If your news is really hot, send it to the news or city editor. If your news item is homier than hard news, send it to the feature editor. Tailor your publicity release to the personality of the medium for which it's intended. A release for a newspaper might be longer and more detailed than a release for a radio or TV station. (The latter usually require brevity and spice).

When writing a publicity release for any medium, use the format that is generally followed and that is appreciated by most media. Put the date in the upper right-hand corner. Type in the name of the person to contact for more information (probably yourself). Be sure to include your phone number. Write the release date next. The item may be for immediate release, in which case you say that—using these exact words: *For Immediate Release.* If it's for release after September 19th, 1999, state so. Next, you have the option of providing a headline. I recommend that you do provide one. If you don't, the newspaper will. And if you supply a headline, the newspaper may change it.

Then type your release. Double-space it. Use 8×11 paper and leave wide margins. Begin one-third of the page from the top. When you move on to a second page, identify your story at the top of that page, in the left-hand corner. Write in short, clear sentences. Do not use long words or adjectives. Do not give opinions. State facts. To indicate the end of your release, type either a ##, a ***, or a -30-, centered, below the last line.

What do you say in your release? Say who it is about, what it is, where it is, when it is, why it is, and how it came about. Say all that in your first paragraph if you possibly can. Read your local newspaper and notice how deftly reporters include the who, what, where, when, why, how data at the beginning of most articles.

It helps immensely if your release is accompanied by a very short note. It's fine if your note is handwritten. On the note, explain in as few words as possible why you are sending the release. When you can, and when it is appropriate, enclose an 8×10 black and white glossy photo. The photo should be interesting— newspapers want to be as interesting as they can. It helps to type a caption on a blank sheet of paper and attach it to the photo. To stand apart even more, put your materials into an attractive folder, including a comprehensive and up-to-date company background, and a business card. Now you've got a press kit.

What do guerrillas do to augment their press kits? They enclose extra photos or slides. Are you announcing a product, a new location, a major personnel change, or other event that would be enhanced with pictures? If you want to include color pictures, use slides, because they provide top quality and processing flexibility.

The press kit

Guerrillas also include brochures and reprints and use them when sending the kits to members of the press who may be unfamiliar with their company. They often enclose a competitive table. A general market overview should already be in your company background piece. A competitive analysis highlights your strengths when compared to your competitors. Guerrillas make sure each press kit is accompanied by a press guide or Q&A. This document anticipates the key questions a reporter might ask about their company or its announcement and then answers them. Finally, many entrepreneurs enclose references. When announcing a product or service, include references from some of your most satisfied customers, one or more industry analysts who will comment favorably on your company, and perhaps even names and key contacts of your major competitors. Takes guts. Gets attention.

Don't overlook the little guys

Guerrillas love the free press coverage they get from the big newspapers, but they rarely overlook the small ones. There are many of them and nearly all of them count. They never send more than one release at a time, and they are quick to learn of the myriad of PR opportunities on-line, discussed in *Guerrilla Marketing Online, Second Edition*. There I go again, blowing my horn and pumping up your profits. Guerrillas are most delighted to hand their press release to a real live person, but they also know that faxing of releases is now acceptable.

When you're armed with a perfect release and you send it to the right person, there's still a good chance that it will be ignored. If you give it to the right person, there's less of a chance. If you give it to the right person over lunch, that's even better. And if you give it to the right person over lunch and that person is an old friend of yours, that's best of all, though no guarantee of publication. This is why publicity contacts are so very important. If you lack those contacts and the time to have lunch with all the editors and news selectors at the various media, you'll have to keep phoning the person to whom you mailed your release until it gets published. That's where persistence comes in. Don't forget, there

Squeaky wheels get the ink

are many people trying to get their stories in. Squeaky wheels receive the grease . . . or ink!

Send your release about ten days in advance of the date you wish it to appear. This allows you time to phone the editor and suggest that the newspaper or other medium cover your story, and you can make suggestions for other picture possibilities. It gives the paper—or the station—time to fit the story in, thereby increasing its chances of being used. Also, you'll be absolutely certain that the release is delivered in time.

Suppose you are Super Handyman. You want free publicity. You decide it would be newsworthy to build a unique barbecue pit in the local park. You secure permission, then write your release. Accompanying it is an 8 × 10 black and white glossy photo of you working on a project of which you are very proud. You include an outline or caption pasted (not clipped) to the bottom of the photo and folded back. It says, "Award-winning patio being built by patio designer Marvin Reskin, owner of Super Handyman, Clancy Avenue." The accompanying release says:

How Super Handyman got free PR

April 15th, 1998

Contact: Marvin Reskin (510) 555-3463
SUPER HANDYMAN, sponsor
115 Clancy Avenue
Berkeley, CA 91554

FOR IMMEDIATE RELEASE

DESIGNER TO BUILD BBQ PIT AS GIFT TO CITY

Marvin Reskin, of Super Handyman, a local contracting firm, will construct a barbecue pit of his own design in Glenn Park on Friday, April 28th, as a gift to the city.

    Reskin, whose patios, sun decks, and barbecue pits have won awards for design excellence, said, "I've drawn up a design that will fit right in with the city's personality. I don't think there's a barbecue pit in America quite like it."

    The gift to the city, to be constructed on the third anniversary of Super Handyman, has been approved by the town planning commission. "The people in this town have been very receptive to my designs," said Reskin. "I feel it is high time I express my gratitude."

    Reskin will cook and serve hamburgers on the newly designed barbecue pit when it is completed Friday evening. The public is invited to view the new addition to Glenn Park and to enjoy the hamburgers—while they last.

*   *   *

    The best thing that could possibly happen would be for the newspapers to publish the release as sent, then do a follow-up story on the celebration following the completion of the barbecue pit, complete with a photo of Super Handyman and his creation. Perhaps you can't build a barbecue pit for your city, but you can still gain free publicity if you do things such as teach classes in your area of expertise, publish a newsletter on it (a nifty marketing tool in itself), pen a column, or write articles. All of these things help establish you as an authority. Because of the free media

The best thing that could happen

coverage you'll get for your work, word of your expertise will spread, and it will sink into the minds of your prospects.

The best marketing plans usually call for a combination of advertising and public relations. The two go hand in hand. One is highly credible but gives you no control. The other has less credibility but gives you complete control. Together, they supply most of the pieces of the marketing puzzle.

Be newsy

Even if you have the best of contacts and the most dogged of attitudes, the bottom line is still that you have to provide news to get a free publicity story or interview. If a Martian lands on the roof of your store, you'll have made that news without even trying. But usually you've got to generate the news, as Super Handyman did when he built a barbecue pit for the city.

There are ten ways guerrillas can create news all by themselves. Most likely, you can garner free publicity by employing at least one of them.

Nine ways to create news

1. Tie in your marketing with the news of the day. If you're a computer tutor, if you can teach people how to operate computers, you can issue statements that pertain to the news stories about computers. Position yourself as the expert. Stage an event—a computer fair or a free computer seminar—during which you show the public how computers work. When enormous floods hit northern California, the Ford Motor Credit Company rose to the occasion by sending letters saying, "We hope you were not affected by the flooding in your area. But if you were, please accept our sympathy and concern. Ford Credit understands that you may experience temporary financial problems due to conditions beyond your control. We stand ready to help you if you need it. We can offer payment extensions allowing you to skip your next one or two monthly payments. Just call our Customer Service Center at our toll-free number." This is good customer relations, good PR, and good humanity, rolled into one by a huge corporation acting like a guerrilla.

2. Release useful information. In your copious reading, maybe you'll come across an item in which your community will be interested. Include it in your press release. You can obtain such useful business data from directories such as those published by American Business Directories. Call them at 402-593-4600 and ask for their free brochure.

3. Form a committee to study how computers can help the com-

munity—by lowering taxes, for instance. It need not be that, but find some slant.

4. Give an award or a scholarship each year. People love awards, and perhaps you can invent one that ties in with computer education.

5. Make a prediction using your computer. If it is startling enough, and pretty likely to be true, it will be news and will enhance your reputation as an expert.

6. Celebrate your own business anniversary by providing free computer lessons for a week. This is the same principle as Super Handyman's donation of a barbecue pit.

Happy anniversary to you

7. Do something incredible. Maybe you could keep a talking parrot at the place where you give computer lessons. The parrot, naturally, would talk computerese ("Polly wants a print-out"). Maybe you could get married in your computer classroom. Maybe you could paint a mural of a computer on the outside of your building. Keep it in good taste, but make it amazing.

Do something incredible

8. Surprise your prospects—and media—by giving something away for free such as a computer course scholarship, an award for kids using computers, an appearance by a local celebrity, a public demonstration of computer technology.

9. Locate a memorable spokesperson who will serve as a living, breathing marketing weapon. It might be a local entrepreneurial success, a local sports star who uses a computer, an inexpensive, recognizable person who will appear at your demos and trade shows, maybe even in your other marketing weapons. Some of my clients have secured the services of the trainer of the professional football team. Trainers get little if any publicity and are often delighted to be your spokesman for very little compensation other than the fame. If your offering has anything to do with physical fitness, that trainer is ideal.

So as not to leave you only halfway home in your quest to be your own PR pro, here are ten guidelines that will help you get the coverage you want:

1. Determine exactly what sets your product or service apart from your competitors'. The media are not looking for humdrum news.

Guidelines for obtaining coverage

2. Practice communicating your message. Actually rehearse

what you'll say to the media. Put it in writing. Say it aloud. Keep it clear, crisp, and concise.

3. Become a familiar name at local clubs, organizations, and associations likely to support your effort. Good research will pay off here.

4. Introduce yourself to newspaper, magazine, TV, and radio pros. You know all about the importance of contacts.

5. Find media biggies at social meetings, local conventions, and events likely to attract them, such as fundraisers. Join their clubs and hangouts. This includes their bars and restaurants.

6. Study all your options—magazines, newspapers, radio, TV, supermarket circulars, trade journals, free event listings, new publications, public service announcements on local radio stations, even public radio and television.

7. Watch and listen to talk shows. If you have a talk-show topic, call the host. If you don't have one, develop a hot topic. Good guests are hard to find.

8. Call radio stations and request a free media kit. This will give you ideas on how to prepare your own kit.

9. Realize that the media always need *hard news* of interest to their readers. If you have any, tell them of it.

10. Consider staging your own special events to attract prospects, sell to customers, and generate media attention. This is often an easily obtainable ticket to PR.

Another part of public relations is to join civic clubs and community organizations. That may be your most important marketing tool. Although you will be doing your duty as a member of the community, you will also make lots of contacts with people who can give you business and with people who will refer business to you. I hope you don't join just to obtain business. In fact, if you do, your true motivation may be discovered, causing you to lose business. But if you join to aid your fellow man, you'll most likely end up with important contacts. If you work hard and diligently for the community, folks will assume that you run your business the same way, and they'll want to do business with you.

The most effective marketing tool can be to join organizations—the only marketing many successful entrepreneurs do is to join as many clubs as possible. I'm sure you've heard that a lot of business is conducted on golf courses. Just as much is conducted in meetings, at lunches, in steam rooms, at dinners, and over cocktails with fellow members of a club.

A true guerrilla puts as much effort into public relations as possible. To a guerrilla, everything that one does publicly is really public relations. That includes the sponsoring of events, teams, floats, tournaments, and more. You'll obtain sales more slowly from sponsoring a Little League team, bowling team, or homecoming float than you will from certain other marketing methods, but entrepreneurs report that the sponsorship of events does help other methods of marketing take effect more quickly. There's no question that you will make sales. You will gain credibility as you support your community. You'll cause folks to feel good about you. Don't underestimate the power of favorable association. Some major advertisers who spend millions on TV commercials test those commercials to find out only if they have resulted in the company's product having a more favorable association in the minds of viewers. So it is true that sponsoring events will cause more favorable public association in a hurry. But sales in a hurry? No way.

Join in

Still, if you want to establish yourself as part of the community, consider sponsorship. Sponsor a turkey race at Thanksgiving, a toys-for-the-homeless collection at Christmas, Little League teams during the summer, and bowling teams during the winter. This will do everything good for you—except win instant sales. Because you are a guerrilla, however, you'll get those sales through other marketing methods. And since that's the case, perhaps you should spring for a sponsorship. It doesn't cost all that much—a few hundred bucks in most cases. And what it doesn't buy in quick profits it buys in good will.

Who should consider sponsorship

Among those who should consider sponsorship are new businesses that need to establish their identity, companies that sell items intended for the audiences of the events sponsored—for example, sporting goods stores sponsoring any type of athletic team—and companies that feel they must become more involved with the community. Sometimes community involvement is beneficial for political reasons.

Sponsor something

Consider your own business. If there is not a good reason for you to sponsor teams or events, you probably should not do it. Don't do it just for your ego, and don't do it because your kid asked you to. But do it if you can, for a true guerrilla utilizes as many marketing tools as can be properly employed. And it doesn't take much cash to employ this particular tool properly. But it means you should show up for games—even if your team has one win and ten losses. Such dedication to a community team will translate, and rightly so, as dedicated treatment of your customers.

Actually, doing it for your kid isn't always bad marketing. If your company has been earning money for many years within the community, there is absolutely nothing wrong with giving some of those profits back. If you sponsor a Little League team and outfit the team in snazzy uniforms that herald your company name, you are making a charitable contribution and marketing at the same time. Nothing wrong with that!

Frankly, many teams and events are sponsored for the benefit of the sponsor's ego. If you want to massage yourself the same way, be sure you know why you are doing it.

It may be that you can take advantage of the timing of certain events. For instance, if a homecoming parade, featuring floats and queens and brass bands, ties in with a specific promotion you are having, join right in. Sometimes you can collaborate with a fellow entrepreneur and co-sponsor a float.

Doing it for your kid and your community

Many astute people believe that you should not become involved in community relations for the profit motive alone. They believe that if you sponsor teams or events for the sake of the community you will prosper, but that if the sole purpose of sponsorship is to earn extra dollars you will fail to prosper. Give that some thought. I believe it to be true. Deep down, I feel that you do owe something to your community if you are succeeding.

Not for profits only

Sponsorship lubricates the marketing wheels that are already turning for you. People aren't going to buy from you because they saw your name on a uniform, but they may buy from you if they saw your ad in the newspaper *and* your name on a uniform.

There is still another reason why some companies sponsor events: they don't want to be resented. If you operate in a small town where most of the businesses sponsor teams, you'll have to pay those civic dues—or run the risk of offending the members of the community. And it's true that the success of your business may depend upon the health and stability of your community. If you sponsor an event or a team, you contribute to that health. This helps you in two ways: it helps your region and it helps your business. Without doubt, sponsoring events, teams, causes, or floats gets you recognized as a solid citizen, as a kind, generous helpful, friendly human being—a pillar of the community. And that helps your business, regardless of your intent. Guerrillas can be philanthropists, too. No law against it.

The cost of sponsorship is going to be time as well as money. Not too much of each, but some of both. You can't sponsor a team and fail to show up for its games. You can't back an event and then divorce yourself from it entirely. Word will get out that you are in it for the money alone, and that will cause you to lose more sales than you'll gain.

In some cities there are no events or teams to sponsor. Although you may want to, you may be unable to add this weapon to your marketing arsenal. If that's the case, perhaps you can create an event. Think about doing that if you have the opportunity. If yours is a growing community, your initiative, which costs very little now, will be worth a lot later. You will have positioned yourself in the right way, in the right place, at the right time. Perhaps you'll never again have that chance. Perhaps one of your competitors will start a cause, a league, or an event and assume a leadership position. Don't let that happen. As a guerrilla, you should take the leadership position.

Creating an event

A client of mine sponsored a 10-kilometer run and donated the proceeds to the town's favorite charity. Each of the entrants received a free T-shirt with the name of the event on the front and the name of the sponsor on the back. The race is held once a year. The T-shirts are worn *throughout* the year.

The payoff from sponsorships will differ from that connected with other marketing tools. Don't shortchange that payoff, however. It might be a feeling of warmth toward your business by the community at large. It might also be a new contact, a new customer, a new source of profits for your business. Perhaps at a league meeting you'll meet someone who can direct fifty new customers your way. Maybe you'll be awarded a gigantic sale seven years after you've sponsored the event. This is not at all uncommon.

The payoff

By sponsoring events, you create the opportunity to meet new people, make new friends. And because your business, rather than you, is doing the sponsoring, it will probably be the benefactor of the gratitude. Little political favors may fall your way, such as better positioning in the local newspaper for your ads, better timing on the local radio station for your commercials, new contracts coming your way. None of this will be measurable, in the classic sense, but little of it will be accidental. Your sponsorship will be the cause. Increased profits will be the effect. Will it always work that way? Not always, but sometimes. Now that you know the value of sponsorship, look into it.

In her fascinating book *The Zen of Hype*, Raleigh Pinsky explains the exact differences between advertising, sales promotion, publicity, and guerrilla PR. When the circus comes to town and you put up a sign, that's advertising. If you put that sign on the back of the elephant and you walk the elephant through town, that's sales promotion. If the elephant, with the sign on his back, tramples the mayor's flower garden and the paper reports it, that's publicity. If you can get the mayor to laugh about it and forgive the elephant and then ride in the circus with no hard feelings, then you truly understand guerrilla PR.

The elephant and the guerrilla

The canny Ms. Pinsky reminds us that advertising is the most expensive method of getting out the word. Direct marketing is the next most expensive method. On-line marketing is third when it comes to expense. PR is the least expensive, but is the most time-consuming.

A truth to remember as we depart an old century for a new one is that presidents, kings, and CEOs don't really run the world; their PR firms have taken over that responsibility.

If you know PR, you should know what the media do not like. It's a pretty obvious list: hemming and hawing, wasted time, frivolous questions, incomplete sentences, bad writing, people who cannot take no for an answer, people who don't really believe in what they're calling or writing about, ugly persistence, demanding natures, bad listeners, people who constantly interrupt, lack of common sense, and blatant attempts to advertise under the guise of real news.

What the media do not like

Why does well-intentioned PR go awry? For the same reason that businesses fail, marketing fails, and advertising fails: *failure to follow up*. If you're too busy to make an average of four phone calls for every media outlet you've contacted, turn your PR over to a pro who has the time and expertise you may lack.

If you have a yogurt shop and send out a release that says, "Best yogurt in town," you'll be greeted by a big ho-hum. But if you sponsor a charity drive, put up a display and sign in front of your store, hand out samples of your yogurt to passersby, link up with a local celebrity, and then invite the media to investigate your business for a story, the media have a valid reason to do a story about your yogurt shop. Did I say it was easy? Never did. Did I say it helps your business? I certainly say that now.

Here are examples of mindful ideas for a PR campaign:

Examples of guerrilla PR ideas

- If you own a beauty shop, offer lessons in hair care to the elderly.
- If you own a pet store, take some animals to visit an orphanage.
- If you run a green nursery, offer saplings to kids and get the city to let them plant the samplings on public property.
- If you own a video store, set up a free or low-cost lending library to an orphanage or a nursing home.
- If you are a carpenter, do what Super Handyman did—give a gift to the city.
- If you play an instrument, give free lessons to the disabled.
- If you run a bookstore, sponsor an annual essay contest.

I haven't even mentioned the plethora of public relations and sponsorship opportunities now available on the Internet. Chances abound for you to spread the good word about yourself in cyberspace, as you'll soon discover during your weekly surf. Sponsor sites visited by your prospects. As with off-line PR, most on-line PR is free. It requires tireless research on your part, but it's worth your effort.

There are many on-line sources for building your own media list. Don't rely totally on free resources for your publicity efforts. They typically are not updated frequently enough to be totally accurate or complete. A good way to collect media names that are current: look for writers' names and contact information when reading trade magazines. Personalized news services can send you articles about your industry, and you should comb those articles for the writers' names. Many free media lists have links only to the Web sites of publications or other media outlets. Then you'll have to visit each site and gather the information needed to send a release. The name of the specific writer you need to contact may not be listed, however.

Building your own media list

With MediaINFO Links from Editor & Publisher, you can search for media by category, frequency, and geographic location. Link to these sites from here. You'll have to research further to locate a contact for your news release. Go to http://www.mediainfo.com/emedia/.

Parrot Media Network is a service that offers databases on disk, directories in print, and broadcast fax services (fee based). Included are contacts at TV and radio stations, cable systems, and newspapers. Find them at http://www.parrotmedia.com/guidebar. html.

US All Media E-Mail Directory features targeted media lists via E-mail and fax broadcast to media contacts at magazines, daily and weekly newspapers, news services and syndicates, and TV and radio stations. They're at http://www.owt.com/dircon/.

Gebbie Press allows you to contact editors at U.S. radio and TV stations, daily and weekly newspapers, and trade and consumer magazines on mailing labels or disks. Try http://www.gebbieinc.com/index1.htm.

Bacon's Media Lists lets you customize your media list at newspapers and magazines, radio, TV, and cable. Request the list on labels, ASCII files, or E-mail. Bacon's will also handle the distribution for you. Bacon's is well known in the PR world. They're at http://www.baconsinfo.com/e/index.htm.

"Mr. Smith E-Mails The Media" is a site that provides a graphical user interface for sending E-mail to members of the media. You select the media category, the specific media outlet from a list provided, enter your release, and send it. This service is free. You'll find it at http://www.mrsmith.com/.

Media Online Yellow Pages is a service that links you to the Web sites of TV stations, news sites, trade magazines, and associations. It's handy if you're developing a list for a highly specialized geographic area and includes European and Asian resources. Easy to find in cyberspace at http://www.webcom.com/~nlnnet/yellowp.html.

And then there's the Media UK Internet Directory, a link to radio stations, on-line national and local newspapers, TV stations, and on-line business and consumer magazines in the United Kingdom. On the Net, it's at http://www.mediauk.com/directory/. Hard work to find all these sources? It is. But remember what the smartest of the PR pros say: without publicity, a terrible thing happens—nothing.

27

Professional Marketing

It's possible to have a first-rate product or service, a well-conceived marketing plan, brilliant positioning, a dynamite creative strategy, a topflight business location, a gorgeous package, an ideal name, and a memorable theme line, but to fail in business. It's not only possible but commonplace. Why? Your marketing materials look just awful. Your words sound horrible. Your advertising is a real turn-off. You have sunk all your money into media, and you have skimped on production. That is a mistake no guerrilla would ever make. A diehard practitioner of guerrilla marketing knows that marketing has an intangible quality that defies number, defies logic. It is the way marketing "feels." And that "feel" is determined by the look and sound of the marketing. If it is bad, you can't hide it. You can't hide it if it is good, either, but you won't want to.

Nonguerrillas measure advertising strictly by CPM. That stands for "cost per thousand," and it refers to the cost in media dollars to reach one thousand people. If a radio commercial costs $100 and it reaches ten thousand people, your cost per thousand—your CPM—is $10. That is considered a relatively high CPM. Some CPMs get down to $4, as is the case with widely viewed TV shows. And $4 is not a high price to pay to reach one thousand people.

But true guerrillas look far past the CPM. First, guerrillas realize that the *cost per prospect is* more important than the cost per thousand. Second, guerrillas are highly sensitive to the *metamessage* of their marketing. The metamessage is the unspoken part of the marketing process. It is the true emotional impact of the advertising, which really cannot be measured at all. As you might sense, it is the "feel" of your marketing.

Beyond
CPM

The metamessage of your marketing reaches not merely the conscious mind of your prospects but also the unconscious. That is why it is so difficult to measure. I suppose it can be gauged only by sales results over a long period of time. One thing is certain:

Your
metamessage

you have complete control over it. That's the good part. Here's the better part: it used to cost a bundle to send out a positive metamessage. It used to be expensive to produce professional marketing materials. Technology—desktop publishing—has changed that. It also costs little to produce unprofessional marketing materials. In fact, it costs so little that many would-be guerrillas are wooed away from success by the temptation to save a buck on production.

Reflecting on my own experience with clients over the years, I realize that 40 percent of them, usually the big ones, spent too much on production. This did wonders for their egos, but not their sales. They confused their prospective customers with too much style and not enough substance. Their electronic marketing—radio and TV—reeked with so much fluff and unnecessary window dressing that the message became cloudy. Another 40 percent of my clients, usually the smaller ones, spent too little on production. They invested in media advertising but not in artwork and production. They bought a lot of time and space but not a lot of talent. They decided that they could write the copy themselves and that their friends could do the artwork. They allowed radio stations to write their radio spots. They allowed newspapers to lay out their newspaper ads. The result was usually schlocky-looking marketing that had an amateurish feel. They produced marketing like cheapskates, and it showed. That means that *only 20 percent of my clients spent the right amount on production.*

Overspending and underspending

Keep in mind that it is very easy to overspend, and even easier to underspend. You will be advised to spend far more than you ought to, possibly by a friend or associate, frequently by a production facility, maybe by an advertising agency. You will also be advised to spend less than you ought to, probably by a media rep who wants extra dollars for the commission on extra media purchases by you. Bad advice, all of it. Don't let it ruin an otherwise good marketing effort. Advice on spending less money may also come from your accountant and a few fellow employees. You might want to listen to them, but I'd suggest taking that advice with a grain of salt.

10 percent ought to do it

Here's some *good* advice: reserve about 10 *percent of your marketing budget for the production of marketing materials.* That means you should set aside quite a few dollars for creating professional ads and commercials, handsome signs and brochures, and motivating messages. Most likely, you'll spend a lot of that production budget up front. That's how it usually works out. You can amortize those funds over a long period of time. Let's say you plan to spend $36,000 over one year to market your product. That comes to $3,000 per month. This means that you should spend $3,600 producing ads and marketing materials.

If you are a new company, or an old company coming to your senses, you may want to invest in a logotype, or logo. This is your symbol—a visual representation of your company such as McDonald's golden arches or Shell's station. It should include your name, though Shell's doesn't and really doesn't have to after nearly a century of exposure. Nike's "swoosh" logo doesn't need the Nike name for identification, and Nike didn't need a lot of time to implant its logo in our collective consciousness because their financial investment was great. Your logo will appear on your signs, in your ads, on your business cards, stationery, and brochures, and on all of your materials. It will become associated with you. To produce a logo, a good art director will charge anywhere from $250 to $50,000. You'd be overspending if you went the $50,000 route—though large corporations have spent more than double that—and you'd be underspending if you paid an art student $50—unless he or she was a highly talented student destined for marketing greatness. They do exist, and art schools are where you find them.

Your symbol

Because you'll be using it for a long period of time and in many different applications, invest in a first-class logo. If this means you write a check for $500 to $1,500 up front, you can amortize that expenditure over the length of time you are in business. In the long run, it may come to only a few dollars per month. Truth is, you should not even consider the money you spend for a logo as part of your production budget. It's above and beyond that budget.

A first-class logo

Say you are quoted a price of $500 to produce an ad. Sounds like a lot. But if you run that ad over the course of four months, it comes to only $125 per month—a small sum for production. And $500 should buy you a darned good-looking ad. Naturally, you won't want to spend a lot money on an ad you'll run only once—but remember, guerrillas do run their ads more than once. They run them until the ads stop pulling in business. If you let your newspaper lay out your ad, and if you write the copy, it may only cost you $50 to produce an ad, but it may never pull in any business—so it's really not much of a savings for you. It amazes me when a person signs up for a $10,000 TV schedule, then wants to run a $150 commercial. Seems to me that's a savings in the $150 department and a waste in the $10,000 department. Don't let it happen to you.

Three ways to
produce ads

There are three ways that guerrilla marketers can produce advertisements or commercials. One way is to *do it by yourself.* You handle the graphics, the writing, and the ad production. If you are a creative genius and have experience producing ads, that will save you a lot of money. It may eat into the time you spend running your business, but if you're the best person to write your copy and create your layout, a rare bird in my experience, go to it.

A second way to produce your advertising is to *turn the work over to an advertising agency.* For many entrepreneurs, that's a good idea. Advertising agencies earn 15 percent of your media dollars. In effect, though, you get their services free. If you buy $10,000 worth of radio spots, it will cost you $10,000. If you use an ad agency, it will still cost you $10,000, but it will cost the ad agency only $8,500 (accredited advertising agencies are given a 15

Good things
about ad
agencies

percent discount from the media). So you get the ad agency's expertise, its planning ability, the time it invests placing the advertising for you, and even its writing talents—and you don't pay anything for services rendered. You pay only for type, illustrations, and a camera-ready ad. But these days, most standard advertising agencies charge on a fee basis, the fee depending upon the amount of work and time required to service your account.

As a guerrilla, you may want to set up your own house ad agency so that you can earn the 15 percent discount, but perform your own services. It's a fair amount of work, but can save a fair amount of money for you.

If you have too small a budget, most ad agencies will turn up their noses at you. But if your budget is hefty, advertising agencies can save you a lot of time and trouble. And they provide a great deal of much-needed expertise. A warning: if your budget is small, your advertising account, while pitched by senior management, will probably be assigned to green-behind-the-ears employees. That's not always bad, but it's a gentle hint that if you're going to use an ad agency, use a small one that will treat your small company like an important client.

How to produce
marketing
materials

Most entrepreneurs, however, produce their marketing materials a third way. They use *independent contractors to enhance* their marketing plans. A success-oriented entrepreneur will hire a smart marketing consultant to help draft a marketing plan and a creative strategy. The consultant is paid a fee—one time—and that's it. The fee covers either several projects or anywhere from one to three months. If he or she is needed down the road, then another fee is charged. You may want to keep a consultant by paying a monthly retainer fee for continuing counsel.

A smart entrepreneur might also have an ongoing relationship with an art director. That person designs the logo, the ads, the brochures, the circulars, the Yellow Pages ads, the mailing pieces, the signs—everything that needs designing. The art director is paid by the hour, by the ad, or by the project. Usually, it is by the hour. If you have a regular need for artwork, perhaps a monthly retainer fee can be established.

You might also hire a copywriter who charges by the hour or by the ad. And you might employ a media-buying service to place all your ads for you, at a charge of from 3 to 10 percent of the cost of running the ads. Since a media-buying service can save you 15 percent, the 10 percent it may charge actually amounts to a savings of 5 percent for you. At times, you might also wish to hire a professional research firm that charges by the project. And you might need the services of a photographer or an illustrator. Be sure they all follow your marketing plan and pull in the same direction.

Hiring a copywriter

As marketing emerges from its infancy and companies wise up to its requirements, they look to a wide variety of sources for new ideas. A 1997 study revealed that 59 percent of them look for innovative thoughts from in-house teams, while 21 percent look to advertising agencies. Another 16 percent look to consultants, and 9 percent enlist the aid of creative boutiques. The unmistakable trend is toward the hiring of outsiders—with 48 percent of the firms saying they use them to supplement strategic thinking and 42 percent saying they're using more outside sources than ever before.

As I have counseled a number of times, and will continue to do because it is so important, you should use as many methods of marketing as you *properly* can. The same holds true for marketing production. Do as much of it yourself as you can do properly. And remember that you can do more of it with current technology than at any other time in history. Farm out the rest to talented professionals. In all likelihood, you are a pro at your business. And you should use people who are pros at the business of advertising production. That combination of pro and pro is a tough combination to beat.

Use properly or not at all

An effective printed piece, be it ad, brochure, circular, or point-of-purchase sign, requires expertise in at least six different areas.

The first idea is the idea. *Don't forget that all great marketing starts with a great idea.* It is not important that you be the person who gets the idea. It is very important that you be able to judge the idea. If you can't distinguish a good idea from a bad idea, find someone who can. That's the most important part of marketing.

The second area is *copywriting*. To begin with, somebody has to come up with a winning headline. To be successful, the headline should either state the idea succinctly or interest people so much that they'll want to read the copy. The copywriter must have the ability to write flowing, motivating copy. No particular style is right or wrong. But in general, copywriting should be clear, easy to follow, crisp, and believable. Many people believe that because they can write, they can write copy. If that were the case, there wouldn't be so many copywriters earning in excess of $250,000 per year for their golden prose. There is a huge difference between writing in the English language and writing advertising copy de-

signed to create a desire to buy. Ernest Hemingway was quick to admit that advertising copywriting was a lot harder than fiction writing because it required people to act rather than feel.

The third area is *graphics*. The most important aspect of graphics is the design and layout. An art director must take the words and pictures and arrange them in such a way that the reader's eye will flow from one element to the next, free and easy. There must be no hint of confusion. The ad should look appealing, should invite readership by its look. It is not easy to create such ads. That's why some art directors are paid high salaries, also in excess of $250,000 yearly, to lay out advertisements. They possess a graphic sense that combines aesthetics with motivation, art

with psychology. They know that readers scan a page in a C-*shaped* pattern, starting in the upper right-hand corner, then moving down to the lower left-hand corner and then to the lower right-hand corner. You need an *ad maker* to design ads, not merely a designer. An ad that merely looks good is a bad ad. The ad must look good and also communicate exactly what you wish to communicate.

The fourth area is *pictures*. The pictures may be illustrations or photos, black and white or color, small or large, one or many. The art director makes that decision. The illustrator or photographer then takes over and draws or shoots the picture that helps bring the marketing plan to life. I have had clients pay $12,500 for a single photo session and feel that the shots were worth every cent. I've had clients spend $150 for a photo session, too. They weren't as captivated as the big spenders, but the $150 helped them grow into a company that could afford the higher figure. If you are superb with a camera or if you can illustrate with pizzazz, perhaps you can handle the picture portion of your advertising. Chances are, though, that you'll be better off hiring a pro. Fortunately, most people recognize their lack of talent at art. Unfortunately, most fail to recognize their lack of talent at writing.

The fifth area is *typography*. There are books and books of typefaces you can select. With such a wide selection, which is the right kind of type for your advertising? Your computer's word processing program probably gives you a galaxy of typestyles. Should yours be a serif typeface—one with letters that have little tails and curlicues? Or should it be a sans serif typeface—one with clean, streamlined letters? Should you use italics? boldface type? all uppercase letters? What is the right size of type for the headline? the subhead? the body copy? the theme line? A type expert or art director must be able to answer all of those questions and answer them correctly. Otherwise, a great deal of money may go down the drain. I've seen many ads that had everything right except that the type was unreadable—either unclear or too small. An ad with unreadable type is a terrible waste of money, space, time, and energy. Daily I see typefaces that give me headaches.

What's the right type for you?

The sixth area is *production*. Today, most production is accomplished with a computer, and computer proficiency is *mandatory*. Guerrillas use computer software and a scanner to create a final layout consisting of the type that has been set, the headline, the illustration or photograph, the logo, the border, and any other element that goes into the ad or whatever item of marketing you are producing.

It is the rare guerrilla who possesses expertise in all six areas. Even the most proficient ad makers are expert in but a few. Generally, one person thinks up and writes the ad, a second person serves as art director, and a third person handles the production. This is *generally* the case (more than 50 percent of the time). In many situations, however, the art director thinks up the ad. In others, one person does the writing, a second person handles all graphics and production responsibilities, and either of the two people gets the idea for the ad. A good idea can come from anybody!

The rare guerrilla

Your job, as a guerrilla, is to exercise the correct judgment in all of these areas. You need not be able to do any one of these tasks, but you must be able to distinguish good from bad in all six areas.

One of the most successful entrepreneurs I have ever known, Mike Lavin—a true guerrilla in every sense of the word, owner of European Mattress Works, a Berkeley showroom that became a local landmark because of his marketing—had no talent in all six areas but had exceptional judgment and resourcefulness. His judgment helped him recognize his own limitations, helped him distinguish a good ad from a bad ad, a good commercial from a bad one, good copy from bad copy. His resourcefulness led him to the people who could supply the talent he needed to run quality ads. Although he didn't contribute one word to his copy, he never ran a bad ad. His success, both financial and personal, was astonishing. He built a company that used all of the media—and I mean *all*. First he sold waterbeds; then he added other beds; then futons; then he invented a breakthrough mattress design; and then he added space-saving furniture and children's furniture—changing with the times and the needs of his market. Responding to the needs of his particular marketplace, he began specializing in beds from Europe and America. There was not a single major marketing tool that he failed to use. And yet he had no innate marketing talent, merely brilliant marketing judgment and instincts. That's all you need to be a guerrilla. That plus patience and aggressiveness.

Needless to say, it will cost you money to secure talent in the six areas required. And remember, I'm just talking about printed marketing materials. You'll require other talents for television marketing. And radio advertising calls for professionalism in six areas: the idea, the writing, the voicing, the music, the sound effects, and the mixing. As with print advertising, you yourself don't have to have talent in these areas, merely good judgment. And you must know how to locate expert production studios.

As with cognac, you usually, but not always, get what you pay for when it comes to marketing production. Learn what you'll be paying for by checking the portfolios of the pros you plan to select.
Be wary of those who talk of awards. Be attracted to those who speak of results.

And by all means, be attracted to technology when it comes to the production of marketing materials. I do not love using the new age word *empowered*, but that's the perfect word to describe what technology can do for you when it comes to marketing. It enables you to save a fortune on production because it makes production a matter of clicking a mouse rather than drawing a picture. It makes production a matter of selecting from existing designs rather than starting from scratch to create your own. Computer technology lets you—yes, *you*, without any help—create a marketing weapon in half an hour that used to take eight hours to create and cost five times as much.

You are now empowered

Until a few years ago, technology was not associated much with small business marketing. Perhaps it was connected with databases or inventory control, maybe with electronic spreadsheets and word processing. But it was complicated and expensive, and its effect on small business didn't stretch into the arena of marketing. But times, especially these times, change.

Technology has recently been revolutionizing small business, enabling many small-business owners to dream new dreams and then attain them in surprisingly brief time spans. Sure, technology assists all businesses, but it assists small businesses in the greatest ways. Technology gives small businesses a blatantly unfair advantage because it allows them to look big and act big without having to spend big. The price of credibility has plummeted while the achievement of credibility has become more precious. Technology provides small-business owners with the tickets to credibility—in fact, lifetime tickets. Until now, the advantages that small business could boast over big business were more personalized service, extra flexibility, and speed. Today, guerrilla business owners have a secret weapon.

Your unfair advantage

The secret weapon is technology. Technology is more simple than ever—so simple that high-tech is becoming easy-tech. It's also becoming so inexpensive that in 1998 you can invest a low four-figure sum to purchase what in 1982 took a mid-six-figure sum.

Technology has evened out the playing field, removed the dome from the top and opened the entire world to the entrepreneur. On-line, that practitioner of free enterprise can connect up with allies and customers anywhere in the community and the planet. That small-business owner has learned that virtual is a state of mind and that it really means "connected," for technology makes teamwork easier than ever possible.

The playing field is now even

To many guerrilla marketers, technology is to be lauded because it has put them on-line, giving them access to the speed of E-mail, the power of fresh information, the warmth of closely con-

What virtual really means

nected people, and the marketing muscle of the World Wide Web. To others, technology is the hero because it allows them to flourish in a home-based business. New, easy-to-use software lets you create your own first-rate marketing materials—giving you a Rolls-Royce marketing identity at Tootsie Roll costs.

Tootsie Roll costs

Regarding the areas where technology adds potency to marketing, ten are especially intriguing if you seriously enjoy consistent profits and know how to turn on a computer. You can produce every single one of these weapons while doing your desktop publishing at a fraction of what it would have cost you when the original edition of this book was published in 1984.

Ten weapons you can produce yourself

1. *Web sites.* A computer can help you design and post a Web site. Just remember, that can't help you unless you know marketing. The Internet is a marketing medium, perhaps the best and most comprehensive ever, but you must be an ace marketer to market on-line successfully.
2. *Newsletters.* Good ones are mailed to customers and prospects on a regular basis and follow the rule of 75 percent giving and 25 percent selling.
3. *Flyers.* Distribute them in a variety of ways, as signs, in orders, to fusion marketing partners to distribute as you distribute theirs.
4. *Postcards.* They eliminate the hassle of having to open the envelope. Your computer can make them eye-stopping.
5. *Brochures.* Perfect forums for including all the details; they should be offered for free in your other marketing and posted on-line.
6. *Catalogs.* You can increase revenues through catalogs, now easy and inexpensive to design and produce, a potentially big profit center.
7. *Gift certificates.* People are on the lookout for gift ideas, and a gift certificate might be perfect. Mention them on signs, in brochures, in ads.
8. *Coupons.* Offer discounts, free merchandise, services, anything to intensify the prospect's desire for your product. Coupons are versatile.
9. *Signs.* Guerrillas use them on community bulletin boards, at the point-of-purchase, and at trade shows. They transform some signs into posters.
10. *Computer-designed proposals.* These add credibility, visibility,

and excitability while instilling confidence in you beyond any price tag.

Of course, there are far more than a mere ten marketing weapons now at your disposal for next to nothing. Technology lets small business gain credibility and economy while providing speed and power in an age when credibility is crucial, economy is a necessity, speed is revered and power comes from being part of a team. Credibility is earned by creating professional-looking marketing materials, and it is economical to do so on your own computer. Speed comes with cellular, wireless, pager, fax, E-mail, and voice-mail technology. Power is gained from networking and sharing technology.

Credibility, economy, speed, and power

If you're guerrilla marketing with technology, you're headed in the right direction. If you're guerrilla marketing without technology, you're not really guerrilla marketing at all.

In most parts of the country, marketing seminars are often presented for entrepreneurs. Many are geared to teaching you how to produce your own marketing materials with computers. If such seminars come to your area (check with a local community college, a chamber of commerce, or the extension division of a local university), sign up for one. Sign up for more than one if creating marketing materials turns you on. But even if it does, ask yourself, "Is this the best use of my time for the business?"

Now that you are taking the marketing process seriously, start developing a radar for good marketing and bad marketing. Both kinds are all around you. The more you observe, the more you learn, and the more you learn, the better you'll be able to market.

With all of my recommendations that you handle much of the marketing yourself, I encourage you to hire a pro to create your marketing materials *at first*. Unless it is something at which you really excel, you are usually better off consulting with a pro — or several pros. To find them, merely set aside a few days to visit graphic-art firms and view the work they have done for others. Visit writers and art directors and look at ads they have created. Listen to radio spots they have written and produced; view TV commercials that they've created. By doing so, you will get a feel for the marketplace. When looking at the work of these people, ask two questions: (1) How much did it cost to produce? (2) What were the sales results? Concern yourself more with the answer to question two than question one. You'll find *Adweek* to be a rich

Use a pro at first

Two questions to ask a pro

source of local marketing talent. And you'll find another source when your computer partners up with the person reading these words.

You can save sacks of money and get to use beautifully produced ads, commercials, brochures, and signs if you make use of co-op advertising. If you are a manufacturer, you can gain a lot in local sales by joining a good co-op program. If you are a retailer or distributor, you can gain welcome funds for your marketing **Co-op funds for** budget by obtaining co-op money. Co-op funds and materials are **the asking** made available to entrepreneurs by large companies. If you deal with one, ask about their co-op advertising program. If they don't have one, ask them to create one for you. Never hurts to ask. To obtain first-class marketing help in the way of money, ads, and more, co-op advertising is an area worth exploring.

Only after you have assembled the proper marketing aids will you be able to combine the best-stated message with the best metamessage. It is the combination of the two that will result in success. One without the other just won't do it.

When thinking about marketing—an activity in which you **How to think** should engage more and more—think long-term *and* short-term. **about marketing** Don't look only at the week ahead. Look also at the months and years. Your marketing efforts will add up. Your identity will not come easily or quickly but will be built over time. And everything you do in the way of marketing will contribute to that identity. If you see that you may have to spend $1,000 to produce an advertising piece, think of other ways the piece can be used. Maybe you can turn it into a sign. Perhaps it can also serve as a customer handout. Possibly it can be the basis for a brochure. Maybe it can be used with interchangeable headlines and become two ads. Perhaps it can be the major part of a mailing. And you may be able to use it for five years or longer. By getting the most mileage out of your marketing materials, you will save a lot of money. Suddenly, that $1,000 figure looks a lot more reasonable. Why, with enough deep thought on your part, it might even seem inexpensive.

In addition to getting as much mileage as possible from your **Become a** marketing, do everything you can to create brand names for your **brand name** products. People trust brand names. They have confidence that a brand-name item will perform better than a non-brand-name item. Don't make the mistake of thinking that brand names belong only in the province of the big guys. Brand names can be used by anyone who wants to create them. Smart marketing people, big and small, want to create them.

According to the *Harvard Business Review,* entrepreneurs are going to have to start developing their own brand names. There is a new selling environment. People want uniqueness, want names they can trust. Creating a brand name gives the people what they want and gives you what you want: customer confidence. A good approach to take is to give your customers *more than their money's worth.* If you sincerely try to do that, to go the extra distance, provide the extra service, give the extra quality, you'll be able to convey that attitude in your marketing. You'll be a better marketer if you think that way. And word will spread, too.

Nordstrom is famed for its customer service—its name is synonymous with superlative service. One day, the store received a call. The customer had purchased an item that had broken, and the customer wanted it fixed—pronto. That day, Nordstrom had a salesperson stop by the person's house to make the repair. The broken item hadn't come from Nordstrom, after all, but from another department store. The Nordstrom person fixed it anyhow, charged nothing, and contributed yet another tale to the treasure trove of service stories that has made Nordstrom a name that people know they can trust. Do that for your company, too.

There is no mystique to marketing. It is fairly easy to dissect. But marketing is difficult to do properly. Never forget that regardless of what you sell, *people will think of it as your marketing portrays it.* If you run cheap-looking ads, people will think of your product or service as cheap. Don't believe people who tell you that you'll never go broke underestimating the intelligence of the American public. Instead, figure that the American public is about as intelligent as your mother. And you know that she is no dodo. In reality, she is a good representative of the public. She won't be won over by gimmicks and special effects.

Involve your employees

If you have employees, make sure they are completely aware of your marketing program. They must reflect all that is conveyed in your marketing. After all, people will come to you because of that marketing, and they will expect certain things from you. Your salespeople or representatives must have attitudes that are consistent with the messages you have been putting forth. Guerrillas not only have all employees and associates read their marketing plans but also insist that all employees read every ad and hear every commercial. If they do, they'll be able to relate that much better to customers and will know what the customers are looking for. They will know what is being communicated in advertising and will be able to help the business live up to its marketing.

One of the most important attributes a guerrilla can have is patience. Wait for that marketing place to take hold. Stick with it. If you have thought it through, it will pay rich dividends. If you expect instant results, your plan will never have a chance to shine, to motivate, to sell. Lean on your marketing materials as much as you can. Post your ads on the door, in your window, on your walls. Be proud of them. Create each ad with the care you would use if it were your only ad.

Pretend it's your only ad

You are probably reading this book because you own your own business or because you are considering owning your own business. I doubt that many people would invest money and time in a marketing book unless they were involved in the marketing process. It may be that you are in the marketing department of a company. But it is more likely that you have your own company. Merely by purchasing or taking the time to read this book, you have proven that you already know the crucial importance of marketing. In our competitive society it is more important now than ever. Because you purchased a book dealing with guerrilla marketing, you are a person who wants to market more effectively than your competitors. You are now equipped to put better marketing to work for you.

Entrepreneur magazine, a worthy publication for any person who considers himself or herself an entrepreneur, publishes an entrepreneur's credo in each issue. Because I suspect that you are a small businessperson who wishes to become a big businessperson, and because I believe you are an entrepreneur, I will repeat the credo by which you may already live:

Words to live by

I do not choose to be a common man. It is my right to be uncommon—if I can. I seek opportunity—not security. I do not wish to be a kept citizen, humbled and dulled by having the state look after me.

I want to take the calculated risk, to dream and to build, to fail and to succeed.

I refuse to barter incentive for a dole; I prefer the challenges of life to the guaranteed existence; the thrill of fulfillment to the stale claim of Utopia.

I will not trade freedom for beneficence or my dignity for a handout. I will never cower before any master or bend to any threat.

It is my heritage to stand erect, proud, and unafraid, to think and act for myself, to enjoy the benefit of my creations, and to face the world boldly and say, "This . . . I have done." All this is what it means to be an entrepreneur.

Now you have risen above the level of entrepreneur. The guerrilla has advanced beyond the entrepreneur, being a mite harder working, a bit sharper, more of an explorer, and often more successful. As the age of the entrepreneur and individual enterprise comes to the forefront in America, the resources of the guerrilla are more important. And to be a guerrilla requires an attack.

V
Launching Your Guerrilla Marketing Attack

A well-equipped army led by a top-rate general in possession of a well-conceived battle plan will win no battles—unless those battles are launched. In real life, that army can assure a blessed peace merely by its presence. But marketing isn't as simple as real life.

You are constantly under attack by your competitors—all vying for that limited disposable income to be spent by your prospects. Your presence, plan, and general don't amount to a hill of Rice Krispies if they just sit there, snapping, crackling, and popping. You're going to have to launch your own attack. To some people, this is a sorry situation. They don't have the smarts, the stomach, or the imagination to launch, much less succeed at, an attack.

But you do. You've got it all—the data, the motivation, the insights, and the arsenal of weapons to stake out a territory and get your fair share, even more. You'll be able to achieve your goals because you know what those goals are. They are clearly spelled out in your marketing plan.

You've got what it takes

You also must now realize that if you don't attack, you'll lose the battle. Others are coming down the pike by the hundreds of thousands, and they're all bent on victory. You are dead meat unless you act. So you've got to do something. You've got to do it with the acumen of a guerrilla, and although you must act with patience, you must also act now—right after you complete this book. No shilly-shallying around.

One of the hallmarks of the guerrilla is a penchant for *action*. When they hear there's a battle coming up, they plan, anticipate, visualize, and understand victory. They take the actions that victors take, and they keep up the attack permanently, always aware

A hallmark of the guerrilla

of what the heck is going on—information most small-business owners lack.

These people have learned that marketing is not an event but a *process*. It begins in a room where they map their battle plan. Then they take it to the streets in the form of mini-media, maxi-media, and nonmedia—using their weapons with skill. Armed with an understanding of how and why marketing works, they remember their thirteen-word guerrilla credo: commitment, investment, consistent, confident, patient, assortment, subsequent, convenient, amazement, measurement, involvement, dependent, and armament. They are ready to take the actual steps to launch an attack.

Not all at once

Do they launch all of their weapons at once? Of course not. That would be time-consuming, confusing, intimidating, and expensive. Guerrilla marketing attacks are precise, easy to control, inexpensive, and intimidating only to the competition. Success requires knowledge of specific aspects of the science of psychology, plus an unstoppable inner will to win. The knowledge and the will aren't usually to be found between the covers of a book. But they're in this manual for guerrillas, and they're coming in just a moment.

Step back and look

But first, step back and take a look at marketing in the context of business, in the context of you. Use this perspective for honest self-evaluation. I'm asking you to do this because in a study to determine why so many products fail, the answer turned out to be painfully obvious: *the boss*.

The number one reason for product failure

An Innovation Survey from Group EFO Limited showed the number one reason for product failure isn't the competition, the trade, the recession, a failure of creativity, or a shortage of ideas. It's the chief, the honcho, the top banana. A startling 63 percent of new-product managers report that *top management at their companies do not have a clear strategic vision of the role of new products*. "Lack of strategic direction" is the leading factor in new-product failure. Absence of management commitment tied for second with such factors as price-value relationship, product delivery, and point of difference. Guerrilla marketing can't save companies that have low marks in those areas.

Management for the twenty-first century must master new skills and be able to fill management roles, old and new, in addition to running the marketing show. As a manager, you'll have to be your own guerrilla. You'll have to:

- Scale economies
- Offer speed and flexibility
- Understand data processing
- Familiarize yourself with the on-line world
- Know the Internet
- Mine a database for profits
- Create intelligently
- Know exactly how to position
- Know how to maximize profits
- Know how to respond lightning fast to change
- Know how to create value
- Constantly refine your operation
- Consistently reexamine your strategy

**How to be your
own guerrilla**

How will you possibly do all these things? By being a true entrepreneur and not an implementer, by developing coaching and not just controlling skills, by identifying and nurturing employees with the right attitudes, and most of all, by understanding your customers inside and out, backward and forward, upside and down.

You may think you're in the software business, but that's not all. You may think you're in the retail business, but there's more to it than retailing. You may consider yourself to be in the manufacturing business, but you're more than merely a manufacturer.

No matter what business your card says you're engaged in, you're really in three businesses: your primary business, the marketing business, and the people business.

**The three
businesses
you're in**

Every business on Earth eventually must sell what it is offering. When that happens, you're in the marketing business. If you haven't seen that up till now, see it clearly beginning today. You've got to market what you sell to your employees, to your salespeople, to your distributors and suppliers, and also to your customers. All these people can help move your business forward.

Focus as much as possible on your primary business—creating quality, value, and desirability. Instead of thinking expansion and diversification, think excellence. Concentrate on your strengths. Don't let success mislead you to thinking that you are now assured of success in fields beyond your specialty.

**Failure to focus
is costly**

When Gerber's Baby Food put their name on other items created for babies, nonfood items, they thought the Gerber name was associated with babies and that they could succeed in any baby-related field. It cost them several million dollars in losses to realize that Gerber's was related to baby food only and not to babies. Their failure to focus was an extremely expensive mistake for them. Coca-Cola thought they knew beverages, so they purchased a winery. Big mistake. Coke has since sold the winery because they soon learned that they're in the soft drink business, and that doesn't make them experts in every other beverage business.

Every business deserves complete focus. Instead of diluting that focus, a business should hone it by sharpening their marketing skills and their people skills.

As you are always eventually in the marketing business, you are also always eventually in the people business. You may toil away in a lab, a factory or an office. But the rubber will meet the road when you emerge from your workplace and factor in the component of human beings.

Your employees must sense your passion and enthusiasm. Your salespeople must share your vision. Your distributors must get onto your wave length. And then, human beings must be aware of why they should purchase what you are selling. If you lack crucial **Know what** people skills, all the toiling you have done will have been in vain, **makes people** for it is real people who will end up buying—or not buying—what **tick** you offer. And if you don't know what makes them tick, you're in for a dismal journey.

When you focus on your own business, focus on the marketing of your service or product. You must become as much an expert in marketing as you are in your own field. I implore you to go on-line and get yourself a Web site, but I also know that you will fall flat on your cyberface if you don't understand *marketing*. You must know marketing and the need for fast response time, individual attention, and a continually fresh on-line presence.

You also should recognize that it's important to know *people*. People make your product. People render your service. People buy your product. People purchase your service. People recommend your offering to other people. No matter what you do or produce, **It all comes** eventually it comes down to *people*. And if you don't understand **down to** that you're in the people business, the consequences will be dire. **people** The guerrilla knows his or her own business like nobody else on earth. But the guerrilla is also a whiz when it comes to marketing and knows that he or she better market more effectively than the competition or else. And finally, the guerrilla understands human beings and what their hot buttons are, why they buy, what turns them on, what turns them off, what makes them happy. If you don't know you are truly in the people business, you'll probably soon learn what it means to be out of business.

There is now a more direct relationship between marketers and individuals than ever before as we head into what many have termed "the one-to-one future." Motorola makes how many pagers? Take a guess. One? Three? Five? Try 20 million—each one tailored to the needs of each customer.

20 million pagers

The Dallas Morning News inserts coupons for dog food in papers delivered to dog owners, coupons for cat food in papers delivered to cat owners.

The name of the game is no longer mass marketing. Instead, it's individual marketing. And that name is a clear indication that you're in your primary business, you're in the marketing business, and you're in the people business. The sooner you address all three businesses and focus upon all three, the sooner your profits will rise to record-breaking levels.

Your customers comprise the most special minority group on Earth. The more you know what's on the minds of your customers, the better you can push their hot buttons, gain repeat business from them, obtain word-of-mouth recommendations, enjoy referrals from them—and create the kinds of products and services they want. All this takes is a knowledge of human behavior—and you'll gain that knowledge when you turn the page.

The most special minority group on Earth

28

How Guerrillas Use Psychology

The field of psychology has undergone a major transformation since I was majoring in the subject at the University of Colorado. I remember how upset I felt upon hearing, as we approached graduation, that there were no fixed laws in psychology, only theories.

Here I had spent nearly four years of my life learning theories (and skiing) instead of hard, tangible facts. No wonder so many people majored in engineering, where the numbers add up in no uncertain way, or English literature, where the words are unarguably printed right there on the page. But psychology and theories? Didn't sound very solid, though it certainly was fascinating.

Since my college days, psychology has changed even more than I have. Many of the theories have been discarded after proving worthless or false. Other theories have emerged, and marketing guerrillas have learned how some of these aspects of human behavior can be applied in marketing.

Where purchase decisions are made

The best example of this—and the one you've just got to remember as long as you market—is that *purchase decisions are made in the unconscious mind.* You do not, as you may have thought, consciously select a brand to purchase. Instead, your unconscious mind, that inner, deeper portion that comprises about 90 percent of your brainpower, figures out what brand you should purchase, then sends its message to your conscious mind. There, where the words are spoken, you order or pick up a specific brand. You thought you were making a conscious decision, but your conscious mind was merely a tool of your unconscious one.

How to access the unconscious

All alone, that's a fairly shocking piece of information—different as it is from the conventional wisdom. But marketing geniuses do not look at that law all alone. They also are entranced by the law that tells us *how to access the unconscious mind.* We didn't know how to do that while I was studying about minds in college.

We figured that hypnosis was one way, but we weren't sure. *Today we are sure that you can access the unconscious mind through repetition.* Advertising leaders from Rosser Reeves to Leo Burnett have frequently made the same point.

So you put two and two together and you see that by repetition of your message, you can gain admission to that holy place where purchase decisions are made. Empowered by that simple fact, you begin to understand why marketing works the way it does. And you make a mental note to apply this new awareness in all of your future marketing. It will manifest itself in repetition. That will be one of the "secrets" to your profitability.

When I was in school, none of the professors talked about left-brained people and right-brained people. Today, still, not many advertisers, even the biggies, act upon the enormous economy this discovery represents to enlightened entrepreneurs.

Left-brained and right-brained

Studies reveal that 45 percent of Americans are left-brained and react to logical appeals while ignoring emotional appeals. Another 45 percent are right-brained and are stimulated by emotional appeals, disdaining logic for the most part. The final 10 percent of us are balanced. Because most marketing is created without regard to this psychological reality, nearly half of mass marketing is wasted. Many marketing campaigns aim in the opposite direction of about 50 percent of a potential audience. As a guerrilla, you can hit 100 percent of the people to whom you market if you aim your marketing at *both left- and right-brained people.*

Left-brained people love logical, sequential reasoning. You offer them a brochure with ten reasons to buy from you and they'll read every word. Is that good? Not necessarily. Since half the population is left-brained and half is right-brained, you're missing half of your market. Those right-brained people, who are influenced by emotional, aesthetic appeals, have zero interest in your ten reasons to buy. So you create a brochure with gorgeous graphics and words that tug at their heartstrings. Is that good? Not necessarily, because such a brochure would miss out on all those left-brained people who don't care a whit for pretty pictures and mushy words.

Guerrillas, therefore, are very careful to aim their marketing materials at both left-brained and right-brained people. They know that their target audience is left-brained *and* right-brained. So they put forth logical appeals to buy—blended with emotional reasons.

Aim at two targets

Nobody is overlooked. Their brochures have both the ten reasons to buy *plus* the appeals directly to the heart. This is not a big deal, but the losses suffered by ignorance of this aspect of human behavior are a humongous deal.

There are exceptions to the left-brained, right-brained aim I advise you to take. If your audience is computer scientists, they're probably left-brained to begin with, so your marketing can be the very model of logic.

However, if your audience is artists, most likely they are right-brained and will buy because of emotion. And you should know that except for the most analytical of souls, almost everyone is influenced by appeals to the basic emotions. To add force to your marketing by giving your prospects motivation to buy, you can rely on one of the following emotional appeals:

The basic appeals
- Achievement
- Pride of ownership
- Security
- Self-improvement
- Status
- Style
- Conformity and peer pressure
- Ambition
- Power
- Love

Your job is to find out which of these emotions will most set your customers and prospects into motion—or to find another that will do the job better.

As you can benefit by appealing to emotions, maybe you're in a business where you can also appeal to the *senses*. Do it whenever you can and consider yourself lucky to have the opportunity. Guerrillas do all they can, by conversation and observation, to learn which senses most motivate their prospects. These examples show how they put their findings into action by enlisting the senses as allies:

Sense their senses

Sight: "That looks great on you."
Sound: "Hear the massive power in that engine?"
Touch: "Feel the richness of those fabrics."
Smell: "The clean, fresh aroma is pure delight."
Taste: "These are remarkably delicious tomatoes."

As you can surmise, guerrillas are both emotional and sensible. This sensibility manifests itself in their understanding of the need to create powerful bonds.

Repeat business occurs because of bonds. The guerrilla knows that the strongest bonds are braided with the strength of a human bond. The guerrilla first makes the human bond, then the business bond. As the years pass, both bonds are intensified, strengthened, made permanent. This does not mean that the guerrilla spends a lot of time socializing with his or her customers. Instead, it means that in all interactions, the person is treated first like a human being—with a family, a business, hobbies, interests, opinions—and then like a customer. When the human bond is powerful, the business bond is lasting. If the business bond exists without the human bond, its existence is fragile.

The human bond

Psychologists have asserted that one of a human's most powerful needs is for an identity. A way to cater to this need is to form a club and make the customer a "member" of your "customer club." Membership privileges might include a membership card, framable certificate, newsletter, special discounts, advance notice of special events or sales, free gifts, car window decal, refrigerator magnet, a greeting card or gift at holiday time, maybe even a birthday card. Sometimes it includes a gift that is personalized with the names of both the guerrilla marketer and the customer. This further strengthens the individual's sense of identity with your business.

Make yourself part of their identity

Stay in touch with your members, offering them new products, new services, and offerings of your fusion marketing partners. Naturally, these offerings will be in the best interests of your customers, so life is good as your customer benefits first and you benefit as a direct result.

To add more power to your human bond while increasing your members' sense of identification with your company, educate them on how to better succeed at their businesses. Sometimes that will mean purchasing from you; sometimes it will mean purchasing from others—or not purchasing at all. Educational marketing is effective, potent, rare, and just the ticket for a guerrilla. By helping your customer—even if there is no immediate gain for you—the eventual gain will make the wait worthwhile.

Educate your customers

The concept of "eventually" takes on special meaning to guerrillas who know that most, but not all, people respond to determination—another law of human behavior.

Dennis Holt, a friend who happens to own what may be

the world's largest media-buying service, tells this story about himself: while he was about halfway through a sales presentation for his company to an advertising executive, the exec, his face only inches from Holt's, snarled, "I don't like you. I don't like what you do. I don't ever want to see you again. I'm insulted that you came into my agency to pitch me. Get out." Holt got up, pulled out a pencil and paper, and said, "I'm putting you down as a firm maybe."

Holt never let up. He called the executive weekly. The first four years the agency chief refused to take his calls. The fifth year, he finally picked up the phone only to beg Holt to stop calling. Thirteen years after their first encounter, that same executive hired Holt's company, and more specifically, Dennis Holt, to handle his media buying. Holt's determination, along with the fact that he is *always a pleasure to be with*—a crucial guerrilla tactic— is why his little media-buying service now purchases billions of bucks' worth of media each year. Determination alone wouldn't do the job. Charm was part of the recipe. And courage.

Thirteen years to success

Don't think you're limited in canvassing and sales presentations to only the approximately 250,000 words commonly used in the English language. Guerrillas aren't limited by such paltry numbers. They've boned up on the latest findings from the psychology world, and they know there are 600,000 nonverbal gestures they can use. *People respond more to nonverbal cues than to verbal ones.* Guerrillas learn the proper stance, the right facial expressions, when to smile, when to lift an eyebrow, and what crossed arms and a furrowed brow mean. Nonverbal communication, that is, body language, is part of communication and therefore part of marketing.

600,000 nonverbal gestures

The colors you use in your marketing weapons—stationery, signs, office decor, brochures, business cards—play an important role in motivating people. Colors speak loudly and clearly about your business. But they give forth mixed messages. Guerrillas know well the hidden language of color, and they know that colors speak louder than words. Colors stimulate emotions, excite, impress, entertain, persuade. They generate negative reactions if you don't understand them. Lasting impressions are made within 90 seconds and color accounts for 60 percent of the acceptance or rejection. Therefore, you must consider the meaning of color. This is what colors mean to people in their emotions and in a business context:

The language of colors

- Red evokes aggressiveness, passion, strength, vitality. In business, it is great for accents and boldness, stimulates appetites, is associated with debt.
- Pink evokes femininity, innocence, softness, health. In business, be sure you're aware of its feminine implications and associations.
- Orange evokes fun, cheeriness, warm exuberance. In business, it's good to use orange to highlight information in graphs and on charts.
- Yellow evokes positivity, sunshine, and also cowardice. In business, it appeals to intellectuals and is excellent for accenting things. Too much is unnerving.
- Green evokes tranquillity, health, freshness. In business, its deep tones convey status and wealth; its pale tones are soothing.
- Blue evokes authority, dignity, security, faithfulness. In business, it implies fiscal responsibility and security. Blue is universally popular.
- Purple evokes sophistication, spirituality, costliness, royalty, and mystery. In business, it's right for upscale and artistic audiences.
- Brown evokes utility, earthiness, woodsiness, and subtle richness. In business, it signifies less important items in documents.
- White evokes purity, truthfulness, being contemporary and refined. In business, it enlivens dark colors and can be refreshing or sterile.
- Gray evokes somberness, authority, practicality, and a corporate mentality. In business, it is always right for conservative audiences.
- Black evokes seriousness, distinctiveness, boldness, and being classic. In business, it creates drama and is often a fine background color.

Learning to speak the language of color is part of the guerrilla growing-up process. Learning the power of sophisticated sales training techniques is another part. Today's guerrillas videotape their top salespeople, then show the other sales staff members the video—pointing out the nonverbal gestures that lead to sales. Dissected, a fifteen-minute sales pitch may have five hundred nonverbal gestures, most subtle, many highly effective. When you learn

Sophisticated sales training

that in most organizations, 20 percent of the people accomplish 80 percent of the sales, you've got to figure that the 20 percent do a lot of nonverbal communication—unless they're in telemarketing. In that case, their voice inflections, volume, and pitch do as much selling as the words they use. Do they understand the science of speaking effectively? They do. They do. Success hardly ever happens by accident.

Make each prospect feel unique

Guerrillas pay close attention to another critical maxim of marketing that focuses on the psychology of human beings: *Make every customer and prospect feel unique.*

This guerrilla tactic leads right to the vault, yet is the most unusual to see in practice. It describes the best possible way for your customer or prospect *to feel* after an encounter with you— either by phone or in person. It's almost like asking you to be a psychologist.

I admit it is difficult to get people to feel this way without appearing phony. It is also difficult because it requires hard work and cannot simply be finessed with a warm smile or a firm handshake.

Still, you've got to make each customer and prospect feel unique and important, not like a consumer, not like a member of a demographic group, not even like a well-treated customer. Instead, each should be made to feel like the special individual that he or she is—with feelings, beliefs, values, problems, and personality traits unlike those of any other human being on Earth. If you convey knowledge of the person by your remarks, actions, and service, you will go a long way toward making that person feel unique. This is not easy to do. But if you do it, you will have a customer for life—*because hardly any other companies do it.* Even if they know the importance of making a person feel unique, they haven't got the knack, the data, or the information to accomplish it. As a guerrilla, you've got the small size to do it with every one of your customers.

Ask yourself this question: When was the last time a business owner made me feel unique—like an extraordinary, one-of-a-kind person? Maybe once or twice, but probably never. That's because it's too hard to collect the information and remember it when dealing with the person. But that's a piece of cake to a guerrilla because the guerrilla has made customer reverence part of his very essence. That's your job.

Guerrillas shy away from marketing strategies based solely upon low price. They realize that low prices attract the worst kind

of customers—the disloyal variety, who are wooed away from you
by even lower prices elsewhere. Low prices do not lead to long-
term relationships. They are less important than you think.

Adweek magazine asked, "What matters most to you—getting
a good bargain or buying the best?" Overall, 32 percent of people
said a good bargain, while 61.5 percent said buying the best. Only
22 percent of men opted for the bargain, while 42 percent of
women went for it. Keep in mind that of all the product leaders in
the United States, none are those with the lowest price.

Experts report that price is the major consideration of anywhere from 15 to 35 percent of customers, though many companies act as if 100 percent are price-obsessed.

If you're looking for reasons for people to buy from you—let
them help you aid a social cause. If they patronize your business,
they'll gain all the benefits you offer—*plus* they can help save the
environment, or stop AIDS in its tracks, or cure multiple sclerosis,
or save whales. Maybe they will buy from you simply because
you're an American and they're worried about the state of the
economy in the United States, so they patronize businesses that
are American.

If you align yourself with a noble endeavor, you can engage in
cause-related marketing, a method of overcoming the "purchase
guilt" that many customers feel. If you encourage your customers
to feel that they've helped the world while buying your product,
you're doing a favor for them, for you, and for the world. Cause-related marketing is an act of philanthropy on your part, and the
world needs and appreciates it. There are many sick, homeless,
displaced, and disabled people who need all the help they can get.
If your business can devote even a small percentage of its profits—
or better still, its sales—to a good cause, there's a good chance that
many winners will emerge.

**Help the world as
you help your
company**

The 1980s was a "greed" decade; the '90s are a "green" decade, with more awareness of environmentally safe or damaging
products than at any other time in history. And we're getting
greener every year. A Roper Poll revealed that consumers said
they'd be willing to pay a 5.5 percent premium for green products.
The recycling of newspapers, glass, and cans is popular in all
parts of the country, and it is mandatory in many communities.
Seventy percent of consumers are against postponing tougher
emission standards for the automotive industry. The world is always changing.

As you pursue the psychological edge that can make or break

Buy American a sale, these days, a call to patriotism in purchasing is often heard and heeded. The appeal to buy American is strong. The percentage of people who believe that when they buy imports they're responsible for putting Americans out of work has risen dramatically. Retailers report that "made in America" promotions of domestically made apparel increase their sales from 25 to 50 percent. Wal-Mart, America's biggest retailer at this writing, has gone on record as being deeply committed to American sources. The company says it has repatriated 130,000 jobs based on that decision.

The downside of this patriotic marketing is that it might appear to cater to the hate and fear instincts in people. Be sure if you embrace cause-related marketing, especially the red, white, and blue variety, that it is not at the expense of other peoples or ethnicities. Guerrillas never alienate potential prospects.

Relationship marketing Another phrase that has come into vogue is *relationship marketing*, the title of a book by Regis McKenna. The authors Don Peppers and Martha Rogers explained it well in their own book about one-on-one marketing. An article in a 1998 issue of the *Harvard Business Review* discussed their newsletter, *Inside 1:1*, in which they wrote about phony relationship marketing, which they term "faux relationship marketing."

In the newsletter they asked aloud if relationship marketing is in danger of suffering a premature death. Their answer: "Unfortunately, a close look suggests that relationships between companies and consumers are troubled at best." The article pointed out that consumers are being overloaded with a barrage of marketing messages and requests for personal information. They are being overwhelmed by the proliferation of choices on their store shelves and in their mailboxes. Their quality of life is suffering.

Peppers and Rogers wrote, "We don't disagree with those points, but we do challenge the underlying premise. Very few of the practices the authors document as irritating to consumers actually come from the discipline of relationship marketing. They are, however, excellent examples of 'faux relationship marketing'—what relationship marketing looks like when it is implemented according to traditional marketing principles.

"Relationship marketing is not synonymous with junk mail or telemarketing. Neither does it involve over-surveying of customers, product line extensions, or purchasing new customers with rebates and special deals. Instead, these are the classic symptoms of a traditional marketing discipline on speed. This is what happens when addressable, interactive media and high-capacity customer databases are used for traditional, product-oriented marketing, with no attention paid to the completely different, customer-oriented business model represented by genuine, one-to-one relationship marketing.

"A genuine relationship with a customer, like a relationship with a friend, must be based on things like trust, emotional support, privacy protection, and tolerance for other relationships. But the most important aspect of any genuine relationship is its inherent individuality. You might have relationships with many friends, but you don't have the 'same' relationship with 'all' of your friends. The one-to-one marketer recognizes that every relationship is different, that it is based on the inputs of 'both' parties, and that its context continues to build and change over time. A relationship marketer should never ask a customer the same thing twice, any more than you would ask your spouse how she likes her coffee.

"So a bank that mails out solicitations to 'target' customers it already has isn't practicing relationship marketing. Nor is a credit card company that gives special rates only to new customers. These are just examples of using computers to practice traditional marketing in a more targeted fashion.

"Probably, neither firm has any idea who its best customers actually are. Consumers are certainly getting tired of mass marketing, target marketing, and phony relationship marketing. Traditional marketing is in its death throes. But, as the enthusiasm of our newsletter's readership consistently demonstrates, true one-to-one relationship marketing is just beginning what promises to be a long, successful life."

Take their words to heart. Guerrilla marketing is more than a collection of buzzwords and buzzphrases. Instead, it's a manner of thinking, of connecting, of communicating—none of which can be accurately encapsulated by a buzzword. It's a knowledge of human behavior and action based upon those psychological insights.

To gain the closest psychological bonding with your prospects and customers, be certain that you know the most possible about them, then marry that information to the understanding you have of your own product or service. Just what is its identity? What does it symbolize to your market? What are its inherent emotional appeals? Logical appeals? Cultural appeals? As true product differ-

What relationships are based on

Don't ask the same thing twice

No buzzwords for guerrilla marketing

entiation is harder to come by and even tougher to sustain, perceptual associations will play a greater role in setting products and services apart from one another.

A large number of business people, 71 percent as I write this, feel overwhelmed by the number of messages that they receive. We're talking E-mail, voice-mail, pagers, faxes, cellular phones, car phones, overnight delivery, and snail mail. This communications blizzard diminishes quality thinking time, forcing people to work weekends and evenings. They fight back against overly aggressive communicators by not responding.

Overwhelmed by communications

Guerrillas know there is a fine line between being persistent and being pushy. They try not to cross it and are able to do that by having not a policy, but a sensitivity to each prospect and customer.

Persistent but not pushy

The American Dream is constantly changing. In 1996, a study reported that financial security was the most important to us, followed by home ownership, having a family, a secure job, and happiness. Knowing what people want helps you serve them. When baby boomers were asked what the American Dream represented to them, 97 percent said "being true to yourself and not selling out"; 96 percent said "feeling in control of life," "finding satisfaction with self," "making enough to insure a comfortable future," and "a job that gives professional satisfaction." Only 42 percent said "being wealthy."

The new American Dream

Can I overestimate the power of small details? In the context of guerrilla marketing, I cannot. Remembering or noting tiny items such as what a customer said during your last conversation, especially about topics unrelated to business, connects you closer to your customer. If it's something you do as a matter of course, you may be a born guerrilla.

Different age groups respond in their own way to advertising. People in their twenties are more likely to specify, recommend, or purchase a product because of the advertising; in fact, 63 percent of them report being influenced. Of those in their thirties, 55 percent say the same, and 57 percent of people in their forties and fifties say they are motivated by ads and commercials. Younger people are less loyal to brands and more willing to experiment. Therefore it's so crucial to understand *precisely* what your business stands for in the minds of your target audience. Research can tell you. Ideally, it's what you want it to stand for. If not, changes are in order. Understanding what your offering means to your market is

See yourself as others see you

something you should always strive for. You must be aware that the public perception of your product or service will probably change over time, necessitating continuing research via questionnaires.

Guerrillas know of the studies that indicate whom today's consumers trust. Family is trusted by 87 percent, friends by 80 percent, environmental organizations by 79 percent, doctors by 75 percent, scientists by 59 percent, trade unions by 28 percent, religious organizations by 22 percent, the media by 15 percent, companies themselves by 12 percent, and the government by 8 percent. You think you've got an uphill battle? Think of what they're up against in Washington.

Who do consumers trust?

People who shop at stores have changed their shopping habits. Nine out of ten shoppers who go to the store for frequently purchased items go armed and ready with a specific shopping strategy in mind for saving money. These shoppers have been categorized into five basic groups:

- *The practical loyalists.* 29 percent of shoppers look for ways to save on the brands they will buy anyway. The confidence they have in these brands cannot be shaken by low price alone.
- *The bottom-line price shoppers.* 26 percent of all shoppers buy the lowest-priced item with little or no regard for brand. This number is up from 14 percent in the mid-1980s.
- *The opportunistic switchers.* 24 percent of shoppers use coupons or sales to decide among brands and products that fall within a mentally preselected group.
- *The deal hunters.* 13 percent of shoppers look for the best "bargain" and are not brand-loyal. Understand that "bargain" refers more to value than to price.
- *The nonstrategists.* Only 8 percent of shoppers do not spend the time and effort to strategize their shopping.

The psychology of shoppers

As you might expect, an economic recession was largely responsible for this fundamental change in consumer behavior, yet the behavior is expected to continue even with economic recovery in full swing. Although confidence will reign supreme as the unconscious motivator for selecting one brand or business over another, recessions cause consumers to clip coupons, cut corners, shop in bulk, and patronize warehouses and price clubs.

In the '90s, consumers learned to become savvy shoppers, buying on pure benefit and price relationships. And although the

The new breed of customer

largest group of them are loyal to their brands, increasing numbers are loyal to their dire financial straits and are forced to forsake longtime loyalties. Guerrillas do all they can to maintain their current customers while winning over the new breed of sophisticated yet savings-minded consumers.

They maintain an eagle eye for the new trends in the lives of their customers and their prospects. Although there are countless changes going on in the world at the same time, and more changes now than ever, guerrillas try to keep up with the most important trends so they may adjust their marketing and their product or service mix. Today, ten trends, as identified by author Joyce A. Schwarz, are changing the way Americans live:

The trends of today

1. They're gaining knowledge electronically. I don't have to tell you that means they know their way around the Internet.
2. They're opting for more visual experiences. And they get it through entertainment, more and more of it interactive entertainment.
3. They're connecting to people more than locations. They realize that people don't have to be seen to make their contributions to each other.
4. They are moving the workplace to home. The result is more work efficiency and personal freedom blended with lower costs and less traffic.
5. They are learning at an accelerated pace. Credit for this goes to self-improvement materials, skill development opportunities, and cyber-tutors.
6. They are creating a home-centric lifestyle. New electronic entertainment, appliances, and on-line commerce make this possible.
7. They're becoming part of the global community. The Internet is why.
8. They're moving toward proactive commerce. They engage in it with direct marketing and interactive marketing now more than ever.
9. They're reducing their fear, uncertainty, and doubt. New tools to ensure security at work and home are leading to more peace of mind.
10. They're putting more value on products created by humans. As more machines create products, those made by people are more valuable.

Unlike traditional companies, guerrillas are very big on the idea of expressing their attitude, knowing that leads to an increased awareness of them. You might offer award-winning quality and superlative service, but if your company is hesitant about marketing, your attitude may not be conveying your excellence. Since your attitude is probably the first way you'll be noticed, it's crucial to have one and to let it sing out about you, loud and clear. It's great that you have an attitude, but do your customers know it?

Your attitude

Your most potent method of communicating your attitude is through your marketing. If you don't market, people will be unaware of your attitude. A private attitude is not going to make you profitable—you must go public with your attitude.

Begin by writing down your company's identity—who you really are and what you stand for. And after you do a first-rate job of that, let your public sense that attitude. They'll sense it through your aggressiveness in the marketing arena. They'll pick up on the fact that you're proud of your company, that you really mean business, that you're trying hard and that you're a key player in your field.

That aggressive attitude will be clearly communicated through the visibility you gain with your marketing—in the mass media, in the direct media, and on-line. If people see or hear of you all over the place, they can't help but notice you and be aware of your attitude. When it's time to make a purchase, they'll be drawn to companies with an attitude far more than invisible companies that don't express theirs.

Your attitude is also expressed by the professionalism of your marketing materials. If they look shabby, that shabbiness will become part of your attitude. If they look exciting and inspire confidence, that too will become part of your attitude. Each marketing weapon you employ will contribute to or detract from that attitude. None is too insignificant.

How you express your attitude

The reach of your marketing also reflects your attitude. And so does the frequency. Your commitment to your marketing program also conveys your attitude. Your consistency does, too. If you keep switching around your media and your message, people will be unclear about your attitude other than thinking that you're not sure of yourself. If you are consistent with your format and your identity, people will figure that you know what you're all about—and that generates confidence. All guerrillas know that

Attitude alone is not enough

confidence in a seller influences a buyer more than any other factor.

Your attitude comes across by means of your offers, headlines, copy, graphics, typestyle, media selection, and the execution of your marketing strategy. It will be conveyed by the message of your marketing. If people continue to see and hear about you, they are aware of your attitude. If you cease to market and fade into the woodwork, they'll forget your attitude. People forget marketing lightning fast and if you don't play at the forefront of their minds, somebody else will—somebody who realizes the power of attitude.

There are a large number of movie stars and rock stars who lack the sheer talent to succeed but have the attitude. Madonna comes to mind. Bette Midler comes to mind. Bruce Willis comes to mind. Brooke Shields comes to mind. John Wayne sure had far more attitude than talent. And a lot more will come to your mind, especially politicians. These people have created and capitalized upon their attitude so much that millions of folks think they also have an immense talent. You sure can't succeed on attitude only. You've also got to have something to back it up. Many product category leaders succeed with attitude over excellence, with attitude over low price, with attitude over lavish spending. All automobiles can get you from point A to point B, but some do it with a more stylish attitude.

Your attitude must come shining through in all of your marketing. And the attitude you express should be consistent from one **Cohesion is** medium to another. Cohesion is an ally of the guerrilla. That **your ally** means all marketing weapons should be pulling in the same direction, expressing the same attitude, conveying the same identity.

Your attitude comes across by what you say, how you say it, where you say it, and how frequently you say it. Even the world's best attitude will lead to little but frustration if you aren't out there communicating it. That's why guerrillas rarely are out of their public's eye. They go for impact with their marketing, but they also go for awareness. They know good and well that a share of mind leads to a share of market. They make up in a big attitude what they lack in a big marketing budget. And they are aware that the more they market, the better they are conveying their attitude.

A few questions for you to ask to yourself are:

- What is my company's attitude?
- Does that attitude come across on a regular basis?

- Is that attitude different from my competitors'?
- Does that attitude accurately reflect my honest identity?
- Are my customers aware of my attitude?

Just remember that most of life and all of marketing is attitude. Now that you know such an important truth, it's time for you to know an important word, one of the most important in marketing. Marketing people learned long ago that the most important word in the lexicon of marketing is "free," but "Swim with the Sharks" author Harvey MacKay disagrees. He says the most important word is "Rolodex." He says a measurement of his success is the many thousands of names in his Rolodex. And he says that when his daughter was graduated from Stanford, he was less impressed by her high grade point average than by the number of names in her Rolodex.

Most of life and all of marketing is attitude

The most important word

If you really and truly want to infuse your business with customers, relationships, and profits, and you want to do it lightning fast, consider throwing a Rolodex party, as suggested by Sam Decker in his *Inc.* magazine article of June 1997. Such a party is best when hosted by yourself and a friend, associate, or fusion marketing partner.

A marketing consultant from Virginia hosted such a party with his architect friend. Their party was strictly for each other and their party activities consisted of making phone calls for an entire afternoon to people and groups whose names were in their Rolodexes. The purpose of the calls: for the marketing person to promote the architect and for the architect to promote the marketing consultant. Please understand that I am not talking rocket science here.

The marketing guy called his clients to ask if they were considering the notion of renovating their offices. If not, it was a brief, friendly contact. If so, he put the architect on the phone. At the same time, the architect called associations of which he was a member and asked if they could use a speaker on marketing for any upcoming meetings or conferences.

Reading about this is one thing. Acting upon this information is something else entirely. The marketing consultant and the architect spent a total of four hours making these phone calls. The architect ended up with seven jobs. The consultant booked four speaking engagements.

You'll ask yourself how much money it costs to lure in all this new business and you'll realize that it didn't cost money at all.

Like all guerrilla marketing, it required time—to plan the party and make the calls, all of one paltry afternoon. It took energy—to execute the plan, which was no more than bringing along their Rolodexes and being somewhere with two phones. And it took imagination—to realize that one of the biggest names in the game is contacts, and another word for contacts is Rolodex. It's not how much you know, it's how many names are in your Rolodex.

Use their name

It's also how much you're paying attention to how profoundly psychology influences your power to motivate. Interviewers interrogating Korean prisoners during that war found that if they used the prisoner's name five times in the first five minutes, they had a successful interrogation. The same concept applies to addressing your customers.

Using psychology involves a whole lot more than ads and brochures, attitudes and Rolodexes. People look for a lot more than what you think they look for. The best predictor of preference for McDonald's is not price or hamburgers, but clean restrooms and good french fries. Clean restrooms convey a metamessage of cleaner kitchens, safer food, and better-trained employees. Proving again the insignificance of price, McDonald's 55-cent Big Mac was a Big Flop. Mobil Oil's sales increased more than other oil companies during a price war because Mobil focused on friendly attention, attractive, well-lit stations, and clean, spotless restrooms.

Clean restrooms as guerrilla marketing

If you use psychology in your marketing, you'll do every single thing in your power to cater directly to your audience and capitalize not only on its universal buying habits, as I've just described, but also on its special idiosyncrasies, regardless of how wild this may make your marketing appear to the outside world.

A *Mad* example

Mad magazine, known for its irreverent humor and wacky views of American life—also for its consistent profitability—gave a free pin to all new subscribers. In keeping with its identity, it didn't treat the pin as it deserved to be treated, as an insignificant object, but instead wrote of it in terms that only its subscribers could love:

"Each and every *Mad* Pin is precision crafted by machines that are turned On and Off by hand. These *Mad* Pins will not be sold in any store—we know, we tried getting any store we could find to sell them and nobody would touch them. Due to the special nature of this offer, the number of Official *Mad* Pins commissioned shall never exceed the demand. Each Official *Mad* Pin is so valuable it will be personally delivered to your home by an official United States Government employee, dressed like a mailman."

You can be sure that each person who received a pin felt unique and identified just a wee bit closer to *Mad*.

Do I recommend this tactic to all guerrillas? I definitely recommend the tactic of being sensitive to your own market. The accuracy of your marketing attack will depend upon that sensitivity.

29

How Guerrillas Win Battles

There is absolutely no mystery as to why guerrillas prevail when others fall by the wayside. They know how to launch a marketing attack and when to do it. They know which battles to fight and which to ignore. They know where to turn for support. They have learned how to win, beginning with one battle, and continuing as the battles get larger and more numerous. They have also learned how to avoid the greed and blind instinct to grow beyond their capabilities and into a heap of trouble. Of greatest significance, they know that marketing is a process and not an event.

Working backward, assuming you're going to do what it takes to be a guerrilla, be sure you know how to deal with success. Most people lack the skill. It is an infrequently encountered talent, and yet without it, you're going to find yourself in deep waters. A good rule of thumb is to *engage in no expansion until you have eliminated all of the mistakes in your current operation.* Otherwise, your mistakes will be magnified and multiplied. When you begin to hit new profit highs month after month, you'll be tempted to go for the gold and grow. If that's what you really want, go for it—but not until you've fine-tuned your mistake-radar to the realities of your company. Any mistakes you find are red flags warning you against growth. Don't ignore those flags.

Eliminate errors

To get to the point where you even seriously *consider* expansion, you're going to have to engage in the ten steps necessary to launch and succeed with your marketing attack, then launch it at the right time.

The ten steps

The ten steps seem to get harder as you take them, but it helps to take the easiest steps in the beginning to build your confidence.

Step one: research your marketplace. That means research your market, product, service, media options, competition, industry, prospects, customers, technology that can help you, benefits you offer, the Internet, and potential fusion marketing partners, on-line and off-line.

Step two: write a benefits list. This is no time to be modest. It's the time to call a meeting, inviting your key personnel and at least one customer. The sole purpose of the meeting is to come up with a list of the benefits that you offer. The reason to invite a customer is that you offer benefits you may not realize are truly benefits. Before I spoke at a national convention of booksellers, I asked my wife why she patronizes the bookseller five miles away rather than the one a mile away. "Their carrot cake!" was her excited reply. Their carrot cake? You can be sure that the bookstore had a benefits list that focused on their selection, trained personnel, extended hours, superb lighting, and willingness to take phone orders. But unless they invited a customer to their benefits list meeting, they probably wouldn't realize the appeal of the carrot cake served in their cafe.

When you've created your list, select a competitive advantage because that's where you'll be hanging your marketing hat. The automobile detailing firm in my community was one of many, and they were in a tough competitive situation. Then they created the competitive advantages of house calls—detailing autos at the homes or offices of their customers. This competitive benefit broke the bank for them. Your task is to spot or create a competitive edge that does the same for you.

Step three: select the marketing weapons you'll use in your attack. Decide the priority order of launching your weapons, who will be responsible for launching each, who will be responsible for tracking each, and the exact date when each weapon will be launched.

Step four: create your marketing plan. After you've completed the first three steps, this one is kind of easy. It's where you force yourself to focus upon the specific goals you want your marketing to achieve for you. This is the plan you'll be developing after consulting with your employees, the one you'll show them to get them onto your wave length. It's the one described in juicy detail in Chapter 4. Along with your marketing plan, now is when to create a creative plan. You read how to do it in Chapter 5, and now is the time to do it. It will breathe life into your marketing plan by elaborating upon the ways you'll communicate with prospects and customers. These written plans will also be a major help to anyone who creates marketing materials for you. I've done a considerable amount of freelance work for bankers and remember always being impressed by the Wells Fargo Bank because along with the assign-

Create your marketing plan

ment, they also gave me a copy of their marketing plans. Helped me immensely.

Step five: create a guerrilla marketing calendar (like the one described and illustrated in Chapter 6). Having it will make decisions easier and emergencies nearly nonexistent.

Where to find fusion marketing partners

Step six: make arrangements with fusion marketing partners. These are the businesses that can help you increase your marketing exposure while sharing your marketing costs. They should have the same kinds of prospects and same lofty standards as you do. Find them in your community, through your local chamber of commerce, through their own marketing, and all over the Internet.

Step seven: launch your guerrilla marketing attack by firing the weapons. The guerrilla knows that there is no reason to launch all the weapons at the same time. He or she knows that guerrilla marketing attacks are most effective when *launched in slow motion.* A sane way to look at it is to figure on about eighteen months, maybe a year, to launch all the weapons you said you'd launch. Launch your attack at a speed that is comfortable to you emotionally and financially.

Launch in slow motion

You should never feel overwhelmed by the marketing actions you're taking and never feel as though you're overinvesting in the process of marketing. There rarely has to be or should be a rush. Every weapon must be used properly or not at all. The people responsible for launching your weapons know who they are; those same people know when to launch them, so there are no surprises—except to your competition.

Step eight: maintain the attack. Sorry, this is no arena for devotees of instant gratification. Little that you do will give you instant results. Feedback will be sparse or nonexistent. You won't be able to stop yourself from questioning your marketing plan. But don't ask too much of it. Remember the Marlboro man and take a horseback ride into the sunset. Bide your time.

Hang in there

Unless you maintain your attack, there is no way it will succeed for you. The money—and the time, energy, and imagination—you have invested in marketing will be lost forever. It would be like shredding a stock certificate because the stock dropped a couple of points. This is the way it's *supposed* to be. It is tough to continue investing your money while seeing little or no return. Some business owners might construe this state of affairs as a failure on their part. But guerrillas know that people don't fail; they only quit trying. They cease maintaining.

This is the time to hang in there and win that all-important confidence that guerrillas are supposed to win. But, sadly, this is where most business owners get cold feet and sweaty palms. They panic, abandon their marketing plan, change their media, fire their advertising agency, and decide that newspapers, direct mail, telemarketing, television, or any combination of these doesn't work for them. Of course it doesn't! It has to be maintained over a period of time—three months to a year—to work.

Once a client excitedly called to tell me that he was overloaded with business. I wasn't surprised. He was shocked! He had been actively marketing for six months, and during the first five, not much happened. During the sixth month, *everything* happened. And it all was good. Those prospects he had spoken to five months earlier decided that now was a good time to take him up on his offer. Those *other* potential customers he contacted, also five months ago, figured that this was a good time to buy from him. His telephone was ringing incessantly and the callers were all ready to undergo that magnificent transition from prospect to customer. The seeds had been planted; they had been lovingly nurtured. Now the harvest was taking place and the farmer was shocked! If you maintain, you'll harvest. If you don't, you won't. Maintenance is not glamorous work. But it does work. And don't be shocked when it does.

Step nine: measure your attack. This is where you will work the hardest, because it is one royal pain to measure the effectiveness of marketing, but it's your job—and if you do it, you can double the effectiveness of your marketing budget. Stated another way, if you don't do it, you can halve the effectiveness of your marketing budget.

Measure your attack

Only by measuring can you improve your marketing calendar. Only by finding out which weapons worked and which were duds can you maximize the good ones and eliminate the bad ones. You learn about the effectiveness of your marketing by asking people where they heard of you.

Ask them in person, when completing a sales receipt, at the outset, in a questionnaire, at any opportunity—because it is so important for you not to waste one cent of your marketing money. If you don't find out where people first learned of your company, you are wasting your marketing money. That's just no way for a guerrilla to conduct business, and so the guerrilla devises methods and policies that capture this information from every customer, and in many cases, from every prospect.

Measuring becomes a mite easier when you've formalized the procedure for any employees who are in a position to track responses, such as including a blank space on your order form with room for the original source of this customer, "forcing" the employee to ask and learn it. Some businesses that do this or have their phone operators ask prospects "Where did you first hear of us?" say that they've got their measuring chore "on automatic"— that is, they use a system that asks everybody for this data.

Doubling your efficacy

Always remember that measuring actually will double your efficacy and translate to dramatic increases in your profits—which is the whole purpose of guerrilla marketing. The idea is to be aware of all the weapons, fire the ones that you figure are correct for your business, and then use only the arsenal of weapons that have proved themselves in action.

What you should improve

Step ten: improve your attack in all areas. Improve your message. Improve your media selection and your weapons. Improve your budget by investing less and getting more. This isn't difficult, for you've been keeping track and learning what works and what doesn't work. Improve the overall results of your guerrilla marketing attack. Do so every year. Never make changes simply to make changes. Remember that guerrillas are constantly making *improvements*.

The past is not the key to the future

The ideal small business of the twenty-first century will realize that the past is *not* the key to the future. Although the sun continues to rise in the east and Uncle Sam requires you to pay your taxes by the ides of April, marketing will continue to change. Guerrillas are positioned for these changes. To adapt, they know that survival and prosperity are not so much a matter of money as a matter of time, energy, and determination.

An arsenal of profit producers

To market with acumen and success today, you've just got to launch a guerrilla marketing attack. Stock your arsenal with these profit-producing tips for the new millennium:

- Forget the past when planning the future. Changes that represent opportunity will take place in service, technology, prospect sophistication, quality expectations, available options, and competitive marketing savvy. Be ready or be lunch.
- Refocus on your marketing strategy. Anticipate response. Be sure your plan is clear and brief enough for all major employees to read it. Don't change your marketing merely for the sake of change or a bad case of nerves.
- Expand your niche. Expand it by offering what your competi-

tors don't do well. Expand it by targeting markets too small for big competitors. Expand it by discovering the new markets that change creates. Strategies to consider for expanding your niche are *speed, service,* and *specialization.*

- Assess your passion. Assessing is done with your mind, a left-brained activity, as you now know. Passion you feel with your heart—a right-brained characteristic. Combine your mind and heart to see if you truly still feel passion for what you do. If the fire's gone out, move on to your next bliss. No guerrilla attack can succeed without a burning desire to win.

- Trust your marketing. In a world with much change, marketing can stand out by changing the least. Maintain your thrust and identity, but broaden your media, add more target markets, and reexamine your pricing. Trust your spouse, your heart, and your marketing.

Trust your marketing

- Become your customers. The moment you are in their shoes, you'll see changes from their perspective, see your company from their viewpoint, see any changes that are needed.

- Make each customer feel unique. I repeat this because most of your competitors will be unable to do it, and you'll gain an enormous advantage if you can. Learn so much about your customers' lives and businesses that when they see or hear from you, they'll instantly remember that you recognize what makes them special.

- Hang in there. When times change, the normal tendency is to make changes in wholesale lots. This is not necessary. What is necessary is that you make some changes, even make them on a constant basis. Hang in there with your mission, but in service and quality, be a rolling stone.

- Hone your awareness of needs and problems. Guerrillas know that the path to profits is smooth when it is directed to filling needs and solving problems. Needs and problems change, but guerrillas have methods for spotting them.

- Practice fusion marketing. Many businesses, large and small, are aware of changes yet unaware of how to act. One way to act is to team up with new collaborative marketing partners who can help you spread the marketing word and cut marketing costs—benefiting both fusion marketing partners.

- Know what your prospects and customers expect. Be assured that they expect more and better. You've got to be ready to exceed those expectations, even new ones.

- Create a new competitive advantage. Change opens many

doors, and guerrillas rush through to offer exactly what new consumers want. They want speed. They want service. They want value. They want technology that works.

Be a follow-up fanatic

- Do more follow-up with existing customers—and prospects— than ever. Do more than any competitor. If I could put this tip into neon type, I'd do it because it is that important to me that you know it deep in your bones.
- Lean on your customers for their awesome referral power. You've treated them well and stayed in touch with them, so they want you to succeed and will happily give you the names of potential customers or recommend your business to friends and associates.
- Engage in constructive discontent. Stop talking up your business with your associates, and start questioning it. Informed criticism helps you keep abreast of changes.
- Don't lower your prices just because others are doing it. Instead, consider maintaining or even raising your price, then justifying it with more service or increased convenience.
- Develop a reverence for measurement. Become an accountability freak, measuring marketing weapons, employees, staff and company performance. Every component is accountable.
- Recognize that your best marketing investment is yourself.
- Remember that marketing is attitude and you should constantly be expressing it.

A core of top talent

- Develop a core of top talent—people you can turn to in order to give more muscle to your marketing, both the strategy and the executions. They are easier to find than ever because many of them are opting for the life of an entrepreneur, freeing themselves from the corporate hierarchy and becoming available to help you.
- Focus on customer loyalty. A successful restaurateur treats his regulars like royalty and his new customers like regulars. Attracting customers is no easy task. That's why it makes so much sense to concentrate upon keeping them as customers.
- Treat your business as though it were your flesh and blood. Just like kids, businesses require constant attention when young and then more attention when teenagers. With support, nurturance, and love, they may grow strong.
- Know your industry in and out. Shop your competitors. Go to trade shows. Read industry magazines. Make friends with others in your industry. Find a few great industry-related sites on

the Internet and visit them frequently. The greatest source of new information is the Net, and guerrillas are keen on keeping up to the moment.

- Resist focusing on trends. You must know what is going on around you, and at the same time, you've got to beware of trendoids, those things that may look and act like trends but are really fads that pass in the night. **Beware of trendoids**
- Invest time and energy learning to negotiate the subtle intricacies of change in your marketing and your managing.
- Learn to feel at home on-line, at home with technology, at home with change. Never let normal progress impede you. The world that is coming requires not that you learn one thing well but that you learn new things consistently. Truth and reality are changing.

The times, your competition, your marketing, the marketing process itself, and you—they are all a-changing. To keep you in touch with what is really happening on this orb called Earth, here's a reality check: if we could shrink the Earth's population to a village of precisely 100 people, with all existing human ratios remaining the same, it would look like this: **Everything is a-changing**

There would be 57 Asians, 21 Europeans, 14 from the Western Hemisphere (North and South), and 8 Africans. Fifty-one would be female; 49 would be male; 70 would be non-Christian; 30 Christian. Fifty percent of the entire world's wealth would be in the hands of only 6 people, and all 6 would be citizens of the United States. Eighty would live in substandard housing; 70 would be unable to read; 50 would suffer from malnutrition. One would be near death, one would be near birth.

That's the real world these days. And that's not the only world you'll have to live in. To be a guerrilla marketer, you must live mentally on two planets. The first planet, Conceptual, is a place ordinary people don't live. Most people don't even know it exists. It is where ideas formulate, where minds meet. The second planet, Earth, is the world of the people who hire you and buy what you sell. They take heed of what you communicate or ignore you completely. You must know what is most important to them. You must know what they want and what they need. This only happens if you live in the same world they do, if you experience what they experience, if you are aware of the changes that they are aware of. **The real world** **The two planets where you live**

These realities are all working for you when you launch your

When to launch guerrilla marketing attack. The two best times to launch it are
your attack exactly the same as the two best times to plant a tree: twenty years
ago—and today.

Action is the purpose of guerrilla marketing. Once you take
the actions described in these pages, you'll discover that guerrilla
marketing will transform you into a guerrilla in other facets of
your business.

Regardless of your lofty achievements, regardless of your successes, regardless of the size to which you grow, it will always be
possible to bring to marketing the imagination, the ingenuity, and
the comprehensiveness of thought of a guerrilla. If you approach
your task with the soul and the spirit of a guerrilla primed for the
times, in spite of the hordes of competitors, my bet's on you. I'll
see you in the trenches. And at the bank.

There has never been a better time than right now to give
wings to your dreams through marketing. There has never been a
better way to market than with the insights and attitudes of the
guerrilla.

Acknowledgments

The acknowledgments may be the least enjoyable section of a book for the reader, yet writing it is one of the most enjoyable parts for the author. It is only in the Acknowledgments that the people responsible for the spirit of the book receive the recognition they deserve.

First on the list is Michael Larsen, my agent. Upon hearing me speak on marketing at a luncheon meeting, he dashed up to me and told me that I ought to write a book based upon my speech. From that moment on, *Guerrilla Marketing* started taking shape. Gerard Van Der Leun, my original editor at Houghton Mifflin, earned my gratitude for believing in the book and adding crucial touches of spark and soul. My current editor, Marnie Patterson Cochran, gets a high-five for much of the scope and style of this updated edition. Debra Kahn Schofield gets a wink and an appreciative smile for her bibliographic research. Bill Gallagher Jr. gets a hearty pat on the back for escorting guerrilla marketers into cyberspace. And Bill Shear gets countless plaudits for shepherding guerrilla marketing into the consciousness of more than half the world. I have dedicated this book to the guerrillas I have met along the way and thank each one for mighty contributions, many sprinkled throughout this book and throughout my mind.

More than ever, I am impressed by my daughter, Amy, who leads a guerrilla life while improving the lot of humankind with her work in state government and in the media while raising three kids—Sage, Seth, and Natty—each one a winner. I offer superabundant appreciation to Alexes Miller, who keeps my home and office running smoothly. As always, I offer the most gratitude and the wettest kiss to my wife, Patsy, who keeps me happy, makes me think, encourages everything I do except hang-gliding, and fills me with her love. I am inspired by her in every way.

I feel blessed to owe acknowledgments to so many outstanding people.

Information Arsenal
for Guerrillas

Acuff, Daniel, Ph.D. *What Kids Buy and Why: Psychological Secrets to Creating Products That Kids Love*. New York: The Free Press, 1997.

Adams, Bob. *Streetwise Small Business Start-Up*. Holbrook, IL: Adams Media, 1996.

Albrecht, Donna G. *Promoting Your Business with FREE or Almost-Free Publicity*. Englewood Cliffs, NJ: Prentice Hall, 1997.

Ambler, Tim. *Marketing from Advertising to Zen*. London: Pitman, 1996.

Anderson, Kristin, and Ron Zemke. *Delivering Knock-Your-Socks-Off Service*. 2nd ed. New York: AMACOM, 1997.

Anthony, Joseph. *Kiplinger's Revised and Updated Working for Yourself*. Washington, D.C.: Kiplinger Books, 1995.

Applegate, Jane. *Succeeding in a Small Business: The One Hundred and One Toughest Problems and How to Solve Them*. New York: NAL/Dutton, 1992.

Arkebauer, James B. *The McGraw-Hill Guide to Writing a High-Impact Business Plan*. New York: McGraw-Hill, 1995.

Astle, Richard M. *The Common-Sense MBA: The Seven Pursuits of Enduring Business for the Entrepreneur*. New York: St. Martin's Press, 1994.

Aurich, Barry, and Len Gill. *Event and Entertainment Marketing*. Chicago: Probus, 1994.

Bade, Nicholas. *Marketing without Money*. Lincolnwood, IL: National Textbook Co., 1994.

Bangs, David H. *The Market-Planning Guide: Creating a Plan to Successfully Market Your Business, Products or Service*. Dover, NH: Upstart, 1994.

Baron, Gerald R. *Friendship Marketing*. Grants Pass, OR: Oasis Books, 1997.

Barrett, Gavin. *Forensic Marketing: Optimizing Results from Marketing Communications*. New York: McGraw-Hill, 1995.

Barter Publishing Staff. *Barter Referral Directory: Small Business Edition*. Denver: Prosperity and Profit Unlimited, 1992.

Beatty, Jack. *The World According to Peter Drucker.* New York: The Free Press, 1998.

Beckwith, Harry. *Selling the Invisible: A Field Guide to Modern Marketing.* New York: Warner Books, 1997.

Beemer, C. Britt, and Robert L. Shook. *Predatory Marketing.* New York: William Morrow, 1997.

Bell, Chip, R. *Customers as Partners: Building Relationships That Last.* San Francisco: Berrett-Koehler, 1994.

Bendinger, Bruce. *The Copy Workshop Workbook.* Chicago: The Copy Workshop, 1993.

Blackwell, Roger D. *From Mind to Market: Reinventing the Retail Supply Chain.* New York: Harper Business, 1997.

Blechman, Bruce Jan, and Jay Conrad Levinson. *Guerrilla Financing: Alternative Techniques to Finance Any Small Business.* Boston: Houghton Mifflin, 1991.

Bobrow, Edwin E., CMC. *The Complete Idiot's Guide to New Product Development.* New York: Alpha Books, 1997.

Bond, Jonathan, and Richard Kirschenbaum. *Under the Radar: Talking to Today's Cynical Consumer.* New York: Wiley, 1998.

Brandenburger, Adam, and Barry Nalebuff. *Co-opetition: A Revolutionary Mindset That Combines Competition and Cooperation.* New York: Currency/Doubleday, 1996.

Bredin, Alice. *The Virtual Office Survival Handbook: What Telecommuters and Entrepreneurs Need to Succeed in Today's Nontraditional Workplace.* New York: Wiley, 1996.

Brooks, William T. *Niche Selling: How to Find Your Customers in a Crowded Market.* Burr Ridge, IL: Irwin, 1992.

Burg, Bob. Endless Referrals: *Networking Your Everyday Contacts into Sales.* New York: McGraw-Hill, 1994.

Burgett, Gordon. *Niche Marketing for Writers, Speakers and Entrepreneurs.* Santa Monica, CA: Communications Unlimited, 1993.

Bygrave, William D., and David Ackroyd. *The Portable MBA in Entrepreneurship.* 2nd ed. New York: Wiley, 1997. Also available on Dove Audio.

Cafferky, Michael E. *Let Your Customers Do the Talking: 301+ Word-of-Mouth Marketing Tactics Guaranteed to Boost Profits.* Chicago: Upstart Publishing, 1996.

Caple, John. *The Right Work: Finding It and Making It Right.* New York: Dodd, Mead & Company, 1987.

Chapman, James. *Street-Smart Business Tactics.* San Mateo, CA: Human Intellect Press, 1990.

Clancy, Kevin, and Robert S. Schulman. *Marketing Myths That Are Killing Business: The Cure for Deathwish Marketing.* New York: McGraw-Hill, 1994.

Cohen, William A. *The Marketing Plan.* 2nd ed. New York: Wiley, 1998.

Connor, Dick, and Jeff Davidson. *Getting New Clients.* New York: Wiley, 1993.

Crandall, Rick. *Marketing Magic, Proven Pathways to Success.* Corte Madera, CA: Select Press, 1996.

Cyr, Donald G., and Douglas Gray. *Marketing Your Product.* Bellingham, WA: Self-Counsel Press, 1994.

Davidson, Jeff. *Marketing on a Shoestring.* New York: Wiley, 1994.

Debelak, Don. *Marketing Magic: Action-Oriented Strategies That Will Help You.* Holbrook, IL: Bob Adams, 1994.

Decker, Sam, ed. *310 Do-It-Yourself Marketing Ideas from America's Most Innovative Small Companies.* Boston: Goldhirsh Group, 1997.

Dennison, Dell. *The Advertising Handbook for Small Business.* Bellingham, WA: Self-Counsel Press, 1994.

Desatnick, Robert L. *Managing to Keep the Customer Happy.* San Francisco: Jossey-Bass, 1987.

Dewitt, Paula Mergerhagen. *Targeting Transitions.* Chicago: Probus, 1994.

Dobkin, Jeffrey. *How to Market a Product for Under $500.* Merion Station, PA: Danielle Adams Publishing, 1996.

Donnelly, James H., Jr. *Close to the Customer.* Burr Ridge, IL: Irwin, 1991.

Dunckel, Jacqueline, and Brian Taylor. *Keeping Customers Happy.* Bellingham, WA: Self-Counsel Press, 1994.

Dru, Jean-Marie. *Disruption: Overturning Conventions and Shaking Up the Marketplace.* New York: Wiley, 1996.

Edwards, Mark, and Ann Ewen. *360-Degree Feedback.* New York: AMACOM, 1996.

Edwards, Paul, Sarah Edwards, and Laura Clampitt Douglas. *Getting Business to Come to You.* New York: Tarcher/Putnam, 1991.

Elton, Kim. *Net Benefits: The Internet Beyond the Technology and Down to the Bottom Line.* Victoria, B.C.: N.B. Publishing, 1997.

Falk, Edgar A. *1001 Ideas to Create Retail Excitement.* Englewood Cliffs, NJ: Prentice Hall, 1994.

Feig, Barry. *Marketing Straight to the Heart.* New York: AMACOM, 1997.

Fisher, Roger, and William Ury. *Getting to Yes: Negotiating Agreement Without Giving In.* 2nd ed. New York: Penguin Books, 1991.

Floyd, Elaine. *Marketing with Newsletters.* St. Louis, MO: Newsletter Resources, 1996.

Floyd, Elaine. *Quick and Easy Newsletters.* St. Louis, MO: Newsletter Resources, 1998.

Fortini-Campbell, Lisa. *Hitting the Sweet Spot: How Consumer Insights Can Inspire Better Marketing and Advertising.* New York: AMACOM, 1994.

Frause, Bob, and Julie A. Colebur. *Environmental Marketing Imperative.* Chicago: Probus, 1994.

Fournles, Ferdinand F. *Why Customers Don't Do What You Want Them to Do—and What to Do About It.* New York: McGraw-Hill, 1994.

Goetsch, Hal. *Developing, Implementing and Managing an Effective Marketing Plan.* Lincolnwood, IL: NTC Business Books, 1994.

Gill, Michael, and Sheila Patterson. *Fired Up! From Corporate Kiss Off to Entrepreneurial Kick-Off.* New York: Viking/Penguin, 1996.

Gordon, Josh. *Tough Calls: Selling Strategies to Win Over Your Most Difficult Customers.* New York: AMACOM, 1997.

Green, Chuck. *The Desktop Publisher's Idea Book.* 2nd ed. New York: Random House, 1997.

Griffin, Jack. *The Do-It-Yourself Business Promotions Kit.* Old Tappan, NJ: Prentice Hall, 1994.

Griffin, Jill. *Customer Loyalty: How to Earn It.* San Francisco: Jossey-Bass, 1997.

Gumpert, David E. *How to Really Create a Successful Marketing Plan.* Boston: Goldhirsh Group, 1997.

Hahn, Fred E., and Kenneth G. Mangun. *Do-It-Yourself Advertising and Promotion.* 2nd ed. New York; Wiley, 1997.

Hall, Robert E. *The Streetcorner Strategy for Winning Local Markets.* Austin: Bard Books, 1994.

Hamper, Robert J., and L. Sue Baugh. *Strategic Market Planning.* Lincolnwood, IL: National Textbook Co., 1998.

Harding, Ford. *Rain Making: The Professional's Guide to Attracting New Clients.* Holbrook, IL: Bob Adams, 1994.

Harrell, Wilson. *For Entrepreneurs Only: Success Strategies for Anyone Starting or Growing a Business.* Franklin Lakes, NJ: Career Press, 1995.

Hiam, Alexander. *Marketing for Dummies.* Foster City, CA: IDG Books, 1997.

Hiebing, Roman G., Jr., and Scott W. Cooper. *How to Write a Successful Marketing Plan.* Lincolnwood, IL: National Textbook Co., 1997.

Horner, Jody. *Power Marketing for Small Business.* Grants Pass, OR: Oasis Press/PSI Research, 1993.

Hughes, Arthur M. *Strategic Defense Marketing.* Chicago: Probus, 1994.

Hunter, Victor L., and David Tietyen. *Business to Business Marketing: Creating a Community of Customers.* Lincolnwood, IL: National Textbook Co., 1997.

Jackson, Robert R., and Paul Want. *Strategic Defense Marketing.* Lincolnwood, IL: National Textbook Co., 1994.

Jones, John Philip. *When Ads Work: New Proof That Advertising Triggers Sales.* New York: Lexington Books, 1995.

Kabodian, Armer J. *The Customer Is Always Right! Thought-Provoking Insights on the Importance of Customer Satisfaction from Today's Business Leaders.* Cambridge, MA: Harvard Business School Press, 1996.

Kawasaki, Guy. *How to Drive Your Competition Crazy: Creating Disruption for Fun and Profit.* New York: Hyperion, 1995.

Kawasaki, Guy. *Selling the Dream: How to Promote Your Product, Company, or Ideas—and Make a Difference—Using Everyday Evangelism.* New York: McGraw-Hill, 1995.

Kennedy, Dan S. *How to Succeed in Business by Breaking All the Rules: A Plan for Entrepreneurs.* New York: E. P. Dutton, 1997.

Kotler, Philip, and Eduardo L. Roberto. *Social Marketing: Strategies for Changing Public Behavior.* New York: The Free Press, 1989.

Krass, Peter. *The Book of Business Wisdom: Classic Writings by the Legends of Commerce and Industry.* New York: Wiley, 1991.

Kremer, John, and J. Daniel McComas. *High-Impact Marketing on a Low-Impact Budget.* Rocklin, CA: Prima Publishing, 1997.

Kremer, John. *The Complete Direct Marketing Sourcebook.* New York: Wiley, 1992.

Lambesis, Barbara. *101 Big Ideas for Promoting a Business on a Small Budget.* Phoenix: Marketing Methods Press, 1989.

Landon, Hal. *Marketing with Video: How to Create a Winning Video for Your Small Business or Non-Profit.* Slate Hill, NY: Oak Tree Press, 1996.

Lant, Jeffrey. *Cash Copy.* Cambridge, MA: JLA, 1992.

Lant, Jeffrey. *Money-Making Marketing.* Cambridge, MA: JLA, 1993.

Lant, Dr. Jeffrey. *The Unabashed Self-Promoter's Guide: What Every Man, Woman, Child and Organization in America Needs to Know about Getting Ahead by Exploiting the Media.* 2nd ed. Cambridge, MA: JLA, 1992.

Levinson, Jay Conrad, and Seth Godin. *Get What You Deserve: How to Guerrilla-Market Yourself.* New York: Avon Books, 1997.

Levinson, Jay Conrad. *Guerrilla Advertising: Cost-Effective Tactics for Small-Business Success.* Boston: Houghton Mifflin, 1994.

Levinson, Jay Conrad. *Guerrilla Marketing Attack: New Strategies, Tactics, and Weapons for Winning Big Profits from Your Small Business.* Boston: Houghton Mifflin, 1989.

Levinson, Jay Conrad. *Guerrilla Marketing Excellence: The Fifty Golden Rules for Small-Business Success.* Boston: Houghton Mifflin, 1993.

Levinson, Jay Conrad. *Guerrilla Marketing for the Home-Based Business.* Boston: Houghton Mifflin, 1995.

Levinson, Jay Conrad, and Seth Godin. *The Guerrilla Marketing Handbook.* Boston: Houghton Mifflin, 1994.

Levinson, Jay Conrad, and Charles Rubin. *Guerrilla Marketing Online:*

The Entrepreneur's Guide to Earning Profits on the Internet. 2nd ed. Boston: Houghton Mifflin, 1997.

Levinson, Jay Conrad, and Charles Rubin. *Guerrilla Marketing Online Weapons: 100 Low-Cost, High-Impact Weapons for Online Profits and Prosperity.* Boston: Houghton Mifflin, 1996.

Levinson, Jay Conrad. *Guerrilla Marketing Weapons: 100 Affordable Marketing Methods for Maximizing Profits from Your Small Business.* New York: Plume, 1990.

Levinson, Jay Conrad. *Guerrilla Marketing with Technology: Unleashing the Full Potential of Your Small Business.* Reading, MA: Addison-Wesley, 1997.

Levinson, Jay Conrad, Bill Gallagher, and Orvel Ray Wilson. *Guerrilla Selling: Unconventional Weapons and Tactics for Increasing Your Sales.* Boston: Houghton Mifflin, 1992.

Levinson, Jay Conrad, Mark S.A. Smith, and Orvel Ray Wilson. *Guerrilla Trade-Show Selling: New Unconventional Weapons and Tactics to Meet More People, Get More Leads, and Close More Sales.* New York: Wiley, 1997.

Levitt, Theodore. *The Marketing Imagination.* New York: The Free Press, 1986.

Lonier, Terri. *The Frugal Entrepreneur: Creative Ways to Save Time, Energy and Money in Your Business.* New Paltz, NY: Portico Press, 1996.

Lonier, Terri. *Working Solo Sourcebook: Essential Resources for Independent Entrepreneurs.* New Paltz, NY: Portico Press, 1994.

Lonier, Terri. *Working Solo: The Real Guide to Freedom and Financial Success with Your Own Business.* New York: Portico Press, 1994.

Lopiano-Misdom, Janine, and Joanne De Luca. *Street Trends: How Today's Alternative Youth Cultures Are Creating Tomorrow's Mainstream Markets.* New York: HarperBusiness, 1997.

Mackay, Harvey. *Dig Your Well Before You're Thirsty: The Only Networking Book You'll Ever Need.* New York: Currency/Doubleday, 1997.

Marconi, Joe. *Image Marketing Using Public Perceptions to Attain Business Objectives.* Lincolnwood, IL: National Textbook Co., 1996.

Marder, Eric. *The Laws of Choice: Predicting Customer Behavior.* New York: Free Press, 1997.

McCrimmon, Mitch. *Unleash the Entrepreneur Within: How to Make Everyone an Entrepreneur and Stay Efficient.* London: Pitman, 1995.

McDonald, Malcolm H. B., and Warren J. Keegan. *Marketing Plans That Work: Targeting Growth and Profitability.* Boston: Butterworth-Heinemann, 1997.

McKeever, Mike. *How to Write a Business Plan.* Berkeley: Nolo Press, 1992.

McKenna, Regis. *Real Time: Preparing for the Age of the Never-Satisfied Customer.* Boston: Harvard Business School Press, 1997.

Misner, Ivan R. *Seven-Second Marketing: How to Use Memory Hooks to Make You Instantly Stand Out in a Crowd.* Austin: Bard Press, 1996.

Misner, Ivan R. *The World's Best-Known Marketing Secret: Building Your Business with Word-of-Mouth Marketing.* Austin: Bard & Stephan, 1994.

Moore, James F. *The Death of Competition.* New York: HarperBusiness, 1996.

Murphy, Dallas. *The Fast-Forward MBA in Marketing.* New York: Wiley, 1997.

Nelson, Carol. *How to Market to Women.* Detroit: Visible Ink, 1994.

Newberg, Jay, and Claudio Marcus. *Target $mart! Database Marketing for the Small Business.* Grants Pass, OR: The Oasis Press/PSI Research, 1996.

Newell, Frederick. *The New Rules of Marketing: How to Use One-to-One Relationship Marketing to Be the Leader in Your Industry.* New York: McGraw-Hill, 1997.

Nulman, Philip R. *Start-Up Marketing: An Entrepreneur's Guide to Advertising, Marketing and Promoting Your Business.* Grants Pass, OR: Oasis Press/PSI Research, 1996.

Parker, Roger C. *Web Content and Design.* New York: MIS Press. 1997.

Parker, Roger C. *Web Design and Desktop Publishing for Dummies.* Foster City, CA: IDG Books, 1997.

Parmerlee, David. *Developing Successful Marketing Strategies.* 2nd ed. Chicago: NTC Business Books, 1997.

Peppers, Don, and Martha Rogers. *The One-to-One Future: Building Relationships One Customer at a Time.* New York: Currency Doubleday, 1997.

Phillips, Michael, and Salli Rasberry. *Marketing without Advertising: Inspire Customers to Rave about Your Business to Create Lasting Success.* 2nd ed. Berkeley: Nolo Press, 1997.

Pinson, Linda, and Jerry Jinnett. *Anatomy of a Business Plan.* Chicago: Dearborn Trade, 1993.

Putnam, Anthony O. *Marketing Your Services: A Step-by-Step Guide for Small-Business Professionals.* New York: Wiley, 1990.

Rackham, Neil. *The Spin Selling Fieldbook: Practical Tools, Methods, Exercises, and Resources.* New York: McGraw-Hill, 1996.

Ramacitti, David. *Do-It-Yourself Advertising.* New York: AMACOM, 1992.

Ramacitti, David. *Do-It-Yourself Marketing.* New York: AMACOM, 1994.

Rapp, Stan, and Thomas Collins. *Beyond Maximarketing.* New York: McGraw-Hill, 1993.

Reichheld, Frederick F., and Thomas Teal. *The Loyalty Effect: The Hidden Force Behind Growth, Profits, and Lasting Value.* Cambridge, MA: Harvard Business School Press, 1996.

Reitman, Jerry I. *Beyond 2000: The Future of Direct Marketing.* Lincolnwood, IL: National Textbook Co., 1994.

Reynolds, Don. *Crackerjack Positioning: Niche Marketing Strategy for the Entrepreneur.* Tulsa: Atwood, 1993.

Rheingold, Howard. *The Virtual Community: Homesteading on the Electronic Frontier.* Reading, MA: Addison-Wesley, 1993.

Reis, Al. *Focus: The Future of Your Company Depends on It.* New York: HarperBusiness, 1996.

Ritchie, Karen. *Marketing to Generation X.* New York: Lexington Books, 1995.

Roberts, Ralph, and John Gallagher. *Walk Like a Giant: Sell Like a Madman.* New York: HarperBusiness, 1997.

Ross, Marilyn, and Tom Ross. *Country Bound! Trade Your Business-Suit Blues for Blue-Jean Dreams.* Chicago: Upstart, 1997.

Rossman, Marlene L. *Multicultural Marketing: Selling to a Diverse America.* New York: AMACOM, 1994.

Sanchez, D., S. Heiman, and T. Tuleja. *The Selling Machine.* New York: Times Business, 1997.

Sanow, Arnold, and Daniel McComas. *Marketing Boot Camp.* Dubuque, IA: Kendall/Hunt, 1994.

Schmitt, Bernd, and Alex Simonson. *Marketing Aesthetics: The Strategic Marketing of Brands, Identity, and Image.* New York: The Free Press, 1997.

Schultz, Don E., Stanley Tannenbaum, and Robert E. Lauterborn. *Integrated Marketing Communications: Pulling It Together and Making It Work.* Lincolnwood, IL: National Textbook Co., 1996.

Shane, Michael. *How to Think Like an Entrepreneur.* New York: Brett, 1994.

Shefsky, Lloyd E. *Entrepreneurs Are Made, Not Born: Secrets from 200 Successful Entrepreneurs.* New York: McGraw-Hill, 1994.

Sinetar, Marsha. *To Build the Life You Want, Create the Work You Love: The Spiritual Dimension of Entrepreneuring.* New York: St. Martin's Press, 1996.

Slutsky, Jeff. *How to Get Clients.* New York: Warner, 1992.

Smith, Jeannette. *Entrepreneur Magazine Guide to Integrated Marketing.* New York: Wiley, 1996.

Smith, Jeannette. *The New Publicity Kit: A Complete Guide for Entrepreneurs, Small Businesses and Non-Profit Organizations.* New York: Wiley, 1995.

Spoelstra, Jon. *Ice to the Eskimos: How to Market a Product Nobody Wants.* New York: HarperBusiness, 1997.

Stanley, Dr. Thomas J. *Marketing to the Affluent.* New York: McGraw-Hill, 1997.

Stansell, Kimberly. *Bootstrapper's Success Secrets: 151 Tactics for Building Your Business on a Shoestring Budget.* Franklin Lakes, NJ: Career Press, 1997.

Sussman, Jeffrey. *Power Promoting: How to Market Your Business to the Top!* New York: Wiley, 1997.

Truax, Pamela, and Monique Reece Myron. *Market Smarter, Not Harder.* Dubuque, IA: Kendall/Hunt, 1996.

Trout, Jack. *The New Positioning: The Latest on the World's #1 Business Strategy.* New York: McGraw-Hill, 1997.

Unruh, James A. *Customers Mean Business: Six Steps to Building Relationships That Last.* Reading, MA: Addison-Wesley, 1996.

Wallace, Carol Wilkie. *Great Ad!* Blue Ridge Summit, PA: TAB Books, 1990.

Wares, Bruce. *Partner$ell: Creating Lucrative and Lasting Client Relationships.* Dubuque, IA: Kendall/Hunt, 1994.

Whitely, Richard, and Diane Hessan. *Customer-Centered Growth.* Reading, MA: Addison-Wesley, 1996.

Wilson, Jerry R. *Word-of-Mouth Marketing.* New York: Wiley, 1994.

Withers, Jean, and Carol Viperman. *Marketing Your Service Business.* Bellingham, WA: Self-Counsel Press, 1992.

Woolf, Brian P. *Customer-Specific Marketing.* Greenville, SC: Teal Books, 1996.

Yohalem, Kathy C. *Thinking Out of the Box: How to Market Your Company into the Future.* New York: Wiley, 1997.

Yudkin, Marcia. *Six Steps to Free Publicity and Dozens of Other Ways to Win Free Media Attention for You and Your Business.* Bergenfield, NJ: 1994.

Ziccardi, Donald. *Masterminding the Store: Advertising, Sales Promotion, and the New Marketing Reality.* New York: Wiley, 1997.

Newsletters

Hudson, Howard Penn. *Newsletter on Newsletters.* Rhinebeck, NY: The Newsletter Clearinghouse. 800-572-3451; fax 914-876-2561.

Levinson, Jay Conrad. *The Guerrilla Marketing Newsletter.* Bi-Monthly. Mill Valley, CA: Guerrilla Marketing International. 800-748-6444, ext. 140, or 415-381-8361; www.gmarketing.com.

Newman, Dan. *Business Ideas Newsletter.* Dan Newman Co., 930 Clifton Ave., Clifton, NJ 07011.

Stansell, Kimberly. *Bootstrappin' Entrepreneur: The Newsletter for Individuals with Great Ideas and a Little Bit of Cash.* Quarterly. Los Angeles: Research Done Write. 310-568-9861. E-mail: ibootstrap@aol.com.

Fast Company. P.O. Box 52760, Boulder, CO 80321-2760. 800-688- **Periodicals**
1545.

Journal of Small Business Management. West Virginia Bureau of Business Research, Box 6025, Morgantown, WV 26506-6025. 304-293-7534.

Marketing News. American Marketing Association, 250 S. Wacker Dr., Ste. 200, Chicago, IL 60606-5819.

Nation's Business. Nation's Business, 1615 H. St. NW, Washington, D.C. 20062-2000. 800-638-6582.

Sales and Marketing Management. 355 Park Ave. South, New York, NY 10010. 800-821-6897.

Small Business Bulletin. Small Business Service Bureau, 554 Main St., P.O. Box 5014, Worcester, MA 01615. 508-756-3513.

Venture. 35 W. 45th St., New York, NY 10036.

Levinson, Jay Conrad. *Guerrilla Marketing: Secrets for Making Big* **Audiotapes**
Profits from Your Small Business. Mill Valley, CA: Cascade Seaview Corporation, 1992.

Levinson, Jay Conrad. *Guerrilla Marketing Attack: New Strategies, Tactics and Weapons for Winning Big Profits from Your Small Business.* Mill Valley, CA: Cascade Seaview Corporation, 1992.

Levinson, Jay Conrad. *Guerrilla Marketing Weapons: 100 Affordable Marketing Methods for Maximizing Profits from Your Small Business.* Mill Valley, CA: Cascade Seaview Corporation, 1992.

Ludden, Laverne L., ed., and Marcia R. Fox. *Be Your Own Business! The Definitive Guide to Entrepreneurial Success.* Indianapolis: Jist Works, 1997.

Mackay, Harvey. *Dig Your Well Before You're Thirsty: The Only Networking Book You'll Ever Need.* New York: Bantam Doubleday Dell, 1997.

Ries, Al, and Jack Trout. *The 22 Immutable Laws of Marketing: Violate Them at Your Own Risk.* New York: HarperAudio, 1993.

Temme, Jim. *Managing Projects, Priorities, and Deadlines.* Skillpath, Inc., 6900 Squibb Rd., P.O. Box 2768, Mission, KS 66201-2768. 800-873-7545.

Bacon, Mark S. *Do-It-Yourself Direct-Marketing Secrets for Small Busi-* **Videotapes**
ness. New York: Wiley, 1994.

Edwards, Paul, and Sarah Edwards. *Best Home-Based Businesses for the Nineties.* Los Angeles: J. P. Tarcher, 1991.

———. *Getting Business to Come to You.* Los Angeles: J. P. Tarcher, 1991.

Holmes, Chet. *Mega Marketing and Sales: How to Absolutely Positively Grow Revenues.* San Rafael, CA: Kaleidoscope Media Group, 1996.

Levinson, Jay Conrad. *Guerrilla Marketing in Action.* Mill Valley, CA: Michelson-Carlson Productions in Association with Guerrilla Marketing International, 1998. 800-748-6444; www.gmarketing.com.

Multimedia   Brenna, Patricia M. *Ten-Minute Marketing.* St. Paul, MN: Devine Multi-Media Pub, 1997.

CD-ROMs   *Jay Conrad Levinson's Guerrilla Marketing.* CD-ROM for Windows. Boston: Houghton Mifflin Interactive, 1996. 1-800-748-6444; www.gmarketing.com.

Index

Marlboro cigarette advertising, 55, 146, 207, 352
Matchbooks, 272
Maxi-media. *See* Media advertising
Measurement of effectiveness. *See* Thirteen marketing secrets
Media advertising
  cost of, *see* Advertising cost
  maxi-media, 161–234
  media list, building your own, 309–10
  mini-media, 89–160, 161–62
  need for, 21
  new types of, 91
  and nonmedia. *See* Nonmedia marketing
  public relations and, 294, 295–96, 297
  what they don't like, 308
  reach and frequency of, 69–70
  selection of media, 58–61, 65
  See also Magazine advertising; Newspaper advertising; Radio advertising; TV advertising
MediaFinder on-line directory, 176
MediaINFO Links, 309
Media Networks, Inc., 78
Media Online Yellow Pages, 310
Media UK Internet Directory, 310
Medicine, trends in, 4
Michener, James, 223
Microsoft advertising, 55
Midler, Bette, 346
Mini-media. *See* Media advertising
Miscellaneous marketing tools, 91, 271–92
  annual reports, 277, 297
  bumper stickers, blimps and buttons, 272
  cellular phones, 281
  contests and sweepstakes, 279–80

cost, 276–77, 280, 284, 285, 290
neatness, 236, 276
new products, 282–83
newsletters, 277–78, 320
photographs, 77, 277, 299
picket marketing, 52, 272, 273
postcard decks, 91, 162, 282
price promotions, 274–75
public relations, 61–62, 293–310
services, 277, 323
smallness as advantage, 275–76
spare time, 276
technology, 33, 162, 273–74, 277, 283–92
unique ideas, 276–77
window displays, 280–81
word-of-mouth, 18, 21–23, 275, 290
See also Free gifts and samples
Mobil Oil, 348
Modern Maturity magazine, 37
Moped marketing, 271–72
Mother Nature cereal, 49, 50, 51–52
Motorola, 331
Movie theater advertising, 272
"Mr. Smith E-Mails the Media," 310

Netscape company, 274
New Media company, 283
Newsletters, 277–78, 320, 340
  designing your own, 76–77, 90
News media. *See* Media advertising
Newspaper advertising, 65, 130, 164–72
  best days to run, 168
  classified, 135, 136, 137, 141
  combined with other types, 150, 169, 206
  cost of, 167
    and barter, 71

GET THE COMPLETE GUERRILLA ARSENAL!

GUERRILLA MARKETING: SECRETS FOR MAKING BIG PROFITS FROM YOUR SMALL BUSINESS, Third Edition

The book that started the Guerrilla Marketing revolution, now completely updated and expanded. Full of the latest strategies, information on the hottest technologies, details about the fastest-growing markets, and management lessons for the twenty-first century. 0-395-90625-3

GUERRILLA MARKETING ATTACK: NEW STRATEGIES, TACTICS, AND WEAPONS FOR WINNING BIG PROFITS

Guerrilla Marketing Attack explains how to avoid running out of fuel by maximizing limited start-up resources and turning prospects into customers and investments into profits. 0-395-50220-9

GUERRILLA FINANCING: ALTERNATIVE TECHNIQUES TO FINANCE ANY SMALL BUSINESS

The ultimate sourcebook for finance, *Guerrilla Financing* is the first book to describe in detail the many traditional and alternative sources of funding available for small- and medium-size businesses. 0-395-52264-1

GUERRILLA SELLING: UNCONVENTIONAL WEAPONS AND TACTICS FOR INCREASING YOUR SALES

Today's increasingly competitive business environment requires new skills and commitment from salespeople. *Guerrilla Selling* presents unconventional selling tactics that are essential for success. 0-395-57820-5

GUERRILLA MARKETING EXCELLENCE: THE 50 GOLDEN RULES FOR SMALL-BUSINESS SUCCESS

Outlining fifty basic truths that can make or break your company, *Guerrilla Marketing Excellence* takes readers beyond do-it-yourself marketing guides, explaining not just how to market but how to market with excellence. 0-395-60844-9

THE GUERRILLA MARKETING HANDBOOK

An essential companion to *Guerrilla Marketing,* this practical guide offers thousands of contacts, ideas, and examples that will help transform plans into specific actions, turning any business into a marketing powerhouse. 0-395-70013-2

GUERRILLA ADVERTISING: COST-EFFECTIVE TACTICS FOR SMALL-BUSINESS SUCCESS

Full of anecdotes about past and current advertising successes and failures, *Guerrilla Advertising* entertains as it teaches the nuts and bolts of advertising for small businesses. 0-395-68718-7

GUERRILLA MARKETING FOR THE HOME-BASED BUSINESS

Using case studies, anecdotes, illustrations, and examples, guerrilla marketing gurus Jay Levinson and Seth Godin present practical, accessible, and inspirational marketing advice and the most effective marketing tools for America's fastest-growing business segment. 0-395-74283-8

GUERRILLA MARKETING ONLINE: THE ENTREPRENEUR'S GUIDE TO EARNING PROFITS ON THE INTERNET,
Second Edition

From building and maintaining a Web site to creating an online catalog and encouraging users to shop on the Net, Jay Levinson and computer book author Charles Rubin will turn entrepreneurs into Internet marketing experts.
0-395-86061-X

GUERRILLA MARKETING ONLINE WEAPONS: 100 LOW-COST, HIGH-IMPACT WEAPONS FOR ONLINE PROFITS AND PROSPERITY

From e-mail addresses and signatures to storefronts, feedback mechanisms, electronic catalogs, and press kits, Levinson and Rubin's weapons will help any business define, refine, and post its message online with ease. 0-395-77019-X

THE WAY OF THE GUERRILLA: ACHIEVING SUCCESS AND BALANCE AS AN ENTREPRENEUR IN THE 21ST CENTURY

A blueprint for future business success, *The Way of the Guerrilla* includes advice on everything from preparing a focused mission statement to sustaining one's passion for work. Entrepreneurs will discover the means to achieving emotional and financial success. 0-395-92478-2

MASTERING GUERRILLA MARKETING: 100 PROFIT-PRODUCING INSIGHTS THAT YOU CAN TAKE TO THE BANK

"No one knows how to use the weapons of the trade better than industry expert Jay Levinson," said *Entrepreneur* magazine. And this is "the book of a lifetime" from the man who has revolutionized small-business marketing strategies.
0-395-90875-2

GUERRILLA CREATIVITY

The guru of guerrilla marketing unveils his methods of optimizing originality and creativity for successful marketing. Levinson focuses on memes, simple symbols that convey complex ideas — how to generate them and how to disseminate them. 0-618-10468-2

GUERRILLA MARKETING FOR FREE: DOZENS OF NO-COST TACTICS TO PROMOTE YOUR BUSINESS AND ENERGIZE YOUR PROFITS

The guru of guerrilla marketing teaches entrepreneurs how to market aggressively without spending a cent. Levinson, the authority on big-business marketing on a small-business budget, proves that aggressive marketing doesn't have to be expensive if you use creative and unconventional means. 0-618-27679-3

Visit our Web sites:
www.houghtonmifflinbooks.com
and **www.gmarketing.com.**

These books are available in bookstores, or order from Houghton Mifflin customer service at **1-800-225-3362.**